Reviewing
U.S. HISTORY
AND GOVERNMENT

Second Edition
(Revised)

Reviewing
U.S. HISTORY AND GOVERNMENT

Second Edition
(Revised)

Dr. Andrew Peiser
Associate Chair and Director
of Graduate Education Programs
Division of Education, Mercy College, New York

Michael Serber
Founding Principal, Academy of American Studies,
New York
Education Coordinator, Gilder Lehrman Institute of
American History, New York

AMSCO

AMSCO SCHOOL PUBLICATIONS, INC.
315 Hudson Street   New York, N.Y. 10013

Dr. Andrew Peiser, is Associate Chair and Director of Graduate Education Programs, in the Division of Education, Mercy College, New York. He served as principal and chair of the Social Studies Department at Sheepshead Bay High School, Brooklyn, New York.

Michael Serber, is Education Coordinator at the Gilder Lehrman Institute of American History, and Principal Emiritus of the Academy of American Studies in Long Island City, New York. He served as chair of the Social Studies Department at Forest Hills High School, New York.

Dr. Andrew Peiser dedicates this book to his wife, Barbara, his children, Richard, Jacqueline, and Brett, his daughter-in-law, Emmy, and his grandchild Jack William, for all their love and support, and the memory of his mother, Marianne.

Michael Serber dedicates this book to his wife, Adele, his children Ellen and Richard, Jeff and Danielle, his grandchildren Daniel, Noah, and Jared, and his mother, Faye, for all their love and support.

Student's Study Guide prepared by *Stephen A. Shultz,* Social Studies Coordinator, Rocky Point Public Schools, New York

Answer Key Prepared by *Ross Bloomfield,* Social Studies Teacher Queens High School for the Sciences, New York City

Reviewer: John M. Schmalbach, Adjunct Professor, Temple University, former Social Studies Department Head, Abraham Lincoln High School, Philadelphia, Pennsylvania

Text design and cover by Howard S. Leiderman
Photo research by Tobi Zausner
Composition by Monotype, LLC

When ordering this book, please specify:
R 7150 P *or*
Reviewing U.S. History and Government, Second Edition (Revised)
ISBN: 978-1-56765-627-5
NYC Item 56765-627-4

Please visit our Web site at *www.amscopub.com*

TEXT ACKNOWLEDGMENT
Pages 216–217: Words and music by Malvina Reynolds, from the song "Little Boxes," © 1962 by Schroder Music Co. (ASCAP), renewed 1990. Reprinted by permission. All rights reserved.

Preface

This revised second edition of *Reviewing U.S. History and Government* is a review text for students preparing to take the 11th-grade New York State Regents examination.

Following an introduction about U.S. geography, there is an initial treatment of the origins and instruments of U.S. government. Chapter 1 describes the founding of the republic, Chapter 2 treats the drafting of the Constitution and Bill of Rights, and Chapter 3 analyzes the federal government and state and local governments as they exist today.

Chapters 4 through 9 present a concise review from the colonial period to industrialization in the post–Civil War United States.

Since an understanding of 20th- and early 21st-century trends and events is critical if Americans are to cope successfully with the changes ahead in this century, the remaining 13 chapters deal with events since 1900.

Throughout, historical topics are presented in *outline form*, arranged in three levels of headings. This format is intended to enhance review work.

Significant changes, additions, and special features reflect the new course of study:

★ a *U.S. geography introduction* emphasizing how geographical features have shaped the American experience

★ a *chapter-opening overview* in three parts: documents, laws, and Supreme Court cases; events; and people

★ influences on the development of our democratic society—*Enlightenment thought* as reflected in the U.S. plan of government, and *federal laws and constitutional amendments* defining and protecting the rights of African Americans

★ expanded coverage of U.S. Supreme Court *landmark cases*

★ inclusion of the experiences of *women and ethnic minorities*

★ *tables, diagrams, graphs, maps, illustrations, and cartoons*—for interest, information, and skill building

★ mid-chapter *In Reviews* to target important subjects and concepts

★ *Chapter Reviews* of Regents-style multiple-choice questions (many testing comprehension of visuals and readings), thematic essays, and document-based questions (DBQs).

Four important features comprise the final portion of the book. (1) A special appendix presents a *student's study guide* for reviewing the entire course and provides proven test-taking strategies for multiple-choice, thematic essay, and document-based questions. (2) For reinforcement, a *glossary* succinctly defines every important vocabulary term that appears in bold type in the text. (3) A comprehensive *index* facilitates easy reference to the content of the text. (4) The book concludes with the most recent U.S. history and government Regents examinations to test student competency.

Our nation derives its unique identity and character from the contributions of many people over centuries of history. As teachers and writers of that remarkable history, we feel privileged to present it to you in a solid review format.

Andrew Peiser
Michael Serber

PICTURE CREDITS

Contents

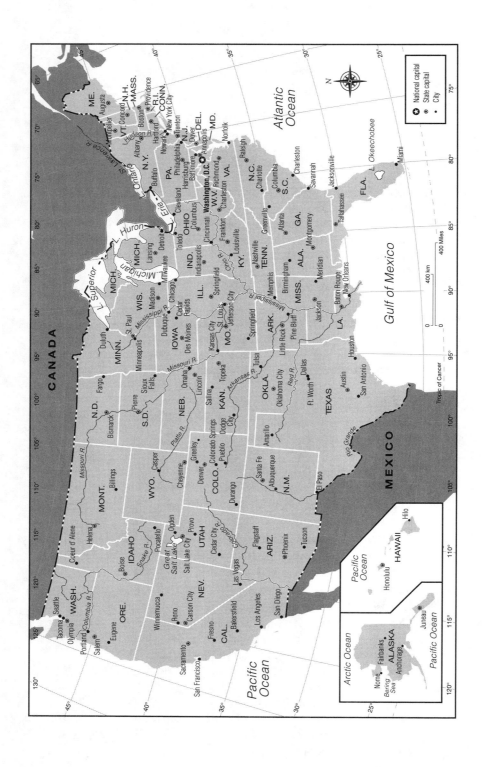

Introduction
Geography of the United States

★ **Objectives**

★ To understand how geography has helped shape the American experience.

★ To identify key U.S. geographic features.

★ To describe how landforms, climate, and vegetation are related.

★ To see how geographic factors help determine economic activities throughout the nation.

Geography and the American Experience

Geography is the study of Earth and its inhabitants. It reveals a given area's physical features, biology, and native culture.

Advantages of Immense Size

In **area**—the measure of how much of Earth's surface one place covers—the United States is the fourth largest country in the world.

Variation in Climate and Vegetation The United States reaches from the Arctic (Alaska) to the tropics (Hawaii). The 48 contiguous states—those sharing an uninterrupted expanse—cover a range of climates. Thus, almost anything can grow somewhere in the United States.

Range and Abundance of Resources Large countries usually have many of the resources on which people and industries depend. U.S. resources are varied and abundant. The United States is the first or second in world production of oil, natural gas, and coal, and a major producer of other minerals needed in modern industries.

Room to Grow **Population density** is found by dividing a place's population by its area. The result is the number of people living in a square mile or kilometer. The U.S. population numbers approximately 280 million. With its relatively low population density—about 78 people per square mile (30 per square kilometer)—the United States has room to grow. China is twice as crowded, India 10 times, the Netherlands 12 times, and Korea 16 times.

Fortunate Location

Oceans for Security and Trade The United States shares no borders with unfriendly neighbors. Wide oceans separate it from the major centers of world power in Europe and Asia.

Such barriers as mountains and deserts do not hamper U.S. trade with the outside world. The Atlantic and Pacific oceans provide easy access for trade. Long coastlines and deep harbors allow ships to load and unload cargoes easily.

★ In Review

1. In what ways does the United States benefit from its great size?
2. Compare the United States to a country that lacks sea or ocean coastlines.

Physical Features

Forces That Have Shaped U.S. Landforms

Landforms are natural features of Earth's surface, including parts that are covered by water.

Continental Drift Scientists believe that the continents were once one or two land masses. They began to break up and drift apart some 240 million years ago. According to the theory of **continental drift**, continents "float" on immense plates of rock. Moving at fractions of an inch a year, they sometimes gain or lose land by colliding with one another. Such collisions in the remote past pushed the surfaces together to form great mountains. When plates broke apart, deep oceans formed.

Volcanoes and Earthquakes Volcanoes and earthquakes occur frequently between shifting continental plates.

Volcanoes occur when hot gases and **magma** (melted rock beneath Earth's surface) build up pressure and spew forth as **lava**. Volcanoes gradually create cone-shaped mountains. Two active volcanoes in the continental United States are Mount St. Helens in Washington State and Lassen Peak in California. There are also volcanoes in Hawaii and Alaska.

Pressures beneath Earth's surface also cause **earthquakes**. The *San Andreas Fault*, for example, is an earthquake-prone fracture running southeast to northwest from southern California to the San Francisco area.

Glaciers **Glaciers** are found in Alaska, in mountainous areas, and near Canada. These ice-packed landforms develop where more snow falls in winter than can melt in summer. Glaciers spread during **ice ages**, when global temperatures dip sharply. During the last ice age, some 20,000 years ago, a glacier stretched from west of what is now Chicago to New York City and south to the Ohio River valley. Moving glaciers can slice off mountaintops, fill valleys with new soil, and gouge out depressions that become lakes.

Erosion **Erosion** is the wearing away of soil by wind, rain, or ice. The older a landform, the longer it has been ground down by erosion.

Mountain Ranges and Plateaus

Mountains are elevated areas of peaks and crests that rise above surrounding countryside. **Plateaus**

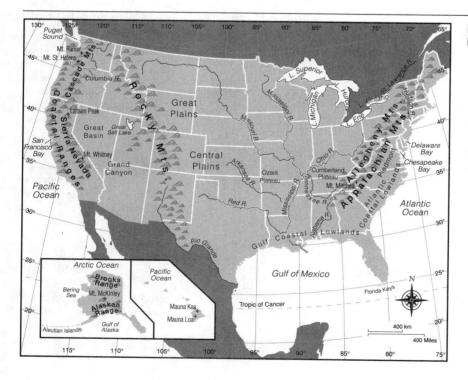

Physical Map of the United States

are flat or gently rolling expanses at high elevations. **Altitude** is the measurement of how high a landform lies above sea level or another surface, such as the ocean floor.

Appalachians The Appalachians, the most prominent mountain range in the East, stretch from Georgia and Alabama northward into Canada. They slowed westward expansion by European settlers. The highest point is Mount Mitchell (6684 feet) in North Carolina.

Western Mountain Ranges The Rockies are the easternmost of three major ranges in the West. The Rockies reach more than 12,000 feet in New Mexico, Utah, Wyoming, Idaho, and Montana, and above 14,000 feet in Colorado. Now a site for big-game hunting and skiing, the Rockies were once the domain of animal trappers.

West of the Rockies is a range with two names—the Sierra Nevada in California and the Cascades in Oregon and Washington. Farther west, the Coast ranges flank the Pacific and extend from Mexico to Alaska.

Alaska and Brooks Ranges The highest U.S. mountain is Mount McKinley (20,320 feet), part of the Alaska Range in south-central Alaska. The Brooks Range lies to the north.

Interior and Coastal Lowlands

Basin and Range Lowland deserts and areas of scrubby vegetation occupy part of the area between the Western mountain ranges. In landforms called **basins**, flowing water collects to form lakes that become very salty as water evaporates. (All water contains tiny amounts of salt.) Utah's Great Salt Lake lies in the Great Basin.

Great Plains, Central Plains, and Interior Lowlands A **plain** is a large area of level land. The Great Plains and Central Plains make up one of the most extensive lowlands in the world. They reach through the central United States from Texas into Canada. The more western Great Plains are drier than the Central Plains. The boundary between the two is defined by the amount of rainfall; it runs from eastern Texas and Oklahoma northward to eastern North Dakota.

The interior lowlands extend through Illinois, Indiana, Michigan, and most of Ohio. Along with the plains, this area is prime farming country.

Coastal Plains and Piedmont Coastal lowlands of the Southeast begin in Texas and extend northward to New York. Between them and the Appalachian Mountains lies the *Piedmont* (French for "foot" and "mountain"). As elevation suddenly drops, rivers flowing from mountains to sea form rapids and waterfalls. This boundary between the Piedmont and the coastal plains is called the **fall line**.

The northernmost part of the Atlantic coastal plain reaches inland into New York State, forming a narrow band on either side of the Hudson River.

Major Water Features

Great Lakes Together, the five Great Lakes make up the largest body of fresh water in the world. (See the map facing page 1.) Lake Michigan is entirely within the United States. Lakes Superior, Huron, Erie, and Ontario straddle the U.S.-Canadian border. First Native Americans and then Europeans used the lakes for fishing and transportation.

St. Lawrence River The Great Lakes empty into the Atlantic Ocean through the St. Lawrence River. In 1959, the United States and Canada finished building a series of canals known as the *St. Lawrence Seaway*. The seaway widens and deepens the St. Lawrence so that ships can travel between Lake Ontario and Montreal. From Montreal to the ocean, the St. Lawrence is **navigable** without canals.

Long before the seaway was built, the *Erie Canal* (completed in 1825) connected Lake Erie near Buffalo to the Hudson River near Albany. Thus, cargoes from the Midwest had a water route to New York City.

Mississippi River The greatest U.S. river, the Mississippi, is 2348 miles long. With its **tributaries** (rivers flowing into it), the Mississippi drains almost the entire area from the Appalachians to the Rockies. It pours into the Gulf of Mexico near New Orleans, Louisiana.

The Mississippi was a means of transport for Native Americans and European explorers into interior North America. An important part of today's industrial economy, the river has fostered the growth of many cities, as have most of the nation's smaller navigable rivers.

Extensive Coastlines

Access to oceans give the United States great advantages for trade and travel. Chesapeake and Delaware bays on the Atlantic coast and San Francisco Bay and Puget Sound on the Pacific coast are examples of protected inlets and bays. Seacoast states often have important fishing industries.

Atlantic, Gulf, and Pacific Fisheries The Atlantic fisheries off the eastern United States and Canada—including the Grand Banks off Newfoundland—contain some of the world's best fishing grounds. Native Americans first fished in these waters, and from colonial days to the present, many New England coastal villages have survived and prospered by fishing. The Chesapeake Bay and more southern coastal regions combine sports fishing with commercial fishing industries.

Gulf of Mexico fisheries are known for shrimp and other shellfish.

The Pacific coastal waters are rich in tuna, sardines, anchovies, and many other fish. The Northwest Coast is famous for the salmon that spawn in rivers flowing into the sea. They are a traditional harvest for Native Americans in the region.

Hawaii Hawaii is an **archipelago**, or chain of islands, formed by volcanic activity. The world's largest active volcano, Mauna Loa, is on the big island of Hawaii. Most Hawaiians live on Oahu.

Mineral and Energy Resources

True Minerals Minerals are solid substances occurring in nature. Most lack organic matter (by-products of living organisms). Since minerals do not replicate themselves, they are **nonrenewable resources**.

Metals are examples of true minerals. The most important for industry are iron, copper, and aluminum. Iron, the main ingredient of steel, is used in a variety of products. Copper is a good conductor of electricity. Aluminum, also an electrical conductor, is one of the lightest metals and, therefore, often substituted for steel in automobiles to lighten their weight. (See the map on page 5 for U.S. sources of metals.)

Energy Resources Coal, petroleum, and natural gas are **fossil fuels**. Since they developed from ancient organisms and minerals over millions of years, they are nonrenewable. The United States is the world's second largest producer of coal and a leading producer of petroleum (crude oil) and natural gas. Oil deposits are located in Texas and Oklahoma and beneath the waters along the Louisiana and California coastlines. Since 1957, however, the United States, in order to meet increasing demands for oil, has bought more crude oil from abroad than it has produced.

Electricity is another form of energy. Slightly more than half of U.S. electricity comes from coal. Another 20 percent comes from **nuclear power**. Uranium, a radioactive mineral used for producing nuclear power, has been found in greater quantities in the United States than elsewhere. Many U.S. sites are suited to producing **hydroelectric power**, generated when falling water turns turbines. Hydroelectric plants produce about 10 percent of U.S. electric power.

Since the 1970s, when industrial nations experienced energy shortages, efforts have been made to develop **alternative energy**:

★ **Solar power**, or energy from the sun, can be exemplified by a greenhouse. Glass walls and ceilings trap the sun's rays to grow plants. Another example is the heat sink, where the sun's warmth heats stone walls that slowly release heat after sundown. Space missions and calculators are run on solar batteries, which tap the sun's power to generate electricity.

★ **Alcohol** produced from corn can be burned by itself or mixed with gasoline (**gasohol**) to run automobile engines. Midwestern states are major producers of gasohol.

★ **Methane** is made by allowing organic matter, such as manure, to rot. Gases emitted are then captured for use in stoves and space heaters.

★ **Geothermal energy**, heat from within Earth, can be used to heat homes or generate electricity. Geothermal electricity plants are located in areas subject to volcanic activity.

★ **Wind power** generates electricity. "Windmill farms" are located at mountain passes, where winds are strong and persistent.

★ **Shale oil** is obtained by heating and crushing oil-bearing rocks.

Many forms of alternative energy are **renewable resources**. The sun's energy and wind can be used without diminishing the supply. Alcohol and methane use resources that can be replicated. Shale oil is nonrenewable.

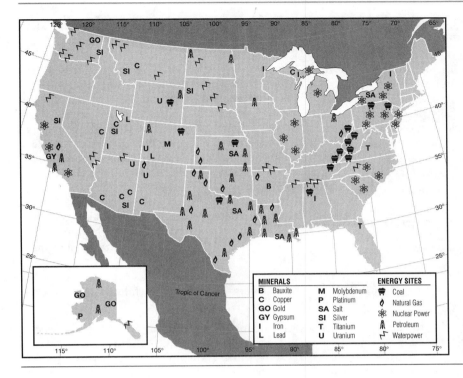

MINERALS

B	Bauxite	**M**	Molybdenum
C	Copper	**P**	Platinum
GO	Gold	**SA**	Salt
GY	Gypsum	**SI**	Silver
I	Iron	**T**	Titanium
L	Lead	**U**	Uranium

ENERGY SITES

Coal
Natural Gas
Nuclear Power
Petroleum
Waterpower

Major U.S. Mineral Deposits and Energy Resources

Importance to the Economy Many Western states have mining industries based on their metal resources. Coal mining has been a traditional activity in the Appalachians, from West Virginia and Pennsylvania to Alabama.

Industries have grown up where local resources are abundant or good transportation routes exist. The steel industries of Pittsburgh in western Pennsylvania and Birmingham in Alabama are based on nearby supplies of coal and iron. Ships and railroads carried the coal of the Appalachians and the iron ore of Minnesota and Wisconsin to the Great Lakes cities that became important centers of industry.

★ In Review

1. Define landforms, continental drift, ice age, plateau, altitude, plain, Piedmont, fall line, tributary, archipelago, fossil fuel.
2. Give examples of *each* of the following natural features of the United States: (a) mountain ranges, (b) interior lowlands, (c) coastal plains, (d) lakes, (e) rivers.
3. Describe U.S. energy resources, making a distinction between renewable and nonrenewable ones.

Major U.S. Geographic Zones

Climate Zones

Climate is the year-to-year weather conditions prevailing over long periods. The United States has a wide range of climates.

Factors Determining Climate

★ **Latitude** is the measurement of how far a place is from the equator, where it is very hot, and from Earth's poles, where it is very cold. Except for Hawaii and Alaska, the United States lies in the middle latitudes of the Northern Hemisphere, neither very near the equator nor the north pole.

★ **Altitude** is the measurement of elevation above sea level or the ocean floor. High altitudes are colder than low altitudes. Even close to the equator, the highest mountaintops may be covered in snow year-round.

★ The direction of **prevailing winds**—the normal direction from which high-altitude winds blow—also affects climate. High-altitude winds carry weather systems around the globe. In the middle latitudes, prevailing winds blow from west to east, so storms generally cross the United States from the Pacific to the Atlantic.

★ Mountains interact with prevailing winds. As storm systems gain altitude to cross over high places, they generally release their moisture. Since U.S. storms typically move from west to east, the western sides of mountains receive rain or snow, while the eastern sides remain dry.

★ Other landforms that influence climate are oceans and lakes. Generally, the closer to an ocean a place is, the more rain or snow it will receive.

Large bodies of water lose or gain heat slowly, so they hold their heat into early winter and remain cool in early summer.

★ Oceans have currents that circulate water from one area to another. In the Atlantic Ocean, the *Gulf Stream* carries warm water from the Gulf of Mexico north along the eastern U.S. coastline and then eastward toward northern Europe. This movement makes the eastern United States and much of Europe warmer than most other places at the same latitudes.

When waters of the tropical Pacific are warm, a condition known as *El Niño* contributes to strong storms and bitter winters in the United States. When these waters are cool, another condition, *La Niña*, brings warm winters to the Southwest, cool winters to the northern Midwest, and mild winters to the East.

Temperature Variations U.S. temperatures vary widely from day to day and season to season. The **growing season** is the period between the last frost of spring and the first frost of autumn. Most parts of the country have reasonably long growing seasons, during which farmers can raise a wide variety of crops. Temperatures influence the kinds of homes people live in and the clothes they wear.

Moisture Variations Rain, snow, sleet, and hail are all forms of **precipitation**. The amount of moisture that falls on an area helps to determine what crops can be grown there.

Key Climate Regions The United States has ten major climate regions:

★ The north coast of Alaska along the Arctic Ocean has an **arctic climate**. Winters are long, dark, and cold. Summers last only a few weeks.

★ From its western coast to its interior, Alaska has a **subarctic climate**. The long, dark winters are less cold than in the arctic region. The short summers are warm, with long hours of daylight that allow many types of crops to grow.

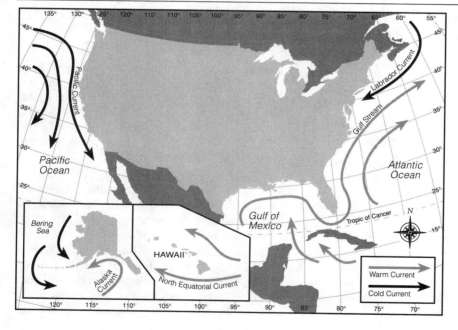

Ocean Currents Affecting the United States

★ A **marine West Coast climate** prevails from southern Alaska to northern California. Winds from the Pacific help keep temperatures cool in summer and mild in winter. Annual rainfall is relatively high (more than 40 to 80 inches) and comes mainly between October and May.

★ Except for its northern coast and much of its interior lowlands, California has a **Mediterranean climate**, with hot, dry summers and cool, rainy winters. The growing season lasts almost all year. Because summers are dry, farmers often use **irrigation** (artificial means of watering crops.)

★ The interior mountain ranges of New Mexico, Arizona, Nevada, Utah, Colorado, Wyoming, Idaho, and parts of California, Oregon, and Washington have a **highland climate**. Depending on altitude, these areas have cool to cold temperatures and much more moisture than the surrounding lowlands.

★ The western Great Plains and the lowlands between the mountains of the West generally have a **steppe climate**, with lots of sunshine and not much rain.

★ Most of the Southwestern lowlands have a dry **desert climate**.

★ The northeastern quarter of the continental United States, from the edge of the Great Plains to the Atlantic, has a **humid continental climate**. "Humid" means moist, and annual rainfall exceeds 40 inches, tapering off to around 20 inches in the western Great Plains. Summers range from short and cool to long and hot, and winters from bitterly cold to mild.

★ The southeastern United States, as far inland as Texas and Oklahoma, generally has a **humid subtropical climate**. Summers are hot, with frequent thunderstorms, while winters are mild, with frequent rain and occasional snow. The growing season is longer than farther north, and rainfall averages from about 30 to 80 inches a year.

★ The tip of Florida and Florida Keys have a mild **tropical climate**. Because of Hawaii's location in the lower northern latitudes, prevailing winds, known in the tropics as **trade winds**, come from the northeast. Blowing off the Pacific, they help keep the islands' temperatures mild, averaging from 72 degrees Fahrenheit in February to 79 degrees in August. Tropical Florida is usually hotter in the summer.

U.S. Climate Regions

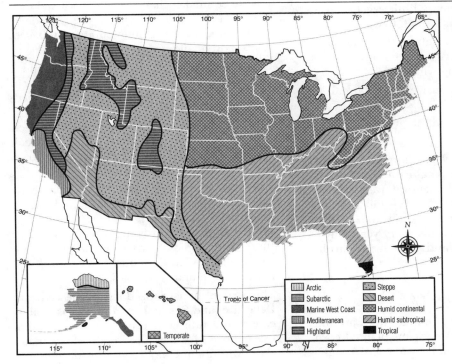

Natural Vegetation Zones

"Natural vegetation" means the plants that would grow in an area even if humans did nothing. **Natural vegetation zones** are bands of territory where climate and other natural conditions produce characteristic mixtures or communities of plants.

Major U.S. Natural Vegetation Zones See the map on page 9 for the locations of U.S. natural vegetation zones, and compare them with the climate regions shown on the map on page 7.

★ The **tundra zone** has very low temperatures, little precipitation, and a short growing season. Typical plants are mosses, lichens, and stunted trees. In much of the zone, the summer sun melts only the uppermost soil, leaving a frozen underlayer called **permafrost**.

★ In the **coniferous forest zone**, the dominant trees are evergreens, which bear their seeds in cones.

★ The dominant trees in the **broadleaf forest zone** are oaks, maples, and other **deciduous trees**, which lose their broad, flat leaves seasonally.

★ The **mixed forest zone** comprises coniferous and broadleaf trees.

★ In the **Mediterranean scrub zone**, hot, dry summers and wet winters limit vegetation to low-growing shrubs and small trees.

★ With relatively low rainfall, the **grassland zone** has no forests. Irrigation, however, makes it excellent for growing wheat.

★ The **steppe zone** has just enough rainfall to support grass.

★ Only scanty scrub vegetation grows in the dry **desert zone**.

Two additional U.S. vegetation zones occur only in Hawaii. In the **tropical rain forest zone**, year-round warmth and plentiful rain sustain many kinds of trees, some extremely tall and with thick undergrowth. Neighboring lowlands experience several short dry seasons every year, which create a **tropical grassland zone** with shrubs and scattered trees.

Agriculture and Industry

Agriculture started in the United States around 2000 B.C., when Native Americans planted corn in what is now Arizona and New Mexico. As agri-culture developed, natural vegetation was supplemented by new plant varieties created by human experimentation and selection. People from outside the region introduced entirely new plant species.

Effect of Culture, Technology, and Nature on Agriculture Culture determines what a region's people choose to eat. Technology determines what tools they use to grow crops. Culture *and* technology determine what crops people use for purposes other than food. These two factors interact with nature to influence what industries are found in an area. Industries that depend on mineral or energy resources tend to be near necessary raw materials. Industries that use agricultural products tend to be where the crops are grown. The proximity of customers to products and the availability of transportation for shipping both raw materials and finished goods also affect agriculture and industry.

Agriculture and Industry by Region The United States can be divided into seven regions with distinctive blends of agriculture and industry:

★ *New England* (Vermont, New Hampshire, Maine, Massachusetts, Connecticut, and Rhode Island) has valleys, hillsides, and mountains. Because of varied terrain, farms tend to be smaller than elsewhere. Much farmland is devoted to hay and pasture for dairy cattle. Other crops include potatoes, tobacco, fruits, and maple syrup.

Because of easy access to ocean transport, New England tapped into world trade early in its colonial history. Its first industries were fishing, shipbuilding, shoemaking, and textiles. Later industries include firearms, precision tools, aircraft engines, and high-tech products. New England's service industries include banking and insurance.

★ The *Mid-Atlantic region* (New York, New Jersey, Pennsylvania, Delaware, and Maryland) has much level land as well as mountains. Because its growing season is longer than New England's, its farmers raise more varied crops. They produce dairy products, poultry, fruit, and vegetables.

This region industrialized early. The Hudson, Delaware, and Susquehanna rivers, as well as canals and railroads, provide transportation. Ocean ports give access to imported raw materials. Mid-Atlantic industries include steel and

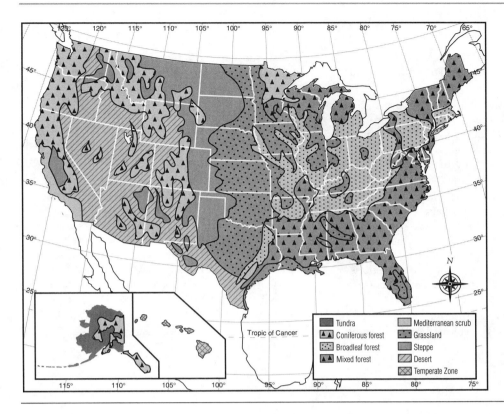

Tundra Coniferous forest Broadleaf forest Mixed forest Mediterranean scrub Grassland Steppe Desert Temperate Zone

Tropic of Cancer

Eight U.S. Vegetation Zones

other kinds of manufacturing, banking, advertising, and publishing.

★ The *South* (Virginia, West Virginia, North Carolina, South Carolina, Georgia, Florida, Alabama, Mississippi, Louisiana, Texas, Oklahoma, Arkansas, Kentucky, and Tennessee) has high rainfall and hot summers. Cotton, whose cultivation requires many laborers, was the South's main crop before slavery was outlawed. Afterwards, farmers began to grow other crops besides cotton.

After the Civil War (1861–1865), the South gradually developed a strong industrial base. Oil and natural gas deposits helped the region develop refining, petrochemical, and plastic industries. Other industries are textile manufacturing, papermaking, fishing and fish processing, and iron and steel production.

★ The *Midwest* (Ohio, Indiana, Illinois, Michigan, Wisconsin, Minnesota, North Dakota, South Dakota, Nebraska, Iowa, Kansas, and Missouri) is relatively flat. Its farms cover hundreds of acres. Much of the nation's corn grows in the "corn belt" from Ohio to Nebraska. Some of it feeds pigs and cattle that are later slaughtered for meat. Wheat is the leading crop on the drier Great Plains farther

west. The Midwest also produces soybeans and dairy products. Wisconsin and Minnesota are known as the "dairy belt."

The Midwest has long been a center of heavy industry, including iron and steel processing and the manufacture of automobiles, farm equipment, machine tools, and computers.

★ Except along its Pacific coast, the *West* (Washington, Oregon, California, Nevada, Arizona, New Mexico, Utah, Colorado, Wyoming, Idaho, and Montana) is dry. Farmers often use irrigation. Major crops are nuts, wheat, sugar beets, beans, alfalfa, wheat, fruits, potatoes, and cotton.

Mining is widespread throughout the West. Today's miners operate immense open-pit coal mines and use up-to-date machinery to extract copper, uranium, molybdenum, petroleum, and other minerals. Western industries include the production of oil and the manufacture of mining equipment, aircraft, ships, and consumer goods.

Hollywood in Los Angeles, California, is the nation's motion picture center. "Silicon Valley," where high-tech industries turn out computer-related products, is located near San Francisco.

★ Despite long winters and cool summers, farmers in *Alaska* raise various fruits and vegetables and run dairy farms.

Logging, fishing, and gold mining are major industries. In the 1960s, oil deposits were discovered at Prudhoe Bay in the far north. A pipeline transports the oil across Alaska to Valdez, where it is shipped to refineries in the lower United States.

★ For decades, sugarcane and pineapple plantations in *Hawaii* drew workers from China, Japan, and the Philippines. Hawaii's rich mixture of races include their descendants, native Polynesians, and U.S. mainlanders. Today, because of competition from other world regions, Hawaiian sugar and pineapple producers are converting to new crops such as peanuts.

Because of its warm climate and extensive coastline, Hawaii has developed an important tourist industry. Its factories process sugar and pineapples and manufacture consumer products.

★ In Review

1. Name six major factors that help determine a place's climate.
2. Name the country's eight main natural vegetation zones, and tell how they relate to climate.
3. In what region or regions of the United States would you be likely to find each of the following: (a) uranium mines, (b) the center of the auto industry, (c) pineapple plantations, (d) sugarcane, (e) the "corn belt," (f) a heavy dependence on irrigation, (g) the "dairy belt"?

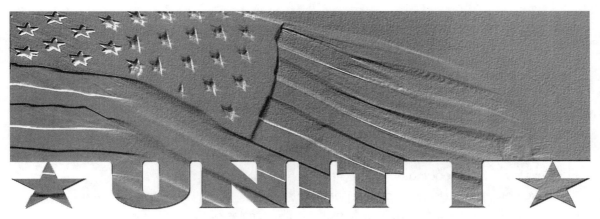

★ UNIT 1 ★

Constitutional Foundations of American Society

Chapter 1
Origins of the Constitution

★ Documents and Laws	★ Events	★ People
Magna Carta (1215)	Glorious Revolution (1688)	John Adams
The Iroquois Confederacy (about 1570)	Zenger Case (1735)	Samuel Adams
	French and Indian War (1754–1763)	Crispus Attucks
Mayflower Compact (1620)		Benjamin Franklin
Habeas Corpus Act (1679)	Boston Massacre (1770)	Patrick Henry
English Bill of Rights (1689)	Boston Tea Party (1773)	John Jay
Stamp Tax (1765)	Battles of Lexington and Concord (1775)	Thomas Jefferson
Coercive Acts (1774)		John Locke
Declaration of Independence (1776)	Revolutionary War (1775–1783)	James Madison
New York State Constitution (1777)	Battle of Saratoga (1777)	Baron Montesquieu
	Battle of Yorktown (1781)	Jean-Jacques Rousseau
Articles of Confederation (1781)	Shays's Rebellion (1786–1787)	Voltaire
Northwest Ordinance (1787)		George Washington
U.S. Constitution (written 1787; ratified 1789)		

★ To explain the influence of the Enlightenment on U.S. political rights and institutions.

★ To describe the experiences of various groups in the American colonies.

★ To explain events leading up to the American Revolution.

★ To evaluate the Declaration of Independence.

★ To describe the strengths and weaknesses of the Articles of Confederation.

Historical Foundations of Representative Government

In a **democracy**, the people govern themselves. In a form of democracy called a **republic**, people elect representatives to make and carry out laws that benefit them. The philosophers of the Enlightenment, as well as events in Britain and its American colonies, influenced the development of U.S. representative democracy.

European Philosophers of the Enlightenment

During the Age of Enlightenment (1600s–1700s), the leading thinkers in western Europe thought that society should be ruled by natural laws rather than the divine right of absolute monarchs:

★ *John Locke* (1632–1704), an Englishman, wrote *Two Treatises of Government* (1690). He stated that life, liberty, and property were **natural rights** that all persons are born with. A government should protect these natural rights. The people have a right to overthrow a ruler who fails to do so. Locke's ideas influenced American patriot Thomas Jefferson. When he wrote the *Declaration of Independence* (1776), he claimed that all people have the right to "life, liberty, and the pursuit of happiness."

★ *Baron Montesquieu* (1689–1755), a Frenchman, wrote *The Spirit of Laws* (1748). In it he argued that government should be separated into three branches: a legislative branch to pass laws, an executive branch to carry out laws, and a judicial branch to interpret laws. Such separation would prevent a person or group from gaining total control of the government. Montesquieu's ideas are the basis of the *U.S. Constitution*.

★ *Voltaire* (1694–1778), a Frenchman, wrote essays, plays, and letters that attacked the French monarchy, class privileges, torture, slavery, censorship, and religious intolerance. Voltaire argued that the best form of government was a monarchy with a constitution, a strong parliament, and civil rights for all—an idea based on the British monarchy. Many characteristics of British government were incorporated in the U.S. form of democracy.

★ *Jean-Jacques Rousseau* (1712–1778), a Swiss, wrote *The Social Contract*, in which he stated that the will of the people should guide the decisions of government. He felt that people are born good but corrupted by society. Rousseau's ideas had a profound influence on the writers of the U.S. Constitution.

Key English Limitations on Government

★ *Magna Carta.* In 1215, a group of nobles compelled England's King John to sign the *Magna Carta*. This document guaranteed (a) trial by a jury of the accused's equals and (b) the right of the Grand Council (group of nobles) to approve a monarch's proposed taxes.

★ *Parliament.* In 1295, King Edward I called on representatives of both the English nobility and the middle class to meet as a **parliament** (advisory group) to consider laws and taxes. Parliament became a check on the monarch's power to make laws and impose taxes. In 1679, Parliament passed the *Habeas Corpus Act* to protect people against unjust imprisonment. It required a judge to rule whether a person should be held in jail.

★ *Glorious Revolution.* In 1688, Parliament forced King James II to give up his throne to King William and Queen Mary. The *English Bill of Rights* (1689) then guaranteed such benefits as the right to a speedy jury trial, protection against excessive **bails** (money to obtain release pending trial) and fines, and Parliament's consent for collecting taxes, suspending laws, and keeping an army.

People in the American Colonies

Native Americans

Origins Native Americans are descendants of Asian peoples who probably migrated from Siberia to North America between 40,000 and 20,000 years ago.

Contact With Spaniards The first contact between Native Americans and Spaniards occurred mainly in Spanish America during and after the voyages of Columbus in the 1490s. Spain then colonized much of the Native Americans' land. The colonists forced Native Americans to work in mines, on **plantations** (large farms with many workers), and in Roman Catholic **missions**. Harsh treatment and European diseases killed off a large number of Native Americans.

Contact With the British The first long-term contact between the British and Native Americans occurred in Jamestown, Virginia, in the early 1600s. Many colonists starved to death during the winter of 1609–1610, but some survived on corn provided by Native Americans. One English leader, John Rolfe, learned how Native Americans grew tobacco. The export of tobacco to England improved conditions in Jamestown. As the colonists sought more land,

conflicts arose with Native Americans. Rolfe won a short period of peace when he married a Native American princess, Pocahontas. But war erupted when the colonists continued to take over Native American land.

Native Americans also helped the English Pilgrims, a religious community, survive the harsh New England winter. In time, however, the Pilgrims also aroused Native American anger by expanding into their territory. The colonists, aided by firearms, easily defeated the Native Americans in battle. Moreover, smallpox brought from Europe wiped out entire Native American villages.

When the Quakers, another religious group, settled in Pennsylvania, their leader, William Penn, set a policy of living peaceably with the Delaware Indians of the region.

French and Indian War

Between 1754 and 1763, Great Britain and France fought for control of North America in the French and Indian War. Both countries arranged alliances with Native American groups. The British were allied with the Iroquois nation, and the French with the Hurons. The British victory gained them control of much of North America, including Canada.

African Slaves

Many enslaved Africans were taken to American colonies against their will. They labored in Spanish America as early as the 1500s as replace-

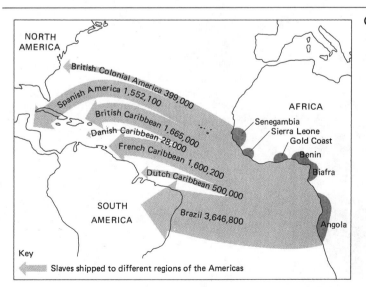

Global Slave Trade, 1700s

NORTH AMERICA

British Colonial America 399,000

Spanish America 1,552,100

British Caribbean 1,665,000

Danish Caribbean 28,000

French Caribbean 1,600,200

Dutch Caribbean 500,000

SOUTH AMERICA

Brazil 3,646,800

AFRICA

Senegambia
Sierra Leone
Gold Coast
Benin
Biafra
Angola

Key

→ Slaves shipped to different regions of the Americas

ments for Native Americans who had died from disease and overwork.

The slaves sold to the British colonists in North America represented about 6 percent of the total number shipped to the Americas. The first slaves in the British colonies arrived in Jamestown, Virginia, in 1619. By the time of the American Revolution, slaves in the original 13 states made up about 20 percent of the population.

Immigrants

A majority of immigrants to the British colonies from 1607 to 1776 came from the British Isles. The Puritans came to escape religious persecution in England. The Quakers sought religious freedom in Pennsylvania under the leadership of William Penn. James Oglethorpe helped criminals, debtors, and the poor seeking new economic opportunities to settle Georgia. Some immigrants came as **indentured servants**, who agreed to work for a number of years in return for their passage to America.

Non-British immigrants came chiefly from France, Germany, Holland, and Sweden.

Difficulties

★ separation from family, friends, and familiar surroundings
★ city dwellers learning to farm
★ diseases
★ attacks from Native Americans
★ dependence on supplies shipped from England.

★ In Review

1. How did the Enlightenment influence the development of the United States?
2. Describe three important events in British history that limited the power of government.
3. Contrast the experiences of Native Americans, African Americans, and European Americans during the colonial period.

Colonial Experience

Charters and Self-Government

House of Burgesses/Mayflower Compact In 1619, the settlers of Jamestown, Virginia, founded the *House of Burgesses*, America's first representative assembly for making laws. In 1620, the Pilgrims drew up the *Mayflower Compact*. It stated that the laws of Plymouth, Massachusetts, would be subject to the colonists' consent. Subsequently, New England townspeople regularly held **town meetings** to discuss problems and to vote directly on laws.

Although English monarchs appointed governors for the colonies founded during the next 150 years, popularly elected assemblies made most of the colonies' laws. By 1760, colonial assemblies enjoyed the **power of the purse**—the right to approve or reject new tax proposals.

Colonial democracy was limited. Only the property-owning minority had the right to vote. Women, slaves, and free males without property could not vote.

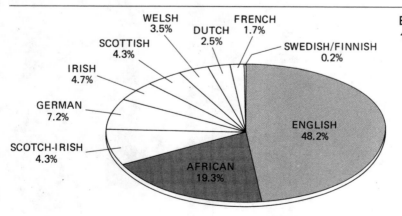

WELSH 3.5%
FRENCH 1.7%
DUTCH 2.5%
SCOTTISH 4.3%
SWEDISH/FINNISH 0.2%
IRISH 4.7%
GERMAN 7.2%
ENGLISH 48.2%
SCOTCH-IRISH 4.3%
AFRICAN 19.3%

Ethnic Groups in the United States, 1790

Albany Plan of Union In 1754, representatives from Britain, from seven of the colonies, and from the Iroquois nation met in Albany to discuss a plan of defense against France. Benjamin Franklin, the representative from Pennsylvania, proposed the *Albany Plan of Union*. It was based on the *Iroquois Confederacy*, in which six Native American peoples had united for mutual defense. The Albany Plan of Union aimed to bring colonial representatives together in a council led by a representative of the British crown but was rejected.

Business and Property Laws

Colonial land was privately owned and purchased through legally binding contracts. Indentured servants were expected to serve their full terms. The monarch gave **joint-stock companies** exclusive rights to trade in specific areas of the colonies. People invested in these businesses in hopes of making a profit.

Under a system called **mercantilism**, colonies were expected to produce only what England needed and to buy everything they needed from England. England did not enforce this policy until the 1760s.

Native American Governments

At first, Native Americans were loyal to their village or clan. In time, however, several villages formed tribal councils to better defend themselves. Loyalty to the tribe rather than to the village increased. Warriors became the most important members of a tribe.

In colonial New York, the six nations of the Iroquois Confederacy had prompted the Albany Plan for Union and may have influenced the plan

Franklin's 1754 cartoon advocating colonial union

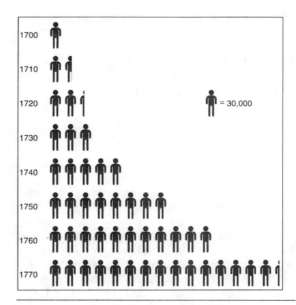

Growth of African Colonial Population, 1700s

of government created by the Articles of Confederation, adopted in 1781. (See page 19.)

Slavery

The South Slavery in the United States first developed in Chesapeake, an area that included both Virginia and Maryland. As demand for the region's major crop, tobacco, grew, so did the demand for slaves. The economies of South Carolina and Georgia depended on the production of rice. When rice exports to Europe grew from approximately 15,000 pounds in 1700 to 80 million pounds in the 1770s, both colonies became reliant on slave labor.

Slavery also developed in the French territory of Louisiana. Captive Africans worked on rural rice and tobacco plantations and in such cities as New Orleans as craftworkers and domesticated servants.

The North The North had few large agricultural enterprises except farms that produced wheat and **provisioning plantations** that produced food and lumber for sugar plantations in the West Indies. These spreads used slave labor. Elsewhere in the North, slaves served as laborers and skilled artisans. Because the slavery system was less advantageous to the Northern economy, it never became as important as in the South.

African Culture

★ music with "call and response" features

★ wood carvings, folk medicines, and charms

★ mixture of Christianity and **animism**, the African belief in nature spirits

★ African names

★ slave houses modeled after West African houses

★ pottery similar to that found in Nigeria and Ghana.

Slavery and Democracy During the American Revolution, opponents of the rebellion noted that the revolutionaries demanded their own freedom while denying it to others. Between the end of the Revolution in 1783 and 1800, slavery ended in the North. At the same time, it expanded in the South. There, the cotton crop (made more profitable by the invention of the cotton gin in 1793) demanded a large, cheap workforce.

Freedom of the Press

The *Zenger Case* expanded colonial rights. When John Peter Zenger published an article criticizing the governor of New York, he was arrested in 1734 for **libel** (writing a false and unfavorable opinion about another person). At his trial, in 1735, Zenger's lawyer argued that the article was true. The jury agreed and declared him innocent of libel. This ruling established the principle of freedom of the press, an important part of the First Amendment to the U.S. Constitution.

Rights of English Citizens

Prior to the French and Indian War, Britain practiced **salutary neglect** in its colonies. That is, it usually allowed the colonists to govern themselves, did not enforce laws requiring the colonies to trade only with England, did not collect taxes, and allowed the establishment of popular assemblies. It did not, however, allow colonists to elect representatives to Britain's Parliament.

American Revolution

Great Britain won the French and Indian War (1754–1763) and gained control of French Canada. This victory soon led the 13 American colonies to revolt against Britain.

Causes

Change in Colonial Policy The French and Indian War put Britain in debt just when it needed money and greater political control to maintain its expanded empire. The government decided to enforce its trade laws, station a permanent military force in the colonies, and collect new taxes there.

Closing of the Frontier The growing movement of colonists west of the Appalachian Mountains provoked Native Americans into attacking new settlements and British forts in the region. Britain's *Proclamation of 1763* forbade such resettlement and even visits there without permission. Colonists, eager for new land and opportunities, were furious.

Resistance to British Taxation Parliament taxed the colonies without their assemblies' consent. The colonists protested against (1) the *Stamp Tax* (1765) on colonial newspapers and legal documents and (2) import taxes (1767) on tea, glass, and other articles from Britain. Resistance took the form of **boycotts** (refusal to buy British goods), riots against tax collectors, and the *Boston Tea Party* (dumping British tea into Boston Harbor, in 1773).

British Retaliation The British soon retaliated. In the *Boston Massacre* (1770), British troops fired on a crowd and killed five colonists, including an African American named Crispus Attucks. As punishment for the Boston Tea Party, the *Coercive Acts* (1774) closed Boston Harbor to shipping.

First Battles: Lexington and Concord On April 19, 1775, British troops marched into Lexington, Massachusetts, and fired upon a small band of armed Americans. Farmers firing from behind trees and stone walls drove back the British as they tried to move on to Concord.

Revolutionary Ideology

In the earliest stages of the war, most Americans wanted only to defend their rights, not to gain independence. *Common Sense*, a pamphlet by Thomas Paine, however, changed the minds of many. Paine wrote that it made no sense for a small island kingdom like Great Britain to rule over the vastly larger American lands at a great distance.

On two occasions, delegates met in Philadelphia to plan a defense of their rights. This body of delegates was known as the *Continental Congress*

Boston Massacre, 1770

and served as the governing body for the American revolutionaries. The *First Continental Congress* (1774) unsuccessfully petitioned the British government to repeal its taxes and other harsh measures. In 1776, the year after the British and

Americans had clashed at Lexington and Concord and at Bunker Hill outside Boston (1775), the *Second Continental Congress* declared the independence of a new nation, the United States.

General Arguments for Independence Drawing on the theories of John Locke, Thomas Jefferson wrote the Declaration of Independence. In it, he stated that governments must be (1) representative of the people and (2) limited in power by a recognition of basic human rights. If any government violates people's natural rights, then they have the right to "alter or to abolish" that government.

Specific Arguments for Independence Specific grievances against the British king demonstrated that the colonists' rights had been repeatedly violated. These included (1) dissolving of colonial assemblies, (2) stationing British troops in the colonies, and (3) "imposing taxes without [the colonists'] consent."

Continuing Importance of the Declaration People in many nations have used the Declaration to justify their own struggles against oppressive governments. Since it states that all men are created equal, the Declaration served as an important document in the fight to end slavery in the United States.

American Colonies, 1763 and 1774

★ ★ ★ ★ ★

THE DECLARATION OF INDEPENDENCE

. . . That whenever any form of government becomes destructive of these ends, it is the right of the people to alter or to abolish it, and to institute new government, laying its foundation on such principles and organizing its powers in such form as to them shall seem most likely to effect their safety and happiness. Prudence, indeed, will dictate that governments long established should not be changed for light and transient causes; and, accordingly, all experience hath shown that mankind are more disposed to suffer, while evils are sufferable, than to right themselves by abolishing the forms to which they are accustomed. But when a long train of abuses and usurpations, pursuing invariably the same object, evinces a design to reduce them under absolute despotism, it is their right, it is their duty, to throw off such government, and to provide new guards for their future security.

Revolutionary Leaders

★ *Benjamin Franklin* assisted in the writing of the Declaration of Independence and represented the Continental Congress in France during the Revolutionary War. He helped establish a republican form of government in the United States.

★ *George Washington* commanded the Continental Army. He was elected first president of the United States and served for two terms.

★ *Samuel Adams* organized a boycott of British goods. He set up the *Committee of Correspondence* by which colonists shared their opinions and activities with one another. He served as a Massachusetts delegate to the Second Continental Congress.

★ *John Adams* served as a Massachusetts delegate to the First Continental Congress and argued against Britain's right to tax the colonies. He served with Thomas Jefferson on the committee that wrote the Declaration of Independence. He was elected second president of the United States.

★ *Patrick Henry* was a Virginia delegate to the First and Second Continental Congresses. His speeches urging independence influenced many colonists to support revolution.

War for Independence

Early Defeats At first, Washington's troops, disorganized and untrained, suffered many defeats. By the end of 1776, British troops occupied Boston and New York. The American capital, Philadelphia, fell to the British the following year.

Turning Points: Trenton and Saratoga American hopes were failing when Washington launched a successful surprise attack on Trenton, New Jersey, on Christmas Night, 1776. A decisive American victory at Saratoga, New York, in October 1777 against British General John Burgoyne convinced France to give the Americans military and naval assistance. This news helped the needy Continental Army survive the severe winter of 1777–1778 at Valley Forge, Pennsylvania.

United States in 1783

Victory at Yorktown Aided by French troops and ships, Washington's army defeated Britain's commanding general, Lord Cornwallis, at Yorktown, Virginia (1781). Two years later in Paris, American and British delegates signed a peace treaty ending the war. Great Britain recognized the United States as an independent nation. The western border of the new nation was to be the Mississippi River.

Contributions of African Americans Approximately 5000 free and enslaved African Americans fought against Britain in the Revolutionary War. After Britain offered freedom to any slaves who fought the colonists, the revolutionists made the same promise to slaves who fought with them. Thus, African Americans fought on both sides. After the war, some ex-slaves who had fought for the British emigrated to the West Indies or England.

★ In Review

1. How did political developments during the colonial period increase the rights of colonists?
2. Explain how slavery influenced the economy of Southern colonies.
3. Identify three acts of Parliament that led to protest in the American colonies.
4. Discuss the ways in which the Declaration of Independence expressed ideas of representative government and limited government.

Early U.S. Government

State Constitutional Governments

During the Revolutionary War, all 13 former colonies declared themselves states and wrote **constitutions** (written plans of government). These documents provided that final authority rested with the people.

New York State Constitution The New York State Constitution (1777) exemplified other state constitutions. It provided for a **bicameral** (two-house) legislative branch, an executive branch, a judicial branch, and a bill of rights. The bill of rights was to guarantee freedom of religion and many of the rights in the English Bill of Rights (see pages 12–13). Such republican principles were later incorporated in the U.S. Constitution.

Abolition of Slavery in the North In 1799, New York passed an act designed to gradually achieve **abolition** of slavery. This law freed future-born males at age 28 and future-born females at age 25. By 1800, all the Northern states had passed laws to end slavery. By 1810, most African Americans in the North were free citizens.

Articles of Confederation

During and after the Revolution, delegates from the 13 states to the Continental Congress drew up the *Articles of Confederation*. This document describing the new government's official powers was approved by the states in 1781:

★ *Organization*. The one-house lawmaking body was the Continental Congress. There was no executive branch to enforce the laws or national court system to interpret them. Each state delegation could cast one vote on each issue.

★ *Powers*. Congress could declare war, make peace, and conduct foreign affairs.

★ *Achievements*. Congress under the Articles brought the Revolutionary War to a successful end. It established the *Northwest Ordinance* (1787), a workable plan for governing the lands between the Appalachian Mountains and the Mississippi River; the ordinance also prohibited slavery there.

★ *Weaknesses*. Congress could not impose taxes and relied on money donated by the states to pay expenses. Laws had to be approved by a two-thirds majority of the states. Congress could not regulate commerce between the states. It issued paper currency that became nearly worthless. Unanimous agreement by the states was necessary to change the Articles.

In the 1780s, economic and political troubles exposed the inadequacy of weak central government. An alarming example was *Shays'* Rebellion (1786–1787), a violent protest by Massachusetts farmers against the collection of a state tax.

★ In Review

1. What features from state constitutions were incorporated into the U.S. Constitution?
2. Describe how the national government was organized under the Articles of Confederation.
3. Summarize why state governments were stronger than the national government under the Articles of Confederation.

Chapter Review

MULTIPLE-CHOICE QUESTIONS

1. The development of a tobacco economy in Virginia, the marriage of Pocahontas and John Rolfe, and the Pilgrims' winter survival show that (1) relations between Native Americans and settlers were sometimes cordial (2) interactions between colonists and Native Americans never happened (3) Native Americans readily accepted British customs (4) war between colonists and Native Americans could have been avoided.

2. The pie graph on page 14 illustrates that in 1790 (1) more than half the colonists were English (2) Africans comprised the second largest ethnic group (3) almost half the population came from elsewhere than western Europe (4) most ethnic groups were English or African.

3. The map on page 17 shows that the Proclamation of 1763 and the Coercive Acts of 1774 (1) expanded settlement into Native American territory (2) permitted free travel between the Canadian colonies and the 13 American colonies (3) defined the boundaries between the Canadian colonies, the 13 colonies, Spanish Florida, and Native Americans (4) enhanced British control of the Mississippi.

4. According to the Boston Massacre illustration on page 17, (1) the crowd provoked the soldiers (2) British soldiers attacked unarmed colonists (3) the British government put its soldiers in a dangerous situation (4) the British government could not control overseas armies.

5. The issue or event that most directly led to the American Revolution was (1) freedom of speech and press (2) taxation by Britain (3) the African slave trade (4) the French and Indian War.

6. The passage from the Declaration of Independence on page 18 illustrates that separation from Britain reflected the ideas of (1) Voltaire (2) Locke (3) Montesquieu (4) Rousseau.

7. Which correctly explains the role of African Americans during the Revolution? (1) They did not participate. (2) They fought primarily on the British side. (3) They fought on the colonists' side when they were allowed to. (4) They fought on both sides.

8. The map on page 18 illustrates that (1) the British promised to leave North America (2) the Americans had captured parts of Canada (3) as a result of the Revolution, the United States gained significant territory (4) the United States was surrounded by Spanish territories.

9. The New York State Constitution (1) had to be changed because of the Revolution (2) created a single-house legislature (3) varied in its toleration of religious differences (4) preceded the U.S. Constitution and promoted republican principles.

10. The most accurate conclusion about the United States government under the Articles is that (1) the national government was powerless and accomplished nothing (2) order ceased to exist in some states but remained strong in others (3) the national government lacked power but succeeded in establishing a plan for the Northwest Territory (4) paper currency was worthless while the value of coined money was inflated.

THEMATIC ESSAYS

1. **Theme:** Colonial Democracy and Self-Government. The 13 American colonies established traditions of democracy and self-government before the Declaration of Independence was written.

   Task: Describe the extent to which there was democracy and/or self-government in colonial America prior to 1776.

   You may use any example from your study of American history and government. Some suggestions include the Mayflower Compact, the House of Burgesses, New England town meetings, and the Zenger trial.

2. **Theme:** Immigration to Colonial America. People came for a variety of reasons:

★ improve economic opportunity
★ to find political or religious freedom
★ because they had no choice.

Task: Choose two of the above reasons for immigration. For each, name the group and describe why they left their home country.

DOCUMENT-BASED QUESTION

*Read each document and answer the question that follows it. Then read the **Task** and write your essay. Include references to most of the documents and additional information you retain about U.S. history and government.*

Historical Context: By the 1760s and 1770s, a number of events and the colonial tradition of self-government led to a debate about independence from Britain.

Document 1: From John Locke, *Second Treatise of Government:*

Whenever the legislators endeavor to take away and destroy the property of the people, or to reduce them to slavery . . . they put themselves into a state of war with the people, who are thereupon absolved from any further obedience and are left to the common refuge which God hath provided for all men against violence.

Question: How does Locke feel that rulers should be treated when they disregard people's rights?

Document 2: From Thomas Paine, *Common Sense:*

Small islands not capable of protecting themselves are the proper objects for kingdoms to take under their care; but there is something very absurd in supposing a continent to be perpetually governed by an island. In no instance hath nature made the satellite larger than its primary planet; and as England and America, with respect to each other, reverse the common order of nature, it is evident that they belong to different systems. England to Europe: America to itself.

Question: Why does Paine feel that the colonies should declare independence?

Document 3: From Lord Mansfield, debate in the House of Lords, 1766, on repealing the Stamp Act:

It must be granted that they migrated with leave as colonies and therefore from the very meaning of the word were, are, and must be subjects, and owe allegiance and subjection to their mother country [England].

Question: How does Lord Mansfield feel about the relationship between colonies and the "mother country"?

Task: Using information from the documents and your knowledge of causes of the American Revolution, write an essay about whether the American Revolution was inevitable.

Chapter 2
The Constitution and Bill of Rights

★ Documents and Laws	★ Events	★ People
Great Compromise, or the Connecticut Plan (1787)	Constitutional Convention (1787)	Samuel Adams
New Jersey Plan (1787)		Alexander Hamilton
Virginia Plan (1787)		Patrick Henry
The Federalist (1787–1788)		Oliver Wendell Holmes
Bill of Rights (1791)		John Jay
Amendments 11 to 27 (1798–1992)		James Madison
Schenck v. *United States* (1919)		Earl Warren
Mapp v. *Ohio* (1961)		George Washington
Engel v. *Vitale* (1962)		
Gideon v. *Wainwright* (1963)		
School District of Abington Township v. *Schempp* (1963)		
Escobedo v. *Illinois* (1964)		
Miranda v. *Arizona* (1966)		
Katz v. *United States* (1967)		
Tinker v. *Des Moines School District* (1969)		
Furman v. *Georgia* (1972)		
Gregg v. *Georgia* (1976)		
Collin v. *Smith* (1978)		
Texas v. *Johnson* (1989)		

★ Objectives

★ To identify and understand the importance of key clauses in the Constitution.

★ To define and illustrate basic principles of the U.S. Constitution—federalism, separation of powers, checks and balances.

★ To know the main provisions of the U.S. Bill of Rights.

★ To evaluate selected landmark cases of the Supreme Court.

★ To understand that the Constitution is a living document that has changed over time.

Constitutional Convention

Representation and Process

Delegates from every state except Rhode Island went to Philadelphia in the summer of 1787 to amend the Articles of Confederation. Among them were Benjamin Franklin, James Madison, and Alexander Hamilton. The convention was headed by George Washington.

James Madison framed a new plan of government, and he and other Virginia delegates persuaded the convention to replace the Articles with this new constitution. The delegates took the document back to their states for **ratification** (approval).

Conflict and Compromise

The delegates disagreed sharply on three issues:

Representation Virginia drew up a plan by which the number of a state's representatives in Congress was proportional to its population. New Jersey's plan called for the same number of representatives per state. The larger states favored the Virginia Plan, the smaller ones the New Jersey Plan.

Slavery Many Southern delegates owned slaves. They proposed that slaves be counted for representation but not for taxes. Northern delegates wanted just the opposite. Most Northerners wanted to end the slave trade. Southerners, fearing that this action could end slavery, opposed it.

Trade Southern delegates were against taxing foreign commerce; the South relied heavily on imported goods from Britain. Northerners manufactured goods that competed with imports and favored taxing foreign goods.

The South shipped large quantities of cotton and tobacco to Britain and opposed a tax on exports.

Compromises

Great Compromise, or Connecticut Plan Congress was to have two houses. In the House of Representatives, states would be represented in proportion to their populations. In the Senate, all states would be represented equally.

Compromises on Slavery

★ Three-fifths of a state's slaves would be counted for purposes of taxation and representation.

★ Congress could not end the slave trade for 20 years, until 1808.

★ The tax on imported slaves could not exceed $10 a person.

Compromise on Trade Congress had the power to tax imports but not exports.

Main Parts of the Constitution

The Constitution consists of the *Preamble*, a main body of seven articles, the Bill of Rights, and twenty-seven amendments adopted at later intervals.

Preamble

The Preamble asserts that the new U.S. government was established by "we the people" (the

Signers of the Constitution, Philadelphia, 1787

entire nation) rather than by the individual states. It also identifies the following goals:

> We the people of the United States of America, in order to form a more perfect Union, establish justice, insure domestic tranquillity, provide for the common defense, promote the general welfare, and secure the blessings of liberty to ourselves and our posterity, do ordain and establish this Constitution of the United States of America.

Three Branches

Articles I, II, and III establish the **separation of powers** by dividing the powers of government among three branches—legislative, executive, and judicial.

Legislative Branch Article I describes the legislative, or lawmaking, branch—the U.S. Congress. It consists of two groups: the House of Representatives and the Senate. This is called a **bicameral** legislature. Besides listing the laws that Congress may make, this article describes (1) methods for electing members of each house, (2) qualifications for election, (3) terms of office in the House and Senate, and (4) lawmaking procedures.

Executive Branch Article II concerns the executive, or law-enforcing branch. It describes (1) powers of the **chief executive**, or president, (2) the term limit (4 years), (3) the method for electing the president and vice president, and (4) the method for removing the president by **impeachment** (accusation of wrongdoing) and trial. It says little about the responsibilities of the vice president.

Judicial Branch Article III describes the federal court system of "inferior" courts (lower courts) and a Supreme Court that interprets the laws in specific cases.

The article describes (1) the term of office for federal judges and (2) Congress's power to establish new courts. Each court is assigned its **jurisdiction** (area of responsibility). Some cases are to go directly to the Supreme Court (the highest court), and some are to be heard first by lower federal courts.

States, Amendment Process, Supreme Law, Ratification

★ *Interstate Relations*. Article IV describes relations among states and their obligations to one another. A person charged with breaking the laws of one state and fleeing to another is subject to **extradition** (return) to the original state. The article also describes (1) how U.S. territories may become states and (2) the government's responsibility for protecting states from invasion and "domestic violence" (rioting).

★ *Amendment Process*. Article V describes ways to amend the Constitution (see page 41).

★ *Supreme Law*. The **supremacy clause** in Article VI states that "the Constitution and the laws of the United States . . . shall be the supreme law of the land." Historic decisions of the Supreme Court making federal laws supreme over state laws were based on this clause.

★ *Ratification*. Article VII describes how the Constitution was to be submitted to the states in 1787 for ratification.

Debate on Ratification

The Constitution describes government by a **federal system**, one in which political power is divided between a national government and state governments. The *Federalists* favored the ratification of the Constitution and such a system while the *Anti-Federalists* opposed them.

Federalist Arguments

James Madison, Alexander Hamilton, and John Jay wrote essays explaining the need to replace the Articles with a federal system. They gave reasons why a representative government with powers evenly distributed among three branches would strengthen the nation and protect personal liberties. The essays were published as a book entitled *The Federalist*.

Anti-Federalist Arguments

Patrick Henry and Samuel Adams, as Anti-Federalists, feared that the central government under the Constitution might not respect people's liberties. It lacked, they said, a bill of rights.

Federalist Victory

Each state called a convention to vote for or against the Constitution. Large majorities in Delaware, Pennsylvania, and New Jersey voted for the Constitution. Massachusetts and Virginia were opposed unless it included a bill of rights. New York voted to ratify by the slim majority of 30 to 27. Ratification by the required nine states was accomplished in June 1788.

Strengths and Weaknesses of the Constitution

Strengths

★ The Constitution is flexible enough to allow for changes required by new generations but still merits respect for its traditional values and principles.

★ The Preamble states that the Constitution is a document of the people, not the states.

Separation of powers and checks and balances prevent one branch of government from gaining absolute power. (See page 39.)

Weaknesses The original Constitution needed amendments to guarantee individual liberties and omissions with regard to equality:

Page from Jefferson's copy of *The Federalist*

```
THE FEDERALIST.      217

   Nothing remains but the landed interest; and this
in a political view, and particularly in relation to
taxes I take to be perfectly united from the wealthiest
landlord to the poorest tenant.  No tax can be laid
on land which will not affect the propietor of millions
of acres as well as the proprietor of a single acre.
Every land-holder will therefore have a common inte-
rest to keep the taxes on land as low as possible; and
common interest may always be reckoned upon as the
surest bond of sympathy.  But if we even could
suppose a distinction of interest between the opulent
land-holder and the middling farmer, what reason is
there to conclude that the first would stand a better
chance of being deputed to the national legislature
than the last? If we take fact as our guide, and look
into our own senate and assembly we shall find that
moderate proprietors of land prevail in both; nor is
this less the case in the senate, which consists of a
smaller number than in the assembly, which is com-
posed of a greater number.  Where the qualifications
of the electors are the same, whether they have to
choose a small or a large number their votes will fall
upon those in whom they have most confidence;
whether these happen to be men of large fortunes or
of moderate property or of no property at all.
   It is said to be necessary that all classes of citizens
should have some of their own number in the represen-
```

★ Without the Bill of Rights, the federal government could abuse its power and deny personal freedoms.

★ Women were denied equality—the right to vote, hold property in their own names, and act as legal guardians of their children.

★ The Constitution did not abolish slavery.

★ White males in some states were unprotected against property qualifications for voting.

★ Several amendments were needed to extend voting rights to all groups of adult age.

★ In Review

1. Describe two conflicts at the Constitutional Convention and the compromise that settled each conflict.
2. How did the Preamble give authority to the people rather than the states?
3. Describe the major function of each branch of the federal government.

Bill of Rights

A **bill of rights** identifies actions that government may *not* take. Its purpose is to prevent abuses of power and to protect personal liberties. In 1789, soon after the Constitution was adopted, Congress proposed ten amendments as the U.S. Bill of Rights. They were ratified in 1791. Originally, they protected citizens from the federal government but were later applied to state governments as well.

Main Provisions

Freedom of Religion Congress may not interfere with a person's choice of worship (First Amendment).

Separation of Church and State Congress may not show special support to any church, synagogue, or other religious institution (First Amendment).

Freedom of Speech, Press, Assembly, Petition Congress may not make any law that interferes with the free expression of ideas in speech and writing. Government officials may not stop **peaceful assemblies** (demonstrations). People may not be punished for making **petitions** (requests in writing) seeking a change in government policy (First Amendment).

Right to Keep and Bear Arms Citizens may not be denied the right to carry weapons for use in a **state militia**, or group of volunteer soldiers for the common defense (Second Amendment).

Protection Against Quartering Citizens are not required to house and feed soldiers in times of peace and, in times of war, must do so only as provided by law (Third Amendment).

Searches and Seizures Government officials must obtain a **search warrant** (judge's permission) before searching a person's property. The warrant must describe "the place to be searched and the persons or things to be seized." A judge may issue the warrant only when convinced that there is "probable cause" of criminal evidence being found (Fourth Amendment).

Rights of Accused Persons The Fifth and Sixth amendments make the following guarantees for accused persons:

★ **Indictments** (accusations) in federal court must be made by a **grand jury**.

★ If acquitted by a **petit jury**, accused persons cannot incur **double jeopardy** (being tried again on the same charge).

★ They cannot be forced to give testimony or evidence that may be used against them at trial.

★ They will have "a speedy and public trial."

★ They will be tried by an impartial jury.

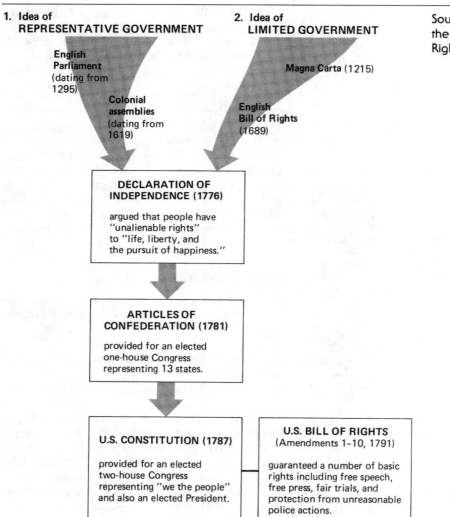

1. Idea of REPRESENTATIVE GOVERNMENT

English Parliament (dating from 1295)

Colonial assemblies (dating from 1619)

2. Idea of LIMITED GOVERNMENT

Magna Carta (1215)

English Bill of Rights (1689)

Sources of Major Ideas in the Constitution and Bill of Rights

DECLARATION OF INDEPENDENCE (1776)
argued that people have "unalienable rights" to "life, liberty, and the pursuit of happiness."

ARTICLES OF CONFEDERATION (1781)
provided for an elected one-house Congress representing 13 states.

U.S. CONSTITUTION (1787)
provided for an elected two-house Congress representing "we the people" and also an elected President.

U.S. BILL OF RIGHTS
(Amendments 1–10, 1791)
guaranteed a number of basic rights including free speech, free press, fair trials, and protection from unreasonable police actions.

★ They will be informed of the criminal charges against them.

★ They will be represented by a lawyer, and the government will help produce defense witnesses.

Due Process   No person may be deprived of "life, liberty, or property without due process of law" (Fifth Amendment).

Bail and Punishment   A person awaiting trial may not be charged excessive bail. A person convicted of a crime may not be punished in "cruel and unusual" ways (Eighth Amendment).

Rights Reserved to the States   Powers neither delegated to the federal government nor denied to the states belong to the state governments and to the American people (Tenth Amendment).

Additional Amendments

After the adoption of the Bill of Rights, the Constitution was amended 17 times, from 1795 (Eleventh Amendment) to 1992 (Twenty-seventh Amendment.) The most important are as follows:

★ The Twelfth Amendment modifies how the president and vice president are elected.

★ The Thirteenth Amendment abolishes slavery.

★ The Fourteenth Amendment guarantees equal rights of citizenship to all groups. (The next section treats this crucial amendment in more detail.)

★ The Fifteenth Amendment guarantees voting rights to citizens of all races.

★ The Sixteenth Amendment provides for the collection of a federal income tax.

★ The Nineteenth Amendment guarantees voting rights for women.

★ The Twenty-sixth Amendment guarantees voting rights to people aged 18 or older.

For a summary of all of the amendments, see pages 28–29.

Fourteenth Amendment   The first ten amendments protected citizens from abuses of the federal government only. The Fourteenth Amendment was adopted in 1868, after the Civil War. Northerners wanted, in particular, to protect freed slaves against unfair state laws, but the provisions applied to all Americans.

The amendment provides that no state may deny its citizens either "due process of law" (from the Fifth Amendment) or "equal protection of the laws." Often in the 20th century, the Supreme Court used the due process clause to apply the protections of the first ten amendments to state laws.

Interpreting the Bill of Rights

In the 20th century, many of the Supreme Court's **landmark** (most important) **decisions** applied the Bill of Rights to specific situations.

Decisions on First Amendment Rights

The First Amendment guarantees every citizen freedom of religion, freedom of speech, freedom of the press, freedom of assembly, and freedom of petition.

Separation of Church and State   The First Amendment states that Congress may "make no law respecting an establishment of religion," that is, to give preference to any religious practice or group.

★ In *Engel* v. *Vitale* (1962), the Supreme Court ruled that prayer in public schools violated separation of church and state and was unconstitutional.

★ In *School District of Abington Township* [Pennsylvania] v. *Schempp* (1963), the Court ruled against Bible reading in public schools.

Freedom of Speech and the Press   Although no one may be penalized for criticizing government officials and policies, under certain circumstances that threaten public safety, free expression of ideas may be limited.

★ In *Schenck* v. *United States* (1919), Justice Oliver Wendell Holmes said that speech that presented a "clear and present danger" could be limited. "Free speech would not protect a man falsely shouting fire in a theater and causing a panic," he said.

★ In *Tinker* v. *Des Moines School District* (1969), the Court ruled that students could not be penalized for wearing black armbands to school to protest the Vietnam War.

★ In the controversial case *Texas* v. *Johnson* (1989), the Court decided that a person who protested by setting fire to an American flag could not be punished by state officials, because flag burning was a form of symbolic speech.

Freedom of Assembly The people have the right to assemble peacefully and petition the government "for a redress of grievances."

★ In *Collin* v. *Smith* (1978), the Court ruled that the American Nazi party had a right to march in Skokie, Illinois, even if this "peaceable assembly" offended other people.

Decisions of the Fourth, Fifth, and Sixth Amendments

In the 1960s, the Supreme Court, under Chief Justice Earl Warren, decided a number of cases that tested the Fourth, Fifth, and Sixth amendments.

Search and Seizure The Fourth Amendment protects citizens against "unreasonable" police searches and seizures of personal property.

★ In *Mapp* v. *Ohio* (1961), the Court ruled that evidence obtained without a search warrant may not be admitted into a state court.

★ In *Katz* v. *United States* (1967), the Court ruled that wiretapping requires a search warrant, because the Fourth Amendment protects privacy as well as property.

Rights of Accused Persons The Fifth and Sixth amendments protect arrested persons from unfair treatment.

★ In *Gideon* v. *Wainwright* (1963), the Court ruled that if an accused person cannot afford a lawyer, the state must provide and pay for one.

★ In *Escobedo* v. *Illinois* (1964), the Court ruled that a person questioned at a police station has the right to be represented by a lawyer.

★ In *Miranda* v. *Arizona* (1966), the Court ruled that an arrested person must be told of the right to remain silent and have an attorney present.

"Cruel and Unusual Punishments"

The Eighth Amendment bans "cruel and unusual punishments." Does this ban include the execution of someone found guilty of a violent crime?

★ In *Furman* v. *Georgia* (1972), the Court ruled that the death penalty is constitutional only if a state has clear and consistent rules for the execution of people of all races and social classes.

★ In *Gregg* v. *Georgia* (1976), the Court ruled that the death penalty is constitutional if imposed solely because of the nature of the crime.

★ In Review

1. Define separation of church and state and due process of law.
2. Explain how the Fourteenth Amendment extended the protections of the Bill of Rights.
3. List three landmark Supreme Court cases, and describe the right that is protected by each case.

★ Summary of the Twenty-seven Amendments to the U.S. Constitution ★

Amendment	Year Adopted	Main Provisions
First	1791	People have freedom of religion, speech, press, assembly, and petition.
Second	1791	People may carry arms for use in a state militia.
Third	1791	People cannot be forced to quarter (house and feed) soldiers during times of peace.
Fourth	1791	People are protected against unfair police searches and seizures.
Fifth	1791	The indictment by a federal court of a civilian citizen of the United States must be made by a grand jury.
		If acquitted, a person cannot be tried again on the same charge (no double jeopardy).

Amendment	Year Adopted	Main Provisions
		People cannot be forced to give testimony or evidence that may be used against them at a trial.
		People cannot be deprived of life, liberty, or property without due process of law.
		Private property cannot be taken for public use without just compensation.
Sixth	1791	People have the right to a jury trial in criminal cases.
Seventh	1791	People have the right to a jury trial in civil (noncriminal) cases.
Eighth	1791	Accused persons are protected against excessive bail while awaiting trial.
		Accused persons are protected against cruel and unjust punishments.
Ninth	1791	People have rights that are not specified in the Constitution.
Tenth	1791	Powers not delegated to the federal government or denied to the states belong to state governments and to the American people.
Eleventh	1798	Citizens of other states or foreign countries cannot sue a state in federal court without that state's consent.
Twelfth	1804	Electors from each state shall cast two separate ballots—one for president, one for vice president.
Thirteenth	1865	Slavery is abolished in the United States.
Fourteenth	1868	All persons born in the United States are U.S. citizens and entitled to due process of law and equal protection of the laws.
Fifteenth	1870	No government in the United States may prevent citizens from voting because of race.
Sixteenth	1913	Congress has the power to collect income taxes without dividing them among the states according to population.
Seventeen	1913	The two U.S. senators from each state shall be elected by direct vote of the state's people.
Eighteenth (Prohibition)	1919	Manufacture and sale of intoxicating beverages in the United States is prohibited.
Nineteenth	1920	No government in the United States may prevent citizens from voting because of gender.
Twentieth ("Lame Duck" Amendment)	1933	The terms of office of president and vice president end at noon, January 20.
		The terms of office of members of Congress end at noon, January 3.
Twenty-first	1933	The Eighteenth Amendment is repealed.
Twenty-second	1951	No person may be elected more than twice to the office of president.
Twenty-third	1961	Residents of the District of Columbia may vote for president and vice president by choosing electors, the number (at present, three) to be determined by population.
Twenty-fourth	1964	No government in the United States may collect a poll tax from citizens who want to vote.
Twenty-fifth	1967	If the cabinet and Congress determine that the president is disabled, the vice president will temporarily assume the duties of president.
Twenty-sixth	1971	No government in the United States may prevent persons aged 18 or older from voting on account of age.
Twenty-seventh	1992	No law increasing compensation of Congress may take effect until an election of representatives intervenes.

Chapter Review

MULTIPLE-CHOICE QUESTIONS

1. At the Constitutional Convention of 1787, how to count slaves was settled by (1) Northerners yielding to Southerners (2) Southerners yielding to Northerners (3) blacks yielding to whites (4) a compromise involving concessions by both Northerners and Southerners.

2. Both the Articles and the U.S. Constitution provided for (1) a Congress with legislative power (2) a president with executive power (3) a Supreme Court with judicial power (4) local governments with veto powers.

3. The Great Compromise settled representation in Congress by (1) giving each state two senators and a number of representatives based on population (2) allowing all states to have equal representation in Congress (3) having an equal number of members in each house (4) limiting the population of large states.

4. The Three-Fifths Compromise dealt with (1) amendments to the Constitution (2) women's rights (3) representation in Congress (4) the rights of the accused.

5. *The Federalist* is important because it (1) helped persuade some states to ratify the Constitution (2) convinced the colonists to rebel against Britain (3) presented the first legal arguments in favor of retaining slavery (4) outlined plans for a confederate system of government.

6. During the debates over ratification, Federalists and Anti-Federalists disagreed most strongly over the (1) division of powers between the national and state governments (2) provision for governing the Northwest Territory (3) distribution of power between the Senate and the House (4) number of amendments in the Bill of Rights.

7. Anti-Federalists opposed ratification because the Constitution (1) gave too much power to the states (2) lacked a bill of rights (3) failed to give Congress enough power (4) was unfair to the smaller states.

Base your answers to questions 8 and 9 on the following statements and on your knowledge of the ratification of the Constitution.

Speaker A: We should reject any plan of government that makes no mention of such basic rights as freedom of speech and freedom of religion.

Speaker B: For every power granted to the executive branch there should be a comparable power granted to the legislative branch.

Speaker C: Our nation should be viewed as a loose compact among the states. The chief concern of the central government should be the conduct of foreign affairs.

Speaker D: The laws of the national and the state governments must both be subject to the supreme law of the land: the Constitution.

8. The kind of government created by the Articles is described by Speaker (1) A (2) B (3) C (4) D.

9. Which two speakers would most likely have voted *against* ratifying the Constitution? (1) A and B (2) B and C (3) A and C (4) C and D.

10. In the ratification debate, an important factor in overcoming objections to the Constitution was (1) political compromise (2) force and intimidation (3) strict devotion to equality (4) distrust of state governments.

THEMATIC ESSAYS

1. **Theme:** Compromise as a Foundation to the U.S. Constitution. The Constitution would never have been written without compromises by all sides. The nation, therefore, was founded on the give and take of debate, discussion, and problem solving.

   Task: Choose two areas of disagreement between delegates to the Constitutional Convention. For each area of disagreement:

★ Describe the disagreement by discussing all sides of the problem.
★ Explain how the disagreement was resolved through compromise.

You may use any examples of compromise at the convention, including representation, slavery, the slave trade, and foreign trade.

2. **Theme:** Interpreting the Bill of Rights. The Supreme Court has ruled in many disputes concerning interpretation of the Bill of Rights. These disputes often involve freedom of speech, separation of church and state, the right to assemble, freedom from illegal search and seizure, rights of accused persons, and freedom from cruel and unusual punishment.

Task: Choose two of the above issues. For each:

★ Describe a dispute over the issue.
★ Discuss how the Supreme Court interpreted the Bill of Rights in order to resolve each dispute.

You *must* use *two* different issues and cases in answering the question. You may, however, use any example from your study of the Supreme Court cases in this chapter.

DOCUMENT-BASED QUESTION

*Study each document and answer the question that follows it. Then read the **Task** and write your essay. Include references to most of the documents and additional information you retain about U.S. history and government.*

Historical Context: A critical period followed the American Revolution. As a result, a new constitution was created to replace the Articles.

Document 1: From Patrick Henry, at a debate in the Virginia ratifying convention, June 5, 1788:

The Confederation . . . carried us through a long and dangerous war; it rendered us victorious in that bloody conflict with a powerful nation; it has secured us a territory greater than any European monarch possesses: and shall a government which has been thus strong

and vigorous, be accused of imbecility and want of energy? Consider what you are about to do before you part with the government. . . .

Question: Why does Patrick Henry feel that the Articles should not be replaced?

Document 2: From James Madison in *The Federalist*, Number 10, 1787:

Complaints are everywhere heard . . . that our governments are too unstable . . . it may be concluded that a pure democracy . . . can admit of no cure for the mischiefs of faction . . . . A republic . . . promises the cure for which we are seeking . . . .

The effect is . . . to refine and enlarge the public views, by passing them through the medium of a chosen body of citizens, whose wisdom may best discern the true interest of their country. . . . On the other hand, men of factious [dissenting] tempers, of local prejudices may . . . betray the interests of the people. . . . The influence of factious leaders may kindle a flame within their particular States, but will be unable to spread a general conflagration [revolution] through the other States.

Question: Why does Madison feel that the new constitution will better serve the people than the Articles?

Document 3: From Benjamin Franklin on the actions of politicians:

Few men in public affairs act from a mere view of the good of their country, whatever they may pretend; and though their activity may bring real good to their country, they do not act from a spirit of benevolence.

Question: What dangers does Benjamin Franklin feel exist in any form of government?

Task: Using information from the documents and your knowledge of the issues involved in ratifying the U.S. Constitution, write an essay in which you:

★ compare and contrast arguments for and against the new constitution
★ write an argument favoring either the arguments for or against ratification.

Chapter 3
The Federal Government and the State Governments

★ Objectives

★ To understand how the legislative, executive, and judicial branches of the U.S. government are organized.

★ To know how government officials are elected or chosen.

★ To evaluate selected landmark cases of the Supreme Court.

★ To understand the organization and responsibilities of state and local governments.

Congress

Bicameral Organization

Congress is divided into two houses: the House of Representatives and the Senate. Each house votes separately on all bills.

Apportionment of Seats in Congress The House is affected by population change, but the Senate is not. Every ten years, a **census** counts the popula-

tion of the 50 states. In a process called **reapportionment**, a state that has gained population relative to other states will gain seats in the House, and one that has lost population relative to other states will lose seats. The total number of House seats is 435. The total number of Senate seats is 100—two for each state.

Special Powers and Rules of the Senate Only the Senate gives "advice and consent" to treaties made by the executive branch. Only the Senate votes on whether to accept the president's nominations of key federal officials.

Senators are allowed unlimited debate. A small group may attempt to defeat a bill favored by the majority by **filibuster**—nonstop speech to delay a vote on the bill and weaken the majority's will to pass it.

Elections to Congress   Elections to Congress are held in every even-numbered year. All House members are elected at the same time. One-third of the senators, who serve six years, are elected at one time; the second third are elected two years later, and the final third two years after that.

Powers

Article I of the Constitution gives Congress power to collect taxes, borrow money, regulate trade, coin money, declare war, raise and support armed forces, and establish a post office.

Elastic Clause   The **elastic clause** is the final legislative power in Article 1. It allows Congress to make all laws necessary and proper to carrying out its other powers. Thus, Congress can use **implied powers** to make laws on matters unconsidered in 1789—airplane traffic, speed limits on interstate highways, minimum wages. Such regulations are viewed as "necessary and proper" means, for instance, of regulating **interstate commerce** (trade crossing state lines) as conditions change. (The Constitution does not mention interstate commerce.)

Limits on Power   The Constitution denies Congress power to (1) impose taxes on exports, (2) grant titles of nobility, (3) favor the ports of one state over those of another, or (4) suspend the writ of **habeas corpus**, which protects citizens from being jailed without good reason.

Procedures for Making Laws

Committees and Subcommittees   Committees in the House and Senate specialize in different areas of lawmaking: agriculture, foreign affairs, armed services, commerce, labor. Such **standing** (permanent) **committees** consider a bill before the House or Senate votes on it. Committees often divide into smaller subcommittees that study a bill and report back to the full committee. The full committee then votes on whether to approve the bill, approve an amended version, or defeat it.

Floor Votes   A bill with committee approval goes to House or Senate for debate and vote. Senators or representatives may debate a bill's merits and propose amendments. To be enacted (passed), the bill must be approved by a majority of those present. After passage by one house, the bill goes to the other house for consideration and vote.

Conference Committee   The two houses may pass similar but not identical bills. Members from both houses then iron out differences in a **conference committee**. If a compromise is reached, two identical bills return to the House and Senate for final votes.

Action by the President   A bill enacted by both houses goes to the president, who may sign it into law or **veto** (reject) it, as follows:

★ If Congress is in session longer than ten days after passing an act, the president must

★ Differences Between the Houses of Congress ★

	House of Representatives	Senate
Number of members	435; seats apportioned to each state according to its population.	100; each state represented by two senators.
Term of member	Two years; may be reelected to unlimited number of terms; all members elected at same time.	Six years; may be reelected to unlimited number of terms; one-third of Senate seats subject to election in same year.
Member's qualifications	At least 25 years old; U.S. citizen for at least seven years; resident of state from which elected.	At least 30 years old; U.S. citizen for at least nine years; resident of state from which elected.
Member's **constituency** (people represented)	Citizens residing in given congressional district of state.	All citizens of state.
Presiding officer	Speaker of the House.	Vice president of the United States.

promptly return it to Congress explaining the veto. Congress can override the veto by a two-thirds vote.

★ If Congress is in session fewer than ten days after passing an act, the president can leave it unsigned, defeating it by **pocket veto**.

Influence of Pressure Groups

How members of Congress vote on a bill can influence their reelection, because they must face the voters on Election Day. Voters can exert pressure on the lawmaking process either as individuals or as members of **special interest groups**.

Individual Action Citizens can write letters to lawmakers or visit their district offices in the home state. Members of Congress often use mass mailings to constituents to ask their opinions on public issues.

Group Action Many businesses, labor unions, and other organizations have a special interest in influencing congressional decisions. Special interest groups organize letter-writing campaigns, place advertisements, and hire **lobbyists** (professional advocates) to visit members of Congress. Many groups form **political action committees (PACS)** to give money to the election campaigns of those they favor.

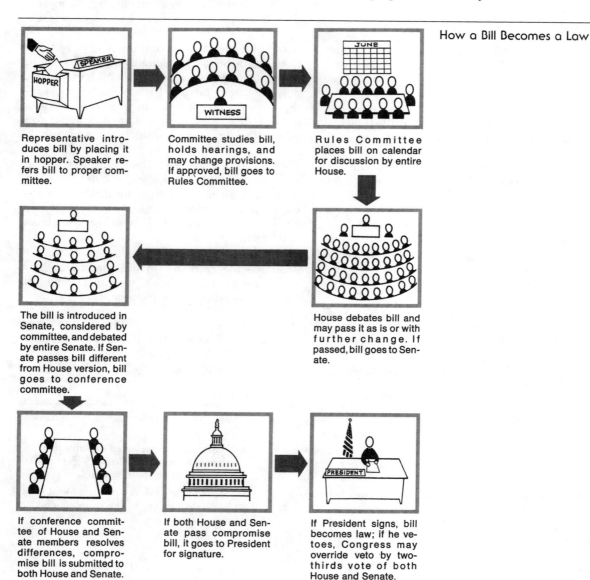

How a Bill Becomes a Law

Representative introduces bill by placing it in hopper. Speaker refers bill to proper committee.

Committee studies bill, holds hearings, and may change provisions. If approved, bill goes to Rules Committee.

Rules Committee places bill on calendar for discussion by entire House.

The bill is introduced in Senate, considered by committee, and debated by entire Senate. If Senate passes bill different from House version, bill goes to conference committee.

House debates bill and may pass it as is or with further change. If passed, bill goes to Senate.

If conference committee of House and Senate members resolves differences, compromise bill is submitted to both House and Senate.

If both House and Senate pass compromise bill, it goes to President for signature.

If President signs, bill becomes law; if he vetoes, Congress may override veto by two-thirds vote of both House and Senate.

President

The writers of the Constitution wanted the executive branch to be equal in power to the other two branches. Many modern historians believe that the presidency has become the most powerful element.

Presidential Leadership

Chief Executive   As chief executive, the president directs cabinet heads and supervises agencies of the executive branch. The president is responsible for enforcing all federal laws and programs.

Among government agencies assisting the president are:

★ *Office of Management and Budget (OMB)*, which prepares an annual government spending plan.

★ *Central Intelligence Agency (CIA)*, which gathers information on foreign matters affecting national security.

★ *National Aeronautics and Space Administration (NASA)*, which directs space exploration.

The president's **cabinet** comprises heads of the departments of the federal government: Agriculture, Commerce, Defense, Education, Energy, Health and Human Services, Homeland Security, Housing and Urban Development, Interior, Justice, Labor, State, Transportation, Treasury, and Veterans' Affairs.

The executive branch employs some 3 million workers and spends more than $1 trillion a year. As chief executive, the president leads this huge staff and recommends its working budget to Congress.

Military Leader   The president is commander in chief of the armed forces. Important military decisions must be approved by the president, who outranks generals and admirals.

Legislative Leader   The president uses the annual State of the Union address to recommend new laws. The president can call Congress into special session after adjournment. The president signs or vetoes acts of Congress.

Diplomatic Leader   As the chief maker of U.S. foreign policy, the president (1) makes treaties (with approval of two-thirds of the Senate), (2) recognizes other countries by receiving ambassadors, and (3) nominates U.S. ambassadors to other countries (with the approval of a majority of the Senate).

Chief of State: Ceremonial Leader   The president, as chief of state, speaks for the nation when abroad and strives to inspire Americans to honor their traditions and ideals.

Judicial Role   The president may grant either a **pardon** (forgiveness for a federal crime) or **reprieve** (delay of punishment). When a seat on the Supreme Court is vacant, the president nominates a new justice and submits the choice to the Senate for **confirmation** (approval).

Election Process

Election of a president and vice president occurs every four years on the second Tuesday in November.

Nomination of Candidates   Presidential candidates seek the **nomination** (selection) of the Democratic party, Republican party, or minor party. The first step is a state **primary election**, at which a party's voters choose a candidate and delegates to a national convention.

In the summer before election, each party holds its convention, at which delegates from the 50 states make nominations for candidates for president. The candidate chosen in a state primary receives most of that state's delegate votes. In recent elections, a single candidate in each party won enough primaries to be assured of nomination. The presidential nominee usually then selects a vice-presidential running mate.

Fall Campaign   The nominees travel across the nation and appear on television seeking votes in the November election.

Electoral College   Voters on Election Day do not vote for president and vice president. They vote for **electors**, who are authorized by the Constitution to cast ballots for president and vice president.

Electors are assigned to each state according to the size of its congressional delegation. In 2004, Nevada, with three representatives and two senators, had five electors. California, with 53 representatives and two senators, had 55 electors.

In all but two states, the candidate who wins a *plurality*, or most, of a state's *popular votes* (those cast by the people) wins all the state's electoral votes. A state's electors make up its **electoral college**. The electors cast ballots for president and vice president one month after the popular election. Almost always, electors cast their ballots for the candidate favored by the plurality of voters.

Lack of a Majority If there are more than two major candidates and no one wins a majority (more than 50 percent) of electoral ballots, the election is decided in the House of Representatives. Each state has one vote. The candidate who wins a majority of the House vote is elected president.

Unusual Elections

Election of 1800: Tie Vote Broken by House
Thomas Jefferson and Aaron Burr had an equal number of electoral votes (73). The House of Representatives broke the tie and elected Jefferson.

Election of 1824: Defeat of the Most Popular Candidate

Candidate	Popular Vote	Electoral Vote
Andrew Jackson	153,544	99
John Quincy Adams	108,740	88
William H. Crawford	46,618	41
Henry Clay	47,136	37

Since no candidate had an electoral majority, the election was decided by the House. The winner was John Quincy Adams.

Election of 1912: Three-way Race

Candidate	Popular Vote	Electoral Vote
Woodrow Wilson	6,296,547	435
Theodore Roosevelt	4,118,571	88
William H. Taft	3,486,720	8

Wilson, the winner, had less than a majority of the popular vote but a huge majority of electoral votes.

Election of 2000: Defeat of the More Popular Candidate

Candidate	Popular Vote	Electoral Vote
Albert Gore, Jr.	50,996,116	266
George W. Bush	50,456,169	271

The winner, Bush, had less than a majority of the popular vote.

Rules of Succession

The **rules of succession** ensure an orderly procedure to replace the chief executive in case of illness or death.

Presidential Succession By a 1947 act of Congress, the vice president automatically succeeds a president who dies. If both die at the same time, the following order of succession applies:

★ Speaker of the House

★ President pro tempore of the Senate

★ Cabinet members in the order in which their departments were created, beginning with the secretary of state.

Twenty-second Amendment (1951) No president may serve more than two elected terms.

Twenty-fifth Amendment (1967) A disabled president may notify Congress of the inability to carry out presidential powers and duties. In this case:

★ The vice president will then serve temporarily.

★ The vice president, supported by a majority of the cabinet, may notify Congress that the pres-

Presidential Campaign 2004: Massachusetts Senator John Kerry (left) and President George W. Bush and First Lady Laura Bush greeting their supporters.

★ Debating the Electoral College ★

Arguments For	Arguments Against
Democratic; electors vote per majority in each state.	Less democratic than direct vote by the people. There is no need for a second election by small number of electors.
Carries out federal system by voting state by state.	Possible danger that electors will vote contrary to the popular plurality.
Good for large urban states, where candidates must appeal to minorities.	Good chance that election involving three or more candidates will be decided by the House.
Good for lightly populated states, which are guaranteed at least four electoral votes.	Gives lightly populated states more weight in election than they deserve.

ident is unable to "discharge the powers and duties of his office."

★ The vice president then serves as acting president.

★ If the president claims renewed capability of carrying out presidential duties and the vice president and a cabinet majority disagree, the president may be overruled by a two-thirds vote of Congress.

Impeachment

The House of Representatives may decide by majority vote on articles of impeachment, accusing a president of "high crimes and misdemeanors." The Senate then meets as a trial court presided over by the chief justice of the United States. A two-thirds vote is necessary for conviction and removal.

Two presidents, Andrew Johnson (1868) and Bill Clinton (1998) were impeached and acquitted. Richard Nixon (1974) resigned from office before the House voted.

Growth of Presidential Power

In 1789, the United States had 4 million inhabitants, a new and untried government, an agricultural economy, and a tiny army and navy. Today, it is a mighty industrial nation and a superpower.

Leadership in Domestic Affairs In the early 1900s, three successive presidents—Theodore Roosevelt, William H. Taft, and Woodrow Wilson—championed reforms to make the government more honest and efficient. (See Chapter 10.) In the 1930s and 1940s, Franklin D. Roosevelt led the nation from the Great Depression to victory in World War II. In the 20th century, the civil rights movement of the 1950s and 1960s enhanced the central

role of four presidents—Truman, Eisenhower, Kennedy, and Johnson.

Leadership in Foreign Affairs As leader of the world's strongest nation, the president meets often with other world leaders at **summit conferences**.

In this age of jet planes, nuclear weapons, and computer-controlled missiles, the response to military attack must usually be entrusted to the commander in chief rather than to the slower deliberation of Congress.

Additional Factors Owing to modern technology, the president can address the entire nation and is seen on television.

Through appointments to federal agencies, the president influences many aspects of our lives.

★ In Review

1. Explain the elastic clause.
2. How does a bill become law?
3. Describe the differences between the electoral vote and the popular vote.

Supreme Court and Lower Courts

Article III of the Constitution empowers a Supreme Court but leaves the responsibility of organizing lower courts to Congress.

Supreme Court Jurisdictions

Original Jurisdiction In a few cases—involving ambassadors and disputes between states—the Supreme Court acts as a trial court, with **original jurisdiction**.

Appellate Jurisdiction When the Supreme Court reviews cases appealed from lower courts, it has

appellate jurisdiction. It may decide either to uphold the decision of a lower court or overturn it.

Justices of the Supreme Court Congress determines the number of justices on the Supreme Court. The first Court had six; today, there are nine, one chief justice and eight associate justices. Cases are decided by majority vote. One of the majority usually gives a constitutional explanation for the decision. A judge in the minority may write a **dissenting opinion**.

Organization of Federal Courts

The Federal Judiciary Act (1789) organized the federal court system, with three **circuit courts** (courts of appeal) to review district court decisions. In 2004, there were 94 district courts, 12 circuit courts, and 1 federal circuit court.

Trial Courts For most trials involving federal laws, district courts have original jurisdiction.

Appeals Process A district court's decision may be appealed to a circuit court. A circuit decision may be appealed to the Supreme Court, "the court of last resort." The Supreme Court may also hear cases begun and appealed in state courts.

The Supreme Court decides whether to hear a case on appeal.

Life Tenure A federal judge holds office for life, voluntary retirement, or impeachment and removal for wrongdoing. This relieves pressure to make decisions favoring politicians or voters.

Landmark Decisions of the Marshall Court

John Marshall was the fourth chief justice of the United States (1801–1835). He made the Supreme Court an independent and influential force in the federal government.

Marbury v. *Madison* (1803) Before leaving office, President John Adams appointed William Marbury as a federal court judge. Thomas Jefferson, the next president, ordered Secretary of State James Madison to ignore the appointment. Marbury appealed to the Supreme Court, arguing that a 1789 law gave the Supreme Court power to force Madison to grant the appointment. Chief Justice Marshall argued that the law cited was unconstitutional—null and void.

His decision established the principle of **judicial review**, the power of the Court to rule on the constitutionality of federal and state laws. Each

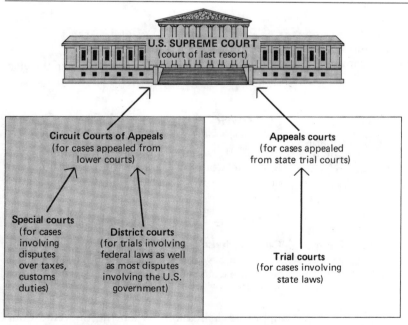

Federal and State Courts:
Appeals Process

U.S. SUPREME COURT
(court of last resort)

Circuit Courts of Appeals
(for cases appealed from lower courts)

Appeals courts
(for cases appealed from state trial courts)

Special courts
(for cases involving disputes over taxes, customs duties)

District courts
(for trials involving federal laws as well as most disputes involving the U.S. government)

Trial courts
(for cases involving state laws)

FEDERAL COURTS   STATE COURTS

Chief Justice John Marshall

This ruling clarified the concept of interstate commerce and increased federal authority to regulate it.

Impact of the Marshall Court Many cases decided under Chief Justice Marshall increased federal power in relation to the states. By repeated application of judicial review, Marshall greatly expanded the power and influence of the Court.

Basic Constitutional Principles

The Separation of Powers

The Constitution prevents domination by one branch of government by distributing legislative, executive, and judicial powers among three branches. This separation of powers gives each one a special area of responsibility (see page 40).

Checks and Balances

Definition and Purpose Each branch has some power to participate in decisions of the others. Thus, each branch must try to gain approval for its policies and decisions. This system of **checks and balances** allows each branch to block actions of the other branches (see page 41).

case that the Court hears involves how the Constitution applies to a unique set of circumstances, because times change. Many cases of the 1880s and 1890s involved the regulation of railroads and oil companies—issues unknown to the Constitution's framers. In the late 20th century, the Constitution was applied to abortion, the death penalty, minority rights, and computer technology.

McCulloch v. Maryland (1819) Maryland wished to collect a tax from a bank chartered by the U.S. government. Marshall argued that states could not tax a federal agency because the Constitution held the federal government to be supreme: "The power to tax is the power to destroy." Marshall also argued that Congress's powers could be interpreted loosely to authorize the creation of a national bank.

This decision permitted **nullification** (cancellation) of a state law that conflicted with a federal law.

Gibbons v. Ogden (1824) New York State granted one steamship company the exclusive right to operate on an interstate waterway, the Hudson River. Marshall stated that trade is commerce, commerce between states is controlled by Congress, and New York's law was invalid.

★ ★ ★ ★ ★

McCULLOCH V. MARYLAND

We admit, as all must admit, that the powers of the government are limited, and that its limits are not to be transcended. But we think the sound construction of the Constitution must allow to the national legislature that discretion, with respect to the means by which the powers it confers are to be carried into execution, which will enable that body to perform the high duties assigned to it, in the manner most beneficial to the people. Let the end be legitimate, let it be within the scope of the Constitution, and all means which are appropriate, which are plainly adapted to that end, which are not prohibited, but consistent with the letter and spirit of the Constitution, are constitutional. . . .

Federalism: Powers of the Central and State Governments

Federalism is the principle by which political power is divided equally between a central government and state governments.

Division of Powers Since the central government under the Articles of Confederation was ineffective, the framers of the Constitution increased its powers while reserving others for the states.

Delegated Powers The Constitution enumerates (names) the powers given to the central government. These **delegated powers** include collecting taxes, coining money, maintaining the armed forces, regulating trade, and making treaties.

Reserved Powers The **reserved powers** granted to the states and people by the Tenth Amendment include any neither delegated to the federal government nor denied to the states, including such matters as health and safety, marriage and divorce, regulation of business, and licensing of professions.

Concurrent Powers **Concurrent powers** are exercised by both the federal and state governments, including building roads and highways, borrowing money, collecting taxes, and operating courts.

★ In Review

1. Define judicial review.
2. Describe two important decisions of the Supreme Court under Chief Justice John Marshall.
3. Define separation of powers, checks and balances, and federalism.

The Constitution: A "Living Document"

The U.S. Constitution is a "living document" because it is flexible enough to be changed either

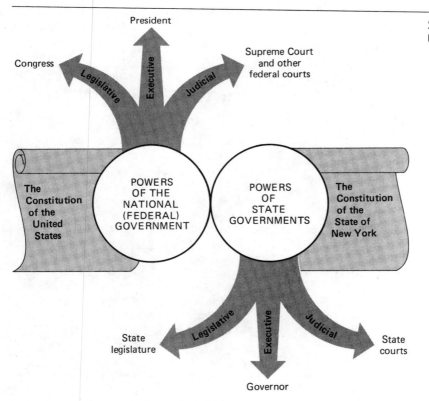

Separation of Powers in the U.S. Federal System

The president acts . . .

1. Makes a treaty with a foreign government.

2. Commits certain "crimes and misdemeanors."

3. Vetoes an act of Congress.

4. Makes an appointment to a cabinet post.

Another branch checks . . .

The Senate rejects the treaty (fails to ratify it by a two-thirds vote).

The House impeaches the president; then the Senate votes to remove the president from office.

Congress overrides the veto by a two-thirds vote of each house.

The Senate rejects the president's nominee.

Congress acts . . .

1. Enacts a bill.

2. Enacts a bill that is signed by the president.

Another branch checks . . .

The president vetoes Congress's act.

The Supreme Court declares Congress's act to be unconstitutional.

The Supreme Court acts . . .

1. Declares an act of Congress unconstitutional.

2. Declares an action of the president unconstitutional.

Another branch checks . . .

Congress proposes a constitutional amendment.

The president appoints a new justice to the Supreme Court (if there is a vacancy).

Checks and Balances in the Federal Government

by formal amendment or informal adjustments and decision making.

Formal Amendment

Article V of the Constitution describes formal procedures for proposing and ratifying amendments, the most common of which follows:

★ Congress proposes an amendment by a two-thirds vote of each house.

★ The proposed amendment is considered by state legislatures. If three-fourths of them ratify the proposal, it is added to the Constitution (see page 42).

Informal Change

Congress and the Elastic Clause The elastic clause in Article 1 of the Constitution empowers Congress to legislate on a vast number of subjects unknown when the Constitution was written. (See page 33).

Presidency and the Unwritten Constitution

The **unwritten constitution** refers to traditions that have become part of the American political system. For example:

★ Most elected officials are either Republican or Democratic, even though the Constitution does not mention political parties.

★ George Washington declined to serve more than two terms, and later presidents followed suit. This tradition was broken when Franklin Roosevelt won a third term (1940) and a fourth term (1944). The Twenty-second Amendment (1951) limited future presidents to two terms.

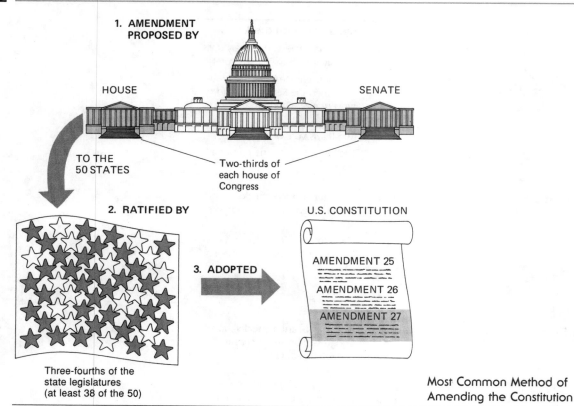

1. AMENDMENT PROPOSED BY

HOUSE

SENATE

TO THE 50 STATES

Two-thirds of each house of Congress

2. RATIFIED BY

3. ADOPTED

U.S. CONSTITUTION

AMENDMENT 25

AMENDMENT 26

AMENDMENT 27

Three-fourths of the state legislatures (at least 38 of the 50)

Most Common Method of Amending the Constitution

★ The Constitution mentions no cabinet, but after George Washington began to meet with four key advisers, presidents relied on a cabinet and added new positions to it.

States in the Federal System

Citizens of the United States are also citizens of their states. State governments are organized like the national government and have authority to deal with local issues. Each one has a constitution, which provides for separation of powers.

Admission of New States

Thirty-seven states were admitted to the Union after the Constitution was written in 1787. Article IV empowers Congress to admit new states, as follows:

★ A territory applies to Congress for statehood.

★ The territory submits a proposed constitution approved by its people.

★ Congress may accept or reject a territory's application by majority vote.

Congress may attach conditions to statehood. When Utah applied for statehood in 1875, it had to disavow **polygamy** (having multiple marriage partners).

The last states, Hawaii and Alaska, were admitted in 1959.

New York State Legislature

New York State has a representative legislature whose members debate and vote on bills affecting such issues as (1) expenditures for education, (2) penalties for criminal behavior, and (3) funding mass transit and highways.

Bicameral Organization Most state legislatures have two houses, both of which approve bills by majority vote. In New York State, the larger house is the assembly and the smaller, the senate.

Redistricting District lines for representation in the legislature reflect shifts in population. The New York State legislature can vote on the new district boundaries.

In a common practice called **gerrymandering**, members of a majority party often draw a district so as to favor their party. The Supreme Court ruled in *Baker* v. *Carr* (1962) that district lines must reflect "one man, one vote." That is, districts must be about equal in population so that all residents are equally represented. Nevertheless, occasional gerrymandering still helps candidates of one party win an election.

New York State Executive

New York State's chief executive is the governor, whose primary role is to enforce state laws. Executive departments and agencies are responsible for various functions. A highway department maintains state roads, and an education department supervises state schools.

Governor's Influence on Legislation The governor proposes a series of bills and tries to persuade a majority of the legislature to vote for it. The governor can veto bills passed.

Every year, the governor of New York recommends a state **budget** (taxing and spending plan). The governor tries to win approval of the budget by use of executive authority, access to the media, and political influence with party leaders.

Other Duties The governor nominates heads of executive departments and agencies. In many states, the governor also appoints state judges. Usually, such appointments require approval of one of the two houses of the legislature.

The governor is commander in chief of the state **national guard** (military force of citizen volunteers). In times of natural disaster or riot, the governor orders it into action and may ask the president for federal troops as well.

The governor may grant a pardon or reprieve to a person convicted of a state crime.

New York State Judiciary

New York State's court system consists of the New York State Supreme Court to try cases and the New York State Court of Appeals (a higher court) to hear appeals.

Function State courts hear criminal cases involving state laws, settle legal disputes between citizens, and resolve cases involving interpretation of the state constitution.

Judicial Process Before a criminal case goes to trial, a **grand jury** decides whether there is enough evidence to indict an accused person. If so, that person is tried by a **petit jury**, which decides on guilt or innocence. A convicted person may appeal the case to a state appeals court. A case involving a federal issue or interpretation of the U.S. Constitution ultimately may be appealed to the U.S. Supreme Court.

In handing down decisions, state courts are guided not only by the state constitution but also by the U.S. Constitution's guarantees of rights.

Interstate Relations

Each state is free to make its own laws and regulations, which may compete with those of other states. Provisions of the U.S. Constitution and interstate agreements help to ease this problem.

"Full Faith and Credit" Article IV of the Constitution requires that states give "full faith and credit" to each other's laws, licenses, and official documents. Thus, the validity of automobile licenses and high school diplomas is recognized from state to state. "Full faith and credit," however, is limited. A state may refuse to acknowledge out-of-state certificates in such professions as medicine, law, and education.

Interstate Compacts Bordering states often recognize a mutual interest in solving common problems. By signing **interstate compacts**, governors of neighboring states set up **regional agencies**. An example is the Port Authority of New York and New Jersey, which operates interstate bridges and tunnels that cross the Hudson River.

Local Governments

Counties, villages, towns, and municipalities (cities), have their own governments. Most municipalities, for example, operate their own police, fire, sanitation, and health departments.

Officials Local chief executives—mayors, city managers, county executives—supervise departments of the municipal or county government. City councils and county boards of supervisors (freeholders) make local regulations called **ordinances**. Legislative and executive decisions must conform to state laws.

Finances Public schools and other local institutions are funded mainly by property taxes on the value of homes and local businesses. Grants from the state and federal governments supplement these revenues.

★ In Review

1. Explain why the Constitution is a "living document."

2. Describe two examples of the unwritten constitution.

3. Explain the principle of redistricting and how it may be abused.

Chapter Review

MULTIPLE-CHOICE QUESTIONS

1. The illustration on page 40 shows that (1) New York State's government is in conflict with the federal government (2) both the federal and New York State governments have a system of checks and balances (3) New York State and the federal government share few powers (4) New York State has no equivalent to Congress.

2. The illustration on page 42 shows that the (1) amendment process is simple and easy (2) president may veto any proposed amendment (3) states have a big role in the amendment process (4) Supreme Court may declare an amendment unconstitutional.

3. Which situation illustrates lobbying? (1) A defeated candidate for the Senate is appointed to the cabinet. (2) A special interest group hires someone to present its views to certain members of Congress. (3) Federal public works projects are awarded to a state. (4) Two members of Congress agree to support each other's bills.

4. The electoral college system influences presidential candidates to (1) make appearances in every state (2) campaign extensively in populous states (3) state their platforms *very* specifically (4) seek endorsements from governors.

5. A power that both state and federal governments share is to (1) regulate interstate commerce (2) issue money (3) declare war (4) collect taxes.

6. In a presidential election, the electoral vote was as follows:

Candidate	A	B	C	D
Percentage of electoral vote	38	38	16	8

Which is a valid statement about the outcome of the election? (1) Candidate A was immediately declared the winner. (2) Candidate A became president and Candidate B became vice president. (3) Another election was held to determine a winner. (4) The president was chosen in the House of Representatives.

7. The principle of federalism provides for the (1) separation of powers (2) ultimate sovereignty of state governments (3) division of power between state and federal governments (4) creation of a republican form of government.

8. How did the Supreme Court under Chief Justice Marshall influence U.S. history? (1) The Court advanced states' rights by agreeing that states could reject acts of Congress. (2) Many of the Court's decisions strengthened the federal government. (3) The Court weakened the judiciary by refusing to rule on controversial issues. (4) The Court became involved with foreign affairs.

9. The Constitution's provisions for federalism and checks and balances suggest that (1) the original 13 states sought to dominate the national government (2) the writers aimed for national control over the states (3) the writers feared a concentration of political

power (4) the people supported a military government.

10. The most accurate statement about the role and function of the president is that (1) the president holds the most power in the government (2) the office of president has a variety of functions—influencing legislation, conducting foreign affairs, and appointing Supreme Court justices (3) laws may not be passed without the president's approval (4) the president has less power than the Supreme Court but more than Congress.

THEMATIC ESSAYS

1. **Theme:** Powers of the President. Presidential power has increased over time to meet new challenges in the nation and the world.

   Task: Choose two instances in which a problem, crisis, or emergency demanded increased presidential power. For each situation:

   ★ Describe the problem, crisis, or emergency.
   ★ Demonstrate how the solution increased presidential power.

   You may use any two situations from your study of the Constitution, the presidency, and U.S. history and government. You may wish to include civil rights, economic depression, need for honest and efficient government, and national emergencies such as war or rebellion.

2. **Theme:** State and Federal Powers: The Constitution provides for a federal system that delegates certain powers to the federal government, reserves others for the states, and provides for concurrent powers between the federal and state governments.

   Task: Choose one power that illustrates each of the following:

   ★ powers delegated to the federal government
   ★ powers reserved for the state governments
   ★ powers concurrent between federal and state governments.

   Explain why the writers of the Constitution created each power that you selected.

DOCUMENT-BASED QUESTION

*Study each document and answer the question that follows it. then read the **Task** and write your essay.*

Include references to most of the documents and additional information you retain about U. S. history and government.

Historical Context: The writers of the Constitution created a government designed to meet the new nation's needs without the exercise of abusive power.

Document 1: From the Constitution of the United States:

> The Congress shall have the power to make all laws which shall be necessary and proper for carrying into execution the foregoing powers and all others vested by this Constitution in the government of the United States, or in any department or officer thereof.

Question: How does the elastic clause help Congress pass needed laws?

Document 2: Refer to the reading on page 39.

Question: What decision did the Supreme Court reach about the power of Congress?

Document 3: From the Supreme Court's decision in *Gideon* v. *Wainwright* (1963):

> We accept *Betts* v. *Brady's* assumption . . . that a provision of the Bill of Rights which is "fundamental and essential to a fair trial" is made *obligatory* [binding] upon the States by the Fourteenth Amendment. We think the Court in *Betts* was wrong, however, in concluding that the Sixth Amendment's guarantee of counsel is not one of those fundamental rights. . . .
>
> Reason and reflection require us to recognize that . . . any person [brought into] court, who is too poor to hire a lawyer, cannot be assured a fair trial unless counsel is provided . . . .
>
> The judgment is reversed. . . .

Question: Why did the Supreme Court reverse a lower court's decision?

Task: Using the documents and your knowledge of U.S. history and government, write an essay that illustrates how the Constitution has been adapted to the needs of changing times but kept secure against abusive power.

Chapter 4
Implementing Principles of the New Constitution

★ Documents and Laws	★ Events	★ People
Alien and Sedition Acts (1798)	Whiskey Rebellion (1794)	John Adams
Twelfth Amendment (1804)	French Revolution (1789–1799)	John Quincy Adams
Monroe Doctrine (1823)	XYZ Affair (1797)	Alexander Hamilton
	Election of 1800	Andrew Jackson
	Napoleonic Wars (1805–1815)	Thomas Jefferson
	War of 1812 (1812–1815)	Francis Scott Key
	Hartford Convention (1814)	Henry Knox
	Election of 1824	James Madison
		James Monroe
		Napoleon
		Tecumseh
		George Washington

★ Objectives

★ To identify important policies of early presidents and evaluate their effects.

★ To understand Hamilton's financial plan.

★ To investigate the unwritten constitution under Washington, Adams, and Jefferson.

★ To evaluate early obstacles to a stable political system.

★ To analyze early U.S. foreign policy.

The U.S. Constitution was only a framework for government. The first five presidents worked out practical details necessary to the systematic operation of government.

Unwritten Constitution Under Washington, Adams, and Jefferson

During his two terms as president (1784–1797), George Washington influenced U.S. government more than any other president. John Adams, the second president, and his successor, Thomas Jefferson, also made major decisions that became part of the unwritten constitution.

First Cabinet (1789)

Officials of the cabinet meet to advise the chief executive. This group is not mentioned in the Constitution. Washington established the cabinet as a permanent executive institution when, in 1789, he appointed a secretary of state (Thomas

Jefferson), a secretary of the treasury (Alexander Hamilton), a secretary of war (Henry Knox), and an attorney general (Edmund Randolph).

Hamilton's Financial Plan

At once, Alexander Hamilton drew up plans to strengthen the new country's finances:

★ means for repaying debts of the states and national government

★ establishment of a national bank in which to deposit tax revenues and private loans to the U.S. government

★ **tariffs** (taxes on imports) to protect new American industries from foreign competition.

Secretary of State Thomas Jefferson and James Madison opposed these policies for favoring Northern business interests rather than Southern agrarian interests. Jefferson believed that Hamilton's plan would give the federal government too much power. Over such objections, Congress enacted the plan, which proved successful.

President Washington (inset) and his first cabinet: (left to right) Henry Knox, Thomas Jefferson, Alexander Hamilton, Edmund Randolph

Stabilizing the Political System

Political Parties While expecting conflicts of opinion within the cabinet, Washington hoped to avoid the formation of political parties, which the Constitution does not mention. Nevertheless, they soon came into being and form the basis of the U.S. political system.

Federalists Conflict over Hamilton's financial plan was one reason why two political parties emerged in the 1790s. Hamilton and Jefferson became the leaders of each party. The policies of Hamilton's party, the Federalists, favored Northern merchants and, to a lesser extent, large plantation owners in the South. The merchants, in particular, liked the plan:

★ It would stabilize and strengthen the national government.

★ A national bank would be a source of loans for new businesses.

★ Tariffs would protect new domestic industries from foreign competition.

Concerning interpretation of the Constitution, the Federalists argued for **loose construction:** Government had many powers implied by the elastic clause.

Democratic-Republicans The policies of Thomas Jefferson's party, the Democratic-Republicans, favored the interests of small farmers and the common people. It opposed Hamilton's financial plan:

★ Full payment of the national debt, achieved by buying back government bonds would benefit **speculators**. Many of them had bought government bonds at a reduced rate and would make a fortune if the government bought them back at full value.

★ A national bank would more readily give loans to Northern merchants than Southern and Western farmers.

The Democratic-Republicans argued for **strict construction** of the Constitution: Government should do no more than what the Constitution specified. Jefferson, as president, softened this position when he purchased the vast Louisiana Territory from France. (See page 70.)

Whiskey Rebellion (1794) To raise revenue, Congress placed a federal **excise tax** (one made on the sale of a domestic product) on the distilling of whiskey. When whiskey-producing farmers in western Pennsylvania protested, Washington sent troops to put down their rebellion. He thus demonstrated that a federal government was more effective than a confederate government, which had been helpless during Shays' Rebellion.

Alien and Sedition Acts (1798) During the presidency of John Adams (1797–1801), a Federalist majority in Congress enacted two laws to intimidate supporters of the Democratic-Republicans. The *Alien Act* authorized the president to deport foreigners thought to endanger public safety. The *Sedition Act* authorized the government to fine and imprison newspaper editors who printed "scandalous and malicious writing" about the government.

Virginia and Kentucky passed resolutions protesting these acts and claimed the right to nullify (disregard) them as unconstitutional. These resolutions expressed the views of Thomas Jefferson, who argued that the Alien and Sedition acts violated citizens' basic rights.

End of the Federalist Era

Election of 1800 During the administrations of Washington and Adams, the Federalists were in control. In 1800, Adams was defeated by two Democratic-Republican candidates, Thomas Jefferson and Aaron Burr. Because Jefferson and Burr had the same number of electoral votes, the election went to the House of Representatives, and Jefferson emerged the winner.

Congress then proposed the Twelfth Amendment to change the electoral college system. The original Constitution had provided that each elector cast two ballots, both for president. The Twelfth Amendment (1804) provided that each elector cast one ballot for president and a second ballot for vice president.

★ In Review

1. How did Hamilton propose to increase the economic strength of the new U.S. government?
2. Explain why the cabinet system and political parties are examples of the unwritten constitution.
3. Contrast Hamilton's and Jefferson's views of the Constitution.

Neutrality and National Security

Foreign policies under the first five presidents aimed for the following goals:

★ **neutrality** (taking no sides in a foreign war)
★ recognition of U.S. **sovereignty** (independence)
★ support for Latin Americans struggling for independence.

As Washington stated in his *Proclamation of Neutrality*, he wanted the United States to remain neutral in European conflicts. The new nation had a small army and navy and was bordered on the

★ First Political Parties ★

	Federalists	Democratic-Republicans
Leaders	Alexander Hamilton John Adams John Marshall	Thomas Jefferson James Madison James Monroe
Geographic strength	Strong support among Northeast merchants	Strong support among farmers of South and West
Position on Hamilton's financial plan	In favor of national bank, funding the debt, protecting new industries	Opposed to all features
Position on constitutional issues	Favored loose construction to maximize federal power	Favored strict construction to limit federal power and safeguard rights of states
Position on foreign policy	Partial to the British but supportive of Washington's Proclamation of Neutrality	Partial to France but supportive of Jefferson's attempts to remain neutral during Napoleonic wars

north by British Canada, on the south by Spanish Florida, and on the west by the Mississippi River, controlled by Spain.

Washington and the French Revolution (1789–1799)

A revolution in France overthrew the monarchy in 1789. Viewing the French republic as a threat to their own monarchies, Britain, Austria, and Spain sent armies to invade and crush it. Although U.S. public opinion was divided, Washington followed a policy of neutrality throughout his two terms.

John Adams and the XYZ Affair (1797)

John Adams adopted Washington's policy of neutrality. During his presidency, the French navy seized American ships and sent French diplomats (identified as X, Y, Z) demanding bribes to stop the French abuses. Angered by the XYZ Affair, many Americans called for retaliation. Adams avoided war, but in 1798, French and American

ships clashed. Adams and Napoleon, new head of the French government, then reached a temporary settlement.

Jefferson and the Napoleonic Wars (1805–1815)

Jefferson as president (1801–1809) also chose neutrality. Napoleon ended the French republic by crowning himself emperor, and was soon at war with Britain. British warships searched U.S. merchant ships, removed cargo, and forced American sailors into British service by **impressment**. The French navy violated U.S. rights as a neutral nation. Congress placed an **embargo** (trade ban) on shipping American goods to Europe. New England merchants and shipbuilders, whose businesses were damaged, protested. The embargo was lifted in 1809.

War of 1812

Madison's Dilemma

The fourth president, James Madison (1809–1817), also tried to defend U.S. rights at sea without going to war. But U.S.-British tensions increased. As settlers took over Native American land near the Great Lakes, the leader Tecumseh led his people against the settlers, who complained that Britain was arming the enemy. Moreover, a congressional faction of Southerners and Westerns—the "war hawks"—argued that the United States might gain Canada through war with Britain. Congress declared war in 1812.

Protest in New England

In December 1814, however, members of the Federalist party met in Hartford, Connecticut, to protest the war. The delegates discussed **secession** (withdrawal of New England from the Union) but took no action.

Consequences of War

An 1815 treaty ending the war said nothing about U.S. neutrality rights and awarded no territory or money to either side. Great Britain, however, stopped seizing American cargoes, and the United States emerged as a respected sovereign nation.

The War of 1812 boosted **nationalism** (loyalty to and support of one's country). For his 1815

Election of 1800

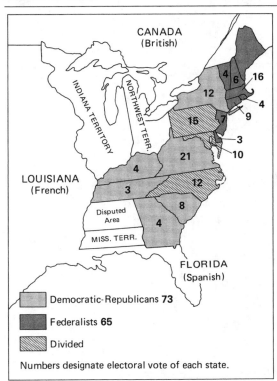

Numbers designate electoral vote of each state.

- Democratic-Republicans **73**
- Federalists **65**
- Divided

victory at New Orleans, Andrew Jackson became a hero. Inspired by watching a battle at Fort McHenry near Baltimore, Francis Scott Key wrote the poem "The Star-Spangled Banner," which was later set to music as the National Anthem.

Era of Good Feelings

The Federalist party, widely condemned for its antiwar stance, ceased to be a major force in U.S. politics. The Democratic-Republican candidate for president, James Monroe, easily won two terms as president (1817–1825). This period has been called the *Era of Good Feelings*.

Monroe and Latin America

Inspired by the American and French revolutions, rebels in South and Central America revolted successfully against Spain, Portugal, and France. Monroe and his secretary of state, John Quincy Adams, warned European powers not to recolonize any part of Latin America. The *Monroe Doctrine* stated:

★ The Western Hemisphere was closed to further colonization by Europeans.

★ The United States would firmly oppose European intervention in the Western Hemisphere.

★ The United States would not involve itself politically in the affairs of Europe.

Great Britain and the new Latin American nations supported the Monroe Doctrine, and it became the foundation of U.S. policy toward Europe and Latin America.

The Monroe Doctrine reflected neutrality, **isolationism** (noninvolvement with foreign entanglements or organizations), and the U.S. concern to end European expansion in the Western Hemisphere. It also protected the interests of the Latin American republics.

Onset of Sectional Conflict

During the Era of Good Feelings, two disputes revealed sectional resentments. One, the *Missouri Compromise*, concerned slavery (see page 64).

The second concerned party politics. By 1824, the Democratic-Republican party had split into several groups, each favoring a different candidate for president. Andrew Jackson, hero of the War of 1812, had more popular votes than the other three candidates. But none had the majority of electoral votes required to win. John Quincy Adams, with the support of candidate Henry Clay, won the election in the House of Representatives. Jackson then charged that the election had been stolen. After this rift, supporters of Adams and Clay called

Snapping turtle "Ograbme" ("embargo" spelled backwards) stops shipment of U.S. goods to Britain.

Burning of Washington, D.C., during the War of 1812

Latin America: Dates of Independence From European Rule

themselves National Republicans. Supporters of Jackson took the name of Democrats.

★ In Review

1. How did the election of 1800 lead to changes in the Constitution?

2. Explain the major causes and results of the War of 1812.

3. To what extent did the Monroe Doctrine reflect sentiments of neutrality and isolationism?

Chapter Review

MULTIPLE-CHOICE QUESTIONS

Base your answers to questions 1 and 2 on the statements made by the following speakers and your knowledge of the early years of the United States:

Speaker A: The federal government must be permitted to do whatever it has to do to establish a sound economy.

Speaker B: If the federal government does not follow the Constitution exactly, tyranny and loss of individual freedom will result.

Speaker C: The Constitution does not permit the establishment of a national bank.

Speaker D: The elastic clause gives Congress broad legislative powers.

1. Which speaker or speakers promote(s) the ideas of Hamilton? (1) Speaker A (2) Speakers B and D (3) Speakers C and D (4) Speakers A and D.

2. The speaker or speakers most likely to support the Democratic-Republicans is/are (1) Speakers A and B (2) Speakers B and C (3) Speakers C and D (4) Speaker D.

Use the map on page 49 to answer questions 3 and 4.

3. Which generalization about the election of 1800 is accurate? (1) Federalists were strongest in the Northeast. (2) Federalists were strongest in the South. (3) Democratic-Republicans lost the election. (4) Democratic-Republicans had greater support in the North than South.

4. Which of the following did *not* participate in the election of 1800? (1) New Jersey (2) people of New England (3) people in the Indiana, Northwest, and Mississippi territories (4) Georgia.

5. The Whiskey Rebellion demonstrated that the federal government (1) had established tyrannical authority (2) had the power to enforce its laws (3) needed the assistance of the Pennsylvania militia to stop the uprising (4) had established the authority to ban the sale and consumption of alcoholic beverages.

Base your answer to question 6 on the following statement and your knowledge of U.S. history and government:

> The Alien Law . . . affects only foreigners who are conspiring against us, and has no relation whatever to an American citizen. . . . The Sedition Act . . . prescribes a punishment only for those pests of society and disturbers of order and tranquillity. . . .
>
> —Timothy Pickering, Secretary of State under John Adams

6. The quotation argues that the Alien and Sedition Acts (1) are necessary and proper for the security of the United States (2) apply only to foreign conspirators (3) are unconstitutional and a violation of the First Amendment (4) should be strengthened.

7. The foreign policies of Washington, Jefferson, and Monroe were similar in that they (1) aided the French Republic (2) favored Britain (3) were hostile to Britain (4) sought to avoid involvement in European affairs.

8. The main purpose of the Monroe Doctrine was to (1) exclude Portugal from Latin America (2) encourage French protection of the Western Hemisphere (3) create an alliance of Latin American nations (4) warn European nations not to interfere in the Americas.

Base your answer to question 9 on the following statement:

> The United States of America . . . [are] fostering revolutions wherever they show themselves . . . they lend new strength . . . and reanimate the courage of every conspirator. If this flood of evil doctrines . . . should extend over the whole of [North and South] America, what would become of our [European] . . . institutions?
>
> —Prince Metternich of Austria commenting on the Monroe Doctrine

9. Metternich takes the position that the Monroe Doctrine is (1) in the best interests of Latin America (2) a U.S. plea to be allowed to remain neutral (3) more helpful to Austria than to the rest of Europe (4) harmful to most European interests.

THEMATIC ESSAY

Theme: Neutrality as Foreign Policy. President Washington decided that the new nation would be best to pursue a foreign policy of neutrality. Succeeding presidents followed his lead with varying degrees of success.

Task: Show how two situations required U.S. presidents to enforce neutrality. For each situation:

★ describe the events that led the president to enforce neutrality
★ evaluate how successful the U.S. policy of neutrality was.

You may use any event you have studied. Some presidents and events you may wish to use are John Adams and the XYZ Affair, Thomas Jefferson and the Napoleonic wars, James Madison and the War of 1812, and James Monroe and the issuance of the Monroe Doctrine.

DOCUMENT-BASED QUESTION

*Study each document and answer the question that follows it. Then read the **Task** and write your essay.*

Include references to most of the documents and additional information you retain about U.S. history and government.

Historical Context: Even though our early presidents followed a policy of neutrality, they could not ignore the rest of the world.

Document 1: From George Washington's Farewell Address:

> Europe has a set of primary interests which to us have no or a very remote relation . . . therefore it must be unwise to implicate ourselves by artificial ties . . . it is our true policy to steer clear of permanent alliances with any portion of the foreign world. . . .

Question: Why did Washington favor U.S. noninvolvement in European affairs?

Document 2: Anonymous author's "Open Letter to George Washington," 1793:

> Had you . . . consulted the general sentiments of your fellow citizens, you would have found them . . . firmly attached to the cause of France. . . . Had even no written treaty existed between France and the United States, still would the strongest ties of amity [friendship] have united the people of both nations; still would the republican citizens of America have regarded Frenchmen, contending for liberty, as their brethren.

Question: Why does the writer tell Washington that the nation should support France against Britain?

Document 3: Thomas Jefferson on France's possible acquisition of the Louisiana Territory:

> The day France takes possession of New Orleans . . . we must marry ourselves to the British fleet and nation. . . . This is not a state of things we seek and desire.

Question: What would Jefferson have to do if France controlled New Orleans?

Document 4: Refer to the map of the Louisiana Purchase on page 70.

Question: How did the Louisiana Purchase prevent the United States from "marrying" the British fleet?

Document 5: Study the cartoon "Ograbme," on page 50.

Question: How does the cartoonist feel the embargo is affecting New England?

Document 6: From James Madison, War Message to Congress, 1812:

> British cruisers have been . . . violating the American flag on the great highway of nations [the Atlantic Ocean], and . . . seizing and carrying off persons sailing under it.
>   . . . British cruisers have been . . . violating the rights and peace of our coasts. They
>   . . . harass our entering and departing commerce [which] has been plundered in every sea. . . .

Question: Why was Madison recommending a declaration of war on Britain?

Task: Using information from the documents and your knowledge of early U.S. foreign affairs, write an essay in which you explain:

★ why the United States followed a policy of neutrality
★ why public opinion made it difficult to maintain neutrality
★ how world affairs placed neutrality in jeopardy.

Chapter 5
Nationalism and Sectionalism

★ Documents and Laws	★ Events	★ People
Missouri Compromise (1820) "Tariff of Abominations" (1828) Ordinance of Nullification (1832) Compromise of 1850 Fugitive Slave Act (1850) *Dred Scott* v. *Sanford* (1857)	Opening of Erie Canal (1825) Resettlement Act (1830) "Trail of Tears" (1838) Irish Potato Famine (1846) Seneca Falls Convention (1848) Harpers Ferry Raid (1859)	Henry Barnard John Brown John C. Calhoun Henry Clay Dorothea Dix Frederick Douglass Robert Fulton William Lloyd Garrison Andrew Jackson Horace Mann Lucretia Mott Elizabeth Cady Stanton Harriet Beecher Stowe Harriet Tubman Nat Turner Denmark Vesey Eli Whitney

★ Objectives

★ To identify the geographic and economic factors contributing to sectionalism.

★ To explain living conditions under slavery.

★ To identify early immigrant groups and their impact on the nation.

★ To identify important policies of Andrew Jackson and evaluate their political effects.

★ To describe how U.S. expansion affected Native Americans.

★ To describe reform movements during the Age of Jackson.

★ To compare and contrast attempts to preserve the Union.

Between 1789 and 1861, several forces preserved national unity and a general feeling that Americans were citizens of the country rather than of individual states. The Marshall Court rulings established federal supremacy over state governments and federal power to regulate interstate commerce. By supporting one of the major political parties, most Americans were organized into two groups rather than many different factions. Finally, industrialization and the building of roads and canals promoted economic interdependence within the United States.

Other forces, however, provoked **sectionalism** (strong loyalty to one region within a nation), which, in 1861, led to the Civil War. The underlying cause was that the North, South, and West had different kinds of economies.

Industrial North

Geography, technology, and U.S. economic policy helped the North industrialize.

Geography

The North's many rivers (1) provided waterpower to drive machinery and (2) served as natural highways for transporting goods. A network of roads and canals connected the rivers. Completion of the Erie Canal in 1825 enabled merchants and farmers to ship goods without transfer between New York City and Lake Erie ports. The North also had ocean ports that facilitated easy and profitable trade with Europe.

Technology

The invention of the steamboat by Robert Fulton and others in the early 1800s speeded up water transportation. In the 1830s and 1840s, railroads began to transport goods by land efficiently.

Economic Policies

Alexander Hamilton's national bank benefited Northern merchants. An 1816 tariff act that taxed imports allowed American textile mills to compete with those in Britain. Also in 1816, the Second Bank of the United States, which replaced Hamilton's national bank, helped industrial growth by providing loans to businesses.

Factory System

New technology spurred the growth of factories. Eli Whitney invented tools to make each part of a

Major Canals and Roads, 1820–1850

device such as a musket a standard size. Manufacture of these **interchangeable parts** was also much faster. The thousands of immigrants arriving every year in Boston and New York provided cheap labor for the new factories.

Women and Children Workers Most workers in New England's textile mills were women and children under the age of 12. At first, working conditions were reasonable, but mill owners soon instituted 12- to 14-hour daily shifts, six days a week. Wages were low and conditions unhealthy and dangerous. Critics of the factory system compared mill workers to slaves.

Urban Problems

Farm people and immigrants flocked to cities in the Northeast, swelling their populations. As the poorer sections grew crowded, open sewers polluted the streets and fresh water became scarce. Diseases such as typhoid and cholera spread rapidly.

Competition for jobs between poor whites and free blacks sometimes resulted in riots. With the influx of poor people, the middle and upper classes moved elsewhere.

Family Life

Middle-class families had comfortable homes. Working-class families crowded in cramped **tenements** (multifamily buildings with few ameni-

ties). In general, middle-class men supported their families while the women ran households and raised children. Their children did not work. In contrast, working–class men, women, and children all worked long hours for low wages and had little leisure time.

Education

Until the 1830s, education was primarily for privileged boys whose parents paid for them to attend private schools. Such reformers as Horace Mann and Henry Barnard argued that democracy depends on people who can read, write, and reason. They advocated public education paid for by the states. Massachusetts and New York established the first free schools for children from eight to fourteen. Attendance was compulsory. By 1850, New York's public education system offered instruction from grade one to grade twelve.

Free Blacks

Most blacks living in the pre–Civil War North were free, but they did not have full rights of citizenship. Except in New England, most cities and towns denied them the vote. Throughout the North, African Americans were usually segregated: Black children went to separate schools, and churches rarely welcomed black members. In some Northern states, blacks could not serve on juries or testify in criminal cases.

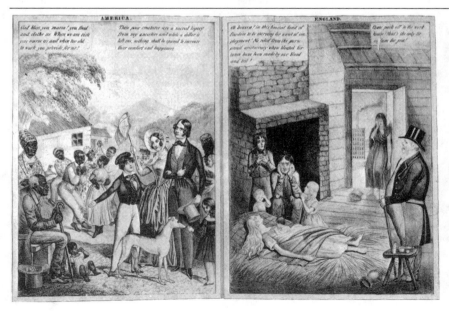

1840s cartoon contrasting Southern slavery with Northern and British "wage slavery"

Development of the South

Role of Cotton

Even in the 1780s and 1790s, the South exported a lot of cotton to British textile mills. By the early 1800s, this region of many plantations had become economically dependent on this single crop.

Cotton grew easily in the South. But removing the seeds from cotton by hand was a slow process. Then, in 1793, Eli Whitney invented the **cotton gin**, which separated seeds from cotton mechanically. This device and the ever-increasing demand for cotton by British and Northern mills made Southern planters wealthy.

Old Southwest

Cotton's one drawback was that it wore out the soil. In search of large tracts of new farmland, Southerners began to move into the Old Southwest—Alabama, Mississippi, Louisiana, Arkansas, and Texas. As a result, Southern wealth and leadership spread to plantation owners in the new regions.

Women on Plantations

Women on plantations supervised the large plantation house, entertained, and provided a "woman's touch" for all events.

Slavery

Laws Most work on plantations was done by African slaves. Southern laws gave plantation owners free reign over their slaves. Beatings were common. Children born into slavery were the property of their owners. It was legal and common to sell slaves and thus separate slave families.

Women Slaves Enslaved women worked along with the men in the fields, maintained homes, and raised families. Women house slaves were cooks, seamstresses, and caretakers of their owners' children. Some male owners expected slave women to have sex with them. Historians believe that Thomas Jefferson had at least one child with Sally Hemings, a slave with whom he had a long relationship.

Child Slaves By the age of six or eight, slave children were expected to work. Escaped slave Frederick Douglass, in his autobiography, stated that he and other black children were poorly fed, inadequately clothed and protected against cold, and kept illiterate. Some, including Douglass, were separated early from one or both parents and their siblings.

Labor As the demand for cotton grew, so did the demand for slaves to plant and pick it. Plantation owners largely ignored the 1808 law against importing slaves. For them, slavery was an economic necessity. Besides serving as field hands and servants, slaves worked as blacksmiths, carpenters, and barrel makers, enabling plantations to be nearly self-sufficient.

Slavery and Religion Slaves were permitted to attend religious services. Most of them became Baptists or Methodists, like the majority of white Southerners. The form of Christianity that they practiced, however, retained many elements from African religions— charms, love potions, and folk medicines. Slaves were particularly attracted to Old Testament stories about the freeing of Hebrew slaves and their return to the Promised Land. When blacks and whites attended the same church, blacks sat in separate pews.

Resistance Some slaves revolted against lifelong bondage, even though it was usually hopeless and

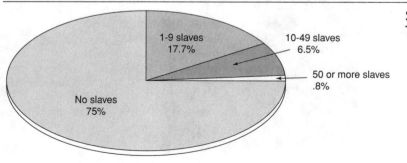

Slaveholding Southerners—and Those With No Slaves

1-9 slaves 17.7%

10-49 slaves 6.5%

50 or more slaves .8%

No slaves 75%

★ United States Labor Force, 1800–1860 ★

(in thousands)

Year	Free	Slave	Total
1800	1,330	530	1,860
1810	1,590	740	2,330
1820	2,185	950	3,135
1830	3,020	1,180	4,200
1840	4,180	1,480	5,660
1850	6,280	1,970	8,250
1860	8,770	2,340	11,110

the penalty was death. In 1822, an uprising planned by Denmark Vesey, a South Carolina slave, was discovered before it began. Nat Turner's 1831 revolt in Virginia resulted in 59 deaths but was quickly put down. Turner was tried and hanged.

Spirituals (religious songs composed by slaves) such as "Go Down Moses" and "Michael, Row the Boat Ashore" expressed the intense desire for freedom. Some songs, such as "Follow the Drinking Gourd," served as codes about escape plans.

In daily life, slaves often slowed their cotton picking. When owners, eager for profits, offered rewards for quicker work, many slaves risked punishment by disobeying.

Some slaves fled. Runaways in the deep South were more easily caught than those farther north.

Frederick Douglass disguised himself as a free black seaman and took a train north from Maryland. "Box Henry" hid himself in a box with a Northern address and was shipped to freedom.

Most slaves escaped on the *Underground Railroad*, a system of routes and safe havens in the homes of white **abolitionists** (persons opposed to slavery). "Conductors" guided escapees to Northern states or Canada.

Pre-Civil War Immigration

★ *The British* came mainly for economic reasons. Unable to find factory work at home, they hoped to do better in the United States.

★ *The Germans*, including many Jews, came in large numbers after 1848. Some were political refugees from the failed 1848 revolution in Germany. Others sought better economic opportunities. As a group, Germans supported the antislavery movement and public education. Many became farmers in the Midwest.

★ *The Irish* were the largest immigrant group before the Civil War. Their numbers soared after 1846, when blight killed the potato crop that the Irish relied on for food. Many escaped famine only by coming to the United States. They made up the first large-scale group of Roman Catholics in American society. Many Irish built the nation's new canals and roads. In the 1860s, Irish immigrants helped build the Union Pacific Railroad. After the Civil War,

"Box Henry" Brown arriving in the North

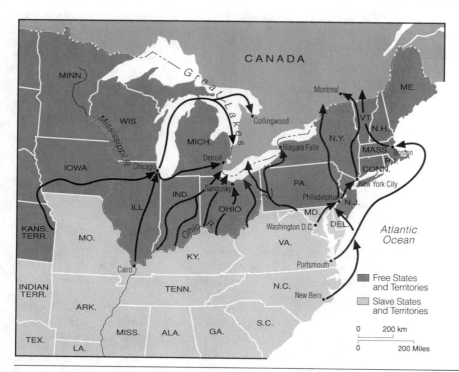

Routes and "Stations" on the Underground Railroad

they worked in coal mines and became active in the campaign for better working conditions there.

Nativist Reactions A **nativist** believes that foreign-born people threaten the majority culture. During the 19th century, nativists tried to exclude Irish Catholics, Jews from eastern Europe, Italians, Chinese, and Japanese.

In the 1850s, Irish Catholic immigrants were the first targets of nativist anger. Groups of American-born Protestants organized a secret society. As a political party, it worked to elect candidates in favor of banning or limiting immigration. Members were called Know-Nothings because, when asked about their society, they answered, "I know nothing."

In Review

1. Compare and contrast patterns of life in the North and the South.
2. How did the nativist movement affect new immigrants?
3. How did African slaves resist their owners?

Age of Jackson

In the election of 1828, Andrew Jackson, a Democrat, decisively won the popular and electoral votes. His presidency (1829–1837) became known as the *Age of Jackson*. Although remembered for reforms, it was also marked by the expansion of slavery, persecution of Native Americans, and sectional conflict.

Reform and Political Change

Universal Suffrage for White Males Between 1800 and 1830, state after state removed property requirements for voting. By the Age of Jackson, most white males aged 21 or older could vote.

Election Campaigns As voting rights were extended, candidates used new techniques to reach voters. Political parties (at this time, the Whigs and Democrats) employed banners, rallies, speeches, and debates. **Caucuses** (meetings of party leaders) were replaced by **nominating conventions**, where party delegates from many states voted for candidates.

In an 1800s nativist cartoon, new citizens—an Irishman and a German—steal the ballot box.

Spoils System After his election, Jackson soon put into effect his motto "To the victor belong the spoils." Under the **spoils system**, his supporters took over most federal jobs in the belief that giving them to "the common man" rather than to the educated and privileged was a democratic reform. Later presidents, Whigs and Democrats alike, followed Jackson's example.

Bank Issue The Second Bank of the United States provoked a bitter dispute. Jackson accused the bank of granting loans to Northeastern businesspeople and denying them to Western farmers. In 1832, he vetoed an act to renew the bank's

charter. Henry Clay, Jackson's Whig opponent in the presidential election of 1832, came out in support of the bank. Jackson won reelection by a huge majority.

Native Americans

Immigrants swelled the number of Americans who, in search of land and economic opportunity, kept pushing Native Americans farther west. Outnumbered and facing superior weapons, Native Americans tried several survival strategies. Some adopted European culture. Others maintained and strengthened their own heritage.

★ U.S. Population by Region, 1790–1860 ★

Year	Northeast[1]	North Central[2]	South[3]	West[4]
1790	1,968,040	—	1,961,174	—
1800	2,635,576	51,006	2,621,901	—
1810	3,486,675	292,107	3,461,099	—
1820	4,359,916	859,305	4,419,232	—
1830	5,542,381	1,610,473	5,707,848	—
1840	6,761,082	3,351,542	6,950,729	—
1850	8,626,951	5,403,595	8,982,612	178,818
1860	10,594,268	9,096,716	11,133,361	618,976

[1]Northeast includes Maine, New Hampshire, Vermont, Massachusetts, Rhode Island, Connecticut, New York, New Jersey, and Pennsylvania.

[2]North Central includes Ohio, Indiana, Illinois, Michigan, Wisconsin, Minnesota, Iowa, Missouri, and the territories of Kansas and Nebraska.

[3]South includes Delaware, Maryland, Virginia, North Carolina, South Carolina, Georgia, Florida, Kentucky, Tennessee, Alabama, Mississippi, Arkansas, Texas, Louisiana, and the Oklahoma Territory.

[4]West includes all area west of the states and territories listed for Northeast, North Central, and South.

"Canvassing for a Vote": Politicians from the Jacksonian era onward sought the common man's vote.

At times, they united in an attempt to stop the incursions into their territories.

When conflicts arose, Jackson favored the settlers over the Native Americans by initiating *Indian Removal*. The *Resettlement Act* (1830), for example, forced Native Americans to abandon their villages and move hundreds of miles west, where whites had not yet settled.

The worst forced removal was the *"Trail of Tears"* (1838). Some 15,000 Cherokees from Georgia were made to trek westward 800 miles through cold and rain; many of them died from exposure and starvation. Chief Justice John Marshall had earlier ruled that the Cherokees had a right to their land, but Jackson ignored the ruling.

Birth of the Reform Tradition

Movements by Women

Women of the 1830s and 1840s worked for their own rights and were also extremely active in other reform movements.

Women's Rights Lucretia Mott and Elizabeth Cady Stanton objected to "male-only" political meetings. To discuss such injustices, Stanton called a convention at Seneca Falls, New York (1848). Delegates drafted a declaration based on the assumption that "all men and women are created equal." It stipulated the following rights:

★ the right of women to vote and hold office

★ the right of married women to hold property in their names

★ the right of women wage earners to manage their incomes

★ the right of women to be legal guardians of their children.

Indian Removal in the 1830s

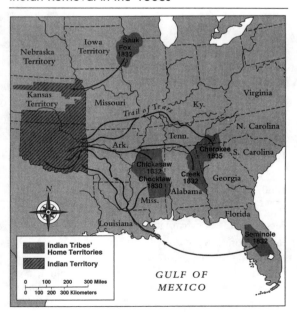

"The Trail of Tears"—
Cherokees' forced
journey to an unknown
land

Stanton fought for laws to grant women long-denied rights and was president of the National Woman Suffrage Association (1869–1890).

Control of Alcohol In the 1840s, women led an anti-drinking campaign called the **temperance movement**. They persuaded several states to prohibit the production and sale of alcoholic beverages in an effort to stop heads of households from spending money on liquor rather than on supporting their families.

Institutions for the Mentally III A former schoolteacher, Dorothea Dix, discovering that the mentally ill were often chained and beaten, called public attention to these horrors. As a result, several states set aside "asylums" where patients received humanitarian care.

Abolition Movement

Political Conflict In the early days of slavery, some Southerners as well as Northerners wanted it abolished by law. But as slave labor became critical to the economy of the South, most whites there viewed slaves as property whose ownership was permitted by the Constitution. Northern states banned slavery, and a small group of abolitionists, mostly Northerners, demanded that slavery end everywhere in the United States. A more moderate group wanted only to stop the spread of slavery beyond the Mississippi.

Abolitionist Leaders

★ *Harriet Beecher Stowe*, a white woman from Connecticut, wrote *Uncle Tom's Cabin* (1852). This novel is about a kind old slave abused by a vicious slave overseer, Simon Legree. The book aroused intense indignation in Northerners and deep resentment in Southerners, who claimed that it depicted Southern society falsely.

★ *Harriet Tubman* escaped slavery as a young woman and became a principal organizer and guide on the Underground Railroad. Tubman also helped free hundreds of slaves during the Civil War and was an advocate of women's rights after the war.

★ *Frederick Douglass*, an escaped slave and skillful orator, argued for abolition. He founded the *North Star*, a newspaper written by African Americans, and wrote his autobiography. He recruited black soldiers for the Union Army during the Civil War.

★ *William Lloyd Garrison*, a white reformer, helped to launch the abolitionist movement by publishing an antislavery newspaper, *The Liberator*, beginning in 1831. He demanded an immediate end to slavery without compensation to owners.

★ *John Brown*, a white abolitionist, believed in using violence to fight slavery. In Kansas in 1856, Brown and his sons murdered five supporters of slavery in retaliation for the deaths of abolitionist settlers. In 1859, he led an attack at Harpers Ferry, Virginia (now West Virginia), a federal arsenal, probably hoping to arm slaves. After Brown was captured and hanged, abolitionists considered him a martyr while proslavery Southerners saw him as a crazed fanatic.

★ In Review

1. How did democracy expand in the first half of the 19th century?
2. How did Andrew Jackson resolve his differences regarding a national bank?
3. How did abolitionists attempt to end slavery?

Abolitionists (left to right): Harriet Beecher Stowe, Frederick Douglass, Harriet Tubman, John Brown, William Lloyd Garrison

Federal Supremacy Versus States' Rights

Nullification

Until the Civil War ended, one of the great constitutional debates concerned **nullification**, a state's right to disregard laws passed by the federal government. An early example occurred in 1798 when Virginia and Kentucky passed resolutions nullifying the Federalist Congress's Alien and Sedition Acts.

Tariff of Abominations During Jackson's presidency, the debate heated up over tariffs. During the War of 1812, when Americans could no longer import goods from Britain, factories in the North sprang up and became profitable. To maintain this advantage, Congress raised tariff rates in 1816, 1818, 1824, and 1828. Besides reducing foreign competition, they encouraged Northern manufacturers to raise prices paid by U.S. consumers.

The tariffs also reduced the market for British-made cotton cloth. This meant that the South sold less cotton to Britain, its chief customer. When Congress again raised the tariff in 1828, Southerners resisted, calling it the *Tariff of Abominations*.

Jackson's vice president, John C. Calhoun of South Carolina, led the resistance. He wrote that every state had a right to nullify an act of Congress that it deemed unconstitutional, and that the Tariff of 1828 should be nullified because

it benefited one section of the country at the expense of another. Jackson declared that Calhoun's ideas were treasonable.

In 1832, Congress reduced the tariff in part, but Southerners remained dissatisfied. South Carolina's *Ordinance of Nullification* threatened secession if the federal government tried to collect tariffs in Southern ports.

Jackson threatened to use troops to enforce the tariff. Senator Henry Clay of Kentucky then proposed a compromise: Congress would pass a new tariff in 1833, providing for a gradual reduction of rates, if South Carolina repealed its ordinance. The compromise was accepted.

Free and Slave States

As new territories were added to the United States, arguments about slavery in the West became more heated.

Missouri Compromise Slave owners who moved to the Missouri Territory brought along their slaves. In 1819, Missouri applied for admission as a state permitting slavery. After much debate, Congress passed the *Missouri Compromise* (1820):

★ Missouri would enter the Union as a slave state.

★ Maine would enter the Union as a free state.

★ All of the Louisiana Purchase north of the 36°30' line of latitude would be closed to slavery.

The agreement did not solve the crisis but merely put it off.

California After the Mexican War (1846–1848), the United States acquired a large tract of land that included present-day California. Settlement there soared after the gold rush of 1849, and California applied for admission as a free state. Southerners were opposed because its admission would upset the balance between free and slave states, as established by the Missouri Compromise, and give the North majorities in the Senate and House. They feared that the Northern majority might prevent them from taking slaves into other territories won from Mexico.

Compromise of 1850 Senator Clay proposed a compromise:

★ California would be admitted as a free state. In other parts of the *Mexican Cession* (lands ceded by Mexico to the United States), including Arizona, New Mexico, Utah, and Nevada, settlers would decide by **popular sovereignty** (majority vote) whether to allow slavery.

★ Buying and selling slaves at public auction would be abolished in Washington, D.C.

★ A *Fugitive Slave Act* would require Northern officials to assist in the capture and return of escaped slaves.

Dred Scott v. *Sanford* (1857)

Facts Dred Scott was a slave from Missouri before his owner took him to Illinois, a free state. Scott returned to a Missouri court and asked to be declared a free citizen on the grounds that he had lived in free territory. His case eventually was appealed to the Supreme Court.

Supreme Court Decision In 1857, Chief Justice Roger Taney, a Southerner, ruled as follows:

★ Free African Americans were not citizens and could not sue in federal courts.

★ Slaves brought into free territory remained slaves because they were property, and owners could not be denied property without due process of law.

★ The Missouri Compromise's ban on slavery in free territory was unconstitutional because it denied slave owners their property rights.

Public Reaction Southerners rejoiced that the Supreme Court had confirmed their views. Many Northerners were shocked at a decision that threw all territories in the West open to slavery.

★ In Review

1. How did the tariff issue heat up the nullification debate during Jackson's administration?
2. How did each of the following attempt to resolve the slavery issue: (a) Missouri Compromise and (b) Compromise of 1850?
3. What were the facts, issues, and decision in *Dred Scott* v. *Sanford*?

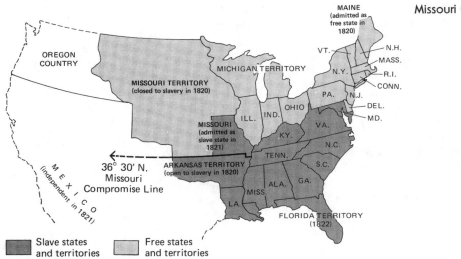

Missouri Compromise of 1820

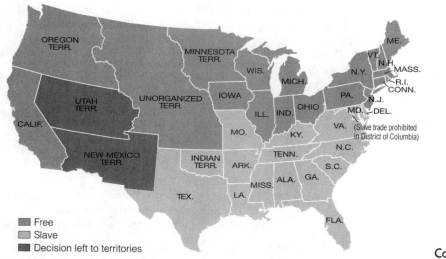

Free
Slave
Decision left to territories

Compromise of 1850

Chapter Review

MULTIPLE-CHOICE QUESTIONS

1. Refer to the map on page 56. The most accurate conclusion to be drawn from the map is that (1) travel between states and territories was becoming more difficult (2) most canals went north-south while most roads went east-west (3) most roads and canals were east-to-west links (4) travel was slow because roads and canals were not connected.

Use the population table on page 61 to answer questions 2 and 3.

2. Between 1790 and 1860, (1) the number of people in all areas rose except for the North Central region (2) the South had fewer people than the Northeast between 1790 and 1810, but the trend reversed itself between 1820 and 1860 (3) by 1850, the North Central population lagged behind that of the West (4) the Northeast population was in decline from 1840 to 1860.

3. The West's population changed between 1850 and 1860 because (1) disease and harsh living conditions caused a decline (2) the dis-

covery of gold caused a migration from the West to the South (3) some territories in the West became states (4) many roads and canals were destroyed by natural disasters.

4. The graph on page 58 shows that (1) some Southern states had no slavery (2) 25 percent of Southerners had no slaves (3) most Southerners owned 50 or more slaves (4) the majority of slaveholders held between one and nine slaves.

5. The map on page 62 shows that in the 1830s, Native Americans (1) migrated from the North to the South (2) were forced to move to Western territories (3) were free to move where they wished (4) abandoned their reservations and returned to the East.

6. Which belief was essential to the nullification doctrine? (1) States had created the federal government and could overturn its laws. (2) The federal government had been created by federal interests. (3) Each citizen could decide whether or not to obey a law. (4) Southern states should not have joined the union.

7. One reason why Westerners opposed the Bank of the United States was that they (1) feared inflation (2) believed the bank favored debtors (3) believed that deposits were mismanaged (4) believed that Eastern business interests benefited most from the bank.

8. During the Age of Jackson, Native Americans (1) moved to cities in large numbers (2) sought alliances with other minorities (3) were forced to move westward (4) chose to adopt the culture of European settlers.

Base your answers to questions 9 and 10 on the following discussion and your knowledge of U.S. history and government.

Speaker A: On all sides we see the national government becoming all-powerful and crushing the liberties of the states.

Speaker B: The time will come—and I rejoice!—when the United States will stretch from sea to sea.

Speaker C: Tariffs are an abomination, and we must resist them forcefully.

Speaker D: The union is one and inseparable, and we cannot permit states to defy congressional law.

9. Which speakers are most likely to support states' rights? (1) A and B (2) A and C (3) C and D (4) B and C.

10. Which speaker is most likely to advocate westward expansion? (1) A (2) B (3) C (4) D.

THEMATIC ESSAYS

1. **Theme:** Sectionalism in the North and South. Between 1800 and 1850, the United States became increasingly divided by sectional differences in the North and South.

   Task: Explain three ways in which the sections differed, and explain the differences. Refer to historical events that contributed to the growth of these differences. Consider such factors as people, geography, work, and lifestyles.

2. **Theme:** Expansion as a Cause of Nationalism and Sectionalism. The expansion of the Western frontier resulted in events that encouraged the unity of nationalism and the disunity of sectionalism.

   Task: Describe one circumstance that promoted nationalism and another that resulted in sectionalism. For each example, include the following:

   ★ background of the circumstance
   ★ how nationalism or sectionalism became an outcome.

   You may use such examples as Eli Whitney's cotton gin and system of interchangeable parts, the Missouri Compromise, the Compromise of 1850, and the Dred Scott case.

DOCUMENT-BASED QUESTION

*Study each document and answer the question that follows it. Then read the **Task** and write your essay. Include references to most of the documents and additional information you retain about U.S. history and government.*

Historical Context: While the period between the 1820s and the 1840s saw democracy expand, many people still had no control of their lives or were second-class citizens.

Document 1: Refer to the cartoon of "Box Henry" Brown's escape to freedom on page 59.

Question: What does the cartoon show about the extremes to which African Americans would go to gain freedom?

Document 2: From Lucretia Mott and Elizabeth Cady Stanton's "Declaration of Sentiments," 1848:

> The history of mankind is a history of repeated injuries . . . on the part of man toward woman, having in the direct object the establishment of an absolute tyranny over her. To prove this, let facts be submitted to a candid world:
> He has never permitted her to exercise her inalienable right to the elective franchise.
> He has compelled her to submit to laws, in the formation of which she had no voice. . . .

Question: What complaints did Mott, Stanton, and other women have about men's treatment of women throughout history?

Document 3: Examine the painting "The Trail of Tears" on page 63.

Question: What does the painting show about the government's treatment of Native Americans?

Document 4: Refer to the cartoon of American slaves and American and British working people on page 57.

Question: What attitude does the artist express in comparing British and Northern factory labor and Southern slavery?

Document 5: Refer to the cartoon of an Irish and a German immigrant on page 61.

Question: How does the cartoon illustrate the view of some Americans about immigrants during the early to mid-1800s?

Document 6: Harriet Martineau, a British author, describes her 1834 visit to the United States:

> I had been less than three weeks in the country and was in . . . awe at the prevalence of . . . external competence [and] intellectual ability. The striking effect . . . of witnessing . . . the absence of poverty, of gross ignorance, or all servility, of all insolence of manner cannot be exaggerated . . . . I had seen every man . . . an independent citizen [or] a landowner. I had seen that the villages had their newspapers, the factory girls their libraries. I had witnessed [candidates'] controversies . . . on some difficult subjects, of which the people were to be the judges.
>
> With all these things in my mind, and with evidence of prosperity about me . . . I was thrown into painful amazement by being told that the grand question . . . was "whether the people could be encouraged to govern themselves, or whether the wise should save them from themselves."

Question: How did Martineau feel about life in the United States in 1834?

Document 7: Look at the painting "Canvassing for a Vote," on page 62.

Question: What does the painting show about election campaigns in the Age of Jackson?

Task: Using information in the documents and your knowledge of the United States during the early and mid-1800s, write an essay in which you show how the period had both democratic and undemocratic aspects.

Chapter 6
Western Expansion and Civil War

★ Documents and Laws	★ Events	★ People
Kansas-Nebraska Act (1854)	Independence of Texas (1836–1845)	Clara Barton
Emancipation Proclamation (1863)	Annexation of Texas (1845)	John Wilkes Booth
Thirteenth Amendment (1865)	Mexican War (1846–1848)	John Brown
	Gadsden Purchase (1853)	Henry Clay
	"Bleeding Kansas" (1855)	Jefferson Davis
	Election of 1860	Dorthea Dix
	South Carolina Secession (1860)	Stephen Douglas
	Firing on Fort Sumter (1861)	Ulysses S. Grant
	Civil War (1861-1865)	Thomas J. "Stonewall" Jackson
	Battle at Antietam (1862)	Robert E. Lee
	Gettysburg Address (1863)	Abraham Lincoln
	Surrender of Vicksburg (1863)	George B. McClellan
	Sherman's March to the Sea (1864)	George G. Meade
	Surrender at Appomattox Court House (1865)	James K. Polk
	Assassination of Lincoln (1865)	Antonio López de Santa Anna
		William T. Sherman
		Harriet Beecher Stowe
		Sojourner Truth

★ Objectives

★ To explain the impact of Western expansion on Native Americans and Mexicans.

★ To examine how the dispute over Oregon was settled peacefully, while others over Texas and the Southwest resulted in war.

★ To identify the causes and consequences of the Mexican War.

★ To compare the Northern and Southern viewpoints on the slavery issue.

★ To identify causes and consequences of the Civil War.

★ To analyze why Lincoln was a great president.

Territorial Expansion

As a Democratic-Republican, Jefferson was committed to states' rights. Yet, his prime presidential duty was to strengthen the nation. Because of his decision to buy the vast Louisiana Territory, he had to modify his view of the Constitution.

Louisiana Purchase

The treaty ending the American Revolution set the Mississippi River as the western boundary of the new nation. New Orleans, at the mouth of the river, and the unexplored expanse of Louisiana to the west were under French rule. By 1800, pioneers had moved into Kentucky, Tennessee, and Ohio, bordering the Mississippi. No more expansion was possible until, in 1803, Napoleon Bonaparte offered to sell New Orleans and the Louisiana Territory to the United States for the bargain price of about $15 million.

Jefferson's Dilemma No clause in the Constitution authorized the federal government to expand U.S. borders. As a strict constructionist, Jefferson could not justify buying Louisiana.

Jefferson finally yielded to the arguments of opponents in the Federalist party. They insisted that the Constitution's elastic clause implied many powers not specified. In 1803, Jefferson asked the Senate to ratify the Louisiana Purchase.

Exploring and Settling the West

Louisiana more than doubled U.S. land area. In 1804, Jefferson sent Meriwether Lewis and William Clark to explore the new lands. The following year, they reached the Columbia River, which was a water route to the Pacific Ocean. Because of these explorations, the United States claimed the whole territory of Oregon.

American fur trappers soon went to the so-called Oregon Country. Known as "mountain men," they became trailblazers for new settlers and for missionaries who wished to convert the Native Americans there to Christianity. By the 1840s, several thousand Americans were in the Oregon Country.

Mormons were among new settlers in the West. Joseph Smith had founded the Mormon Church (Church of the Latter-Day Saints) in western New York State. The growing Mormon congregation tried to set up communities in the Midwest but were persecuted for their beliefs, particularly the practice of polygamy. Led by Brigham Young, the Mormons traveled to Utah, where they founded Salt Lake City.

Spaniards, Mexicans, and Native Americans Present-day Texas, New Mexico, Arizona, and California were originally explored and settled by the Spaniards. Spreading northward from Mexico City, they claimed and occupied much of

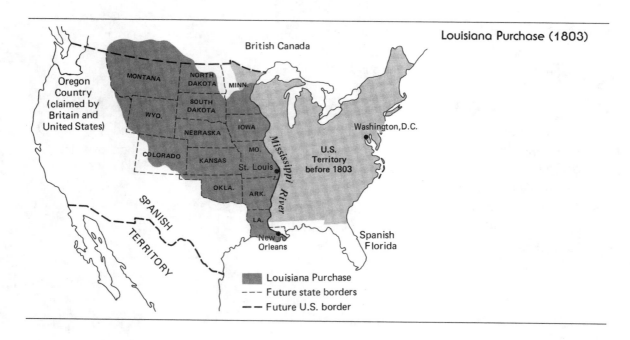

Louisiana Purchase (1803)

the Southwest and established forts, missions, ranches, villages, and towns.

Spanish missions were surrounded by farmlands. The missionaries gave small plots to Native American converts.

Some Native Americans challenged Spanish control of the Southwest. In 1680, the Pueblos drove the Spaniards from Santa Fe, New Mexico. Within a dozen years, however, the region was again under Spanish control.

★ In Review

1. What constitutional dilemma did the Louisiana Purchase present Jefferson with?
2. Discuss the long-term effects of the Louisiana Purchase.
3. Describe the significance of the Lewis and Clark expedition.

Motives for Expansion and Western Settlement

By the 1800s, many Americans believed in a self-evident U.S. right to expand to the Pacific coast and dominate North America. They called it **manifest destiny**. Mexicans, who had already settled large parts of the West, viewed manifest destiny as a threat.

To encourage Western settlement, Henry Clay proposed, and Congress adopted, the **American System**. It called for building roads and canals to the West and placing a high tariff on European imports. The tariff would encourage Westerners to buy from Eastern manufacturers. By aiding both West and East, Clay hoped to unite the nation's economy.

Politics of Expansion

In colonial times, the lands from Texas to California had been Spanish. When the Mexicans revolted in 1821, Texas and California became the northern part of independent Mexico.

Texan Independence and Annexation

In the 1820s, only a few thousand Mexicans lived in Texas, and the Mexican government did not immediately object when U.S. pioneers began to move in. By the mid-1830s, however, there were more Americans than Mexicans there. Americans often defied Mexican laws, including the ban against slavery. When Mexico tried to end immigration, the American settlers revolted and declared Texas independent (1836).

Mexico's president, Antonio López de Santa Anna, led troops in and defeated the Texan defenders occupying the Alamo, a mission serving as a fort. Soon afterwards, the Texans captured Santa Anna and forced him to recognize their independence.

From 1836 to 1845, Texas was an independent nation. The issue of slavery delayed the **annexation** (formal addition) into the Union. Southerners supported it, but Northerners were opposed to another slave state. In 1845, Congress annexed Texas.

Dispute Over Oregon

In the Northwest, both the United States and Britain claimed the Oregon Country as far north as the 54°40' line of latitude in northern Canada. President James K. Polk and other expansionists

Pre-Civil War Agriculture, Mining, and Manufacturing

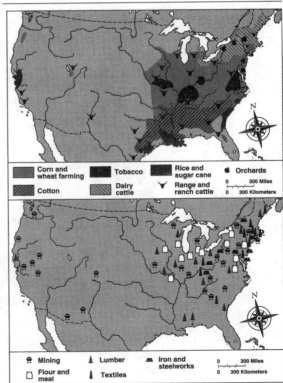

wanted this forested land. In 1845, their supporters adopted the slogan "Fifty-four forty or fight!" War with Britain loomed.

Settlement British-American compromise resulted in a treaty of 1846, which divided the Oregon Country roughly in two; the northern half went to Britain and the southern half (below the 49th parallel of latitude) to the United States. The treaty thus extended the U.S.-Canadian border to the Pacific and improved U.S. relations with Britain.

Mexican War (1846–1848)

Mexico still held present-day Arizona, New Mexico, Utah, Nevada, and California. When the United States offered to buy these lands, Mexico, angry about the annexation of Texas, refused.

Causes of War The expansionism of Polk was largely responsible for a war with Mexico. The immediate cause was a disputed Texas-Mexico boundary. When Mexican troops fired on U.S. troops in the area, Polk asked Congress to declare war.

Peace Terms The Mexican War ended after U.S. troops captured Mexico City and the territory of California. By terms of the *Treaty of Guadalupe Hidalgo* (1848), the United States paid a mere $15

Cartoon of "John Bull" (Britain) laughing at "Yankee Doodle" (United States) in the Oregon dispute

million for all the land west of Texas to the California coast (the *Mexican Cession*).

California Gold Rush

Soon afterwards, an American settler in California discovered gold. Fortune hunters poured

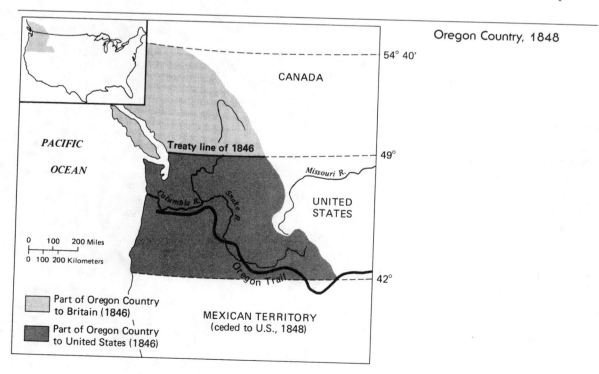

Oregon Country, 1848

CANADA

PACIFIC OCEAN

Treaty line of 1846

Missouri R.

Columbia R.

Snake R.

UNITED STATES

54° 40′

49°

42°

0   100   200 Miles

0 100 200 Kilometers

Oregon Trail

MEXICAN TERRITORY (ceded to U.S., 1848)

☐ Part of Oregon Country to Britain (1846)

■ Part of Oregon Country to United States (1846)

into California. As a result of the 1849 gold rush, California's population grew rapidly, and it soon applied for admission as a nonslave state. The South opposed its admission.

Gadsden Purchase

The United States made a final purchase of land from Mexico in 1853 for $10 million. Called the *Gadsden Purchase*, it consisted of land along the southern border of New Mexico and Arizona.

Impact of Expansion on Mexicans and Native Americans

The Mexican War deprived Mexico of much of its land and natural resources. Mexicans who found themselves living within the United States lost their farms and ranches and took low-paying jobs on farms, in mines, or on railroads. Many Americans looked down on the Mexicans that they had dispossessed.

Western expansion severely reduced the Native American population. U.S. settlers brought diseases such as measles and smallpox against which Native Americans had no immunity. The great buffalo herds on which Plains people depended for survival were destroyed. As the settlers advanced, Native Americans fought to defend their territory. They were no match for the well-equipped U.S. Army, however, and were forced to move to **reservations** (government land set aside for them).

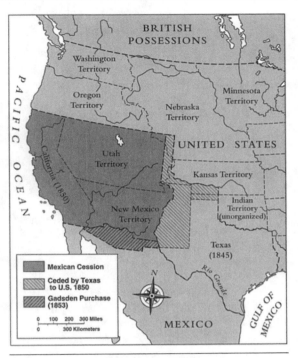

Annexation of Texas, Mexican Cession, and Gadsden Purchase

★ In Review

1. What did Americans mean by manifest destiny?
2. Identify the causes of conflict between (a) Mexico and American settlers of Texas in

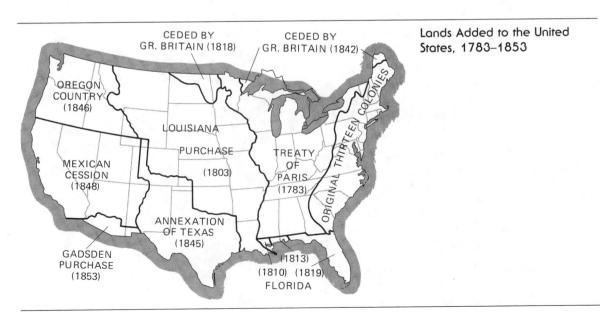

Lands Added to the United States, 1783–1853

"Plucked"—bird symbolizing Mexico before and after its territories were taken by the United States

1836, (b) Britain and the United States in 1845, and (c) the United States and Mexico in 1846.
3. Summarize the impact of Western expansion upon Mexicans and Native Americans.

United States Divided

Western Expansion and Slavery

The territories of Kansas and Nebraska were both north of the 36°30′ line and were, according to the Missouri Compromise of 1820, therefore, slave-free. In the 1850s, Senator Stephen Douglas of Illinois proposed, and Congress passed, the *Kansas-Nebraska Act* (1854):

★ The Missouri Compromise no longer applied to Kansas and Nebraska.

★ They would decide by popular sovereignty whether to allow slavery.

Violent Outcome Fighting broke out in Kansas between Southern, proslavery settlers and Northern, antislavery settlers. "Bleeding Kansas" became a clear omen of civil war.

Disintegration of the Whig Party From the early to mid-1800s, Whigs comprised one of the two major political parties. Having supporters in the North and South, they took no initial stand on slavery. In the 1850s, however, legislation such as the Compromise of 1850 and the Kansas-Nebraska Act pointed up the deep division between Northern and Southern Whigs.

In 1852, the Whig candidate for president won only four states. As the party divided, many Northern Whigs joined the Know-Nothings or American party, which campaigned against im-

migration and Catholicism. The new Republican party replaced the Whigs.

Rise of the Republican Party

Founded in 1854 by such antislavery groups as Whigs, Northern Democrats, and abolitionists, the Republican party drew its support from the North and West. The Democratic party's strength was more widespread—North, West, and South.

The Republican platforms of 1856 and 1860 included the following goals:

★ keeping slavery out of Western territories

★ enacting a high protective tariff to encourage Northern industries

★ building a transcontinental railroad (stretching from the Atlantic to the Pacific).

"Bleeding Kansas" John Brown's Harpers Ferry raid and the Dred Scott decision increased the Republicans' popularity in the North. In the election of 1856, the Republican presidential candidate, John C. Frémont, came in second nationwide and first in the North.

Abraham Lincoln

Abraham Lincoln began his political career in Illinois. As a state legislator, he opposed the ex-

United States After the Kansas-Nebraska Act, 1854

pansion of slavery and supported internal improvements and a high tariff. Lincoln joined the Republican party when the Whig party began to disintegrate. In 1858, he became Republican candidate for the U.S. Senate.

Lincoln-Douglas Debates Lincoln and his opponent, Stephen Douglas, the Democratic leader in the Senate, debated the issue of slavery in the new Western states. Douglas supported popular sovereignty. Lincoln believed that slavery was wrong and should not spread. The popular Douglas was reelected to the Senate, but Lincoln's strong arguments in debate and the closeness of the election won him national attention.

Election of 1860 In 1860, the Republicans nominated Lincoln for president. A majority of Democrats nominated Stephen Douglas, whose views on slavery were moderate. Southern Democrats nominated John Breckinridge, who was a proslavery Southerner. The new Constitutional Union party nominated John Bell. Lincoln won this race with only 40 percent of the popular vote (the heavily populated North gave him enough electoral votes). For the South, it was the worst possible outcome.

Secession of the South

One month after Lincoln's election, South Carolina seceded from the Union. These were the reasons:

★ *Cultural and Economic Differences*. Plantation life was based on one family's ownership of land worked by many slaves. Courtly Southern manners reflected customs of an earlier time, while the industrialized North was developing new values and lifestyles. These differing economies conflicted on important political issues such as the tariff.

★ *Regional Loyalties*. Nationalism was weaker in the South, where people were attached to their region and jealously guarded states' rights.

★ *Belief in Easy Southern Victory*. Many Southerners believed that the North would not go to war over secession since it needed Southern cotton for its mills. If war came, Southerners believed that foreign (especially British) demand for their cotton would mean European support for their cause.

★ *Lack of National Leadership*. Recent presidents—Millard Fillmore, Franklin Pierce, and James Buchanan—were not strong leaders, and congressional leadership was weak. Two nationalist senators, Henry Clay and Daniel Webster, died in the early 1850s.

★ *Slavery as a Moral Issue*. Most Southern whites owned no slaves but supported slavery. More and more Northerners viewed slavery as immoral and unprincipled.

Efforts at Compromise A compromise plan, the *Crittenden Proposal*, called for federal protection of slavery in any U.S. territory below the 36°30' line of latitude, thus allowing slavery in any Southern territory. Territories north of the line would be slave-free. On becoming a state, any territory could choose admittance as a slave or free state. Lincoln rejected the compromise.

Fort Sumter U.S. forces held Fort Sumter, an island fortress in the harbor of Charleston, South

Lincoln-Douglas debate

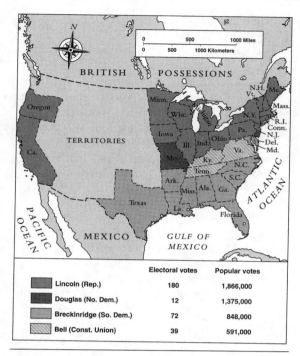

Election of 1860

	Electoral votes	Popular votes
Lincoln (Rep.)	180	1,866,000
Douglas (No. Dem.)	12	1,375,000
Breckinridge (So. Dem.)	72	848,000
Bell (Const. Union)	39	591,000

Military Strategy and Major Battles

Both the North and the South believed that it would win the war quickly. The South relied on its strength as defender of its territory. The North expected that its numerically huge advantage in troops and equipment would defeat the South.

Lincoln's Strategy Lincoln planned to capture the Mississippi River and then defeat Southern armies in the West and East separately. He intended to stop the export of cotton and import of supplies and weapons by blockade. Finally, he hoped that the Union army would inflict major losses on the smaller Confederate army.

Antietam The South won most of the important initial battles. In 1862, however, Union general McClellan stopped a Confederate advance by General Robert E. Lee in Maryland at the Battle of Antietam, with important consequences. England and France decided not to intervene, and Lincoln issued the Emancipation Proclamation. (See p. 79.)

Gettysburg With war supplies running low, Lee invaded the North. After a three-day battle near Gettysburg, Pennsylvania (July 1 to 3, 1863), Confederate troops were badly defeated by well-protected Union troops, and Lee retreated South. Both sides lost thousands of men, but General George G. Meade had won the Union's first major battle and stopped the only Confederate attempt to invade the North.

Vicksburg One day later, Union General Ulysses S. Grant forced the surrender of Vicksburg, a key Confederate port on the Mississippi River. The South's supply route from Texas was blocked.

Sherman's March to the Sea In 1864, Union general William T. Sherman led a campaign of destruction from Tennessee to the Georgia coast and northward through the Carolinas. For the first time, destruction of civilian property became wartime policy, as numerous Southern mansions and farmhouses were put to the torch.

Richmond and Appomattox Richmond in central Virginia was the Confederate capital. On April 2, 1865, a Union army marched into the city, and seven days later, the Civil War ended when Lee surrendered to Grant at Appomattox Court House, Virginia.

Carolina. South Carolina demanded its surrender, and Lincoln refused. A month after the president's inauguration in March 1861, Southern guns bombarded the fort. The Civil War had begun.

★ In Review

1. Explain the major reasons for the decline of the Whigs and rise of the Republicans.
2. List key reasons for Lincoln's victory in the election of 1860.
3. Describe the major steps that led to the Civil War.

Civil War

By spring of 1861, a total of 11 Southern states had seceded and loosely joined under their own constitution and central government, the Confederate States of America. Between 1861 and 1865, Southerners fought for independence and Northerners fought to save the Union and put down the "rebellion."

In general, the South had a better short-term army, and the North the economic resources to win a long war.

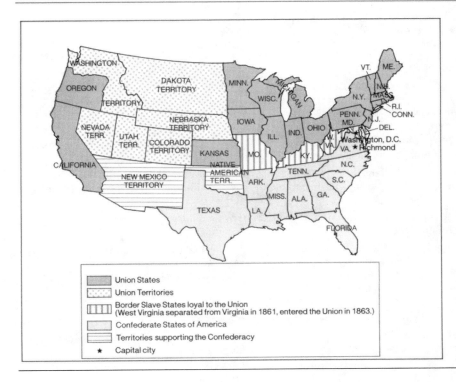

Union States

Union Territories

Border Slave States loyal to the Union
(West Virginia separated from Virginia in 1861, entered the Union in 1863.)

Confederate States of America

Territories supporting the Confederacy

★ Capital city

United States at the
Outbreak of the Civil
War, 1861

Impact on the Home Front

Civil Liberties Lincoln made the defeat of the South his priority and suspended the writ of habeas corpus. Hundreds of people in Maryland, including Baltimore's mayor and police chief and members of the state legislature, were arrested for disloyalty but not tried. Lincoln feared that they posed a threat to nearby Washington, D.C.

By the end of the war, 15,000 individuals had been arrested and imprisoned without trial. Some civilians were tried and convicted by military courts. After the war, the Supreme Court held that military courts could not try civilians where state and federal courts are functioning.

Scholars still disagree about Lincoln's actions. Supporters hold that the Constitution allows the suspension of habeas corpus "when in cases of rebellion or invasion the public safety may require it" (Article I, Section 9). Opponents believe that only Congress may suspend habeas corpus and that such presidential power could lead to **dictatorship** (one-man rule).

Women's Roles Women factory workers, already accustomed to long hours, worked even harder to fill the labor gap left by the fighting men. They earned as little as 25 cents a day producing uni-forms, weapons, and other war goods.

The need for nurses opened up the profession to women. Under the leadership of Dorothea Dix and Clara Barton, women volunteers cared for the wounded on battlefields and in hospitals. After the war, Clara Barton organized the American Red Cross (1881).

The wives and mothers of soldiers on both sides supported the war effort by writing their men letters of comfort and encouragement.

★ In Review

1. Explain how Lincoln's wartime strategies were related to Northern advantages.
2. Was Lincoln right to limit civil liberties during the Civil War? Explain.
3. "Although women did not fight, they played a major role during the Civil War." Do you agree with this statement? Explain.

Wartime Policy

Finances The North financed the war effort by increasing tariffs on imports and excise taxes on domestic goods (such as alcoholic beverages),

★ Resources of the North and South ★

	North: Union	South: Confederacy
Population	22 million (1860)	6 million free citizens, 3 million slaves
Economic Resources	Many factories and farms to produce war goods and food supplies; superior railroad system; control of 70% of nation's wealth	Little industry; farms for growing cotton, not food; poor railroad system; control of 30% of nation's wealth
Strategic position	Difficult: forces required to launch risky offensives on enemy territory	Relatively easy: forces deployed on home ground in defensive positions
Morale	Poor: many civilians initially indifferent to or against war; troops far from home and family	Good: most civilians behind war effort; troops fighting in defense of homes and families
Preparation	Mostly undertrained, raw recruits with no military tradition	Strong military tradition; general expertise in riding and shooting
Military leadership	Inexperienced officers; mediocre or uncooperative generals (e.g., George B. McClellan) until later years (e.g., Ulysses S. Grant)	Experienced officers and superior generals (e.g., Robert E. Lee and Thomas J. "Stonewall" Jackson)
Naval strength	Strong navy able to **blockade** Southern ports and cut off vital supplies	Few ships; dependence on blockade-runners
Political leadership	President Abraham Lincoln: tireless, active, militarily astute	President Jefferson Davis: intelligent, aloof, overly cautious
Foreign relations	Universal recognition as legitimate government	Lack of support and recognition from other nations

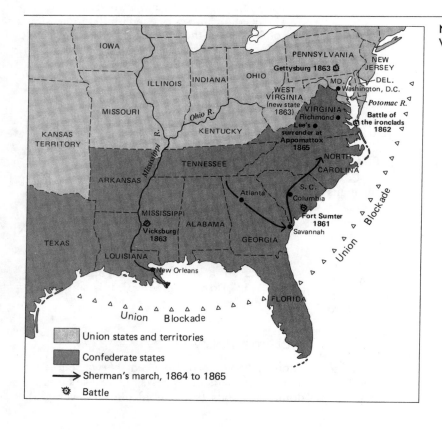

North and South in the Civil War

Union states and territories

Confederate states

→ Sherman's march, 1864 to 1865

✿ Battle

issuing "greenbacks" (paper money), and selling government bonds. Government bonds brought in the most money and rose in value as the Union army began to win.

The South had few ways to raise money. The Union blockade deprived it of foreign goods and limited tariff collections. Dedicated to states' rights, the Southern states opposed taxation by the Confederate government, which printed a large amount of paper currency backed by little gold. As the Southern cause worsened, Confederate money lost value.

National Currency The *National Banking Act* (1863) gave banks in the national banking system the right to issue paper money backed by government bonds. The federal government's success in selling Treasury bonds reinforced the soundness of the new currency.

Homestead Act (1862) The *Homestead Act* provided free public lands to those willing to settle on them. Any citizen or immigrant aspiring to citizenship could acquire 160 acres of federal land simply by farming it for five years.

Emancipation

Although opposed to slavery, Lincoln waited two years before acting on the issue. In September 1862, after the Battle of Antietam, he announced that he would issue an emancipation order in the new year. The *Emancipation Proclamation* (January 1, 1863) declared that slaves in Confederate states were free. Border states that had remained loyal could keep slavery.

Slaves throughout the South made their way to Union lines seeking freedom. The Emancipation Proclamation gave the war a moral basis. Thus, Great Britain, which had abolished slavery in the 1830s, was reluctant to aid the South even to obtain cotton.

Gettysburg Address (1863)

Thousands of soldiers died at Gettysburg. A military cemetery was then dedicated there to honor the Union dead. In his *Gettysburg Address*, Lincoln demonstrated that the Union was fighting not only for victory but also for universal values. His speech ends thus: ". . . that we here highly resolve that these dead shall not have died in vain; that this nation, under God, shall have a new birth of freedom; and that government of the people, by the people, for the people, shall not perish from the earth."

African Americans in the War

At first, neither the North nor the South allowed blacks in its armed forces. As the war progressed, the Union allowed both emancipated slaves and free blacks to serve in army units under a system of **segregation** (separation by race). At first, they were assigned nonfighting duties. In 1863, African American troops (usually commanded by white officers) were trained for combat and sent into battle. By the war's end, more than 180,000 African Americans had joined the Union army and about 38,000 had lost their lives. Sixteen African Americans won the nation's highest military honor, the Medal of Honor.

Draft Riots in the North In 1863, Congress passed a **draft**, which compelled young men of a certain age to join the military. In New York City, whites unwilling to serve rioted by targeting the black population. During four days of violence, countless African Americans were beaten and some lynched (hanged).

Thirteenth Amendment

The Thirteenth Amendment (1865), passed by two-thirds of Congress and approved by three-quarters of the states, made slavery illegal in every state.

Lincoln's Leadership

Historians consider Lincoln one of the greatest presidents, for the following reasons:

★ *Firm political purpose.* All of Lincoln's actions and decisions were focused on saving the Union.

★ *Political shrewdness and courage.* He had a keen sense of when to bend to political pressure and when to risk an unpopular decision. He gave many generals a chance before deciding on Grant's superior capability.

★ *Achievements.* He steadily pursued the war when others might have tried compromise. He kept the Union together. He overcame sectionalism. He freed 4 million people.

Lincoln was reelected in 1864. In April, 1865, an actor and Southern sympathizer, John Wilkes Booth, assassinated him.

African American Union regiment during the Civil War

★ In Review

1. Why did the Union have an advantage over the South in financing the war?
2. Explain why each of the following events was a turning point in the Civil War: (a) Battle at Antietam, (b) Union victory at Gettysburg, (c) Union victory at Vicksburg.
3. Historians consider Lincoln one of the greatest U.S. presidents. Would you agree with this assessment? Explain.

Chapter Review

MULTIPLE-CHOICE QUESTIONS

Use the map on page 70 to answer questions 1 and 2.

1. The map shows that the Louisiana Purchase (1) gave control of the Mississippi and New Orleans to the United States (2) included the territories of Oregon and Florida (3) immediately added several states to the union (4) led to a conflict between the United States and British Canada.

2. The best conclusion about the Louisiana Purchse is that (1) it was unconstitutional (2) the boundaries were somewhat unclear (3) the United States paid too much for a small amount of land (4) Mexico was paid for some of Louisiana.

3. The maps on page 71 show that before the Civil War (1) a lot of manufacturing was done in the Southeast (2) ranching existed only in the Far West (3) cotton growing was important in the Southwest (4) most agricul-ture, mining, and manufacturing took place east of the Mississippi.

4. The labor force table on page 59 shows that (1) slavery caused unemployment among the free (2) the free labor force was consistently larger than the slave labor force (3) slavery forced free people to leave the South for the North and West (4) the free labor force decreased as the slave labor force increased.

Refer to the map on the bottom of page 73 to answer questions 5–7.

5. According to manifest destiny, the United States (1) had to acquire all new land through treaties (2) had no right to purchase Louisiana (3) respected all Mexican land claims in North America (4) claimed a right to control all land shown on the map.

6. In 1783, the United States extended from the Atlantic to the (1) Appalachians (2) Mississippi (3) Rockies (4) Pacific.

7. As a result of the Mexican War and Oregon settlement, the United States (1) approximately doubled in size (2) lost land west of the Mississippi (3) extended to the Pacific (4) gained Texas.

8. The British cartoon on page 72 refers to the dispute over the (1) Mexican War (2) Oregon Country (3) Louisiana Purchase (4) Florida Territory.

9. The map on page 74 shows that by 1854 (1) few territories were still open to slavery (2) the Eastern states had already declared themselves slave or free (3) the Far West was completely open to slavery (4) the Utah Territory would be free.

10. The map and table on page 76 show that (1) Stephen A. Douglas came in last in electoral and popular votes (2) the Constitutional Union party won three states in the upper South (3) Abraham Lincoln received few votes in the far West (4) John C. Breckinridge and the Southern Democrats received no votes in the North.

THEMATIC ESSAYS

1. **Theme:** Slavery and the Civil War. The controversy over slavery's moral justification and expansion into new territories led to sectional conflict and ultimately to civil war.

   Task: Choose two events that caused serious controversy and helped lead to the Civil War. For each event:

   ★ describe the circumstances causing the event
   ★ explain how the events helped lead to the Civil War.

   Some events that you may use are the Mexican War, Compromise of 1850, Kansas-Nebraska Act, Dred Scott decision, and John Brown's raid at Harpers Ferry.

2. **Theme:** States' Rights and the Civil War. Although the Civil War was fought over the morality of slavery, it was also fought to determine if the powers of the federal government (the Union) were greater than states' rights.

   Task: Choose two issues that created great controversy and helped lead to the Civil War. For each issue, *specifically* discuss how states' rights versus federal powers played a part in leading to the Civil War.

Some ideas that you may wish to discuss are the Fugitive Slave Act, popular sovereignty, and the Dred Scott decision.

DOCUMENT-BASED QUESTION

*Study each document and answer the question that follows it. Then read the **Task** and write your essay. Include references to most of the documents and additional information you retain about U.S. history and government.*

Historical Context: Although the United States was originally an Atlantic coast nation, its future rested in expansion west.

Document 1: Study the map on page 70.

Question: How did the United States change as a result of the Louisiana Purchase?

Document 2: Study the map on page 62.

Question: How did the United States remove Native Americans from their tribal homelands?

Document 3: Study the map on page 73.

Question: How did war with Mexico affect U.S. territory?

Document 4: Look at the cartoon on page 74.

Question: How does the cartoonist feel about what happened to Mexicans as a result of war with the United States?

Document 5: Study the map on page 74.

Question: How did the acquisition of Western lands further aggravate the controversy over slavery?

Document 6: Study the map on the bottom of page 73.

Question: How did the United States change between 1783 and 1853?

Task: Using information in the documents and your knowledge of United States history and government, write an essay in which you:

★ describe the opportunities that acquiring land in the West provided for the United States
★ explain how territorial expansion also resulted in issues that had serious consequences for the nation.

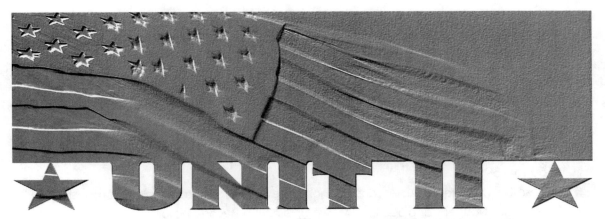

★ UNIT II ★
Industrialization of the United States

Chapter 7
The Reconstructed Nation

★ Documents and Laws	★ Events	★ People
Black Codes (1865)	Reconstruction (1865–1877)	W. E. B. Du Bois
Thirteenth Amendment (1865)	Impeachment of Andrew	Ulysses S. Grant
Freedmen's Bureau (1865)	Johnson (1868)	Jeremiah Haralson
Civil Rights Act (1866)	Election of 1876	John Harlan
Military Reconstruction (1867)		Rutherford B. Hayes
Tenure of Office Act (1867)		Abraham Lincoln
Fourteenth Amendment (1868)		Hiram Revels
Fifteenth Amendment (1870)		Robert Smalls
Force Acts (1870–1871)		Edwin Stanton
Amnesty Act (1872)		Thaddeus Stevens
Civil Rights Acts (1866, 1875)		Samuel Tilden
Compromise of 1877		Booker T. Washington
"Jim Crow" Laws (1881–mid-1900s)		
Civil Rights Cases (1883)		
Plessy v. *Ferguson* (1896)		

★ To evaluate various plans for readmitting Southern states to the Union after the Civil War.

★ To understand the changing nature of American society, especially Southern society, from 1865 to 1895.

★ To describe why African Americans did not achieve full freedom after their emancipation.

★ To compare Northern and Southern viewpoints during Reconstruction.

★ To describe the weakening of Northern Republican control and increase of Southern Democratic control in the post-Reconstruction South.

After the Civil War, the U.S. government faced the problem of how to rebuild the governments of Southern states and readmit them to the Union. The era of Reconstruction lasted from 1865 to 1877.

Plans of Reconstruction

The Civil War had cost Southern planters vast amounts of property and a labor force of 4 million slaves, now freed.

The North had two major problems: (1) On what terms should Southern states be readmitted, and (2) how would the rights of former slaves be protected?

Lincoln's Plan

President Lincoln wanted seceded states to rejoin the Union on an equal status with those of the North. He proposed two conditions: (1) Ten percent of a state's voters would have to take an oath of allegiance to the United States, and (2) the states had to guarantee the end of slavery.

Andrew Johnson's Plan

After Lincoln's assassination, Vice President Andrew Johnson became president (1865–1869). Many Northern Republicans distrusted him because he had been a Democrat from the slaveholding state of Tennessee.

Johnson's Reconstruction plan was the same as Lincoln's, with one addition: A state had to deny important Confederate leaders the right to vote, while granting it to all other Southern white men.

Congressional Reconstruction

A large group in Congress, the *Radical Republicans*, devised a plan to protect former slaves and punish the South:

★ No state could deprive citizenship to any native-born American or withhold the right to vote because of race or former slave status.

★ No Confederate military leader or officeholder could hold any office without congressional pardon.

★ The U.S. army would occupy and govern a state until its new constitution was acceptable to Congress.

Post–Civil War Amendments   The Radical Republicans also passed three amendments to the Constitution:

★ The *Thirteenth Amendment* (1865) declared slavery illegal in every state.

★ The *Fourteenth Amendment* (1868) defined the rights of U.S. citizenship: "All persons born or naturalized in the United States, and subject to the jurisdiction thereof, are citizens of the United States and of the state wherein they reside." It also itemized three prohibitions to ensure that rights protected by the Constitution applied to state and federal governments alike:

1. States could not interfere with the "privileges and immunities" of citizens.

2. States could not deprive a person of life, liberty, or property without due process of law.

3. States could not deny a citizen equal protection of the law.

★ The *Fifteenth Amendment* (1870) stated that voting rights could not be denied because of "race, color, or previous condition of servitude."

Dates refer to year when a state was readmitted to the Union and ( ) to reestablishment of conservative government.

0   100   200   300 Miles
0   100 200 300 Kilometers

Delaware free 1865
Maryland free 1864
Missouri free 1865
W.Va. 1863 free 1865
Virginia 1870 (1869)
Kentucky free 1865
N. Carolina 1868 (1870)
Tennessee 1866 (1869)
Arkansas 1868 (1874)
S. Carolina 1868 (1876)
Miss. 1870 (1876)
Alabama 1868 (1874)
Georgia 1870 (1872)
Louisiana 1868 (1877)
Texas 1870 (1873)
Florida 1868 (1877)

ATLANTIC OCEAN
GULF OF MEXICO
N

Congressional Reconstruction, 1865–1877

Impeachment and Trial of Andrew Johnson

Johnson antagonized the Radical Republicans in Congress by vetoing each step in their Reconstruction plan. The lawmakers overrode each veto.

In 1867, Congress tried to redesign the system of checks and balances in Congress's favor. The *Tenure of Office Act* prohibited the president from firing a cabinet officer without Senate approval.

Freedmen voting in the South

Johnson, believing the act unconstitutional, fired Secretary of War Edwin Stanton. In 1868, the House of Representatives impeached the president. At trial, the Senate fell one vote short of the two-thirds majority needed, and Johnson completed his term.

★ In Review

1. How were the Republicans' Reconstruction plans more "radical" than those of Lincoln and Johnson.
2. Summarize the Thirteenth, Fourteenth, and Fifteenth amendments.
3. Why did the Radical Republicans impeach Johnson? How did this conflict illustrate the system of checks and balances?

Reconstructed Nation

Southern whites considered Northern control of their state governments an insult and continued to champion states' rights. For blacks, Reconstruction was an all too brief period of freedom and equal opportunity under federal law.

Northern Viewpoint

After the war, thousands of Northerners moved south in search of economic gain and political power. Shielded by federal troops, they ran for election to the legislatures created by new state constitutions.

Republican Victories Seven Southern states held elections in 1868. Supported by freed blacks, Northern Republicans won four of the seven governorships, ten of 14 seats in the Senate, and 20 of 35 seats in the House of Representatives.

Extravagant Use of Public Funds The new legislatures' chief task was to rebuild what had been destroyed by war. For this purpose, Republican legislators voted large sums of money and took some of it for personal use.

Southern Viewpoint

Southern whites wanted (1) a revived economy, (2) recontrol of state governments, and (3) a reduction of the political power of Southern blacks.

"Carpetbaggers" and "Scalawags" Southerners called Northerners who descended on them **carpetbaggers** (fortune hunters carrying their belongings in one travel bag). Southern whites who cooperated with the Northerners were known as **scalawags** and deemed to have only one motive—a share in corrupt, moneymaking schemes.

Secret societies such as the Knights of the White Camellia and the Ku Klux Klan (KKK) used violence against blacks and scalawags alike.

Economic and Technological Impacts

The Civil War had accelerated industrialization in the North but devastated infant Southern industries. After the war, the North broke all records for output, invention, and business growth. Historians disagree about whether the business boom would have happened anyway or if the war was a major stimulant for investment.

Trade With Europe

The United States and Europe became more industrialized in the postwar period. An increase in manufactures increased the need for buyers. Industrialized nations also needed more raw materials—cotton, coal, iron, oil, and so on. The resource-rich United States exported its raw goods to Europe, simultaneously building up its industries.

Poster championing white supremacy of the Ku Klux Klan

Trade With Asia

Throughout the 1800s, American merchants were frustrated by the refusal of the Chinese court to import cheap, factory-made U.S. goods. At the same time, Chinese teas, porcelains, and silks were in great demand in the United States.

Japan shared China's lack of interest in trading with Europeans and Americans. In 1853, however, Commodore Matthew Perry arrived in Japan with a U.S. fleet. He persuaded the Japanese to initiate mutual trade. When new leadership in Japan decided to industrialize the nation, it eagerly sought Western technologies. Trade with Japan increased after the Civil War. Nevertheless, the United States imported more from Asia than it exported to Asia.

Transcontinental Railroad

A great postwar achievement was the building of a transcontinental railroad across the Western plains to the Pacific coast. Undertaken by two private companies, the project had considerable federal help.

The railroad was designed to open the West to settlers. The route passed over almost unsettled territory. Congress made huge land grants along the route. Sections were arranged in a checkerboard pattern, half of the squares going to the railroads and half to be kept for sale to settlers.

Other Western railroads were soon completed too. Between 1865 and 1900, U.S. railroad tracks increased from 35,000 to 260,000 miles.

Need for Labor   Immigrants made U.S. industrial growth possible. They built the first transcontinental railroad. They turned Midwest prairies and forests into prosperous farms. In New York, they worked at construction or in garment factories. Some opened small retail stores that grew into large department stores. They went down into mines or manned the steel mills of Pittsburgh, Pennsylvania, and Birmingham, Alabama. They became the technicians, inventors, and scientists necessary for industrial development.

Women joined the workforce because men's wages seldom covered family needs. In the early postwar years, women took low-paying jobs in factories or as servants. New technologies of the 1880s and 1890s, however, opened up jobs for typists and telephone operators.

★ In Review

1. Define carpetbagger. Describe how Southern whites viewed them.
2. In what ways did the North benefit economically from the Civil War?
3. Describe trade with Europe and Asia after the Civil War.

The New South

Land and Labor

During and after Reconstruction, Southern whites owned most of the land, while blacks worked it as tenants and sharecroppers.

Farm Owners   After the war, few plantation owners could afford to keep their huge properties intact. Some were broken up into small sections and sold as farms. Most buyers were white, although there were a few black landowners.

Tenant Farmers   Some plantation owners rented parts of their land to **tenant farmers**, who provided their own seed, mules, and provisions.

Sharecroppers   The poorest Southerners, white and black, were **sharecroppers**. In return for farming a piece of land, they gave some of the crop to a landlord. Worn-out land, low prices for cotton, and high prices for farm supplies kept many sharecroppers in debt. Thus, in spite of the Thirteenth Amendment, many Southerners were still in bondage.

Status of Freedmen

Economic and Political Hopes   In the early years of Reconstruction, Congressman Thaddeus Stevens and other Radical Republicans wanted to give land to freed slaves. The Fifteenth Amendment made African Americans believe that the federal government would protect their right to vote.

Economic and Political Reality   Congress never acted on land distribution. At first, Northern troops protected the right of blacks to vote, but the determination of many white Southerners to end this right eventually prevailed.

Participation in Reconstruction Governments   From 1868 to 1872, many African Americans won seats in Southern legislatures. In one house of South Carolina's legislature, black men were in the majority.

African Americans in Congress   During Reconstruction, 14 Southern African Americans served in Congress, among them Senator Hiram Revels of Mississippi, Congressman Robert Smalls of South Carolina, and Congressman Jeremiah Haralson of Alabama. Half of the black lawmakers were former slaves; half had attended college. As a group, they championed civil rights and federal aid to education.

From Exclusion to Segregation   Many white Americans regarded blacks as inferior. In some Northern and Southern cities, blacks were forbidden to mix with whites in public.

The *Civil Rights Act of 1875* prohibited railroads, restaurants, and other public places from segregating African American customers. For a time, the law was generally obeyed. Beginning in 1881, however, Southern states adopted **Jim Crow laws** enforcing segregation. By the 1890s,

Senator Hiram Revels (far left) and Congressman Robert Smalls

these laws applied to every part of life—marriage, education, health care, public accommodations, even cemeteries.

Struggle for Political Control

Black Codes In 1865, Southerners holding state conventions to organize new governments drew up measures to restrict the rights of former slaves. These **Black Codes** prohibited blacks from (1) carrying firearms, (2) starting businesses, (3) appearing outside after sunset, (4) renting or leasing farmland, and (5) traveling without a permit.

Radical Republican Laws for the South To protect the blacks and punish the whites, Radical Republican leaders pushed through a series of laws.

★ *Freedmen's Bureau (1865)*. This agency helped more than 3 million **freedmen** (former slaves) adjust to freedom. They were provided with necessities of life and new educational facilities. As a result, thousands attended school and college for the first time.

★ *Civil Rights Act of 1866*. Congress moved against the Black Codes by empowering the federal government to protect the civil rights of blacks.

★ *Military Districts*. Congress divided the South into five military districts, each occupied by federal troops responsible to a military governor.

★ *Conditions for Readmission of a Seceded State*. Congress made the state conventions of 1865 illegitimate. A state had to draw up a constitution that recognized the Fourteenth Amendment, including the provisions that former Confederate officers could not hold office.

★ *Force Acts (1870 to 1871)*. Federal troops were authorized to break up organizations such as the Ku Klux Klan that intimidated black voters.

Civil Rights Cases (1883) Black citizens challenged Jim Crow laws on the grounds that they violated the Fourteenth Amendment's equal protection clause.

In a series of cases, the Supreme Court ruled that Jim Crow laws were constitutional because property owners had the right to choose their customers. The Fourteenth Amendment applied only to government officials.

Cartoon of segregated Southern railroad car

Former slaves and their children being educated at the Freemen's Bureau

Debating the Role of African Americans Between 1890 and 1910, two African American leaders took opposite positions on segregation.

★ *Booker T. Washington.* Washington was freed from slavery at the age of nine. In 1881, he founded the Tuskegee Institute in Alabama to provide industrial and vocational training to African Americans. Washington thought that blacks should not seek acceptance by whites but rather improve their economic position by learning high-paying job skills.

★ *W. E. B. Du Bois.* Du Bois was younger than Washington and had earned a Ph.D. from Harvard. In *The Souls of Black Folk* (1903), he stated that education for economic success was important, but not as important as equal civil rights. He urged firm opposition to Jim Crow laws.

★ In Review

1. How did the Southern economy change after the Civil War?
2. What new forms of discrimination against African Americans developed after the Civil War?
3. Compare and contrast the strategies of Booker T. Washington and W. E. B. Du Bois for achieving equality for African Americans.

End of Reconstruction

Northern Republican control of Southern state governments began to weaken in 1869, when those states began to elect governments domi-nated by Democrats. By 1877, there were no more Reconstruction governments.

Reasons

★ *Change in Public Opinion.* Northern whites became less concerned about African American rights and more about their own affairs. By 1875, many wanted to withdraw troops from the South.

★ *Amnesty Act.* Toward the end of Ulysses S. Grant's first term as president, Congress enacted the *Amnesty Act* (1872), restoring voting rights to 160,000 former Confederates.

★ *Increased Terrorism.* Groups such as the Ku Klux Klan grew stronger, and the federal government either could not or would not enforce civil rights laws. Many frightened Southern blacks stopped trying to vote.

★ *Election of 1876.* In the election year of 1876, federal troops occupied South Carolina, Florida, and Louisiana, where the Republican presidential candidate, Rutherford B. Hayes, won. The other Southern states gave their electoral votes to the Democratic candidate, Samuel Tilden of New York. Tilden, however, claimed victory in the occupied states, citing Democratic voting returns that contradicted Republican ones. A commission, called to decide the winner, had a majority of Republicans and went for Hayes. Southern Democrats talked of another civil war.

★ *Compromise of 1877.* In secret, Republican and Democratic leaders agreed to support Hayes's claim. In exchange, Hayes would remove federal troops from the South, abandoning Southern blacks to the rule of the white majority.

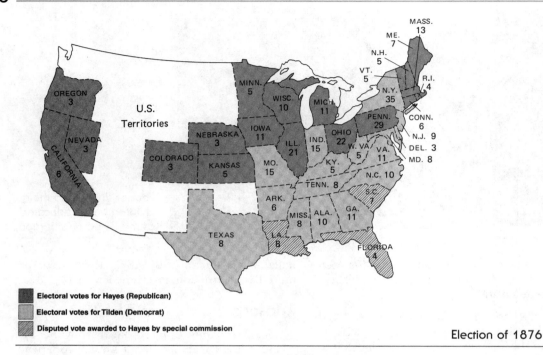

Election of 1876

Electoral votes for Hayes (Republican)
Electoral votes for Tilden (Democrat)
Disputed vote awarded to Hayes by special commission

Restoration of White Control

Solid South Southern whites blamed Republicans for their hardships. After Reconstruction, the South became the *Solid South*, a Democratic-controlled region. From 1880 to 1924, Democratic candidates for president won all the electoral votes of Southern states.

Disenfranchisement The Fourteenth Amendment had briefly punished Confederate officers with **disenfranchisement** (cancellation of voting rights). After Reconstruction, the South disenfranchised black citizens to ensure control by the Democratic party.

Plessy v. *Ferguson* (1896) After Reconstruction, the Supreme Court became less protective of African American civil rights. Homer Plessy, a black man, sued a railroad for denying him entry into a car set aside for whites. In a landmark decision, the Supreme Court ruled that because the railroad provided "separate but equal" facilities for blacks, the equal protection clause in the Constitution had not been violated. One justice, John Harlan, dissented, arguing that segregation threatened personal liberty and equality of rights. For many years, however, the Court's majority used "separate but equal" to justify racial segregation.

★ In Review

1. How did the Compromise of 1877 contribute to segregation?
2. How and why did the Solid South emerge?
3. How did the Supreme Court's ruling in *Plessy* v. *Ferguson* establish a legal basis for segregation.

★ Methods of Disenfranchisement ★

Method	Law	Discriminatory Use of Law
1. **Literacy test**	Voters must pass reading and writing test.	★ Slaves had not been taught literacy skills. ★ State examiners deliberately passed whites and failed blacks.
2. **Poll tax**	Citizens must pay state tax before voting.	Most blacks were too poor to pay the tax.
3. **"Grandfather clause"**	Men whose grandfathers had voted before 1867 could vote without taking literacy test.	Only white males had grandfathers who voted before 1867.

Chapter Review

MULTIPLE-CHOICE QUESTIONS

1. A major result of the Civil War was that (1) North-South disputes ended (2) whites accepted blacks as social equals (3) slavery was ended by an amendment to the Constitution (4) the South returned to its prewar ways.

2. Which statement accurately compares Andrew Johnson's Reconstruction plan with that of the Radical Republicans? (1) Both plans aimed to punish Southern whites. (2) Johnson's plan was more lenient. (3) Radical Republicans wanted to aid Southern whites, while Johnson wanted to aid Southern blacks.(4) Both plans welcomed secessionist states back into the Union with few conditions.

3. A major feature of Reconstruction was that (1) new federal laws and constitutional amendments attempted to ensure equal rights and opportunities for African Americans (2) the South rapidly developed as a major industrial center (3) a spirit of cooperation existed between president and Congress (4) new state governments in the South aimed to end corruption.

4. In addition to awarding citizenship to former slaves, the Fourteenth Amendment (1) guaranteed women the right to vote (2) abolished the poll tax (3) guaranteed equal protection of the laws (4) provided protection against illegal searches and seizures.

5. During Reconstruction, African American voters in the South generally (1) voted Republican (2) voted Democratic (3) showed no preference for Republicans or Democrats (4) refused to participate in elections.

6. A difference between the portrayal of the Ku Klux Klan on page 86 and actual practices of the Klan is that it (1) failed to achieve a popular following (2) used violence only occasionally (3) operated in secret (4) was rarely successful.

7. The map on page 90 shows that, in the election of 1876, (1) Westerners split their votes between Hayes and Tilden (2) New York and Indiana voted for Tilden while the rest of the North voted for Hayes (3) the South was solidly behind Hayes (4) the territories split their vote between Hayes and Tilden.

8. Reconstruction ended when Democrats agreed to the election of Hayes and Republicans promised to (1) withdraw federal troops from the South (2) give each freedman forty acres and a mule (3) do away with the electoral college (4) repeal the Fifteenth Amendment.

9. The purpose of Jim Crow laws was to (1) give full civil rights to African Americans (2) keep African Americans in a separate and inferior position (3) give economic incentives for business growth (4) provide equal opportunities for all citizens.

10. In *Plessy* v. *Ferguson*, the Supreme Court argued that (1) states could segregate people on the basis of race as long as equal facilities were provided (2) segregation based on race was unconstitutional (3) the Fourteenth Amendment outlawed emphasis on racial distinctions (4) separate but equal laws would create separate but unequal facilities.

THEMATIC ESSAYS

1. **Theme:** Reconstruction and Balance of Power. An intense struggle for power between Andrew Johnson and the Radical Republicans took place between 1865 and 1868.

   Task:

   ★ Compare and contrast Johnson's Reconstruction plan and that of the congressional Radical Republicans.
   ★ Show how the dispute between Johnson and the Radical Republicans ended in impeachment of the president, and describe the outcome.

   You may include in your answer differing views on secession, amnesty, pardon, and procedures for readmitting secessionist states to the Union. In addition, describe the controversy over the Tenure of Office Act, which led to Johnson's impeachment.

2. **Theme:** Outcomes of the Civil War and Reconstruction. The Civil War and Reconstruction resulted in change but left serious problems unresolved.

Task:

★ Describe one change that resulted from the Civil War and/or Reconstruction.

★ Show how one problem remained unsolved after the end of Reconstruction.

★ Based on information you have given, react to the following statement: "In some ways, the Civil War was both a victory for the North and a draw for the South."

In writing your essay, you may refer to federal-state relations, the development of Northern industry, the Compromise of 1877, *Plessy* v. *Ferguson* (1896), sharecropping, and tenant farming.

DOCUMENT-BASED QUESTION

*Study each document and answer the question that follows it. Then read the **Task** and write your essay. Include references to most of the documents and additional information you retain about U.S. history and government.*

Historical Context: In spite of emancipation, many former slaves were given freedom only briefly. As Reconstruction ended, African Americans in the South became segregated from white society, with no real rights as U.S. citizens.

Document 1: From the Thirteenth and Fifteenth amendments:

Amendment 13: Abolition of Slavery (1865)

[Slavery Forbidden] Neither slavery nor involuntary servitude [compulsory service], except as a punishment for a crime whereof the party shall have been duly convicted, shall exist within the United States, or any place subject to their jurisdiction.

[Enforcement Power] Congress shall have power to enforce this article [amendment] by appropriate [suitable] legislation.

Amendment 15: Right of Suffrage (1870)

[African Americans Guaranteed the Right to Vote] The right of citizens of the United States to vote shall not be denied or abridged by the United States or by any state on account of race, color, or previous condition of servitude [slavery].

[Enforcement Power] The Congress shall have power to enforce this article by appropriate legislation.

Question: According to the Thirteenth and Fifteenth amendments, what responsibilities was Congress given on behalf of freedmen?

Document 2: Refer to the illustration on the bottom of page 85.

Question: What change had taken place in the South by 1867?

Document 3: From the writings of "Pitchfork" Ben Tillman, a Southerner:

. . . We organized the Democratic Party with one plank . . . that "this is a white man's country, and white men must govern it. . . .

. . . President Grant sent troops to maintain the carpetbag government in power and to protect the Negroes in the right to vote. He merely obeyed the law. . . . Then it was that "we stuffed ballot boxes" because desperate diseases require desperate remedies and having resolved to take the state away, we hesitated at nothing. . . .

I want to say now that we have not shot any Negroes . . . on account of politics since 1876. We have not found it necessary. Eighteen hundred and seventy-six happened to be the hundredth anniversary of the Declaration of Independence, and the action of the white men . . . in taking the [government] away from the Negroes we regard as a second declaration of independence from African barbarism.

Question: How did Southern white Democrats justify their actions?

Document 4: From *Plessy* v. *Ferguson* (1896):

Legislation is powerless to eradicate racial instincts or to abolish distinctions based upon physical differences, and the attempt to do so can only result in accentuating the difficulties of the present situation. If the civil and political rights of both races be equal, one cannot be inferior to the other civilly or politically. If one race be inferior to the other socially, the Constitution of the United States cannot put them upon the same plane.

Question: What did *Plessy* v. *Ferguson* decide regarding segregation?

Document 5: Refer to the illustration on the bottom of page 88.

Question: What does the illustration show about the Civil War, Reconstruction, and the period immediately following?

Task

★ Show in what ways former slaves obtained temporary freedom and equality.

★ Explain how the post-Reconstruction era left Southern African Americans in a segregated and inferior status.

Chapter 8
Rise of American Business, Labor, and Agriculture

★ Documents and Laws	★ Events	★ People
Homestead Act (1862)	Industrial Revolution	Horatio Alger
Morrill Act (1862)	(c. 1750–present)	Alexander Graham Bell
Munn v. Illinois (1877)	Grange Movement founded	Henry Bessemer
Wabash, St. Louis, and Pacific	(1867)	William Jennings Bryan
Railway v. Illinois (1886)	First continental railroad	Andrew Carnegie
Interstate Commerce Act (1887)	(completed 1869)	Grover Cleveland
Sherman Antitrust Act (1890)	Knights of Labor organized	Eugene V. Debs
United States v. E. C. Knight	(1869)	Thomas Edison
(1895)	American Federation of Labor	Henry Ford
Sixteenth Amendment (1913)	founded (1886)	Samuel Gompers
Seventeenth Amendment	Haymarket Riot (1886)	William McKinley
(1913)	Homestead Strike (1892)	Samuel F. B. Morse
	Populist party organized	Mary Kenney O'Sullivan
	(1892)	Terence Powderly
	Pullman Strike (1894)	John D. Rockefeller
	Election of 1896	Adam Smith
	International Ladies' Garment	James Watt
	Workers' Union founded	James Weaver
	(1900)	
	National Women's Trade Union	
	League founded (1903)	
	Lawrence Strike (1912)	

Economic Change

Business Response

The **Industrial Revolution**, which began about 1750, persists today. It has involved the invention of machines and systems to mass-produce goods for domestic and foreign markets. Manufacturing started within homes but now takes place in large factories.

Great Britain The making of textiles such as cotton cloth was the first industry revolutionized by machinery and mass production. British inventors created machines for spinning cotton thread. In 1782, James Watt invented the steam engine, which supplied power for various machines. In 1786, the steam-powered loom speeded up the weaving of thread into cloth.

Machine-made cloth cost less to produce than handmade cloth and could be sold more cheaply at home and abroad. Manufacturers made great profits from textiles, but only after investing large sums to buy machines, build factories, and pay workers.

U.S. Advantages in Industrialization The United States was rich in the resources necessary for industrialization—land and raw materials, labor, and **capital** (tools, machinery, and money for investment).

Capitalism is the economic system in which tools, machinery, and factories are privately owned and managed by competing businesses. U.S. capitalism has the following advantages:

★ *Tradition of Business Enterprise*. Colonial merchants risked capital to make a profit. Their profits enabled U.S. banks to finance new economic ventures.

★ *Patent Laws to Encourage Invention*. The U.S. Constitution empowers Congress to issue **patents** to inventors. These government documents give to creators of an original object the exclusive right to make and sell it.

Post–Civil War Growth of U.S. Industry

Northern industries had already made great strides before the Civil War. Cities were linked by railroads. Production of pig iron (crudely cast iron) increased. In 1844, Samuel F. B. Morse invented the telegraph, which speeded business communications.

In the early 1900s, Henry Ford utilized the assembly line to build cars. As cars moved on conveyor belts past a line of workers, each worker did one job in the assembly process. Thus workers became specialized, faster, and produced more. The rate in turning out goods is called **productivity**. High productivity lowers costs.

Proprietorships, Partnerships, and Consolidation
Early U.S. businesses were usually a **proprietorship** (single ownership) or **partnership** (multiple ownership). Because a proprietor or partner was liable (responsible) for all business debts, raising money for risky enterprises was difficult.

Incorporation By the late 19th century, many businesses were organizing as **corporations**, which were chartered under state law. To raise capital, a corporation sells ownership **shares**, or **stock**, to the public. Stock buyers can lose no more than they have originally invested. If the corporation goes bankrupt, its stockholders are not personally liable for its debts.

Investment in Transportation Railroad and canal companies were also organized as corporations and sold their stock to the public to finance their costly operations. Many people invested in canals and railroads because these improved ways of transporting freight over long distances were the key to the nation's industrial future.

Consolidation

Laissez-faire A Scottish philosopher-economist, Adam Smith, believed that the best government policy toward businesses was **laissez-faire**, that is, to allow them to compete without legal restriction. One way that businesses minimized competition was through **consolidation**, by which several businesses joined together and operated thereafter under one management. A more extreme step was to set up a **monopoly** by consolidating all competing businesses. Because a monopoly became the only seller of a product and controlled its manufacture, it was able to charge high prices with little risk.

Expanding Markets

Domestic Markets Investors and business leaders began to create products that could be sold nationwide. Railroads shipped goods from Eastern factories to the West. Meat and wheat from the West were shipped east to feed the workers in big cities there.

International Markets Global trade increased as the United States was challenged by competition in international textile, steel, machinery, and shipbuilding markets. Western European nations and Japan engaged in **imperialism** by gaining foreign territories for their own economic benefit. Imperialism also increased railroad building and the shipment of consumer goods throughout the world. Thus, new markets were opened for American goods.

Merchandising Changes

Department Stores Until the 1860s, there were only small specialty stores for nonbasic consumer goods, and they catered to the rich. In 1862, A. T. Stewart built a **department store** in New York City that sold such goods at prices that the middle class could afford.

Mail-Order Catalogs To reach Americans on remote farms and in villages, Chicago businessman Montgomery Ward sent out catalogs picturing merchandise that people could order by mail. Two other Chicagoans, Richard Sears and Alvah Roebuck, followed his example and built a second successful mail-order business.

Business and Industrial Growth

Transportation

Prior to the Civil War, roads, rivers, and canals made up the U.S. transportation system.

Railroads The steam locomotive, first built in 1804 in England, led to vast new transportation networks. Although the earlier means of transportation remained important, the new railroad networks truly united the nation. After completion of the first transcontinental (coast-to-coast) railroad in 1869, other Western railroads followed. By the end of the century, the United States was tied together by more miles of railroad track than existed in all of Europe (see map, page 98).

Cartoon of "King Monopoly" and his subjects

Page from a late 1800s Sears Roebuck catalog

Steel

For a long time, people knew that steel was stronger and more durable than iron. But it was slow and costly to make. In 1855, a British industrialist, Henry Bessemer, invented a process for producing steel with no impurities by blowing cold air through molten iron. An American industrialist, Andrew Carnegie, adopted the Bessemer process in 1867. By 1901, the United States was leading the world in steel production.

Energy Sources

Coal Coal became important in the early 1800s when it replaced wood to power locomotives. Coal was mined in the Allegheny Mountains, from Pittsburgh, Pennsylvania, to Birmingham, Alabama. Growing industrialization led to an increase in coal production— from approximately 30 million tons in 1870 to more than 200 million tons by 1900.

Oil Before the Civil War, homes were lighted mainly by lamps that burned whale oil or vegetable oil. In the 1850s, kerosene from petroleum (oil) was discovered to be a relatively clean fuel for home lighting. In 1859, Edwin Drake of Titusville, Pennsylvania, accidentally discovered a source of oil while drilling a well for water. Drilling oil wells and processing oil into kerosene became a big business.

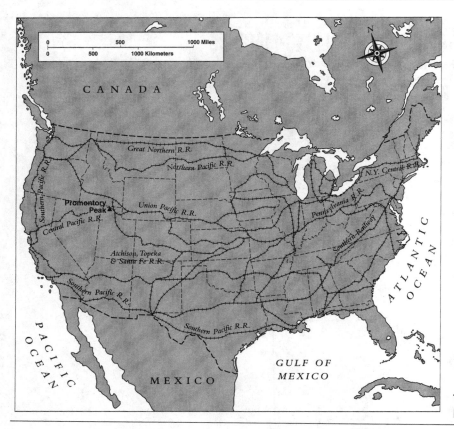

Transcontinental
Railroads, 1865–1900

Electricity Among the nation's most prolific inventors was Thomas Edison. One of his key inventions was the lightbulb (1879), which gives off light when an electric current passes through a filament inside. In addition to the Victrola (early phonograph) and the motion picture camera, Edison also devised a system in which talented people work together on research projects. His "invention factory" of the 1870s and 1880s was the forerunner of modern industrial laboratories.

Communications

The use of electricity to send messages greatly speeded up business communications. Before the Civil War, telegraph wires connected American cities. After the war, Alexander Graham Bell's invention, the telephone (1874–1876), allowed people to talk with each other over long distances.

★ In Review

1. What advantages enabled the United States to industrialize rapidly?

2. What advantages do corporations have over proprietorships and partnerships?
3. How did railroads affect the United States in the 19th century?

Work Methods for Success

Entrepreneurship

John D. Rockefeller In 1865, John D. Rockefeller invested in an oil-refining company. Oil refining was a fiercely competitive industry. To ensure his company's survival, Rockefeller tried to drive all competitors out of business. In 1870, when Rockefeller organized the Standard Oil Company, he had 200 competitors. Ten years later, Standard Oil refined 90 percent of U.S. oil.

Rockefeller crushed his competitors by these means:

★ He persuaded railroads to give Standard Oil **rebates**—that is, they returned to the company a portion of their shipping charges. Rockefeller was then able to charge the lowest prices for oil.

★ Rockefeller offered to buy struggling competitors.

★ To eliminate railroad shipping charges, Rockefeller built pipelines to carry his oil from one place to another.

Andrew Carnegie Andrew Carnegie, a poor immigrant from Scotland, at first worked in a cotton mill. He then got a job working for the president of the Pennsylvania Railroad and invested

John D. Rockefeller (top) and Andrew Carnegie

his savings in railroad sleeping cars, iron mills, and steel. By the 1870s, he owned his own steel company. He paid low wages, drove hard bargains with railroads over their shipping prices, and tried to bankrupt competitors. In 1901, his steel company was worth nearly $500 million.

Work Ethic

When the Pilgrims and Puritans arrived here from England in the early 1600s, they brought with them the tradition of the **work ethic**. It was founded on the teachings of John Calvin, including **predestination**, the belief that every person's afterlife had been determined before birth. Hard work and material success were signs that a person was predestined for a good afterlife. Two Americans who helped solidify this tradition were:

★ *Cotton Mather*. A Puritan minister of Boston's North Church, Mather preached and wrote about the importance of a strong work ethic.

★ *Horatio Alger*. In the post–Civil War era, Alger wrote popular books for young people in which poor boys, by hard work and lucky breaks, rose from rags to riches (like Andrew Carnegie).

Public Good Versus Private Gain

Carnegie and Rockefeller made their industries the biggest and most productive ever. They took huge risks with no guarantee of success. As **philanthropists**, both made huge donations for libraries, schools, hospitals, and other institutions. For their achievements, they were called "captains of industry."

Carnegie, Rockefeller, and other business leaders of their time were also known as "robber barons." They paid low wages, did not tolerate strikes, and used every available means—including secret agreements with railroads and temporary price cuts—to put competitors out of business.

Business Practices and Controls

Government Practices

Laissez-Faire as Government Policy The U.S. government observed laissez-faire in protecting and encouraging businesses. It applied the Fourteenth Amendment's provision that no state may "deprive any person of life, liberty, or property without due process of law" to corporations.

Thus, they enjoyed the same protections as individuals and won favorable rulings in many judicial decisions.

Business Practices

Pooling Railroad lines that had once cut fares to attract business, began to engage in **pooling**; that is, different lines secretly agreed to charge the same high fares. They also shared profits and divided up their once-competitive market. One railroad often had a monopoly on lines servicing small towns and could thus charge higher prices for short trips from one town to another than for longer trips between cities.

Competition and Consolidation

Mergers During the 1870s and 1880s, competition declined as businesses formed **mergers** by joining together as monopolies.

Trusts Rockefeller created a supercorporation called a **trust**. After nearly ruining competitors, he let them exchange their company stock for trust certificates and share in the trust's profits. Other business leaders followed his example, and soon there was a steel trust, a tobacco trust, a sugar-refining trust, and so on.

Holding Companies In the 1890s, corporations were formed that had only one function—to hold the stocks of several businesses in the same industry. By controlling a majority of each company's stock, such **holding companies** could dictate common policy.

Government and Trusts

Sherman Antitrust Act (1890) This act provided that "every contract, combination in the form of a trust or otherwise, or conspiracy, in restraint of trade or commerce . . . is hereby declared to be illegal." Such terms as trust, conspiracy, and restraint of trade, however, were not defined, and no trusts were successfully prosecuted in the 1890s. But the Sherman Antitrust Act established the principle that government should break up trusts and other forms of monopoly.

United States v. *E. C. Knight* (1895) The weakness of the Sherman Antitrust Act was demonstrated in the government's attempt to break up E. C. Knight and Company's control of sugar-refining. The Supreme Court ruled that the federal government had no authority to do so. The Court defined interstate commerce as a business involved in trade or transportation. The sugar refinery, located within one state, did not qualify.

★ In Review

1. What methods did Rockefeller use to maximize profits, reduce costs, and eliminate competition?

1889 cartoon showing business trusts controlling the Senate

★ Changes in Business and Industry ★		
	Age of Jackson (1825–1845)	Mid-century (1845–1865)	After Civil War (1865–1900)
Business organization and manufacturing advances	★ growth of textile mills ★ increase in corporations	★ Isaac Singer's sewing machine plant (1853) ★ Bessemer steel-making process (1865)	★ Standard Oil Trust (1882) ★ trend toward business consolidation
Inventions in transportation and communication	★ Peter Cooper's first locomotive (1830) ★ Samuel Morse's telegraph (1844)	★ laying of New York-London transatlantic cable (1859–1865) ★ first oil pipeline (1865)	★ cable streetcars in San Francisco (1873) ★ Alexander Graham Bell's telephone (1876) ★ Thomas Edison's phonograph (1878)
Inventions in agriculture	★ John Deere's steel plow (1837) ★ Cyrus McCormick's reaper (1831)	★ introduction of grain elevators (1850s) ★ mowing, threshing, and haying machines (1850s)	★ giant harvester-and-thresher combine (1880s) ★ corn-shucking machine (1890s)

2. Discuss whether Rockefeller and Carnegie were captains of industry or robber barons.
3. How did Supreme Court rulings affect efforts to regulate business?

Labor Organization

To minimize costs, most manufacturers kept wages low. Workers put in 60- to 70-hour workweeks in unventilated factories—cold in winter and hot in summer. Accidents from unsafe machinery were common and blamed on the operator. Unable, on their own, to persuade corporate giants to better conditions, workers organized large labor unions.

National Labor Unions

The Knights of Labor (1869) The Knights of Labor, led by Terence Powderly, was the first important union. Unlike earlier ones, it was open to skilled **craft workers** and unskilled **industrial workers** alike, as well as to African Americans, women, and the foreign-born.

For years, the Knights of Labor tried to settle disputes through **arbitration** (judgment by an impartial person). It established cooperatives (see page 104). Its most important goal was to win an eight-hour workday.

Changing tactics in 1885, the Knights of Labor won a major strike against a railroad company. Membership soared to 700,000. Then, in 1886, a bombing in Chicago's Haymarket section

killed several police officers and civilians. The Knights of Labor was wrongly blamed for the incident, workers left in droves, and by the 1890s, the union was almost defunct.

The Haymarket bombing was the work of **anarchists**, those who believed that capitalism and its political system could not be reformed and should be ended through violence.

American Federation of Labor (A.F. of L.) Founded in 1886, this organization, in altered form, survives to this day as the largest American union.

Samuel Gompers, a cigar maker, brought craft unions together in one organization. This federation permitted cigar makers, carpenters, and so on to exist as independent groups. The A.F. of L. leadership set overall policy for achieving common objectives.

Membership grew steadily. By 1900, half a million workers belonged to A.F. of L. craft unions.

Gompers focused on the crucial goals of higher wages, shorter hours, and better working conditions. If a strike seemed the best means to these ends, Gompers approved it.

Most unions in the A.F. of L. discriminated against black workers. The few that admitted African Americans segregated them. Employers often used the excluded blacks to fill jobs of striking union members. Black workers' reputations as "strike breakers" increased racial prejudice within the membership.

The A.F. of L. also excluded women. Mary Kenney O'Sullivan, an activist in the labor movement, persuaded thousands of garment workers

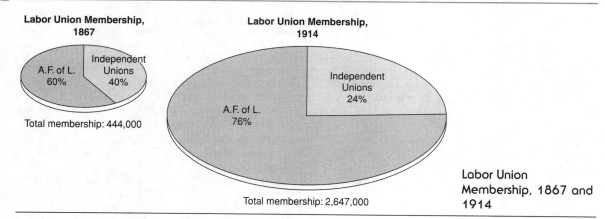

Labor Union Membership, 1867

A.F. of L. 60%

Independent Unions 40%

Total membership: 444,000

Labor Union Membership, 1914

A.F. of L. 76%

Independent Unions 24%

Total membership: 2,647,000

Labor Union Membership, 1867 and 1914

in New York City and Troy, New York, to join local unions. In 1903, she founded a national organization for women called the *National Women's Trade Union League*.

International Ladies' Garment Workers' Union (ILGWU) This union represented workers in the women's clothing industry and protested low pay, long hours, and unsafe working conditions. Most members were Jewish immigrants employed in **sweatshops**—small manufacturing establishments with unsafe and unsanitary conditions. In 1909, the ILGWU organized the first garment strike and won a pay raise and a reduction of work hours per week. In 1910, a second strike of 50,000 mostly male cloak makers won uniform wages, a shorter workweek, and paid holidays. In 1911, after a fire in the Triangle Shirtwaist Company in New York City killed 146 workers, the New York State legislature established strict fire safety codes in factories.

Struggle and Conflict

Homestead Strike In 1892, a union of steel workers refusing to accept a wage reduction struck the Homestead, Pennsylvania, steel plant owned by Andrew Carnegie. Henry Clay Frick, the chairman of Carnegie Steel, called in guards from the Pinkerton National Detective Agency to protect the plant and the replacement workers. Fighting broke out between the guards and the strikers, and many on both sides were killed. After the governor called out the state militia, workers went back to work at lower wages, the union was crushed, and unionization of the steel industry was hindered until the 1930s.

Pullman Strike In 1894, George Pullman, inventor and manufacturer of the Pullman sleeping car, announced a reduction in wages, but no reduction in rents or groceries in the **company town**—one in which workers are dependent on one business for employment, housing, and supplies. Supported by the American Railway Union and its leader Eugene V. Debs, the Pullman workers went on strike, picketed Pullman's railway cars, and prevented them from entering or leaving Chicago. Debs called for a boycott of Pullman cars, and railway workers nationwide refused to handle trains using them, which stopped interstate commerce and the transport of U.S. mail. A federal court granted an **injunction** (court order) against the picketing, and President Grover Cleveland sent federal troops to end the strike. When Debs and other union officials refused to comply, they were jailed and the railway union was broken. The Supreme Court upheld the injunction by ruling that the federal government may prevent "all obstructions to the freedom of interstate commerce or the transportation of the mails."

Lawrence Strike In 1912, the Industrial Workers of the World (IWW) struck the American Woolen Company in Lawrence, Massachusetts. It was led by Joseph Ettor, "Big Bill" Haywood, and Elizabeth Gurley Flynn. Founded in 1905, the IWW was a radical (extreme) labor organization opposed to capitalism and promoting **socialism** (the belief that major industries should be owned and operated by the government). The issue in Lawrence was low wages. Although the governor called in the state militia, the strikers won raises and were not punished for their actions.

Government troops putting down the Pullman Strike, 1894

Public Policy and Public Opinion Most Americans viewed strike leaders as revolutionaries who challenged society's traditional values. But a growing minority sympathized with the unions and recognized that workers were being treated unfairly.

★ In Review

1. Explain how the growth of labor unions was a response to the growth of business.
2. How did the Knights of Labor and the A.F. of L. differ?
3. For the Homestead, Pullman, and Lawrence strikes, prepare a chart listing the (a) conditions that led to the strike, (b) tactics used by both sides, (c) union leadership, (d) role of state or federal government, and (e) outcome of the strike.

Agrarian Organization

Cheap Land

Homestead Act (1862) This law provided that any citizen or immigrant intending to become a citizen could acquire 160 acres of federal land by farming it for five years.

Morrill Act (1862) This act gave huge tracts of federal land to the states on condition that they use it for colleges that taught agricultural and mechanical arts. These land-grant colleges taught farmers new technology for increasing crop yields.

Dependence on Railroads, Merchants, and Banks

Although farmland was cheap, machines, tools, buildings, seed, horses, and crop storage and transportation were not. Farmers needed capital to buy equipment and supplies.

Farmers sought bank loans and credit from merchants. Several years of bad weather, poor crops, and low prices, however, would leave a farmer unable to repay these debts. The bank would then take possession of the farm by **foreclosure**.

Public Domains and Land Grants to Railroads

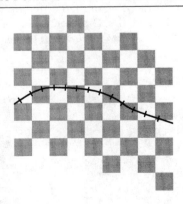

☐ Public domain (held by U.S. government for sale to settlers)

▨ Granted to railroad company

During the 1870s, 1880s, and 1890s, crops were good but prices for farm products grew worse, as dictated by the **law of supply and demand**. As formulated by Adam Smith, this law states that if supply of an item is low, sellers can charge a high price for it. As supply increases, price is lowered in the competition for customers. Thus, as prices sank, farm debts soared.

Grange Movement

The Grange was founded in 1867 to bring farm families together for social purposes. Its meetings, however, soon focused on economic problems.

Grievances Farmers complained about the cost of transporting goods by rail. Railroads competed for business over long routes and therefore charged low rates. They made up their losses by overcharging farmers who had to ship over less competitive short routes. They also charged farmers high rates for storing their wheat and corn in railroad-owned grain elevators.

Cooperatives Grange members set up their own grain elevators by contributing money to a **cooperative** (an enterprise owned and operated by those using its services). Besides giving farmers access to low-cost storage, Grange cooperatives lowered prices for supplies by buying in large quantities.

Laws To fight high railroad rates, the Grangers persuaded several state legislatures in the 1870s to regulate railroad freight and storage rates.

Supreme Court Decisions Companies facing such regulation challenged the Granger laws. In the landmark case of *Munn* v. *Illinois* (1877), the Supreme Court decided that a state could set maximum rates for grain storage. The Court reversed itself in 1886 in the case of *Wabash, St. Louis, and Pacific Railway* v. *Illinois* by ruling that railroads were a part of interstate commerce and their rates could be regulated only by the federal government. The next year, Congress enacted the *Interstate Commerce Act*, which created the Interstate Commerce Commission. It was in existence for over a century (see page 106).

Populism

As farm prices fell in the late 1880s, farmers joined a movement that became a new political party—the *People's party*, or *Populist party*.

Platform of 1892

In 1892, the new party announced its **platform** (statement of political ideas), which was radical for the time:

★ **graduated income tax** (the higher the income, the higher the tax rate)

★ establishment of savings banks in U.S. post offices

★ government ownership and operation of railroads

★ government ownership and operation of telephone and telegraph companies

★ election of U.S. senators by direct vote of the people rather than by state legislatures

★ eight-hour workday for all factory workers

★ state laws granting the **initiative** (voters' power to initiate ideas for new laws) and **referendum** (voters' power to mark ballots for or against proposed laws).

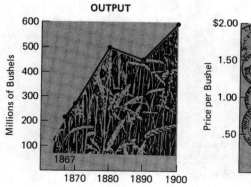

Rising Wheat Production (left) and Falling Farm Prices, 1870–1900

Cartoon showing effects of the railroad monopoly on farmers

Monetary Policy

Between 1873 and 1890, the U.S. government had minted and circulated only coins of gold. Because gold was more valuable than silver, these coins were often hoarded (kept and not spent). As money became scarce, farmers saw a connection between the scarcity of money and the low prices they got for cotton and corn. The Populists felt that if the government coined 16 silver dollars for every gold dollar, farm prices would rise. In effect, the Populists wanted the government to create **inflation** (constantly rising prices). Silver miners, who liked this idea, became enthusiastic Populists.

Early Triumphs

The coinage of silver and other Populist reforms appealed to voters. The 1892 Populist presidential candidate, James Weaver, won more than a million votes (almost 9 percent of the total) as well as 22 electoral votes. Other Populists were elected to seats in Congress and in state legislatures of the South and West—an impressive showing for a new party.

Election of 1896

In 1892, Grover Cleveland, a Democrat, was elected president. He believed that gold was "sound money" and that silver coins would damage business confidence. Most Democrats of the North and East supported his stand, while those of the South and West favored the "free and unlimited coinage of silver."

Democratic Nomination of Bryan At the Democratic convention of 1896, Congressman William Jennings Bryan of Nebraska thrilled the "silver Democrats" with a rousing "cross of gold" speech. Declaring that farmers would prevail over city bankers, he brought the convention to its feet with his last sentence: "You shall not press down upon the brow of labor this crown of thorns, you shall not crucify mankind upon a cross of gold." Bryan was nominated for president.

Populist Nomination of Bryan The Populists also nominated Bryan as the candidate most able to rally the nation behind the cause of silver.

Republican Victory Bryan lost to the Republican candidate, William McKinley, who supported gold. Bryan carried the South and much of the West but failed to win crucial Eastern electoral votes. Many Eastern workers feared inflation and believed McKinley's prediction that silver money would cause high prices, a depression, and the loss of jobs.

Contributions

Bryan's defeat and improved farm prices after 1896 caused a rapid decline of the Populist party. After 1900, no more Populists were elected to Congress.

Nevertheless, many Populist reforms were adopted. Two Populist ideas became the basis for constitutional amendments:

★ graduated income tax—Sixteenth Amendment (1913)

★ popular election of U.S. senators—Seventeenth Amendment (1913).

Early Regulation of Business

Until 1887, the federal government encouraged business growth through tariffs, land grants, and patents but did little to regulate business practices. In the 1880s, however, Congress, responding to public pressure, enacted a law that marked the beginning of government regulation of business.

Interstate Commerce Act (1887)

To regulate certain practices of railroad companies, Congress created the *Interstate Commerce Commission (ICC)*, with power to enforce the following rules:

★ Railroad rates had to be "reasonable and just."

★ Pools were illegal.

★ Returning rebates to favored customers was illegal.

★ Railroads could not charge more for a short haul than for a long haul.

Later amendments to the law expanded the commission's powers.

★ In Review

1. What problems did small farmers experience, and what economic solutions did the Grangers propose?
2. To what extent was the Populist party successful in resolving the problems of the farmers?
3. What features of the Populist agenda were eventually legislated?

Chapter Review

MULTIPLE-CHOICE QUESTIONS

1. "The problem of our age is the proper administration of wealth, that the ties of brotherhood may still bind together the rich and poor in harmonious relationship. . . ."

   —Andrew Carnegie

   Which of the following statements best describes the quotation? (1) The rich should contribute to the betterment of society. (2) We need a constitutional amendment providing for a graduated income tax. (3) Government should never tax what is inherited. (4) Anyone who is wealthy must have become so through corruption.

2. Which of the following was most likely to write a letter to the editor opposing the viewpoint in the cartoon on page 96? (1) Terence Powderly (2) John D. Rockefeller (3) Samuel Gompers (4) "Big Bill" Haywood.

3. A conclusion to be drawn from the ad on page 97 is that (1) to increase sales, the graphophone manufacturer reduced its price (2) the graphophone was used mainly in offices (3) by 1898, a great amount of music was recorded (4) most people could afford a graphophone.

4. Which conclusion may be made from the two pie graphs on page 102? (1) The A.F. of L. was taking control of all U.S. unions. (2) In 1867, few workers joined the A. F. of L. (3) By 1914, most workers were in a labor union. (4) The A. F. of L. organized 76 percent of U.S. union members in 1914.

5. The graphs on page 104 show that from 1870 through 1890 (1) farmers earned great profits as wheat production increased (2) the price of wheat dropped as production increased (3) value of the dollar increased (4) as the price of wheat fell, farmers produced other crops.

6. The map on page 98 illustrates that, after the Civil War, the transcontinental railroads (1) continued to promote sectional interests (2) further isolated the North from the South (3) extended U.S. influence into Mexico and Canada (4) connected most sections of the nation.

7. The best title for the political cartoon on page 100 is (1) "The People's Court" (2) "The Senate Runs the Country" (3) ". . . of the Trusts, by the Trusts, for the Trusts" (4) "Checks and Balances in Action."

8. "Show me the country in which there are no strikes and I'll show you the country in which there is no liberty!" This statement was probably made by (1) Samuel Gompers (2) Grover Cleveland (3) George M. Pullman (4) Henry Ford.

9. During the late 1800s, farmers supported free unlimited coinage of silver because they believed it would lead to (1) government farm price supports (2) lower rates charged by railroads (3) lower prices for consumer goods (4) higher prices for farm products.

10. A major aim of the Grange and Populist movements was (1) establishment of a gold standard (2) mandatory policies to end inflation (3) laws for public control of railroads (4) unlimited immigration of Asians.

THEMATIC ESSAYS

1. **Theme:** The Federal Government as a Partner of Big Business. In spite of its policy of laissez-faire, the federal government cooperated with and assisted in the growth and development of private business.

   Task

   ★ Discuss *two* specific ways in which the government helped private business expand.
   ★ Evaluate how each example had a positive or negative impact on a *specific* group in the United States.

   You may discuss land grants, railroad subsidies, and tariff and monetary policies, with their impact on any group, including farmers, Native Americans, consumers, and industrial workers.

2. **Theme:** Impact of Railroads on the Nation. Completion of the transcontinental railroad in 1869 marked a major change for the people in the states and territories.

   Task: Choose two groups and show how railroads caused major changes in their lives.

   Examples you may choose are farmers, immigrants, city dwellers, and Native Americans.

DOCUMENT-BASED QUESTION

*Study each document and answer the question that follows it. Then read the **Task** and write your essay. Include references to most of the documents and additional information you retain about U.S. history and government.*

Historical Context: Because of excesses by businesses, banks, and the federal government, industrial workers and farmers organized unions and political parties to make their voices heard.

Document 1: Refer to the illustration on page 103.

Question: Why did President Cleveland use the U.S. army during the Pullman Strike?

Document 2: An infamous sign in a sweatshop:

> IF YOU DON'T COME IN SUNDAY,
> DON'T COME TO WORK MONDAY!

Question: How were the factory owners who posted the sign taking advantage of their workers?

Document 3: From Samuel Gompers's "Letter on Labor" in *Industrial Society Forum*, September 1894:

> . . . man's liberties are trampled underfoot [by] corporations and trusts, rights are invaded and laws perverted. . . . wherever a tyrant has shown himself he has always found some willing judge to clothe that tyranny in . . . legality, and modern capitalism has proven no exception . . . .

Question: How does Gompers feel about government's attitude to labor and the common people?

Document 4: Refer to the cartoon on page 105.

Question: How does the cartoonist feel about the railroads' treatment of farmers?

Document 5: From a speech by Populist orator Mary Lease in 1890:

> This is a nation of inconsistencies. The Puritans fleeing from oppression became oppressors. We fought England for our liberty and put chains on four million blacks. We wiped out slavery and by our tariff laws and national banks began a system of white wage slavery worse than the first.
>
> . . . It is no longer a government of the people, by the people, and for the people, but a government of Wall Street, by Wall Street, and for Wall Street. . . .
>
> . . . Kansas suffers from two great robbers, the Sante Fe Railroad and the loan companies. The common people are robbed to enrich their masters. . . .

Question: How was Lease comparing the problems of Kansas farmers to those of slaves?

Document 6: From William Jennings Bryan's "cross of gold" speech at the Democratic National Convention, 1896:

> You . . . tell us that the great cities are in favor of the gold standard; we reply that the great cities rest upon our broad and fertile prairies. Burn down your cities and leave our farms, and your cities will spring up again as if by magic; but destroy our farms and the grass will grow in the streets of every city. . . .
>
> . . . We will answer their demand for a gold standard by saying to them: You shall not press down upon the brow of labor this crown of thorns, you shall not crucify mankind upon a cross of gold.

Question: Why does Bryan say that the gold standard will destroy both farms and cities?

Task: Using the documents and your knowledge of U.S. history and government, write an essay describing how, between the late 1800s and early 1900s, farmers and factory workers organized labor unions and political parties to gain an effective voice in politics.

Chapter 9
Impact of Industrialization

★ Documents and Laws	★ Events	★ People
Chinese Exclusion Act (1882)	Gold rushes (1849, 1859)	Andrew Carnegie
Dawes Act (1887)	Women's suffrage in Wyoming	Willa Cather
Gentlemen's Agreement	(1869)	Samuel Clemens
(1907–1908)	Battle of Little Big Horn (1876)	Charles Darwin
Literacy test bill (1917)	Dedication of Statue of Liberty	William Randolph Hearst
Immigration quota laws	(1886)	Helen Hunt Jackson
(1921–1924)	Battle at Wounded Knee (1890)	Henry James
Indian Reorganization Act	End of the frontier (1890)	Scott Joplin
(1934)	Red Scare (1919-1920)	Chief Joseph
Indian Self-Determination and	Protest at Wounded Knee	Emma Lazarus
Education Act (1975)	(1973)	Joseph Pulitzer
		Jacob Riis
		John D. Rockefeller
		Theodore Roosevelt
		Herbert Spencer
		Frederick Jackson Turner
		Thorstein Veblen
		Edith Wharton
		Woodrow Wilson

★ Objectives

★ To understand the impact of industrialization and urbanization on American life.

★ To trace how industrialization changed the role of women.

★ To appreciate how immigrants contributed to American life in a pluralistic society.

★ To examine prejudice and discrimination against ethnic minorities.

★ To understand how Western settlement affected Native Americans and U.S. society.

Urban Growth

In the late 1800s, millions of people—native-born Americans from rural areas, freed slaves seeking to escape social and economic bondage in the South, and immigrants from Europe and Asia—flocked to Eastern and Midwestern cities.

Attractions of Urban Life

Jobs Industrialists built factories near transportation centers such as railroad terminals and steamship ports. Workers moved near these hubs to get factory jobs. Near the factories, **entrepreneurs** (business investors) rented housing to the workers and opened shops to supply their needs. As city populations increased, so did the variety of goods and services available there.

Public Education City schools were larger, better-equipped, and offered more complete courses of study than rural schools. To serve growing populations, cities raised money for new elementary schools and high schools. Between 1865 and 1900, elementary school enrollments more than doubled. The number of U.S. high schools rose from about 400 in 1860 to more than 6,000 in 1900. Schools also improved in quality as more teachers received professional training.

Earlier educators had concentrated on teaching reading, writing, and arithmetic. After 1900, however, occupational training and citizenship education were considered equally important.

Culture Urban cultural resources—libraries, museums, and concert halls—enriched the education of city children. Moreover, urban life offered a variety of cultural experiences. For example, in the late 1800s, as now, New Yorkers had their choice of restaurants, theaters, beaches and parks, sporting events, and amusement centers.

Urban Problems

Slums As disadvantaged people crowded into cities, they could afford to live only in **slums**—poor neighborhoods with crowded streets and run-down buildings.

Increased Crime Poverty encouraged crime. As cities grew, so did the number of murders, burglaries, and robberies. Tenement youths organized rival gangs.

Inadequate Water and Sanitation Cities dumped sewage into rivers and lakes that provided drinking water. As a result, there were frequent outbreaks of typhoid fever, transmitted by polluted water. Lacking bathtubs and running water, tenement dwellers could not keep clean. Factory smokestacks polluted the air. Horse droppings fouled the streets.

New Urban Architecture

Skyscrapers and Elevators The invention of electric elevators made it possible to erect higher buildings. The first skyscraper, built in Chicago in 1884, was ten stories high.

Tenements The tenements that dotted the slums were cheaply constructed buildings five or six stories high, without elevators. They were breeding grounds for vermin and disease, and built so closely together that fire could spread through an entire neighborhood in minutes.

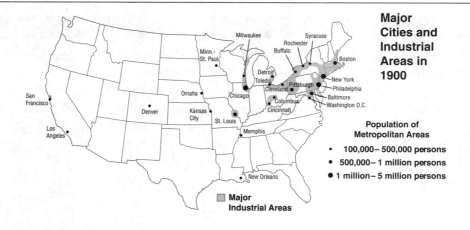

Major Cities and Industrial Areas in 1900

Population of Metropolitan Areas
- • 100,000– 500,000 persons
- • 500,000– 1 million persons
- ● 1 million– 5 million persons

▨ **Major Industrial Areas**

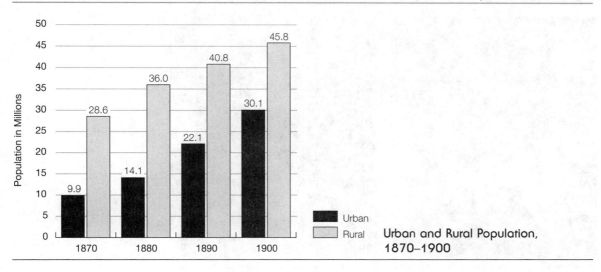

Urban and Rural Population, 1870–1900

Social Classes

Social Darwinism A British biologist, Charles Darwin, advanced the theory that lower forms of life evolved into higher forms as the result of an ongoing struggle for survival. The survivors were the "fittest" of the species. British philosopher Herbert Spencer adapted this theory as **social Darwinism**: It is for the good of society that the strongest and most efficient businesses survive while weaker ones die out. In Spencer's words: "The American economy is controlled for the benefit of all by a natural aristocracy . . . brought to the top by a competitive struggle that weeded out the weak, incompetent, and unfit and selected the wise and able."

Class Divisions

★ *Working-class hardship.* A laborer's wages seldom covered family expenses, so wife and children also had to work. Paid lower wages than men, they sometimes had more job security than men, particularly during an economic depression.

★ *Middle-class contentment.* The middle class had sufficient income to live in modest comfort. After the Civil War, the middle class included shopkeepers, well-educated professionals (doctors, lawyers, teachers, and so on), and office workers. The middle class tended to be conservative—patriotic, politely mannered, and affiliated with religious organizations.

★ *Upper-class display and philanthropy.* In the late 1800s—the so-called Gilded Age—the families of people who had made great fortunes from corporations and trusts comprised the upper class. Such men as Andrew Carnegie and John D. Rockefeller flaunted their wealth. They had yachts, private railroad cars, and racehorses and built enormous mansions filled with masterpieces of art and cared for by many servants. The economist Thorstein Veblen called their buying habits **conspicuous consumption**.

The rich also donated millions for public causes such as libraries, museums, universities, and medical research.

Work and Workers

Factories and People Most factory workers could not better their positions because unskilled work taught them little that was useful. Their wages were so low that even ambitious, clever workers could seldom raise enough capital to start a business. In large factories, business owners and their managers had too little contact with workers to recognize those with promise.

Immigrant Patterns of Settlement Immigrants tended to move to cities, where there were jobs. Since most of them arrived at New York City, many stayed there. Others settled in cities such as Philadelphia, Boston, and Chicago. Wherever they settled, immigrants usually moved into neighborhoods peopled by their own nationality. In New York, people still refer to such neighborhoods as Little Italy and Chinatown.

Gilded Age: The very rich (left) and very poor

Insecurity After 1865, the plight of factory workers increased. Appeals to employers were useless, and those who joined unions or participated in strikes, were fired. Replacement workers were plentiful—immigrants, women and children, youths fresh from their farms, and African Americans who had migrated north.

Jobs were also threatened by new machines that were cheaper and faster than humans. Depressions and financial panics sometimes ended business booms abruptly, and there was no unemployment insurance for those who were fired or laid off.

Women, Families, and Work

Traditional Roles From the mid- to late 1800s, middle-class women were completely under male protection and expected to be wives and mothers rather than professional workers.

Most middle-class women were also allowed to engage in civic and charitable activities. Many single women became teachers, the one calling in which women outnumbered men.

Working-class women had to provide some of the family income. Farm women worked with their husbands, sons, and brothers in the fields. City women became mill or factory hands, servants, or laundresses and did their own housework in the evenings.

Emerging Family Patterns The long hours of working-class women strained family ties but their incomes were badly needed to supplement

their husbands' low wages. Additional strains arose when men wasted their salaries on gambling or drinking.

African American women could generally find work only as domestic help.

Children, the Elderly, and the Disabled Prior to the Civil War, children under 12 earned pennies a day in textile mills. In 1900, about 1.7 million children between the ages of 10 and 15 earned pennies an hour in mines and factories.

Unprotected by law, the elderly and the disabled were often unemployed. They relied heavily upon support from family members and charity.

Religion in a Pluralistic Society

Degree of Tolerance The Pilgrims and Puritans had come to America seeking religious freedom, but they did not grant it to others. They were particularly intolerant of Quakers, who were forced to leave the Massachusetts Bay Colony. In the 1800s, Americans of British descent considered their culture and Protestant faith superior. Religious intolerance—always a problem—increased when Catholics from Italy, Eastern Orthodox Christians from Greece, and Jews and Catholics from Poland and Russia arrived in the United States in large numbers.

Influence of Puritan Beliefs and Values In colonial New England, most Protestant ministers were Puritans, who had split from the Church of England. Their beliefs in predestination, hard work, and the careful management of property are still a part of American values.

Religion and Party Politics   Throughout the 1800s, elected leaders on both national and state levels were Protestants. As more Catholics and Jews arrived in the late 1800s and early 1900s, they began to influence Democratic politics in New York City, Boston, and Chicago. Party leaders sought to win the support of new immigrants at the polls by providing them with financial assistance and social welfare.

Threatened by the number of Catholic immigrants, some Protestants believed that the pope had sent the new arrivals to take over the country. Such extremists joined the American Protective Association, as others like them had joined the Know-Nothings decades earlier.

Fearing a loss of influence in Northern cities where Catholics and Jews had settled, Protestants established religious reform groups aimed at solving such urban problems as overcrowding, poor working conditions, and **machine politics** (organized control of elected officials by party leaders). These reform goals influenced the emerging Progressive movement of the early 1900s.

Changes in Lifestyle

Buying and Selling Goods   New methods of commercial financing encouraged urban middle-class consumers to buy the new products created by industrialization. People who could not afford a new Singer sewing machine could buy it on **credit** and pay for it sometime in the future. Or they could put down part of the price and pay off the rest monthly on the **installment plan**.

Sports and Recreation   City dwellers who could not hunt and fish could enjoy sports as spectators. In 1846, one of the first amateur baseball games was played in Hoboken, New Jersey. Cincinnati had the first professional team—the Red Stockings (today's Cincinnati Reds)—formed in 1869. College football became popular in the 1870s. A teacher in Springfield, Massachusetts, invented basketball in 1892.

Health and Life Expectancy   Doctors developed cures for diphtheria and other contagious diseases that raged through the crowded, dirty cities. New city hospitals met the needs of a growing population. By 1900, improved health care had raised the average life expectancy in the United States from the 35.5 to 47.3 years.

Literature and Music   As prosperity gave the urban middle class more leisure, some turned to the arts. Thus, more American writers, musicians, and artists were able to make a living. Samuel Clemens, the author of *The Adventures of Tom Sawyer* (1876) and *The Adventures of Huckleberry Finn* (1884), became a celebrity under the pen name Mark Twain. Willa Cather achieved fame for *My Antonía* (1918), a novel of Midwestern life. Henry James's *Washington Square* (1880) and Edith Wharton's *The Age of Innocence* (1920) depicted earlier and later manners of upper-class New Yorkers.

In 1883, the Metropolitan Opera House opened in New York City. Scott Joplin, a former slave, composed original, distinctly American music. His piano compositions, such as "Maple Leaf Rag" (1899), were in the style known as ragtime. Its lively, rhythmic musical style had a marked influence on the development of jazz.

Popular Culture   One-penny and two-penny newspapers circulated daily in every city. New York publishers such as William Randolph Hearst and Joseph Pulitzer appealed to the urban masses by featuring articles on team sports and sensational crimes. Some publishers issued dime novels on such exciting subjects as the outlaws of the West.

★ In Review

1. How was Darwin's theory of evolution applied to business?
2. Compare the impact of industrialism on a working-class family and a middle-class family.
3. Identify three ways in which the growth of cities affected American cultural life.

Immigration: 1850–1924

While European immigrants were settling mainly in the East and Midwest, Chinese and Japanese immigrants were settling on the West Coast. By 1910, more than 300,000 Chinese and more than 150,000 Japanese immigrants lived and worked in the United States.

Italians   Italians began a mass emigration in the late 1800s. By 1898, some 205,000 emigrated every year. Between 1898 and 1914, the arrival number increased to about 750,000 a year.

In the 1880s, an agricultural crisis, caused, in part, by increased competition from American

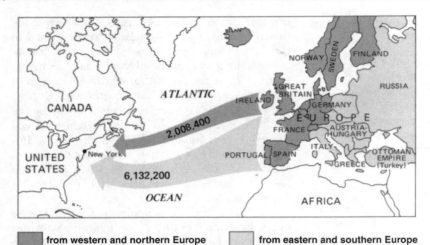

from western and northern Europe | from eastern and southern Europe

Peak Period of "New" European Immigration, 1891–1915

farmers, caused a decline in the Italian standard of living. The price of farm products fell and unemployment increased. Peasants spent about three-fourths of their income on food. In addition, Italy was a country where few could vote or gain an education.

Chinese The Chinese first arrived in California in 1849. They hoped to discover gold and return home rich. They were the first nonwhites to arrive in large numbers of their own free will. Viewed with hostility, Chinese immigrants were prevented from owning property or gaining citizenship.

Chinese labor was essential in the development of the West. Agents of the Central Pacific Railroad recruited thousands to build the western half of the first transcontinental railroad. Thus, Chinese workers dynamited the tunnels through the rugged Sierra Nevada. Overworked and underprotected from both the elements and hazardous working conditions, many Chinese lost their lives.

When a depression hit the nation in the 1870s, Chinese laborers became scapegoats (people unfairly blamed for an event or condition). Further resentment arose when bosses replaced striking workers with Chinese labor. Anti-Chinese sentiment led to the passage of the Chinese Exclusion Act (1882), which halted further immigration. It also prevented Asians and their American-born children from becoming citizens. (For Japanese exclusion, see page 118.)

The Chinese Exclusion Act, the first major restriction on U.S. immigration, was not fully repealed until 1942, when China was a wartime ally.

Chinese immigrants, however, had challenged the law in the Supreme Court. In 1897, the Supreme Court established for the first time the legal right of citizenship by birth in the United States.

Russian Jews Abraham Cahan, who arrived from Russia in 1882, wrote about the experiences of immigrant Russian Jews. The following passage is from his 1888 article, "The Lower East Side in 1898," in the *Atlantic Monthly*:

Sixteen years have elapsed . . . . The Jewish population has grown . . . to about one million. Scarcely a large American town but has . . . an educated Russian-speaking minority forming a colony within a **Yiddish**-speaking colony [Yiddish is the language of many European Jews], while . . . New York, Chicago, Philadelphia, and Boston have each a ghetto rivaling . . . the largest Jewish cities in Russia, Austria, and Rumania. The [Jews] in Manhattan [number] 250,000, making it the largest center of Hebrew population in the world. . . .

The grammar schools of the Jewish quarter are overcrowded . . . for progress and deportment, [immigrant children] are raised with the very best in the city. At least 500 of 1,677 students at New York City College, where tuition and books are free, are Jewish boys from the East Side. . . .

The 5,000,000 Jews . . . in Russia had not a single Yiddish daily paper . . . , while their fellow countrymen and coreligionists . . . in America publish six dailies . . . , not to mention the countless Yiddish weeklies and monthlies, . . . New York [is] the largest Yiddish book market in the world.

New York City's Lower
East Side, 1900

Reasons for Emigration

Population Pressures As Europe industrialized, it became overcrowded. A population of 140 million in 1750 grew to 260 million in 1850 and 400 million in 1914. Farmland was much scarcer than in the United States.

Recruitment Railroad companies with Western lands to sell and steamship companies seeking passengers sent agents abroad to promote emigration. Steamship lines offered tickets to New York City for as little as $25 a person.

Economic Conditions From generation to generation, European farm families divided their land to provide for their sons. Eventually, most farms had become too small to be profitable. After 1880, poor farmers in Italy, Sweden, and Norway found it almost impossible to earn a living.

American Attractions

Labor Shortage Because of rapid industrialization in the United States, Europeans thought that American factory jobs would be plentiful and better-paying than those at home.

Liberty and Freedom Jews in Russia and Poland lived in fear of **pogroms**—sudden violent attacks on their communities. In many eastern European countries, laws required boys of 15 and 16 to do military service.

Ghettos Distinct immigrant groups gathered in **ghettos**—city neighborhoods made up mostly of one nationality or **ethnicity** (group that shares a common culture).

The tenement apartments of poor immigrants were known as "railroad flats"—their rooms were arranged in a straight line, one after the other.

★ European Immigrants: When They Came and Why ★

Nationality	Period of Greatest Immigration	Reasons
Irish	1840s–1850s	Failure of potato crop and resulting famine
Germans	1840s–1880s	Economic depression; oppression following failed revolutions
Scandinavians (Danes, Swedes, Norwegians, Finns)	1870s–1900s	Poverty; shortage of farmland
Italians	1880s–1920s	Poverty; shortage of farmland
Jews from eastern Europe (including Poles and Russians)	1880s–1920s	Political oppression; religious persecution; poverty

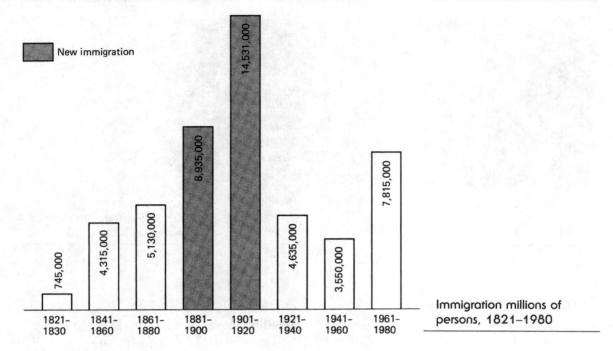

New immigration

| | 745,000 | 4,315,000 | 5,130,000 | 8,935,000 | 14,531,000 | 4,635,000 | 3,550,000 | 7,815,000 |

1821–1830 1841–1860 1861–1880 1881–1900 1901–1920 1921–1940 1941–1960 1961–1980

Immigration millions of persons, 1821–1980

Families often shared an already crowded apartment with relatives and friends newly arrived. The grim living conditions of typical New York City immigrant families were described by Jacob Riis in his 1890 book *How the Other Half Lives*.

"Americanization"

Ghetto life helped immigrants preserve their customs and language, and they had difficulty adapting to strange new ways. Although they tried to speak English, only the children usually adapted readily.

Society pressured new immigrants to undergo "Americanization." School lessons were taught only in English. Sometimes, a teacher changed a student's name to one that was easier for a native-born American to pronounce.

Most immigrants supported the Democratic party, which provided services for the urban poor in return for their support in elections. Since most cities had large immigrant populations, Democratic politicians usually won city elections.

Growing Diversity and Reaction

Between the 1840s and the 1920s, approximately 37 million immigrants arrived in the United States. Until the 1870s, Germans and Irish predominated.

After 1890, the "new immigration"—those from southern and eastern Europe—began to exceed those from other regions. Between 1900 and 1910, total immigration averaged close to a million people a year. Of the total arriving in 1910, about 700,000 people came from southern and eastern Europe and only about 300,000 from all other countries (see map on page 114).

English-speaking, Protestant Americans, as guardians of the dominant culture, feared that the "new immigrants" would not easily adapt to it. Although American values differed from region to region, several were generally agreed upon and cherished:

★ **Immigration by Nationality, 1840s–1920s** ★

Nationality	Number
Germany	About 6 million
Italy	4.75 million
Ireland	4.5 million
England, Scotland, Wales	4.2 million
Austro-Hungarian Empire	4.2 million
Russia, Baltic states	3.3 million
Scandinavia	2.3 million

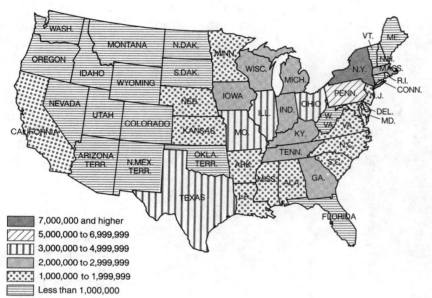

7,000,000 and higher
5,000,000 to 6,999,999
3,000,000 to 4,999,999
2,000,000 to 2,999,999
1,000,000 to 1,999,999
Less than 1,000,000

U.S. Population
Distribution, 1900

★ *Individualism*. Each American was completely responsible for his or her actions. People attained economic success because of strength of character. Failure resulted from weakness of character.

★ *Rough social equality*. Americans of European descent tended to view one another as social equals deserving of mutual cooperation, especially on the Western frontier.

★ *White superiority*. Whites in the North and South believed in the superiority of their "race" and culture. They recognized a mission to bring Western civilization to other regions and peoples.

Methods of Adaptation

Between the peak immigration years (1901–1910), Americans debated three points of view about how immigrants should adapt to their new country:

★ *Assimilation*. Immigrants should quickly learn English and adopt all aspects of American culture.

★ *"Melting pot" theory*. Immigrants would gradually and naturally blend into a new American culture that combined the best elements of many cultures and nationalities.

★ *Cultural pluralism*. There are no superior cultures, and each ethnic group should practice its own customs, respect unfamiliar customs, and adjust to the ways of a larger society.

Resurgence of Nativism

Nativist feelings had not disappeared (see page 60). Faced with the "new immigrants," nativists had four main fears:

★ *Economic*. Immigrants would deprive native-born Americans of jobs by accepting lower wages.

★ *Cultural*. The dominant culture deserved to be protected against foreign influences.

★ *Psychological*. Native-born Americans of European descent were superior by race and nationality, and inferior newcomers from eastern and southern Europe would produce a class of criminals and paupers.

★ *Political*. The "new immigrants" might be connected with radical and revolutionary causes.

Non-nativists voiced their opposition. A New York writer, Emma Lazarus, poetically expressed her recognition of the contributions of immigrants:

> . . . "Give me your tired,
> Your poor, your huddled masses yearning to
>   breathe free,
> The wretched refuse of your teeming shore.
> Send these, the homeless, the tempest-tossed,
>   to me,
> I lift my lamp beside the golden door!"

Lazarus's complete poem is inscribed at the base of the Statue of Liberty, which began welcoming immigrant ships to New York Harbor in 1886.

Cartoon of anti-immigrant citizens and their "shadows"—their immigrant ancestors

Limits on Immigration

In the 1870s, anti-Chinese riots broke out to protest the "yellow peril"—the unfounded fear that Asian immigrants would overwhelm American culture. Two new laws reflected such nativist fear and prejudice:

★ The *Chinese Exclusion Act* (1882) declared that no more Chinese would be allowed into the United States.

★ Japanese schoolchildren in San Francisco were ordered to attend segregated classes. When the Japanese government expressed resentment, President Theodore Roosevelt arranged a compromise, the *Gentlemen's Agreement* of 1907–1908. California would end its offensive school policy, and Japan would stop further immigration of Japanese workers into the United States.

Literacy Testing In 1917, Congress overrode President Wilson's veto and passed a literacy test law. It provided that those unable to pass a reading test in their native language (or any other language) were prohibited from immigrating.

Red Scare In 1917, the Communist-backed revolution in Russia fueled nativist fears that Communists (Reds) and other foreign-born radicals might

Early 20th-century immigrants arriving at Ellis Island, New York City

overthrow the U.S. government. During the Red Scare of 1919 and 1920, President Wilson's attorney general, A. Mitchell Palmer, organized raids, often without search warrants, to arrest and deport immigrants suspected of disloyalty.

Quota Acts of 1921 and 1924 The *Emergency Quota Act* (1921) limited the yearly immigration from any country to 3 percent of the number arriving from that country in 1910. The *Immigration Restriction Act* (1924) limited the yearly immigration from any country to 2 percent of the number arriving from that country in 1890.

These quota laws were designed to cut sharply the number of immigrants from Italy, the Soviet Union (formerly Russia), and other countries of southern and eastern Europe. They were also meant to halt immigration from Asia. Between 1901 and 1910, more than eight million immigrants arrived, most from southern and eastern Europe. In the 1930s, immigrants numbered fewer than 350,000.

★ **Summary of Immigration Laws** ★

Date	Law
1882	Chinese Exclusion Act: Chinese immigration was prohibited.
1882	Paupers, convicts, and mentally defective persons were prohibited.
1891	Prostitutes, polygamists, and diseased persons were prohibited.
1917	Literacy test. Those unable to pass a reading test in their native language (or any language) were prohibited.
1921	Emergency Quota Act: Yearly immigration from a country was limited to 3 percent of the number arriving from that country in 1910.
1924	Immigration Restriction Act: (a) Yearly immigration from a country was limited to 2 percent of the number arriving from that country in 1890; (b) no more than 150,000 immigrants were to be admitted yearly from a single country; (c) no Asians would be admitted.

★ In Review

1. Why did the "new immigrants" leave their countries for the United States?
2. How did the "new immigrants" contribute to American society?
3. What conflicts between American ideals and reality are illustrated by the following laws? (a) Chinese Exclusion Act, (b) Gentlemen's Agreement, (c) literacy test of 1917, (d) Emergency Quota Act and (e) Immigration Restriction Act.

The Frontier: 1850–1900

The U.S. **frontier** was an imaginary line separating settled areas from the wilderness. As trappers, miners, and farmers moved west, the frontier moved with them.

Westward From the Missouri River

Plains and Desert Before 1850, the region between Missouri and California was called the Great American Desert because it seemed dry, barren, and impossible to farm. It consisted of:

★ the *Great Plains*—flat grasslands stretching 400 miles from the banks of the Missouri River to the slopes of the Rocky Mountains

★ the *Great Basin*—a dry lowland stretching about 700 miles between the Rocky Mountains and the Sierra Nevada.

Settlement of the West

Beginning around 1850, Easterners began to realize that the so-called Great American Desert was rich in resources.

Mining Frontier In 1859, news of a gold strike on Pikes Peak in Colorado touched off a rush westward similar to the one in California ten years earlier. Later, many others were lured elsewhere in the Rockies by news of silver in Nevada and copper in Montana, and to the Black Hills of the Dakotas for gold.

Cattle Frontier During the 1860s and 1870s, settlers began to raise cattle on the grassy plains of Texas. The herds were privately owned, but the open range was used by all.

Farming Frontier The 1862 Homestead Act (see page 103) attracted "homesteaders," who set up farms on the Great Plains. Speculators took over some of the newly available land.

Violence in the "Wild West"

Ranchers Versus Farmers The barbed wire that farmers used to fence in their homesteads angered cattle owners, who regarded the grasslands as open range. Gun battles broke out between the factions. In the 1880s, the ranchers conceded defeat and began to fence in their own grazing lands.

Vigilantes Versus Outlaws For many adventurers, it was easier to steal a miner's gold or rustle a rancher's cattle than work for them. Most Westerners carried guns to protect their property, and, sometimes, to settle personal quarrels.

Remote towns could not rely on government officials to capture thieves. Therefore, they carried out the law as **vigilantes** (a self-appointed police force). Suspected outlaws were sometimes hanged without a full trial—or any trial at all.

Industrialization and the West

Railroads and Investment Railroad companies were even more eager than the U.S. government to encourage farmers to go west. A railroad's chief business was transporting freight. Settlers on the plains would expand business.

Railroads were crucial to the cattle drives from Texas. At the end of the cowboys' long journey were the railroad depots in Abilene and Dodge City, Kansas, from which cattle were shipped for slaughter to Chicago. The meat was then sent east. Cattle ranchers needed railroads. In the 1860s, a steer worth $3 in Texas could bring between $30 and $40 when sold to a Chicago meatpacker.

Urban Centers Chicago grew into a great city and the world's largest meatpacking center. Abilene and Dodge City fared well, too. Their stockyards charged cowboys to house their cattle before shipment. During their stay, cowboys spent money at hotels, restaurants, stores, and other businesses. With their prosperity, the towns' populations grew. Soon, **railheads**, as such stopovers were called, became bustling urban centers.

Technology Farmers on the Great Plains faced three problems. Rainfall was slight, there was a scarcity of trees for rail fences to enclose their animals, and the soil was dry, hard, and full of tough grass roots. Windmills provided the power for pumping up groundwater. Barbed wire (invented in 1874) enabled farmers to fence their lands. With improved steel plows, they could cut deep into the hard ground.

Cultural Diversity

Mexicans who had lost their land in the Mexican War often worked as cowboys on American ranches. African Americans, recently freed from slavery, became ranchers and farmers. In the 1860s and 1870s, many immigrants from Europe joined the movement west.

Lifestyles

Sod Houses and Dugouts Lacking trees, homesteaders built their first homes out of bricks

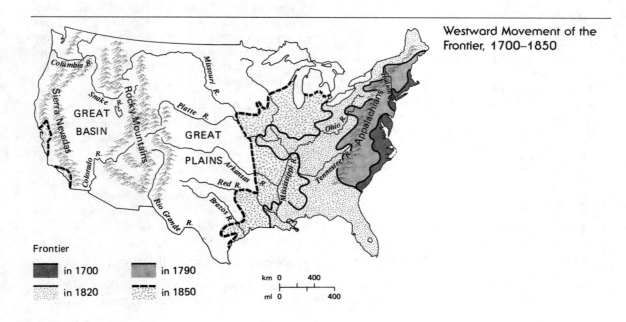

Westward Movement of the Frontier, 1700–1850

Frontier
- in 1700
- in 1790
- in 1820
- in 1850

km 0   400
ml 0   400

made from the prairie sod, with blankets and hides covering doors and windows. On hilly sites, they dug these homes into the hillside. When it rained, the sod roof leaked. In long dry spells, crops withered and dust covered everything. Separated by great distances, farmers only rarely got together. Many farm families on the plains soon moved back east.

Women Women farmed, fed the livestock, churned butter, cooked, sewed linens and clothing, and reared children—often enough, ten or more of them. It was common for a woman to work all morning, give birth in the afternoon, and return to chores the next morning.

In spite of this drudgery, women were a civilizing influence that could turn a rough mining camp or cow town into a more settled, peaceful community. They called for libraries, schools, even theaters. They worked as teachers, missionaries, librarians, and, occasionally, doctors and dentists.

Women of the Wyoming Territory first achieved the right to vote in 1869. Women in most Western states were voting in large numbers by 1910, while Eastern women were still fighting for suffrage.

Impact on American Life

In 1890, the Census Bureau reported that the frontier had ceased to exist. Frederick Jackson Turner, a historian, then wrote an essay about the effects of the frontier on American society.

Turner observed that frontier life was more democratic than life in settled areas. People on the frontier judged each other not by social rank but by ability and strength of character. They felt that everyone had an equal chance for success.

For people from crowded Eastern cities, the frontier meant a new starting point where hardworking people could get land cheaply.

Some scholars, who feel that American democracy owes more to British colonial influences than to the frontier, point out that few poor people could afford covered wagons and supplies necessary for the trip West.

Native Americans

Plains Indians The Great Plains were filled with plants and animals that supported the Native American way of life. Huge buffalo herds supplied Plains Indians with meat for food, hides for clothing and shelter, bones for tools, and dried manure for fuel. Buffalo-hunting tribes (the

Blackfeet, Cheyenne, Comanche, and Sioux) believed that the land and the life it supported were sacred. They could not conceive of dividing land into private plots and using it for personal gain.

Pressures of White Settlement By 1890, Native Americans had been placed on reservations and had lost their rights to the land. White people hunted the buffalo herds of the plains for hides and sometimes merely for sport. By 1890, the once-teeming buffalo herds numbered less than a thousand.

Reservations Reservations were often barren and supported little wild life for hunting. Native Americans were reduced to poverty and hopelessness. U.S. agents who ran the reservations often pocketed funds intended for the inhabitants.

In 1887, Congress passed the *Dawes Act*, which offered 160-acre plots on reservations to the heads of Indian households. Lawmakers viewed it as a form of Americanization by which Indians would adopt the lifestyle of self-supporting white farmers. Native Americans, however, followed a hunting culture, and many of them rented or sold their plots to white settlers.

Treaties and Legal Status U.S. treaties had guaranteed Native Americans the right to their own land. But as settlers moved west in the 1850s, these treaties were ignored. Often, U.S. troops supported the takeover of Native American land. Some African American troops (whom the Indians called "buffalo soldiers") fought against Native Americans as well.

In the 1880s, a reformer named Helen Hunt Jackson published *A Century of Dishonor* (1881), describing how often the U.S. government had violated its treaties with Native Americans.

Indian Wars: 1850–1900 The Sioux of Wyoming were the first Plains people to attack U.S. military posts. In an 1876 battle on the Little Bighorn River in Montana, the Sioux, led by Chief Crazy Horse, killed 210 soldiers, including Lieutenant Colonel George Custer. In 1890, the U.S. Army retaliated by killing about 300 Sioux at Wounded Knee Creek in South Dakota. This battle, in which even women and children were massacred, ended Sioux resistance. They moved to a South Dakota reservation.

Other Native American resistance also failed. In 1877, 500 members of the Oregon Nez Percé fled toward Canada to escape being forced onto a

Native Americans in the West,
Late 1800s

reservation. They were turned back by U.S. troops. So thorough was their defeat that their leader, Chief Joseph, declared that his people's fight was finished forever.

The Apaches of Arizona, who submitted in 1900, were the last Native Americans to engage U.S. troops.

Native Americans lost their wars against settlers and U.S. troops for three reasons:

★ They fought as separate tribes, rather than uniting.

★ Most tribes numbered fewer than a thousand people.

★ Though equipped with bows and arrows and rifles, they lacked such advanced weapons as cannons and machine guns.

Indian Civil Rights

Early in the 20th century, two laws somewhat improved the status of Native Americans. In 1924, Congress granted Native Americans full citizenship. In 1934, the *Indian Reorganization Act* per-

Chief Joseph, around 1870

mitted Indian peoples to own land in common as tribal property rather than as separate farms. At the same time, reservation schools began to teach scientific farming.

★ In Review

1. How did the Industrial Revolution contribute to the economic development of the Great Plains?

2. Identify (a) the Homestead Act, (b) the Battle of Wounded Knee, and (d) Frederick Jackson Turner.

3. Summarize the federal government's attempts to address Native American rights from 1887 to 1934.

Chapter Review

MULTIPLE-CHOICE QUESTIONS

1. Which was most responsible for the rapid economic growth of cities during the 19th century? (1) theaters and libraries (2) industrial growth (3) urban mass transportation (4) mass communication.

2. How did "new immigrants" differ from earlier immigrants? (1) They were considered physically and mentally superior. (2) They arrived before the end of the frontier. (3) They came from different countries. (4) They came from northern and western Europe.

Base your answer to question 3 on the Emma Lazarus poem quoted on page 117 and the following poem by Thomas Bailey Aldrich:

> Wide open and unguarded stand our gates,
> And through them presses a wild motley throng—
> Men from the Volga and the Tartar steppes,
> Featureless figures of the Hoang-Ho,
> Malayan, Scythian, Teuton, Kelt and Slav,
> Flying the Old World's poverty and scorn;
> These bringing with them unknown gods and rites,
> Those, tiger passions, here to stretch their claws.
> In street and alley what strange tongues are loud,
> Accents of menace alien to our air,
> Voices that once the Tower of Babel knew!

> O Liberty, white Goddess! is it well
> To leave the gates unguarded? . . . .

3. Lazarus and Aldrich (1) agreed that American-style democracy should be extended to other nations (2) felt that immigration should be limited (3) desired a quota system (4) disagreed about U.S. immigration policy.

4. The photographs on page 112 show that (1) most families had a lot of leisure time (2) while some Americans were rich, others lived in poverty (3) the divorce rate was high (4) few children went to public schools.

5. The bar graph on page 111 shows that (1) between 1870 and 1900, the number of people in cities was gradually approaching the number in the country (2) urban population would never catch up with rural population (3) urban population would surpass rural population by 1910 (4) agricultural output outperformed industrial output in 1900.

6. The artist of the cartoon on page 60 believed that nativists were (1) cynical (2) correct (3) hypocritical (4) practical.

7. The graph on page 116 indicates that (1) the number of arriving immigrants tripled by 1861 (2) immigration was severely limited in 1911 (3) officials limited entry of British, Irish, and German immigrants (4) between 1881 and 1920, the nature of immigration changed.

8. "U.S. society may be described as a stew in which each ingredient adds flavor but still

retains its distinct identity." This statement best describes the concept of (1) ethnocentrism (2) cultural pluralism (3) nativism (4) social control.

9. What effect did population growth in the 19th century have on Native Americans? (1) It caused them to move to cities in increasing numbers. (2) It forced them westward. (3) It led most of them to adopt the settlers' culture. (4) Most formed alliances with other minority groups.

10. Passage of the immigration acts of 1921 and 1924 showed a determination to (1) restrict immigration (2) continue traditional immigration policies (3) encourage cultural diversity (4) play a larger role in international affairs.

THEMATIC ESSAYS

1. **Theme:** Urbanization. The gradual U.S. population shift from rural to urban areas created new problems that demanded new solutions.

   Task: Choose one change resulting from the growth of cities that created a problem. For this change:

   ★ describe in detail the problem created
   ★ show how people attempted to solve the problem
   ★ evaluate the success of the attempted solution.

   You may wish to consider changes in the areas of housing, immigration, and working conditions.

2. **Theme:** The Shrinking Frontier. As the U.S. frontier moved west, it shrank and disappeared.

   Task

   ★ Define "frontier" and show how its movement west resulted in its disappearance.
   ★ Explain *two* factors that caused the frontier to shrink and disappear.
   ★ Describe *one* outcome of the shrinking frontier.

   Some factors to consider in explaining the shrinking frontier are: discovery of gold in California, Homestead Act, development of railroads, and role of technology.

Outcomes of the shrinking frontier might include, but are not limited to, its impact on Native Americans, immigrants, the environment, and living styles.

DOCUMENT-BASED QUESTION

*Study each document and answer the question that follows it. Then read the **Task** and write your essay. Include references to most of the documents and additional information you retain about U.S. history and government.*

Historical Context: The "new immigration" presented special challenges for newcomers to New York City and other urban centers.

Document 1: Refer to the graph on page 116.

Question: What happened to the number of immigrants from 1881 through 1920?

Document 2: Refer to the map on page 114.

Question: During the period shown on the map, where did most immigrants come from?

Document 3: Refer to the photograph on page 118.

Question: What feelings does this photo convey to you?

Document 4: Refer to the photograph on page 115.

Question: What conditions did many immigrants live in when they first arrived in U.S. cities?

Document 5: Read the excerpt "The Lower East Side in 1898" on page 114.

Question: In Cahan's view, how did life in the United States compare with that in Russia?

Task: Using the documents and your knowledge of U.S. history and government:

★ describe some challenges faced by immigrants who arrived during the late 1800s and early 1900s
★ describe why most immigrants decided to remain in spite of the challenges facing them.

★ UNIT III ★

The Progressive Era

Chapter 10
Reform in America

★ Documents and Laws	★ Events	★ People
Sherman Antitrust Act (1890)	Seneca Falls Convention (1848)	Jane Addams
Newlands Reclamation Act (1902)	Woman's suffrage in Wyoming (1869)	Susan B. Anthony
Elkins Act (1903)	Pennsylvania Coal Strike (1902)	Louis Brandeis
Northern Securities Company v. *United States* (1904)	National Association for the Advancement of Colored People (NAACP, 1909)	Eugene V. Debs
Lochner v. *New York* (1905)	Election of 1912	W. E. B. Du Bois
Hepburn Act (1906)		William Randolph Hearst
Meat Inspection Act (1906)		Robert La Follette
Pure Food and Drug Act (1906)		John Muir
Inland Waterways Act (1907)		Frank Norris
Muller v. *Oregon* (1908)		Gifford Pinchot
Payne-Aldrich Tariff (1909)		Joseph Pulitzer
Sixteenth Amendment (1913)		Jacob Riis
Seventeenth Amendment (1913)		John D. Rockefeller
Underwood Tariff (1913)		Theodore Roosevelt
Clayton Antitrust Act (1914)		Margaret Sanger
Federal Trade Commission Act (1914)		Upton Sinclair
Eighteenth Amendment (1919)		Lincoln Steffens
Nineteenth Amendment (1920)		William H. Taft
		Ida Tarbell
		Lillian Wald
		Booker T. Washington
		Ida B. Wells
		Woodrow Wilson

Pressures for Reform

The *Progressive Era* began in the 1890s. Reformers in this movement aimed to solve problems of industrial growth and change.

Government Power and Reform

Should government regulate business? **Progressives** and their conservative opponents actively debated this question.

Conservative View Conservatives believed in laissez-faire—government should not restrain business from free competition.

Progressive View Progressives wanted to (1) stop unfair competition by businesses and (2) protect consumers and the public from the bad effects of industrialism.

Developing Technologies

New technologies of the late 19th century helped industry grow. Using the Bessemer process, Andrew Carnegie's steel company outproduced all competitors. High-quality steel tracks replaced weaker iron ones as railroads expanded westward. The Westinghouse air brake made railroads safer, and the Pullman car made them more comfortable. Refrigeration enabled railroads to carry shipments of food long distances without spoilage.

Improved transportation helped farmers and miners move west. At the same time, immigrants poured into American cities and brought about the increasing urbanization of the nation. By 1920, more people lived in cities than in rural areas.

The typewriter, Dictaphone, and telephone opened up new jobs for women, which created the foundation for social and political change.

Business Practices and Working Conditions

Reformers weighed the effects of long working hours on women's health. A Chicago social worker, Florence Kelley, helped bring about an Illinois law to limit women's workdays to eight hours. Women in Massachusetts persuaded the legislature to pass a minimum wage law in 1912.

In response, businesses argued in court that state regulatory laws infringed on property rights and were unconstitutional.

Conservative (left) and progressive views of government's role in business

Lochner v. *New York* (1905) A New York law prohibited bakers from working more than a 60-hour week or 10-hour day. The Supreme Court ruled the law unconstitutional because it violated the Fourteenth Amendment's protection of a business owner's right not to be deprived of the use of property without "due process of law."

Muller v. *Oregon* (1908) An Oregon law provided that women could not work more than ten hours a day in factories and laundries. Louis Brandeis successfully defended the law before the Supreme Court by showing scientifically that long hours of physical labor could injure women's health. He later became the first Jew to serve on the Court.

Increasing Inequities in Business Operations

From 1865 through the early 1900s, the gap between great wealth and great poverty widened and became a target for progressive reformers. Railroad millionaires such as Leland Stanford and Cornelius Vanderbilt were able to handsomely endow the universities that bear their names. Rockefeller and Carnegie grew fabulously rich. When Carnegie sold his steel company to J. P. Morgan, he donated most of the proceeds to new libraries and other institutions—notably, New York City's 42nd Street Library and Carnegie Hall. Other multimillionaires of the era included meatpackers Gustavus Swift and Philip Armour.

The new millionaires defended their fortunes by citing social Darwinism (see page 111).

In contrast were the millions who labored long hours for low wages. In the late 1800s, steelworkers worked 12-hour shifts, often seven days a week. Women and children toiled in New York City's garment industry. In Chicago, immigrants earned low wages in dangerous meatpacking jobs. From 1880 to 1900, the number of women working (usually for pennies a day) increased from 2.5 million to almost 9 million.

Influence of the Middle Class and Newspapers
Progressive politicians depended on support from middle-class voters and city newspapers.

The middle class read books, newspapers, and magazines that influenced their economic and political views. Proud of tradition and patriotic in their civic duties, middle-class men voted regularly, and the women joined clubs, charities, and, often enough, reform movements.

New inventions helped publishers sell more newspapers. By the 1870s, machine-driven presses had replaced earlier hand presses. Publishers schemed to increase readership and advertising income. Joseph Pulitzer's *New York World* and William Randolph Hearst's *New York Journal* competed to reach a large public by selling newspapers for only a penny and running scandalous and sensational feature stories. Such methods were known as **yellow journalism**.

Social and Economic Reform/Consumer Protection

"Muckrakers" and Reform

Many writers reported on corruption in city government and the shocking living and working conditions of the poor. These journalists, dedicated to exposing immorality in business and politics, came to be called **muckrakers**.

The *Ladies' Home Journal* and *McClure's* were among the magazines that published muckraking articles. The most influential writers were:

★ *Lincoln Steffens*. In *The Shame of the Cities* (1904), he revealed how corrupt city politicians of his time were.

★ *Ida Tarbell*. Her investigation of John D. Rockefeller's monopolistic methods was first a series of articles and then a book, *History of the Standard Oil Company* (1904).

★ *Frank Norris*. His novel *The Octopus* (1901) dealt with the struggle of California wheat growers against a monopolistic railway.

★ *Upton Sinclair*. His novel *The Jungle* (1906) exposed unhealthy conditions in Chicago's meatpacking plants:

. . . there [came] back from Europe old sausage that had been rejected . . . moldy and white—it would be dosed with borax and glycerine . . . and made over again for home consumption. . . . meat . . . tumbled out on the floor, in the dirt and sawdust, where the workers had tramped and spit . . . . meat [was] stored in rooms, and the water from leaky roofs would drip over it, and thousands of rats . . . race about on it. . . . a man could . . . sweep off handfuls of the dried dung of rats [who were then poisoned]; they would die, and then rats, bread, and meat would go into the hoppers together. . . . there were things

Dreadful tenement conditions—in this case, cholera confronting a slumlord

that went into the sausage in comparison with which a poisoned rat was a tidbit.

The public outcry following publication led to the Meat Inspection Act and the Pure Food and Drug Act (see the next section).

Legislation

★ The *Meat Inspection Act* (1906) gave officials the power to check the quality of meats shipped in interstate commerce.

★ The *Pure Food and Drug Act* (1906) banned manufacture and sale of impure foods, drugs, and liquors. It also required the truthful labeling of commercial medicines.

Social Justice Movement

Other reformers wanted to help people who lived in slums:

★ *Jacob Riis.* A New York City newsman, Riis wrote *How the Other Half Lives* (1890), exposing the misery of slum life and prompting efforts to reduce tenement overcrowding and lack of sanitation.

★ *Jane Addams and Lillian Wald.* Jane Addams and Lillian Wald knew about urban poverty and persuaded state legislatures to protect children against harsh labor. They ran **settlement houses** (Addams's Hull House in Chicago and Wald's Henry Street Settlement

in New York City), where immigrants received help in adjusting to American life and poor children were safe from the dangers of city streets. These institutions also offered free adult education in English, the arts, literature, and music.

Women's Rights/Efforts for Peace

Suffrage Movement Male and female activists for woman's suffrage (voting rights) were known as **suffragists**. The movement, begun at the Seneca Falls Convention in 1848 (see page 62), continued into the Progressive Era. One leader, Susan B. Anthony, wanted to amend the Constitution so as to guarantee voting rights for women in every state. When the amendment was introduced in Congress in 1878, male lawmakers rejected it. Suffragists introduced it during every session for the next 40 years.

Suffragists asked how a democracy could fail to grant women the vote. A new generation led by Alice Paul and Carrie Chapman Catt replaced Susan B. Anthony and Elizabeth Cady Stanton. In 1919, Congress passed the *Nineteenth Amendment*, giving women the vote, and it was ratified by the states in 1920.

Margaret Sanger and Birth Control A nurse to immigrant families in New York City, Margaret Sanger saw that frequent pregnancies increased hardships for poor women. She began publishing a magazine on birth control in 1914, opened the first U.S. birth-control clinic, in Brooklyn, and wrote *What Every Girl Should Know* (1916). Her ideas and work gained strength in later decades.

Peace Movement In 1915, during World War I (see Chapter 11), an international conference of women met at The Hague in the Netherlands, founded the *Women's International League for Peace and Freedom*, and elected Jane Addams president. Later, they denounced the peace treaty for creating conditions for a future war.

Black Movement

The best-known African Americans of the Progressive Era were Booker T. Washington and W. E. B. Du Bois. (For their points of view about racial segregation, see page 89.) White business leaders and politicians conferred with Washington about preparing young black people for

Reformer and educator Booker T. Washington (top) and W. E. B. Du Bois, African American activist against racial discrimination

skilled industrial jobs. Washington was a frequent adviser to President Theodore Roosevelt.

In 1905, Du Bois launched the *Niagara Movement* at a meeting of black reformers in Niagara Falls, Canada. Its focus was to publicize and protest injustice against African Americans.

NAACP In 1909, members of the Niagara Movement and white reformers organized the *National Association for the Advancement of Colored People (NAACP)*. Its aim was to protect the civil rights of African Americans and defend black suspects unfairly accused of crimes because of race. Its magazine, *The Crisis*, was edited by Du Bois.

The NAACP won a number of civil rights cases in the Supreme Court, which, between 1915 and 1917, declared the following unconstitutional:

★ "grandfather clause" (see page 90)

★ segregated housing

★ denying African Americans the right to serve on juries

★ denying African Americans the right to run for office in party primaries.

Ida Wells One of the NAACP's founders was a Tennessee reporter named Ida B. Wells. She wrote a book about the outrage of lynching—between 1900 and 1914, more than 1,100 African Americans had been lynched by white mobs—and dedicated her career to racial justice.

Marcus Garvey In 1916, Marcus Garvey came to the United States from Jamaica. He was deeply offended by the second-class status of African Americans. In Jamaica, he had organized the *Universal Negro Improvement Association (UNIA)* and its "Back to Africa" movement, which attracted about 500,000 U.S. members. Garvey urged African Americans to shun the white majority, build their own institutions, and return to Africa. His leadership ended in 1925 when he was convicted of mail fraud. In 1927, he was deported to Jamaica.

Temperance/Prohibition

The many women of the temperance movement urged people not to drink alcohol and wanted public sale of it banned. Drinking alcohol, they argued, increased working-class poverty. The most famous crusaders were Frances Willard and Carrie Nation. In 1919, the *Eighteenth Amendment* was passed, and, until its repeal in 1933, the manufacture and sale of alcohol in the United States was prohibited.

Anti-Defamation League (1913)

Jewish immigrants from Europe were so often the target of nativist prejudices that Jewish

Illiteracy by Race, 1890–1910

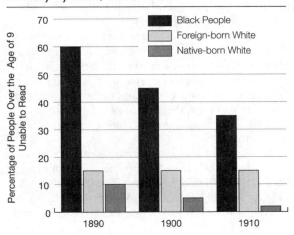

Americans organized the *Anti-Defamation League* in 1913. Its purpose was to combat unfair statements made about Jews.

★ In Review

1. How did the Supreme Court both assist and retard progressive reforms?
2. Define progressivism, muckraker, social justice, settlement house, and suffragist.
3. Describe the efforts of women and African Americans to bring about democratic reforms.

Progressivism and Government Action

From about 1890 to 1900, progressives focused on enacting laws at the local and state levels.

Urban Middle Class and Political Reform

Unlike the Populist party, progressives were concerned with reform in the cities. By 1900, approximately 30 million of the 75 million Americans lived in urban areas. As urban populations grew, so did the middle class—lawyers, doctors, middle-management employees, teachers, and clerical workers.

Municipal Reform In the late 1800s, many cities were controlled by political machines. Government provided no unemployment insurance or welfare for the poor. Instead, they looked to the local party boss for rent and food in exchange for loyalty at the polls. Political leaders took bribes for contracts and jobs.

Large cities badly needed bridges, subways, electric trolley cars, gas and electricity, and telephones. Reformers feared that the growth in services would lead to more corruption in government. The urban middle class supported progressive attempts to break the power of party bosses, reduce the cost of government, lower taxes, and end corruption.

In the early 1900s, progressive mayors in several large cities broke the power of political machines. Two Ohio mayors, Tom Johnson in Cleveland and Samuel ("Golden Rule") Jones in Toledo, provided efficient transportation and honest government. Often enough, however, re-

form politicians could not keep power when they failed to meet the needs of growing ethnic minorities.

State Reform

Wisconsin: Robert La Follette In Wisconsin, as elsewhere, railroads, political bosses, and business interests had great influence. Governor Robert ("Battling Bob") La Follette challenged them. Besides providing tax reform, business regulation, and technical expertise, he fought for the following:

★ The *direct primary*: Instead of state nominating conventions, voters would nominate candidates by direct popular vote in a primary election (an early election before the general election in November).

★ The *initiative*: By signing a petition, a small percentage of voters could force the state legislature to consider a proposed law.

★ The *referendum*: A proposed law could be submitted to the people and voted on in an election.

★ The *recall*: The people, by special election, could vote on whether to remove an elected official from office before term's end.

Wisconsin became known as a "laboratory for democracy."

New York: Theodore Roosevelt As president of the New York board of police commissioners, Theodore Roosevelt tried to end police corruption. As governor of the state in the late 1890s, his dedication to civil service reform angered several important state politicians. They were happy to have him selected as vice-presidential candidate on the 1900 Republican ticket with William McKinley and get him away from the state arena.

Political Reforms Elsewhere Oregon first used the initiative and referendum. Many states also adopted the **Australian ballot**, whereby voters could mark in secret a ballot printed not by a political party but by the state.

Economic, Environmental, and Social Reforms By 1914, most states had enacted child labor laws. As more children attended school, mandatory education requirements were established. Engineers and urban planners were developing new methods of sanitation and garbage removal, designing bridges and tunnels, and installing street lighting. Building codes increased safety in new housing.

President Theodore Roosevelt (1901–1909) and the Square Deal

At the age of 42, following the assassination of President McKinley, Theodore Roosevelt became the youngest president in U.S. history. He promised a Square Deal to all Americans—labor and business, poor and rich.

Stewardship Theory Throughout the late 1800s, government policy toward business was laissez-faire. When presidents intervened at all, they favored big business. Roosevelt, however, believed that presidents should be stewards (guides) of the nation's economy and politics. A depression in the 1890s convinced him to try to improve conditions.

Roosevelt demonstrated the Square Deal when Pennsylvania coal miners struck in 1902. He did not call in troops to support the mining company; he invited union and company leaders to the White House. The company agreed to a shorter workday and a 10 percent wage increase, and the strike was settled.

Railroad Regulation and Consumer Protection Roosevelt persuaded Congress to enact the following laws to reform railroads:

★ The *Elkins Act* (1903) allowed the Interstate Commerce Commission to punish railroads that granted rebates.

★ The *Hepburn Act* (1906) empowered the Interstate Commerce Commission to fix railroad rates and limit free passes for politicians and business owners.

Roosevelt also persuaded Congress to pass the Pure Food and Drug Act and the Meat Inspection Act (see page 128).

"Trust Busting" Using the Sherman Antitrust Act for the first time, Roosevelt prosecuted the Northern Securities Company, a powerful holding company controlling several Western railroads. In *Northern Securities Company* v. *United States* (1904), the Supreme Court ruled the president's move to break up Northern Securities constitutional. Roosevelt broke up other business combinations as well, including Standard Oil.

Popularly known as a **trust buster** (breaker of monopolies), Roosevelt was not an enemy of big business. He encouraged "good trusts," which acted responsibly, and broke up "bad trusts," which ignored the public interest.

"Teddy" Roosevelt, trust buster

Conservation of Nature, Land, and Resources

Roosevelt was wary of mining and lumbering exploitation of the wilderness. He sought public support for **conservation**—wise management and careful use of the natural environment. Thus, Congress passed two major conservation laws:

★ The *Newlands Reclamation Act* (1902) set aside money from the sale of Western desert lands for irrigation projects.

★ The *Inland Waterways Act* (1907) provided that a commission be appointed to study how major rivers were being used.

Using an already existing law, the *Forest Reserve Act*, Roosevelt established 149 publicly owned national forests totaling more than 190 million acres, to be controlled by the National Forest Service.

Gifford Pinchot and John Muir

★ *Gifford Pinchot*. Theodore Roosevelt appointed Gifford Pinchot head of the Forest Service. Pinchot had long tried to get private lumber companies to plant new trees to replace those cut down. He asked that only full-grown trees be cut down.

★ *John Muir*. Prior to Roosevelt's administration, John Muir had supported bills to create a national park in Yosemite Valley, California. Under Roosevelt, he supported setting aside additional forestland and establishing national parks in Mesa Verde, Colorado, and the Grand Canyon, Arizona.

Controversy Under President Taft (1909–1913)

Roosevelt chose his secretary of war, William Howard Taft, as Republican presidential nominee for president in 1908. Taft won the election easily.

Taft was often a zealous progressive. He prosecuted 90 businesses for antitrust violations (Roosevelt had prosecuted 44.)

But Taft did not please progressives who favored lower tariffs and better conservation. Over the protests of progressives in Congress, he signed the *Payne-Aldrich Tariff* (1909), which raised prices on many products.

Even more upsetting was Taft's firing of Gifford Pinchot. Roosevelt was especially angered.

Woodrow Wilson (1913–1921) and the New Freedom

Wilson was only the second Democrat (after Grover Cleveland) elected president after the Civil War. In his inaugural address, he announced a program called the *New Freedom*, including a lower tariff, more effective business regulation, and a reformed banking system.

Progressivism and the Election of 1912 In the 1912 election, the Republican party was split. Conservative Republicans nominated Taft. Progressives supported Roosevelt and formed the Progressive party—also known as the "Bull Moose" party because Roosevelt described himself as "strong as a bull moose."

Woodrow Wilson, popular and progressive governor of New Jersey, won the Democratic nomination.

The Socialist party had gained strength and numbers by championing industrial workers and proposing that major industries be owned and operated by the government. Its presidential candidate was labor leader Eugene Debs.

In this race of four self-acclaimed reformers, Wilson won over the divided Republicans with 435 electoral votes.

Underwood Tariff Wilson appealed for lower tariffs. The *Underwood Tariff* (1913) lowered prices of many consumer goods and deprived big business of protections it had long enjoyed.

Graduated Income Tax The *Sixteenth Amendment* (1913) empowered Congress to collect an income tax that was *not* apportioned according to state populations. At first, it was collected only from people with very high incomes. A **graduated income tax**, its rate schedule rose as reported income increased.

Clayton Antitrust Act Wilson persuaded Congress to enact the *Clayton Antitrust Act* (1914). It strengthened the Sherman Antitrust Act by listing as illegal such business practices as (1) holding companies that prevented competition, (2) **interlocking directorships** (the same people serving as directors of several companies), and (3) secret agreements to fix an industry's prices. In addition, labor unions could no longer be prosecuted as monopolies.

Federal Trade Commission Under pressure from Wilson, Congress passed the *Federal Trade*

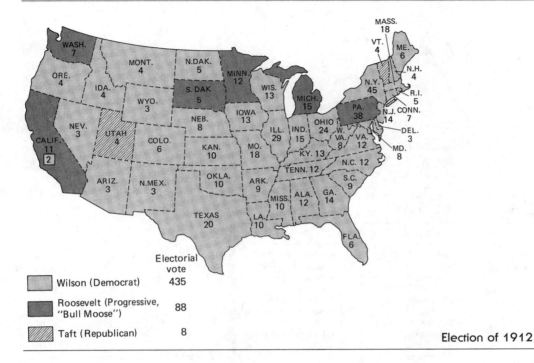

Electorial vote

Wilson (Democrat) — 435

Roosevelt (Progressive, "Bull Moose") — 88

Taft (Republican) — 8

Election of 1912

Commission Act in 1914. It created the Federal Trade Commission (FTC) to (1) investigate suspicious business practices and (2) order companies to "cease and desist" from illegal acts.

Federal Reserve System Before Wilson, there was no federal system to control the supply of money (currency) needed by business. Thus, private banks often had too little currency in reserve (kept in their vaults). If many customers withdrew their money at the same time, a bank with a low reserve might fail. The failing of many banks at once would cause an economic depression.

Wilson supported the progressives who called for a federal reserve system. Private banks would deposit cash reserves in 12 regional banks. Officials of the Federal Reserve Board would supervise those regional banks, which could make loans to private banks at interest rates set by the board. The loans would be in the form of paper currency printed by the government as Federal Reserve notes (dollar bills). Americans have used such currency ever since the *Federal Reserve Act* was passed in 1913.

Under the act, money supply may be increased or decreased according to need. The Federal Reserve Board sets interest rates that affect all banks and, therefore, the national economy.

Expanding and Contracting Democracy

Direct Election of Senators The *Seventeenth Amendment* (1913) required that senators be elected by the voters of their state rather than state legislatures. This reduced the influence of special interests, particularly big business.

Women's Suffrage Women's struggle for voting rights ended with the passage of the *Nineteenth Amendment* (1920). It stated: "The right of citizens of the United States to vote shall not be denied or abridged by the United States or by any state on account of sex."

Segregation Under Woodrow Wilson Rights of African Americans did not expand under Wilson. He ordered segregation of the washrooms in federal buildings in the nation's capital. And he angrily dismissed a group of African Americans who came to the White House to protest.

World War I and Domestic Reform

In 1917, the United States entered World War I. Government and big business cooperated to produce the greatest amount of war supplies in the

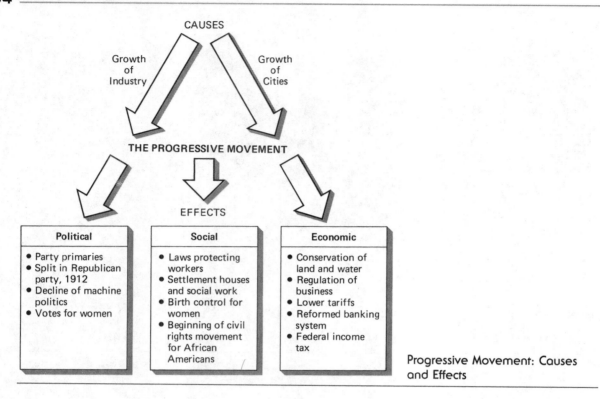

CAUSES

Growth of Industry

Growth of Cities

THE PROGRESSIVE MOVEMENT

EFFECTS

Political	Social	Economic
• Party primaries • Split in Republican party, 1912 • Decline of machine politics • Votes for women	• Laws protecting workers • Settlement houses and social work • Birth control for women • Beginning of civil rights movement for African Americans	• Conservation of land and water • Regulation of business • Lower tariffs • Reformed banking system • Federal income tax

Progressive Movement: Causes and Effects

Suffragists celebrating the Nineteenth Amendment

shortest time. Government regulation of business ceased. After the war, most citizens were more interested in goods and services than reform. As a result, the three conservative Republican presidents after Wilson returned to a policy of laissez-faire.

★ **In Review**

1. Define initiative, referendum, recall, direct primary, and Australian ballot.

2. For each of the following concerns, describe a progressive reform associated with it: (a) consumer safety, (b) trusts, (c) natural resources, (d) tariffs, and (e) banks.

3. Describe the main features of Theodore Roosevelt's Square Deal and Woodrow Wilson's New Freedom.

Chapter Review

MULTIPLE-CHOICE QUESTIONS

Use the cartoon on page 126 to answer questions 1 and 2.

1. The cartoon takes the position that (1) the progressive view of the proper relationship between government and business meets most people's needs (2) laissez-faire is the best means of protecting the public and business from corruption (3) workers should take part in running U.S. corporations (4) a combination of early and late 19th-century business practices is needed for a strong economy.

2. Who would most disagree with the viewpoint of the cartoon? (1) John D. Rockefeller and Andrew Carnegie (2) Samuel Gompers and Eugene Debs (3) Theodore Roosevelt and Robert La Follette (4) Upton Sinclair and Lincoln Steffens.

3. A muckraker is (1) a conservative cartoonist (2) a reporter in the Age of Jackson (3) a Roosevelt conservationist (4) a writer who investigates political corruption.

4. What problem did Elizabeth Cady Stanton and Susan B. Anthony hope to correct? (1) scarcity of free public schools (2) lack of legal and political rights for women (3) inadequate medical care (4) unfair treatment of ethnic minorities.

5. The main purpose of initiative, referendum, and recall is to (1) reduce federal control of local government (2) enlarge citizens' control of state and local governments (3) stimulate economic growth (4) restore the balance between state and federal power.

Use the map on page 133 to answer questions 6 and 7.

6. A conclusion to be drawn from the map is that (1) third parties rarely have political influence (2) the Progressive ("Bull Moose") party received more votes than the Republicans (3) the nation was tired of progressive ideas (4) Roosevelt carried the popular vote but lost the election.

7. An explanation of the election results is that (1) President Taft failed to pursue trust-busting policies (2) Wilson's platform appealed to African Americans for the first time (3) the Republican party split between followers of Taft and Roosevelt (4) people did not want Roosevelt to serve a third term.

Use the chart on page 134 to answer question 8.

8. The chart shows that the Progressive movement was (1) brought about by ambitious politicians from cities and industry (2) primarily a Western rural experience (3) a result of the abuses caused by rapid industrial and urban development (4) started by corporations and political organizations such as the New York Central Railroad and Tammany Hall.

9. What best reflects the beginnings of the civil rights movement for African Americans? (1) passage of antilynching legislation (2) court

decisions outlawing Jim Crow laws (3) President Wilson's policies (4) the work of W. E. B. Du Bois and Booker T. Washington.

10. A chief function of the Federal Reserve System is to (1) make loans to farmers (2) regulate international trade (3) balance the federal budget (4) regulate the amount of money in circulation.

THEMATIC ESSAYS

1. **Theme:** Progressive Era and Reform. The Progressive Era involved broad reforms that had far-reaching effects on the society at large.

   Task: Choose *two* areas in which reform was attempted. For each reform chosen:

   ★ describe the problem trying to be corrected
   ★ show how the reform tried to correct the problem
   ★ evaluate the success of the reform.

   You may wish to include in your answer consumer protection, poverty and immigration, women's rights, and the attempts of African Americans to gain civil rights.

2. **Theme:** Progressive Era and Presidential Power. The Progressive Era was brought about largely through activism by presidents Roosevelt and Wilson.

   Task: Select one example of presidential activism by Roosevelt and another by Wilson.

   ★ Show how each president tried to correct a specific problem. (Do not treat the same problem for both presidents.)
   ★ Demonstrate how each president expanded federal power.

   You may select trust busting and conservation for Roosevelt, and tax reform and monetary policy for Wilson.

DOCUMENT-BASED QUESTION

*Study each document and answer the question that follows it. Then read the **Task** and write your essay. Include references to most of the documents and additional information you retain about U.S. history and government.*

Historical Context: Progressive reforms were a response to many problems resulting from the Civil War, industrialization, and urbanization.

Document 1: From *Lochner* v. *New York* (1905):

Statutes . . . [that limit] hours in which grown and intelligent men may . . . earn their living, . . . [meddle with] rights of the individual, and [cannot be defended] by the claim that they are passed in the exercise of the police power and upon the subject of [an individual's] health . . . , unless there be some fair ground . . . to say that there is material danger to the public health, or to the health of the employees, if the hours . . . are not curtailed.

Question: Why did the Supreme Court declare the New York State law limiting bakers' hours unconstitutional?

Document 2: From *Muller* v. *Oregon* (1908):

. . . as healthy mothers are essential to vigorous offspring, the physical well-being of woman becomes an object of public interest and care in order to preserve the strength and vigor of the race. . . .

. . . Differentiated by these matters from the other sex, she is properly placed in a class by herself and legislation designed for her protection may be sustained, even when [it] is not necessary for men . . . .

Question: Why did the Supreme Court protect female workers?

Document 3: Refer to the excerpt from Upton Sinclair's *The Jungle* on pages 127–128.

Question: What was Sinclair telling his readers about the meatpacking industry?

Document 4: Refer to the cartoon on page 128.

Question: Why does the cartoonist feel that cholera might spread?

Document 5: Refer to the graph on page 129.

Question: How does the graph show *both* progress and problems for African Americans between 1890 and 1910?

Document 6: Refer to the cartoon on page 131.

Question: How does the cartoon show what President Roosevelt did about "bad trusts"?

Task

★ Describe two problems existing at the end of the 19th and beginning of the 20th century?
★ Choose one problem you selected and show to what extent it was solved or remained a problem.

Chapter 11
Rise of American Power

★ Documents and Laws	★ Events	★ People
Monroe Doctrine (1823)	Acquisition of Hawaii (1898)	Venustiano Carranza
"Open Door" Notes (1899–1900)	Sinking of the *Maine* (1898)	Grover Cleveland
Foraker Act (1900)	Spanish-American War (1898)	Dupuy de Lôme
Platt Amendment (1901)	Battle of Manila Bay (1898)	George Dewey
Roosevelt Corollary (1904)	Battles of San Juan Hill and El Caney (1898)	Cyrus Field
Fourteen Points (1918)	Boxer Rebellion (1900)	George W. Goethals
Schenck v. *United States* (1919)	Russo-Japanese War (1904–1905)	William C. Gorgas
Treaty of Versailles (1919)	Construction of Panama Canal (1907–1914)	Warren G. Harding
Kellogg-Briand Pact (1928)	U.S. intervention in Haiti and Dominican Republic (1915-1934)	John Hay
	Assassination of Archduke Francis Ferdinand (1914)	William Randolph Hearst
	World War I (1914-1918)	Oliver Wendell Holmes
	Sinking of the *Lusitania* (1915)	Victoriano Huerta
	Russian Revolution (1917)	William McKinley
	Zimmermann Telegram (1917)	Alfred Thayer Mahan
	League of Nations established (1920)	John J. Pershing
	Washington Naval Conference (1921–1922)	Joseph Pulitzer
	Statehood for Hawaii (1959)	Theodore Roosevelt
		Josiah Strong
		William H. Taft
		Pancho Villa
		Woodrow Wilson

★ To analyze reasons for U.S. involvement in Asia and Latin America, 1890–1920.

★ To evaluate arguments for and against U.S. intervention in Latin America.

★ To identify causes of World War I.

★ To explain why U.S. foreign policy changed from neutrality to involvement.

★ To understand how war affected the civil liberties of Americans.

★ To evaluate U.S. contributions to peace after the war.

New U.S. Power and Diplomacy (1865–1900)

Communications Technology

Before the Civil War, the telegraph and Morse Code led to speedier long-distance communication. After the war, Cyrus Field successfully completed a transatlantic cable. As rapid messages between the United States and Europe became possible, the two continents seemed closer than ever.

Attitudes Toward an International Role

After industrialization, U.S. leaders considered a policy of imperialism.

Arguments for Expansion

★ *Economics.* As the frontier disappeared, business leaders looked for new markets and investment opportunities abroad. Belief in manifest destiny (see page 71) justified increasing the U.S. role in world affairs.

★ *Culture.* Many Protestant ministers, Josiah Strong among them, argued that undeveloped regions would benefit from contact with advanced Western civilization. Their belief that Christianity and American civilization were linked benefits was based on a variation of social Darwinism—superior nations and cultures survive while weaker ones die out.

★ *Strategy.* In the 1890s, Alfred Thayer Mahan, a U.S. naval captain, pointed out that U.S. security depended on having a strong navy like Britain's. Because ships were powered by coal, the nation had to establish strategic island bases in the Atlantic and Pacific where ships could pick up coal. Moreover, increased U.S. trade with Asia and Latin America would require naval protection against rivals.

Arguments Against Expansion

★ *Morality.* Some Americans felt that the cause of democracy would suffer from a U.S. takeover of foreign lands and their people. Many also believed that manifest destiny had rightly ended with American expansion to the Pacific Ocean.

★ *Practicality.* Some Americans feared that foreign involvement would lead to foreign wars. Such wars would do more to harm than help overseas trade.

"Opening" of Japan (1854)

Japan had avoided trading with the West. In 1853, however, Commodore Matthew Perry arrived there with a U.S. fleet. To persuade the Japanese to open trade and assist shipwrecked U.S. sailors, he gave gifts exemplifying industrial technology and fired the fleet's guns as a show of force.

In 1854, Japan signed a trade treaty with the United States. Soon afterwards, new Japanese leadership, eager to industrialize the nation, asked about Western technologies.

Imperialism and China

Japan's 1895 defeat of China in the *Sino-Japanese War* showed two things: China could not withstand imperialism, and the newly industrialized Japan was a major power in East Asia. Japan then occupied Korea and the Chinese island of Taiwan and won economic control of Manchuria in northern China.

Manchuria became a Japanese **sphere of influence** (area dominated by an imperialistic power). Russia disputed Japan's control of Man-

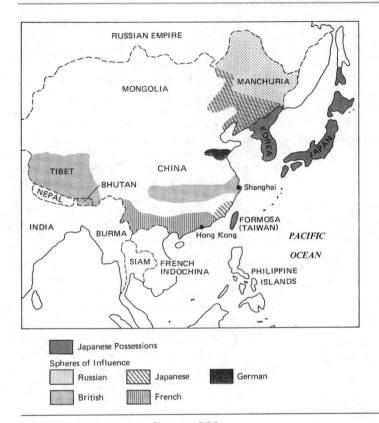

RUSSIAN EMPIRE

MONGOLIA

MANCHURIA

KOREA

JAPAN

TIBET

BHUTAN

NEPAL

CHINA

Shanghai

INDIA

BURMA

Hong Kong

FORMOSA
(TAIWAN)

PACIFIC

OCEAN

SIAM

FRENCH
INDOCHINA

PHILIPPINE
ISLANDS

■ Japanese Possessions

Spheres of Influence

▨ Russian ▨ Japanese ■ German

▨ British ▨ French

Spheres of Influence in China, 1900

churia until 1904, when Japan defeated Russia in the *Russo-Japanese War.*

Other Spheres of Influence France, Germany, Russia, and Great Britain also forced China to grant them spheres of influence. The U.S. government feared that its trade with China might be cut off.

"Open Door" Notes U.S. Secretary of State John Hay, therefore, wrote two diplomatic notes. In one (1899), he asked the European powers and Japan to agree to an *Open Door Policy*; all nations would have "equal trading rights" in China and pay equal port fees and taxes. In the second note (1900), he suggested that all powers in East Asia respect China's **territorial integrity**; that is, no nation would compel China to give up control of any territory.

The U.S. government maintained this policy until the early 1940s, when Japanese troops occupied much of China.

Boxer Rebellion Many Chinese, resentful of Western imperialism, joined a secret terrorist or-

ganization, the Boxers. In 1900, they attacked Westerners and their embassies to drive the "foreign devils" from China. Many Christian missionaries, including some Americans, lost their lives. To rescue those trapped in the capital of Peking (now Beijing), the United States, Japan, and the European powers formed an international army and crushed the *Boxer Rebellion.*

Most of the victors threatened China with harsh terms and demanded an **indemnity** (payment to cover damages and deaths). The United States remained committed to territorial integrity of China and insisted that the others do likewise. It also returned its portion of the indemnity, which so impressed China's government that it applied the money to scholarships for Chinese students attending U.S. colleges and universities.

Other Pacific Overtures

Acquisition of Hawaii In 1893, a group of American sugar growers in Hawaii, helped by U.S. marines, overthrew Queen Liliuokalani. President Grover Cleveland opposed imperialism and rejected a plan to turn Hawaii over to the United States. In 1898, however, President William McKinley pushed to make Hawaii a U.S. territory.

Naval Bases in Samoa Samoa is a group of Pacific islands far southwest of Hawaii. The United States, Germany, and Britain all wanted Samoa as a naval base. In the 1880s, Germany and the United States almost went to war over Samoa.

Spanish-American War

In 1895, Cubans rebelled against Spanish rule. Three years later, the United States sided with Cuba by declaring war against Spain. The swift and decisive U.S. victory demonstrated American military and economic power.

Causes

American sympathy for Cuban rebels played a large role in bringing about the war. Several factors accounted for that sympathy.

Yellow Journalism Hearst's and Pulitzer's New York City newspapers specialized in yellow journalism (see page 127). Both publishers sensationalized the conflict in Cuba. Reporters described, and sometimes exaggerated, the terrible suffering of Cubans and the brutal acts of Valeriano Weyler, a Spanish general nicknamed "Butcher" Weyler.

De Lôme Letter Early in 1898, Hearst's *New York Journal* printed a stolen letter written by the Spanish minister to the United States, Dupuy de Lôme. Its description of President McKinley as "weak and a bidder for the admiration of the crowd" outraged many Americans.

Sinking of the *Maine* A few days later, the U.S.S. *Maine*, a battleship anchored in the harbor of Havana, Cuba, exploded and sank, killing abut 250 of the crew. The cause was never discovered, but the newspapers suggested Spain's guilt. Editorials called for U.S. liberation of Cuba from Spain.

Additional Reasons

★ *Strategy*. Military and naval planners saw in Cuba an ideal naval base for U.S. ships, and they argued that an island 90 miles from Florida should not belong to a European power.

★ *Economics*. By replacing a hostile Spanish government with a friendly Cuban one, Americans could protect their $50 million of investments in Cuba's sugar and tobacco plantations.

Decision for War

Some U.S. business leaders feared that the war might destroy American-owned properties in Cuba. Moreover, after the sinking of the *Maine*, Spain had agreed to all U.S. demands, including Cuba's eventual independence. Nevertheless, Pres-

Cuba as a pawn in the U.S.-Spanish power play

ident McKinley decided that most Americans wanted war and persuaded Congress to declare war against Spain in April 1898.

"Splendid Little War"

The *Spanish-American War* lasted four months, and the United States won every major battle. One American called it a "splendid little war."

In Cuba, the Rough Riders, led by Theodore Roosevelt, won instant glory by charging up San Juan Hill. African Americans took part in the charge and also spearheaded another attack in El Caney. The battles of San Juan Hill and El Caney forced the Spanish surrender of the port of Santiago. Neighboring Puerto Rico—a Spanish island colony since 1508—also fell to the Americans.

In the Pacific, the U.S. Navy under Commodore George Dewey decisively defeated the Spanish fleet in Manila Bay, the Philippines. Filipinos—like Cubans—had already been fighting for independence from Spain. After Manila Bay, they were bitterly disappointed by the U.S.-Spanish peace treaty.

Results of the War

The terms of the treaty, signed in December 1898, were as follows:

★ The United States gained Puerto Rico in the Caribbean and Guam in the Pacific.

★ Spain granted Cuba independence.

★ Spain sold the Philippines to the United States for $20 million.

Puerto Rico For economic reasons, Puerto Rico wanted to be part of the U.S. empire. The *Foraker Act* (1900), allowed Puerto Ricans to elect their legislators, but their governor was appointed by the president.

Cuba The U.S. position on Cuba's independence was unclear. McKinley and Congress finally decided to allow it under conditions listed in the *Platt Amendment* (1901):

★ Cuba would sell or lease a piece of land for use as a U.S. naval and coaling station.

★ Cuba would permit no other power to acquire Cuban territory.

★ Cuba would allow U.S. intervention to protect American citizens in Cuba.

Cubans strongly protested these terms but finally accepted them when the United States made them firm conditions for removing its troops.

Debate About the Philippines

Some Americans wanted the Philippines to become a U.S. territory. Others wanted to see the islands independent.

Anti-Imperialist Argument William Jennings Bryan led those who favored Filipino independence. These anti-imperialists warned that the United States would abandon its commitment to democracy by ruling overseas territory. And they feared that possession of Asian islands would lead to involvement in Asian politics and wars.

Imperialist Argument Imperialists, including Theodore Roosevelt, argued that acquisition of Pacific islands would ensure the U.S. reputation as a great world power. They also felt that the Philippines were likely to fall under some foreign influence and that U.S. control would be more democratic than control by Germany or Russia.

Filipino Rebellion Unwilling to trade one colonial power for another, Philippine rebels rose up against U.S. forces in 1899. McKinley sent in 70,000 additional troops. After nearly three years of fighting, U.S. troops finally forced the last rebel band to surrender in 1902.

Disposition of Territories

As a result of U.S. actions in the late 1800s and the Spanish-American War, the following territorial changes had taken place:

★ In 1900, a treaty for the annexation of Hawaii was approved by the Senate. (Hawaii became the 50th state in 1959.)

★ In the late 1890s, Germany and the United States agreed to divide Samoa, each taking control of different islands.

★ Cuba became a U.S. **protectorate** (nation whose foreign policy is partly controlled by a foreign power).

★ The Philippines remained a U.S. territory until July 4, 1946, when it gained independence.

Constitutional Issues

Did citizens of colonial U.S. territories have the same rights as American citizens, including the right to protection? In the *Insular Cases*, the Supreme Court in 1901 ruled that the Constitution did not fully apply to possessions. The extent to which it did apply would be determined by Congress.

Latin American Affairs

Interventions by Roosevelt, Taft, and Wilson (1900–1920)

Roosevelt Corollary to the Monroe Doctrine Implied in the Monroe Doctrine of 1823 was the idea that the United States would protect Latin America from outside interference (see page 50). Also implied was the U.S. right to send troops into a threatened country there. The Platt Amendment making Cuba a protectorate was one example.

Roosevelt added a corollary (logical extension) to the Monroe Doctrine when several Latin American countries failed to repay funds borrowed from Britain, Germany, and other European nations. Roosevelt, fearing that the Europeans might use the debts as an excuse for taking over Latin American territory, announced that the United States might intervene in Latin America when debts were overdue. The *Roosevelt Corollary* read:

> Chronic wrongdoing may in America, as elsewhere, ultimately require intervention. In the Western Hemisphere the adherence of the United States to the Monroe Doctrine may force the United States, however reluctantly, in flagrant cases of such wrongdoing . . . to the exercise of an international police power.

Many Latin Americans saw in this an unfair expansion of U.S. military power into their affairs—not for their protection but to maintain U.S. dominance.

West Indies Protectorates Applying his corollary in 1904, President Roosevelt sent troops to the Dominican Republican, an island nation in the Caribbean. The troops stayed until the Dominican Republic paid its debts.

Haiti, which shared the same island, was also treated as an American protectorate.

Roosevelt and the Panama Canal

Intervention is a policy by which a nation's military and naval power achieves its political goals. Roosevelt used this policy to build the Panama Canal.

Early Attempts In the 1850s, there were vague but ambitious plans to dig a canal through the Isthmus of Panama, a 30-mile strip of Central American land between the Atlantic and Pacific oceans. Such a canal would cut in half sailing time from New York to San Francisco, help inter-

The United States (Theodore Roosevelt) as the world's policeman

national trade, and eliminate the dangerous voyage around the tip of South America. Jungle diseases and inadequate funds frustrated a French attempt to construct a canal in the 1880s.

Quarrel With Colombia When Roosevelt became president in 1901, he was eager to begin a canal through Nicaragua or Panama, a province of Colombia. Preferring the Panama route, he offered Colombia $10 million to lease the land. Colombia's refusal angered Roosevelt, who, in 1903, decided to support a Panamanian rebellion.

Acquisition The uprising lasted only a few hours. U.S. naval forces blocked Colombian interference, and Roosevelt immediately recognized the new Republic of Panama, which quickly agreed to U.S. terms for a canal zone. Work began soon afterward.

Evaluating Roosevelt's Intervention Roosevelt boasted: "I took Panama," but Colombians called the move imperialist robbery. Years later, President Woodrow Wilson persuaded Congress to award Colombia $25 million in compensation.

Construction Construction of the canal began in 1907. A marvel of the 20th century, it was supervised by George W. Goethals, an army engineer. A 10-mile-wide strip of jungle had to be cleared, a huge dam built to control the canal's water level, and towns raised for workers.

Two mosquito-transmitted diseases—malaria and yellow fever—threatened the enterprise. Dr. William C. Gorgas, who had curbed the breeding of deadly mosquitoes in Cuba during the Spanish-American War, came to Panama. Although he saved many lives, thousands died of malaria and yellow fever—most of them African Americans (they accounted for 4500 of the 5500 canal workers).

Taft's Dollar Diplomacy

President William H. Taft believed that the United States should protect its business investments in Latin America and that the United States had the right to force a Latin American country to repay its debts. This policy, called *dollar diplomacy*, resulted in U.S. intervention in Nicaragua in 1912, where civil war threatened to prevent repayment of a large U.S. loan.

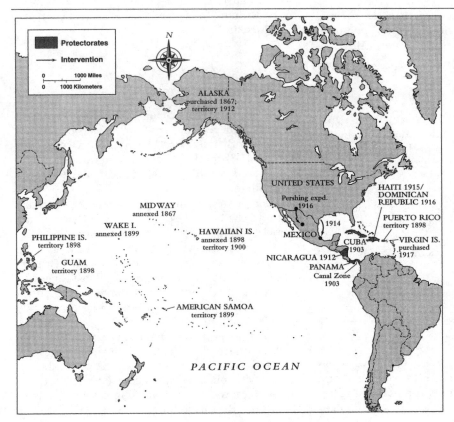

U.S. Territories and Protectorates, 1917

Wilson's Continued Intervention

President Woodrow Wilson disavowed dollar diplomacy but believed in keeping order in areas near the United States. In 1915, he sent marines to quell a civil war in Haiti. Two years later, he intervened in the Dominican Republic for the same reason. The Dominican Republic remained occupied until 1925 and Haiti until 1934. Latin Americans deeply resented such interventions.

Wilson distrusted the ruthless Mexican dictator Victoriano Huerta. Instead of recognizing Huerta's government, Wilson followed a policy of *Watchful Waiting* to see if Huerta would be overthrown.

In 1914, several U.S. sailors in Mexico were jailed, which gave Wilson a reason to take action against Huerta. U.S. occupation of the Mexican port of Vera Cruz greatly offended both Huerta and his enemies. Wilson withdrew the troops after the "ABC Powers" (Argentina, Brazil, and Chile) urged Huerta to resign. The new Mexican president, Venustiano Carranza, was immediately challenged by rebels under Pancho Villa.

In 1916, Villa raided a town in New Mexico, killing 19 Americans. A punitive expedition entered northern Mexico, but war was averted when Wilson withdrew the troops in 1917 and recognized the Carranza government. Bitter memories of these U.S. interventions led to poor Mexican-U.S. relations for many years.

★ In Review

1. Define sphere of influence, Open Door Policy, Boxer Rebellion, de Lôme Letter, Platt Amendment, anti-imperialist, protectorate, Roosevelt Corollary, and Watchful Waiting.
2. Evaluate (a) the U.S. decision to go to war with Spain and (b) the U.S. decision to take possession of the Philippines.
3. Describe Latin American reaction to U.S. intervention in Mexico, Nicaragua, and Haiti.

World War I

Long-Range Causes

The long-range causes of World War I were: nationalism, imperialism, and **militarism** (nation's policy of glorifying its armed forces and aggressive spirit). In addition, a system of alliances made it likely that a war between two European nations would grow into a larger war involving the allies of each nation.

Before 1914, tensions between rival European powers had been building. Britain worried about Germany's colonial ambitions, strong navy, and growing industrial strength. Austria-Hungary worried about rebellious Serbs and other Slavs within its empire—and, especially, about Russia's support of Serbia. Russia worried about Germany's support for Austria-Hungary.

Short-Range Causes

The immediate cause of World War I was the assassination in June 1914 of heir to the Austro-Hungarian throne Archduke Francis Ferdinand and his wife in Sarajevo (present-day capital of Bosnia-Herzegovina). The assassin was a Serbian terrorist committed to independence for Serbs within the empire.

Austria-Hungary presented Serbia with an **ultimatum** (final demands). Even though Serbia mostly agreed, Austria-Hungary declared war.

The allies of each side became involved. By early August, all major powers in Europe were at war—Britain, Russia, and France against Germany and Austria-Hungary.

Neutrality (1914–1916) and "Preparedness"

In 1914, most Americans, including President Wilson, believed that the war in Europe did not involve U.S. interests. The Atlantic Ocean shut them off from European problems. Many remembered Washington's advice against permanent alliances.

As a neutral country, the United States traded with all the countries of Europe. A German victory largely depended on keeping supplies from its enemies. German submarines began sinking passenger and merchant ships nearing Britain. Many carried American cargo and passengers.

In May 1915, a German submarine torpedoed the British liner *Lusitania*, and more than 1,000 people, including 128 Americans, were killed. Wilson's protests persuaded Germany to stop sinking unarmed ships without warning.

After German submarines sank a number of passenger ships, Wilson accepted the need for "preparedness." He asked Congress for funds to build up the armed forces and established a

Council of National Defense to increase cooperation between the military and private industry.

Long-Range Causes of U.S. Involvement

Sympathy for Britain and France Most Americans felt strong ties to Britain and France—a common language with Britain and memories of French aid during the Revolutionary War. Both countries also had democratic governments while Germany and Austria-Hungary were directly ruled by monarchs. Moreover, most U.S. trade during the period of neutrality was with Britain and France.

Fear of German Power U.S. military leaders worried about American security and trade if Germany controlled the Atlantic Ocean. Would Germany then hesitate to intervene in South America?

British and French Propaganda Germany's military aggressiveness was stressed by British and French **propaganda** (facts, ideas, and rumors spread to help one cause and harm an opposing one). Invented stories of German cruelty were widely reprinted in U.S. newspapers.

Conditions in Europe By the end of 1916, millions of soldiers had died from artillery fire, poison gas, tank attacks, and machine-gun bullets, without significant gains on either side. Civilians suffered as much as soldiers. The Germans and Russians were near starvation.

Short-Range Causes of U.S. Involvement

Submarine Warfare In January 1917, Germany announced a renewal of submarine attacks without warning in British waters. Germany knew that it risked provoking U.S. entry on Britain's side but hoped to win the war before U.S. troops could be trained for combat.

Zimmermann Telegram The German foreign secretary, Arthur Zimmermann, telegraphed a German diplomat in Mexico with the message that Germany might help Mexico regain lost territories in the American Southwest if Germany and Mexico both declared war on the United States. After the telegram was intercepted and published in American newspapers, anger toward Germany soared.

Revolution in Russia In March 1917, the terrible suffering in Russia led to the overthrow of the czar, who was replaced by a constitutional government. Thus, Wilson felt that he could lead the United States to war on the side of democracies.

Decision for War

In April 1917, Wilson, arguing that "the world must be made safe for democracy," asked Congress for a declaration of war against Germany. Congress voted almost unanimously for the declaration.

Mobilization

Wilson recognized that all the nation's resources had to be a part of the national war effort. For an entire year after the U.S. entry into the war, its main contributions to the Allies were large supplies of food, guns, ships, airplanes, and other goods.

Factories Business leaders were asked to coordinate the war effort. Bernard Baruch headed the new *War Industries Board*. He told thousands of

In a 1917 cartoon, Germany's kaiser honors Senator La Follette for his antiwar stance.

corporation presidents how to convert their products and methods to wartime needs, and American factories produced vast quantities of war materials.

Food Supply Herbert Hoover, head of the *Food Administration*, sent out pamphlets explaining how to save food badly needed by the British. Americans responded by having a "meatless" day and "wheatless" day every week.

Jobs for Women and Minorities As young men entered the armed forces, women took their places in shipyards and factories. African Americans, who had begun to migrate North before the war, were drawn in increasing numbers by new wartime job opportunities.

Between 1917 and 1920, about 100,000 Mexicans settled permanently in Texas, New Mexico, Arizona, and California to replace enlisted Americans as farm workers.

Fighting the War

Weapons New weapons included (1) machine guns, (2) poison gas carried by the wind, (3) armored tanks, (4) submarines, and (5) airplanes that fought one another in the sky and detected enemy positions on the ground.

Final Campaigns and Armistice In 1918, large numbers of U.S. soldiers, led by General John J. Pershing, were sent to combat in France. After several months, they began to play a major role in forcing a German retreat. The Allied push continued until Germany was defeated and signed an armistice conceding defeat on November 11, 1918.

United States and the Russian Revolution

In November 1917, a second revolution in Russia overthrew the new democratic government. The new revolutionaries were Bolsheviks, or Communists. They ended Russian suffering by making peace with Germany, thus enabling Germany and Austria-Hungary to concentrate their strength on the Western Front.

In 1918, U.S. troops went to the aid of Russian forces known as the "Whites" in their attempt to overthrow the new Communist government of the "Reds." The U.S. troops failed and withdrew.

In 1921, Herbert Hoover organized a program to send millions of tons of food to help the starving Russians.

In 1922, the Communist government in Russia renamed the country the Soviet Union.

★ In Review

1. Describe the U.S. response to Germany's submarine policy from 1915 to 1917.
2. Identify the two causes of U.S. involvement in World War I that you think were most important. Explain each choice.
3. Describe the effects of U.S. participation in the war on (a) women and minorities and (b) industry.

Wartime Constitutional Issues

Most Americans supported the war, but a few **dissenters** openly disagreed and refused to cooperate. The First Amendment protects a person's rights to speak on any issue in peacetime. When national security is at stake, however, the Constitution may be interpreted differently.

Draft Issue

An army can be recruited by (a) calling for volunteers and (b) compelling service by a draft of persons from every social class and ethnic group.

Wilson, believing that the draft was more efficient and democratic, asked Congress to pass the *Selective Service Act* in May 1917. All male citizens aged 21 to 30 were required to register. Those who passed a medical examination were required to serve.

Some opposed the draft as a threat to democracy and a step toward militarism. Many socialists and anarchists thought war was a capitalist scheme to make money. Still others—**pacifists**—regarded war as legalized murder.

Espionage and Sedition Acts

Congress passed the *Espionage Act* (1917) and the *Sedition Act* (1918). They imposed heavy fines and prison sentences for (1) spying and aiding the enemy, (2) interfering with recruitment, (3) speaking against the sale of government bonds, (4) urging resistance to U.S. laws, and (5) using "disloyal, profane, scurrilous, or abusive language" about the government, flag, or military

In a 1917 poster, Uncle Sam backs up the draft.

uniform. In addition, the U.S. Post Office was empowered to remove antiwar materials from the mails.

About 1,500 dissenters were arrested. The socialist Eugene Debs was sentenced to ten years in prison for antiwar speech. The anarchist Emma Goldman received a two-year prison term for antiwar activities.

Schenck v. United States

Another jailed dissenter, Charles Schenck, had mailed leaflets urging draftees to refuse to serve. Convicted of violating the Espionage Act, Schenck appealed to the Supreme Court, arguing that his First Amendment rights to freedom of speech had been denied.

In *Schenck* v. *United States* (1919), the Court ruled against Schenck. Justice Oliver Wendell Holmes noted that speech must be judged according to circumstances. Thus, the First Amendment "would not protect a man in falsely shouting fire in a theatre and causing a panic." The question to be asked was whether speech posed "clear and present danger" to the public.

Postwar Peace and Arms Control

Fourteen Points

In January 1918, Wilson announced *Fourteen Points* that he considered integral to any peace settlement. The key features were:

★ end to secret treaties
★ freedom of the seas for all nations in peace and war
★ reduction of weapons
★ **self-determination** in Europe, whereby people with a common culture could unite as an independent nation
★ establishment of a *League of Nations* to resolve international disputes
★ placing European colonies in Africa, Asia, and Latin America under the League's control.

Treaty of Versailles

Wilson sailed to France to meet with the Allied leaders and negotiate a peace treaty. The discussions took place in the palace of Versailles, near Paris.

Allies' Revenge The British, French, and Italian leaders wanted to punish Germany and Austria-Hungary. They were determined that Germany remain weak militarily and pay heavy war damages.

Treaty Provisions The *Treaty of Versailles* contained the following provisions:

★ Alsace-Lorraine, seized by Germany in 1871, would be returned to France.
★ Poland would be independent and gain from Germany the Polish Corridor, a strip of land connecting Poland to the Baltic Sea.
★ Germany would lose its colonies, including Cameroon, German West Africa, and German East Africa.
★ Germany's Saar Basin, a major coal-producing region, would be controlled by France for 15 years.
★ Germany would pay huge reparations.
★ Germany would disband its armed forces.
★ Germany would be forbidden to manufacture and import war materials.
★ Germany would accept full responsibility for the war.

★ The League of Nations would be created to reduce the chance of future wars.

A separate treaty with Austria ended the Austro-Hungarian Empire, reduced Austrian territory, and created several new nations, including Hungary.

Analysis Wilson regarded the treaty as harsh and at odds with his Fourteen Points. He was somewhat appeased that formation of the League of Nations was part of the treaty.

League of Nations

All U.S. treaties must be approved in the Senate by a two-thirds vote. Wilson's Democratic party generally supported the Versailles treaty, but many Republican senators feared that a clause concerning the League of Nations might draw the United States into a war that Congress had not voted for. Opponents of the treaty included (a) isolationists, who felt that it involved too many commitments abroad and (b) reservationists, who would accept the treaty only if it contained some modifying clauses. Senator Henry Cabot Lodge, an opponent of Wilson's, was the leading Republican reservationist.

Votes in the Senate In 1920, a majority voted in favor of Senator Lodge's reservations. The form of the treaty did not win two-thirds approval, because Wilson instructed Democrats to vote against it. A vote for the treaty without reservations also failed.

The United States thus also rejected the League of Nations. A separate U.S. peace treaty with Germany was signed by Republican president Warren Harding in 1921. It contained nothing about the League of Nations and was approved by the Senate.

U.S. Postwar Foreign Policy

Washington Naval Disarmament Conference President Harding called the *Washington Conference* (1921–1922) to reduce international military rivalry. The United States and other naval powers agreed to limits on ship construction according to the following ratio: United States (5), Great Britain (5), Japan (3), France (1.67), Italy (1.67). The ratios helped reduce U.S. and British expenses but did not limit potentially dangerous competition among the naval powers. Japan had wanted full **parity** (equality) with its Western rivals and, in the 1930s, ignored the agreed limits

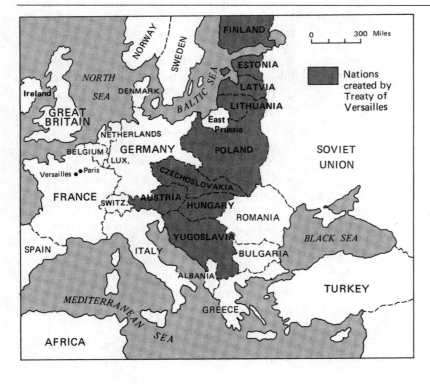

New Nations
of Eastern Europe, 1919

1918 cartoon "Interrupting the Ceremony": U.S. congressional opposition to Wilson and the League of Nations

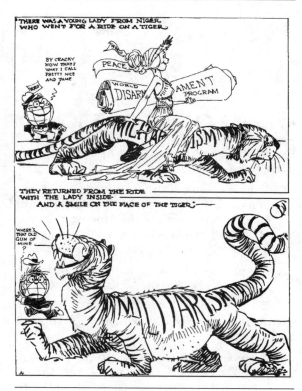

1926 cartoon depicting hopes for world disarmament swallowed up by the tiger of militarism

by building a navy strong enough to challenge both U.S. and British forces.

Reparations and War Debts The Allies fixed German reparations at $33 billion. The United States was unable to propose a more reasonable sum because its new policy of isolationism did not allow it to participate.

The European Allies had borrowed more than $10 billion from the United States to purchase war materials for the conflict. Thus, the United States in the 1920s became the world's greatest creditor nation (one to which debts are owed). France, for one, argued that its debts should be canceled since it had lost more lives and fought longer than the Americans. U.S. presidents, however, insisted on a sizable repayment of Allied debt.

Kellogg-Briand Pact In 1928, the United States signed the *Kellogg-Briand Pact*, by which participating nations agreed to "renounce war as an instrument of national policy." Unfortunately, it was unenforceable because it contained no requirement that the signers had to act against aggression.

World Court The Permanent Court of International Justice, or World Court, was a branch of the League of Nations. Nations could settle disputes peacefully by arguing their cases before the Court's judges. The United States could have joined the World Court without joining the League, but isolationist senators feared that even an "advisory opinion" of the Court might draw the United States into a war.

★ In Review

1. Explain the significance of: the draft, dissenters, *Schenck* v. *United States*, self-determination.
2. What factors contributed to the Senate's failure to ratify the Treaty of Versailles?
3. To what extent did the Treaty of Versailles and postwar diplomacy reflect Wilson's principles?

Chapter Review

MULTIPLE-CHOICE QUESTIONS

Use the cartoon on page 142 to answer questions 1 and 2.

1. The cartoon shows that in 1905, the United States was (1) neutral (2) warring with European violators of the Monroe Doctrine (3) settling disputes between nations (4) limiting foreign involvement to Latin America.

2. The president in the cartoon is (1) Theodore Roosevelt (2) William McKinley (3) Grover Cleveland (4) Woodrow Wilson.

Use the map on page 139 to answer questions 3 and 4.

3. The map shows that, at the time when Hay issued the Open Door notes, the United States (1) was very involved in China (2) controlled Japan (3) had no sphere of influence in China (4) planned to set up shipping between the Philippines and Shanghai.

4. The map shows that one Boxer grievance was (1) Chinese isolation (2) foreign dominance (3) decreased trade with the United States (4) disputes over the border with Korea.

Use the cartoon on page 140 to answer question 5.

5. The main idea is that (1) the United States was correcting Spanish atrocities (2) the United States should not have defended Cuban revolutionaries (3) the United States was attacking Spain (4) neither Spain nor the United States was truly interested in improving life in Cuba.

Base your answers to questions 6 and 7 on the statements of the following speakers:

Speaker A: By our genius and growth in power, we have become a determining factor in history; after that happens, you cannot remain isolated.

Speaker B: Wars between nations come from contact. A nation with which we have no contact is a nation we should never fight.

Speaker C: Nations must respect the territorial integrity and political independence of others.

Speaker D: We cannot meddle in Europe and expect that Europe will not meddle with us.

6. Which speakers would most agree with establishing the League of Nations? (1) Speakers A and D (2) Speakers B and C (3) Speakers A and C (4) Speakers C and D.

7. Which speakers would endorse isolationism? (1) Speakers A and B (2) Speakers C and D (3) Speakers A and D (4) Speakers B and D.

Use the cartoon on the left of page 149 to answer questions 8 and 9.

8. The cartoon illustrates that (1) there was widespread U.S. support for the League of Nations (2) Congress opposed U.S. membership (3) many foreigners immigrated by marrying U.S. soldiers (4) in 1918, the federal government took over the state power of creating marriage laws.

9. Which constitutional principal is at issue? (1) federalism (2) unwritten constitution (3) judicial review (4) checks and balances.

Use the cartoon on the right of page 149 to answer question 10.

10. The artist feels that (1) there should be more attention to wildlife conservation (2) attempts at disarmament were unsuccessful (3) armies cannot be controlled (4) since peace is impossible, each nation should maintain a large army.

THEMATIC ESSAYS

1. **Theme:** Spanish-American War. The war was, to a great extent, a "newspaperman's war," which led to acquisition of overseas territory.

   Task

   ★ Describe how newspapers influenced the U.S. government to declare war on Spain.

★ Explain how the results of the war represented a second phase of manifest destiny.

2. **Theme:** Emerging U.S. Global Involvement. Overseas involvement took place mainly in Latin America, the Caribbean, and Asia.

Task: Select one example of overseas involvement in Latin America or the Caribbean and another in Asia. For each example:

★ describe circumstances leading to involvement

★ show whether the involvement had a positive or a negative impact on each area chosen.

You may use, but are not limited to, Panama, the "big stick," and dollar diplomacy for Latin America and the Caribbean; Commodore Perry, the Open Door Policy, and acquisition of the Philippines for Asia.

DOCUMENT-BASED QUESTION

*Study each document and answer the question that follows it. Then read the **Task** and write your essay. Include references to most of the documents and additional information you retain about U.S. history and government.*

Historical Context: U.S. entry into World War I marked a consensus among citizens unprecedented in U.S. history.

Document 1: Refer to the poster on page 147.

Question: How did the poster encourage young men to support the war?

Document 2: Senator Robert La Follette in the *Congressional Record*, 1917:

The President proposes alliance with Great Britain . . . a hereditary monarchy . . . ruler . . . House of Lords . . . landed system, with a limited . . . suffrage for one class and a multiplied suffrage . . . for another, and with grinding industrial conditions for all the wageworkers. The President has not suggested that we make our support . . . conditional [on home rule in] Ireland, or Egypt, or India. We rejoice in . . . democracy in Russia, but [if Russia were still autocratic] we would [still] be asked to [ally] with her . . . . [All] of the countries with whom we are to enter into alliance, except France and . . . Russia, are still of the old order. . . .

. . . This war is being forced upon our people without their knowing why and without their approval.

Question: Why does Senator La Follette oppose U.S. entry into the war?

Document 3: Refer to the cartoon on page 145.

Question: How does the cartoonist feel about Senator La Follette's opposition?

Document 4: From a release by George Creel, Director of the U.S. Committee for Public Information, 1918:

Now let us picture what a sudden invasion . . . by these Germans would mean . . . .

. . . While their fleet blockades the harbor [of New York City] and shells the city . . . their troops . . . advance toward the city in order to cut its rail communications, starve it into surrender and plunder it. . . .

. . . They pass through Lakewood . . . New Jersey . . . demanding wine . . . and beer . . . they pillage and burn . . . they demand $1,000,000 . . . One feeble old woman tries to conceal $20 . . . she is taken out and hanged . . . The Catholic priest and Methodist minister are thrown into a pig-sty . . . officers quarter themselves in a handsome house . . . insult the ladies of the family, and destroy and defile the contents of the house.

. . . Robbery, murder, and outrage run riot. Most of the town and beautiful pinewoods are burned, and then the troops move on to treat New Brunswick in the same way. . . .

This is not just a snappy story. . . The general plan . . . has been announced repeatedly by German military men. *And every horrible detail is just what the German troops have done in Belgium and France.*

Question: What is Creel saying could happen if Germany invades the United States?

Task

★ Describe how the U.S. government promoted and encouraged conformity to make victory in World War I more likely.

★ Explain how some people opposed to the war were treated.

UNIT IV
Prosperity and Depression

Chapter 12
War and Prosperity: 1917–1929

★ Documents and Laws	★ Events	★ People
Eighteenth Amendment (1919)	Harlem Renaissance (1920s)	Calvin Coolidge
Nineteenth Amendment (1920)	Sacco-Vanzetti case	Countee Cullen
Village of Euclid, Ohio v.	(1921–1927)	F. Scott Fitzgerald
Ambler Realty Company	Scopes trial (1925)	Henry Ford
(1926)		Sigmund Freud
Twenty-first Amendment		Warren G. Harding
(Repeal) (1933)		Ernest Hemingway
		Langston Hughes
		James Weldon Johnson
		Sinclair Lewis
		Carrie Nation
		Paul Robeson
		Edith Wharton

★ To describe social changes in the 1920s.

★ To examine positive and negative changes in the lives of women, African Americans, and other minorities.

★ To examine the economic policies of the 1920s.

★ To understand the effects of mass consumption on cultural values.

★ To describe constitutional and legal issues that arose between 1917 and 1929.

After World War I, the United States enjoyed prosperity, its government resumed a policy of laissez-faire, and its citizens ceased promoting progressive reforms.

Impact of War

Gender Roles and Minorities

During World War I, as men fought in Europe, women filled their jobs at home—as factory workers, railroad conductors, farmers, and so on. They served as army and navy nurses. As more telephone operators, secretaries, and salespeople were needed, women comprised the majority in these occupations.

African American men had fought for their country and, more than ever, resented treatment as second-class citizens. During the 1920s, confrontations between blacks and whites increased, and organizations challenging discriminatory practices became strong and numerous.

The 1920s were a difficult time for immigrants. Many from eastern Europe were thought to be Communist sympathizers. Those from Asia, whose numbers were increasing, were distrusted by the white population.

Northern Migration of African Americans Between 1910 and 1930, the number of African Americans in the North grew from one million to 2.5 million. Southern blacks moved north partly to find good-paying work and partly to escape Jim Crow laws. Blacks who defied such laws risked jail or lynching. In 1927, 24 lynchings occurred in the South.

Race Riots The arrival of blacks in large numbers threatened many Northern whites. Segregation was as strict and common in the North and at times led to race riots. Race riots broke out. In 1919, a riot on a segregated Chicago beach resulted in the deaths of 38 people, black and white.

Such confrontations also rocked Southern cities. One of the most serious took place in Tulsa, Oklahoma, in 1921. A rumor that a black man had attacked a white woman sent an army of whites on the offense in the black section of the city. Many black-owned homes and businesses were burned and many people killed, most of them black.

Politics and Economics of the 1920s

Business Boom and False Prosperity

Postwar Recession During World War I, prices of many goods exported or used by the military increased. Wages, however, remained low. By 1920, wartime production was in decline, unemployment was rising, and many businesses were failing. Neither the employed nor unemployed could afford goods and services. Farm income also declined as European farmers resumed raising crops that had been imported during the war. The U.S. **recession** (period of business decline) lasted from 1920 to 1922. Then, the economy experienced a business boom that masked problems that would lead to disaster in 1929.

Return to "Normalcy" In 1920, the Republican presidential candidate, Warren G. Harding, won by a huge majority. He had promised to lead the nation back to *normalcy*—the quieter time before war and Wilson's progressive politics. Harding's laissez-faire policy toward business recalled the 1880s and 1890s. Such a domestic policy failed to take into account that society and the economy were changing fast.

Prosperity Under Coolidge Vice president Calvin Coolidge became president when Harding died suddenly in 1923, and he was reelected in his own right in 1924.

"The business of America is business," summed up Coolidge's support of unregulated big business, high protective tariffs, less government spending, and lower taxes.

Farmers and Workers in Trouble

The general prosperity of the 1920s did not include farmers or the urban working poor.

Productivity, Mortgages, and Technology During World War I, European farmlands were turned into battlefields. American farmers expanded production to meet the growing demand for crops, and farm income rose to new heights. After 1921, foreign demand for U.S. farm products fell, as did U.S. farm prices. Improved farm machinery, which produced wheat and corn surpluses, also lowered prices. Moreover, to buy the new machinery, farmers took **mortgages** (money borrowed against the value of property) on their land and homes. Lower prices for crops often made it impossible to repay such loans, and farmers lost their land by foreclosure.

Decreased Government Supports Laissez-faire hurt urban workers as well. The government was no longer committed to improving living conditions and wages. Union efforts to force factory owners to raise wages usually failed.

Business Boom and Wider Investment

During the 1920s, there was no trust busting. By 1929, the 200 largest U.S. corporations controlled 49 percent of all corporate wealth.

"It Works Both Ways": cartoon criticizing high tariffs in the early 1920s

New machinery and new work methods resulted in greatly increased productivity, which reduced the cost of manufacture. Workers' wages also increased in the 1920s, but far less than increases in productivity.

This business boom encouraged Americans with average incomes to invest in major corporations. As people invested more in the stock market, stock prices rose to record levels in a great **"bull market"** (condition when public confidence in stocks causes stock prices to soar).

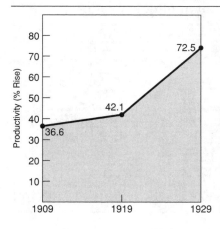

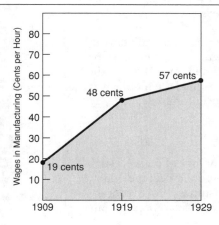

Gains in Productivity and Wages, 1909–1929

★ In Review

1. Describe the effects of World War I on women and African Americans.
2. What were the causes and effects of the African American migration north after World War I?
3. How did uneven distribution of wealth and farm overproduction show that the prosperity of the 1920s did not include everyone?

Effect of Mass Consumption

While prosperity lasted, most Americans cared more about exciting new amusements than about politics. Movies, major league sports, new dance steps, and fast-paced jazz music—mainly the creation of African Americans—became very popular. As a result, the decade became known as the *Roaring Twenties*.

Automobile

Model of Productivity   Henry Ford mass-produced his Model T cars so that they could be sold cheaply. His assembly-line method (see page 95) saved time, cut production costs, and lowered the Model T's 1916 price to $400. Ford's methods were widely copied.

The number of American cars manufactured increased from 1.5 million in 1919 to 4.7 million in 1929. By 1930 Americans owned more than 25 million cars. The success of the automobile industry helped other industries to grow. The rubber industry produced more tires. The oil and gasoline industries provided fuel. The steel industry produced millions of tons for auto bodies. Roadside hotels and restaurants to cater to motorists sprang up everywhere.

Problems   The automobile brought problems as well: drunken driving, fatal accidents, parking problems—and later, polluted air. But in the 1920s, most Americans welcomed the mobile way of life made possible by the automobile.

Installment Buying

Only in the 1920s did technological marvels such as the telephone and automobile become widely available to American consumers. To encourage sales, businesses encouraged customers to buy on the installment plan (see page 113.) Many people went so deeply into debt that they had to use all their resources to make monthly payments on what they had already bought.

Real Estate Boom and Suburban Development

Subways, buses, and electric trolleys made urban transportation easy. By the 1920s, the residents in cities outnumbered those in rural areas.

To escape city crowds, many people moved to the **suburbs** (residential communities near cities) and commuted to their city jobs by car. Land outside the city became more valuable, the real estate business flourished, and new roads to serve the suburbs became a construction priority. New railroad lines also connected suburban and urban areas. Better urban-suburban transportation encouraged businesses to move to the suburbs as well.

Advertisment in a 1920s magazine

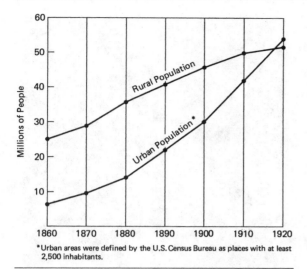

Urban and Rural Population, 1860–1920

Regional Politics and Economics

Counties, small cities, and towns developed alternate forms of government. In Suffolk County, Long Island, New York, for example, county boards and executives regulated property taxes, road building, environmental codes, and schools. Town governments provided police protection, welfare, clean water, and garbage removal, and town residents elected boards of education. Thus, political parties developed new areas of influence.

Suburban **zoning** became increasingly important. Local governments regulated business and home locations, land use, and allowable acreage for building sites. Zoning sometimes became a means to limit housing to the well-to-do. The Supreme Court usually upheld zoning regulations. In *Village of Euclid, Ohio* v. *Ambler Realty Company* (1926), the Court agreed that municipalities had a right to regulate health and safety through zoning.

Entertainment and a Common Culture

By 1920, popular entertainment had undergone a revolution—phonograph records of classical and popular music, radio broadcasts, and bigger and better motion pictures, produced in the new movie capital, Hollywood, California. Such stars as Charlie Chaplin and Mary Pickford acted in early silent movies. In 1927, Al Jolson starred in *The Jazz Singer*, the first "talkie."

The new entertainment created a common culture. Americans everywhere enjoyed the same movies and radio programs and, with one voice, idolized such celebrities as aviator Charles Lindbergh, movie actor Rudolph Valentino, and baseball hero Babe Ruth.

Repeated magazine and radio advertising made Americans feel that they had a culture in common. Some people expressed fear that regional differences would disappear, blended into a uniform way of life.

Issues About Differing Rural and Urban Values

Although life in the 1920s was generally good for the white middle class, it was otherwise for ethnic minorities and the foreign-born. Rural people, especially, often distrusted urban Italian and Jewish immigrants. Nativists held them responsible for city slums and crime even though they were usually hardworking and law-abiding.

Threats to Civil Liberties

The Communist revolution in Russia made nativists fearful that foreign-born radicals would try to overthrow the U.S. government (see pages 117–119). Such fears persisted throughout most of the 20th century.

"The Only Way to Handle It": cartoon of U.S. immigration quotas in the 1920s

In the 1920s, the Ku Klux Klan (see Chapter 7) made a comeback. The revived Klan's targets were African Americans, Roman Catholics, Jews, and immigrants. As its membership grew, it became important in the politics of many states. The governors of Oregon and Indiana owed their election to Klan support.

In 1921, Nicola Sacco and Bartolomeo Vanzetti were convicted by Massachusetts of armed robbery and murder. The evidence of guilt was weak, and the judge appeared biased against them. Liberals blamed antiforeign prejudice for their conviction. In spite of worldwide protests and appeals for clemency, Sacco and Vanzetti were executed in 1927.

Prohibition and the Volstead Act

The work of temperance reformers such as Carrie Nation bore fruit with the adoption of the Eighteenth (Prohibition) Amendment (1919), which prohibited manufacture and sale of alcoholic beverages in the United States. Congress passed the National Prohibition Act (Volstead Act) to enforce the amendment.

Supporters believed that Prohibition would reduce crime and make Americans healthier.

Cartoon summing up fear of foreign terrorists during the Red Scare

Prohibitionist disposing of a dandelion that might be processed into homemade wine

Instead, it caused millions of otherwise law-abiding citizens to drink illegally. Alcohol was either manufactured illegally or smuggled across the border from Canada. **Bootleggers** (suppliers of illegal beverages) made huge profits and organized gangs that evaded the law by bribing the police. In addition to a huge increase in organized crime, many Americans were poisoned from contaminated liquor produced illegally and without quality control. In 1933, the Eighteenth Amendment was repealed (abolished) by the Twenty-first Amendment.

Scopes Trial

In 1925, another clash between urban and rural cultures arose in a famous trial. John Scopes, a biology teacher, defied a Tennessee law against the teaching in public schools of Darwin's theory of evolution. Darwin's ideas offended fundamentalist Protestants, many of them rural, who interpreted the Bible strictly. Many city people tended to support the theory. The following is a portion of the examination by Clarence Darrow, Scopes's defense lawyer, of the prosecution's chief witness, William Jennings Bryan:

Mr. Darrow: Do you claim that everything in the Bible should be literally interpreted?

Mr. Bryan: I believe [it] should be accepted [as is]; some of the Bible is given illustratively. For instance: "Ye are the salt of the earth." I would not insist [on a literal reading] . . . it is used in the sense of salt as saving God's people.

Mr. Darrow: But when you read that Jonah swallowed the whale—or that the whale swallowed Jonah . . . how do you literally interpret that? . . .

Mr. Bryan: One miracle is just as easy to believe as another. . . .

Mr. Darrow: Perfectly easy to believe that Jonah swallowed that whale? . . .

Mr. Bryan: Your honor . . . . [Mr. Darrow's] only purpose . . . is to slur at the Bible, but I will answer his question. . . . I want the world to know that this man, who does not believe in God, is trying to use a court . . . .

Mr. Darrow: I object . . . .

Mr. Bryan: [Continuing] to slur at it . . . .

Mr. Darrow: I object . . . . I am examining you on your fool ideas that no intelligent Christian on earth believes.

Scopes was convicted but fined only a token $100, and a higher court later reversed the verdict. In recent years, the conflict between teaching science vs. religion in the classroom has reemerged.

Shifting Cultural Values

Morals and Manners

Fads **Fads** are vivid, usually frivolous, forms of social expression that last only briefly. One fad of the 1920s was a fast dance called the "Charleston." Another was the slang expression "23 skiddoo" (good-bye).

Flappers Many young women of the 1920s shocked their elders by bobbing their hair, raising their hemlines, dancing to ragtime, and smoking in public. Traditionalists worried that the new freedoms of these "flappers" would lead to a breakdown of the family.

Freud Sigmund Freud was an Austrian psychiatrist whose ideas became popular in the United States. He held that people could resolve emotional problems through **psychoanalysis**, which involved a "talking cure" of free association, reliving troubling experiences, and recall and interpretation of dreams. Freud's theory that sexual repression was a major cause of emotional problems found a receptive audience during the newly liberated 1920s.

Women's Changing Roles

Suffrage The Nineteenth Amendment gave all American women the right to vote. During their struggle for suffrage, women had organized public demonstrations and used such tactics as petitioning, picketing, and hunger strikes. They succeeded in influencing public policy.

Women in the Workforce After World War I, women were reluctant to give up working and keep house again. Such labor-saving appliances as refrigerators, washing machines, and vacuum cleaners enabled middle-class women to enter the workforce in record numbers. Most jobs were in support services—as secretary or typist to a male boss. Other jobs that became available were telephone operator, clerk, and teacher. Women earned less than men doing the same work and were expected to leave when they got married. Nevertheless, jobs gave young women the chance to live on their own and experience independence.

Women's health improved as they exchanged heavy physical labor such as farm work for less strenuous white-collar work. Moreover, as city dwellers, they had better access to doctors and medical facilities.

Literature and Music

During the 1920s, a number of writers wrote about American life. Sinclair Lewis, in his novel *Main Street* (1920), exposed the attitudes of smug small-town Americans. In *The Sun Also Rises* (1926), Ernest Hemingway depicted Americans abroad who cast off traditional values but found no alternatives to help them understand themselves or the world. In *The Age of Innocence* (1920), Edith Wharton satirized the social manners and arrogance of upper-class New Yorkers. In his novel *The Great Gatsby* (1925), F. Scott

Women ship
construction workers,
Puget Sound, Oregon,
1919

Fitzgerald lent a tragic note to the American dream of material success and social acceptance.

Harlem Renaissance In the 1920s, a number of talented African Americans brought new acclaim to Harlem, a black neighborhood of New York City. Their creativity became known as the *Harlem Renaissance*. Best known of the Harlem poets were James Weldon Johnson, Langston Hughes, and Countee Cullen. Hughes's poem "What happens to a dream deferred?" expresses the frustration of African Americans still living in an age of segregation.

Paul Robeson, a black actor and singer, starred in several Eugene O'Neill plays. He also appeared in Jerome Kern's 1927 hit *Showboat*, the first American musical to (1) highlight problems faced by black Americans and (2) bring black and white performers together on the same stage. Josephine Baker sang and danced in nightclubs in Philadelphia, New York, and Paris. Eubie Blake and W. C. Handy composed songs that are still popular today.

African American musicians began playing jazz in New Orleans around 1900. By the 1920s, this music was popular in Chicago and New York City. Among the greatest of the jazz musicians were bandleader and songwriter Duke Ellington, trumpet player and singer Louis Armstrong, and blues singer Bessie Smith.

Discrimination in the Entertainment Industry In spite of their popularity, African American entertainers often faced discrimination. In the movies, they were cast in stereotypical roles as servants and figures of fun. Chorus lines were generally all-white. Even in Harlem's famous Cotton Club, most blacks were admitted only as entertainers.

★ In Review

1. Explain the significance of installment buying, the Eighteenth Amendment, Sigmund Freud, the Nineteenth Amendment, and the Harlem Renaissance.
2. How did the growth of the automobile industry stimulate growth in other industries? How did it influence American lifestyles.
3. How did each of the following contribute to the literary scene during the 1920s: Sinclair Lewis, Ernest Hemingway, Edith Wharton, F. Scott Fitzgerald, and Langston Hughes?

Chapter Review

MULTIPLE-CHOICE QUESTIONS

Use the cartoon on page 155 to answer questions 1 and 2.

1. The cartoon (1) endorses 1920s U.S. trade policy (2) is critical of U.S. tariff policy (3) demands isolation of Europeans for causing World War I (4) shows that the United States does not need foreign trade.

2. The cartoonist probably feels that (1) the United States should retaliate against foreign tariffs (2) immigration restrictions go hand in hand with high tariffs (3) high tariffs hurt U.S. business (4) the United States should be totally isolated.

Use the graphs on page 155 to answer question 3.

3. An examination of the graphs shows that (1) higher productivity lowered product prices between 1909 and 1929 (2) productivity and wages rose in proportion to each other (3) both productivity and wages rose, but not proportionally (4) there was little relationship between productivity and wages.

Study the advertisement on page 156 and answer question 4.

4. The ad shows that 1920s automobiles were (1) considered luxuries (2) becoming affordable (3) used only in cities (4) uncomfortable and unreliable.

5. "The nation became urbanized, a process to which the automobile especially, as well as the radio, moving picture, and newspaper, contributed." The first period in U.S. history to which this statement applies is (1) 1890–1900 (2) 1901–1910 (3) 1910–1920 (4) 1920–1928.

Use the cartoon on page 157 to answer question 6.

6. The cartoon shows that the United States (1) continued earlier immigration policies into the 1920s (2) limited immigration during the 1920s (3) cut off all immigration (4) stopped admitting immigrants from eastern and southern Europe.

Study the cartoon on the left of page 158 and answer question 7.

7. The cartoonist felt that Prohibitionists were (1) cynical (2) intelligent (3) practical (4) extremist.

Read the following excerpt from a Brooklyn, New York, newspaper during the 1920s, and answer question 8.

> And the pistol's red glare,
> Bombs bursting in air
> Gave proof through the night
> That Chicago's still there.

8. The excerpt refers to (1) protests against immigration quotas (2) the rise of organized crime (3) Ku Klux Klan violence (4) postwar strikes by unions.

Read the trial dialog on page 159 and answer question 9.

9. The dialog is taken from a court case that decided whether (1) prohibition was constitutional (2) a public teacher had broken the law by teaching evolution (3) the book *On the Origin of Species* should be removed from public libraries (4) fundamentalists had the right to interpret the Bible literally.

THEMATIC ESSAYS

1. **Theme:** Tradition Versus Change. The 1920s were a time of great change in the United States. Changes, however, provoked resistance to change and a longing for "the good old days."

Task

★ Choose one change during the 1920s. Describe its cause and impact on the United States.

★ Give one example of how some Americans tried to resist a change, and evaluate their success in stopping or slowing it. (You may use the same change or a different one.)

You may wish to discuss migration of African Americans, women's roles, and mass consumption.

Some examples of resistance to change are attitudes toward immigrants, Prohibition, and the fundamentalist response to science.

2. **Theme:** Return to "Normalcy." During the presidential election of 1920, soon-to-be-elected Republican candidate Warren G. Harding promised a return to "normalcy."

Task

★ Describe what Harding meant by "normalcy."
★ Choose two events or circumstances from the 1920s. For each, explain how it stemmed, in part, from U.S. participation in World War I.
★ Use each example to evaluate whether the United States had returned to "normalcy."

You may use, but are not limited to, the treatment of immigrants, stock speculation, foreign policy, mass consumption, and changing cultural values.

DOCUMENT-BASED QUESTION

*Study each document and answer the question that follows it. Then read the **Task** and write your essay. Include references to most of the documents and additional information you retain about U.S. history and government.*

Historical Context: World War I left an aftereffect of fear for some and hope for others.

Document 1: Refer to the cartoon on the right of page 158.

Question: What does the cartoon say about immigrants and foreigners?

Document 2: Hiram W. Evans, Imperial Wizard of the Ku Klux Klan, in *North American Review*, 1926:

The greatest achievement so far has been to formulate and [recognize] the idea of preserv-

ing and developing America . . . for the benefit of the children of pioneers . . . . The Klan [did not create] this idea—it has long been a vague stirring in [plain people's] souls. But the Klan can fairly claim to have given it purpose, method, direction. . . .

. . . there are three great racial instincts . . . [in] the Klan slogan: "Native, white, Protestant supremacy."

Question: Whom does Evans feel that the nation was created to benefit?

Document 3: Refer to the photo on page 160.

Question: How does the photo show that women's role had started to change by the end of World War I?

Document 4: James Weldon Johnson in *Harper's*, November 1928:

. . . [T]here is a common, widespread, and persistent [stereotype of] the Negro, . . . that he is here only to receive; to be shaped into something new and . . . better. The common idea is that the Negro reached America intellectually, culturally, and morally empty, and . . . is here to be filled . . . with education, . . . religion, . . . morality, . . . culture. . . .

Through his artistic efforts the Negro is smashing this . . . stereotype . . . . He is [showing] that he [has] a wealth of natural endowments and . . . has long been a generous giver to America. . . . that he is an active and important force in American life; that he is a creator as well as a creature; that he . . . is the potential giver of larger and richer contributions.

In this way the Negro . . . has placed himself in an entirely new light . . . . through artistic achievements the Negro has found a means of getting at the very core of . . . prejudice . . . by challenging the Nordic superiority complex. A great deal has been accomplished in this decade of "renaissance."

Question: Why does Johnson feel that there was a change in attitude toward African Americans following World War I?

Task

★ Describe why Americans were *both* fearful and hopeful immediately following World War I.
★ Show how one of the fears or hopes is still important in the new millennium.

Chapter 13
The Great Depression

★ Documents and Laws	★ Events	★ People
Federal Farm Board (1929)	Stock Market crash (1929)	Mary McLeod Bethune
Hawley-Smoot Tariff (1930)	Great Depression (1929–1942)	Father Charles Coughlin
New Deal legislation (1933–1938)	Congress of Industrial Organizations (C.I.O.) established (1938)	Amelia Earhart
Reconstruction Finance Corporation (1932)		William Faulkner
Indian Reorganization Act (1934)		Lillian Hellman
Schechter Poultry Corp. v. *United States* (1935)		Herbert Hoover
Wagner Act (1935)		Huey Long
Fair Labor Standards Act (1938)		Frances Perkins
Twenty-second Amendment (1951)		Franklin D. Roosevelt
		Alfred E. Smith
		Norman Thomas
		Dr. Francis Townsend
		John Steinbeck
		Robert Weaver

★ Objectives

★ To examine causes of the Great Depression and its effect on people and institutions.

★ To understand worldwide financial and economic interdependence.

★ To examine how Herbert Hoover and Franklin D. Roosevelt responded to the depression.

★ To evaluate the impact of the New Deal on the U.S. economy.

★ To examine cultural life during the depression.

ONSET OF THE DEPRESSION

A **depression** is a severe economic decline marked by business failures, high unemployment, and low production and prices.

Weak Economy

Overproduction/Underconsumption A nation's economic strength depends on whether its citizens can afford what factories and farms produce. As wages in the 1920s failed to keep up with productivity, goods went unsold and many businesses failed.

Much of the nation's wealth belonged to a small number of people. The richest 5 percent had 25 percent of total income.

Overexpansion of Credit In the 1920s, it was a common practice to buy stocks "on margin," that is, to pay a small percent of the purchase price and finance the rest with a loan.

Stock Market Crash

Herbert Hoover succeeded Calvin Coolidge as president in 1928. Economic prosperity continued for about six months, and Hoover ran the executive branch well.

The **"bull market"** on New York City's Wall Street crested in September 1929. Then, prices started to drop. Bankers tried to halt the decline in stock prices, but on October 29—"Black Tuesday"—thousands panicked and ordered their brokers to sell at any price. A record 16.5 million shares were traded, almost all at a loss. By the end of December, the combined prices of Wall Street stocks had lost one-third of their peak value in September.

There were four harmful consequences. First, billions of dollars that people had invested in stocks were wiped out. Second, many investors had bought on margin and went bankrupt. Third, banks failed because loans were not repaid. Fourth, people lost confidence in the economy and, for years afterwards, preferred savings over investments.

Worldwide Financial Interdependence World War I produced an imbalance in the world economy. The peace treaty forced Germany to pay the Allies huge reparations. The European Allies owed vast sums to the United States for wartime consumption of American goods. In the 1920s, the United States became the world's largest creditor nation.

By 1930, most nations were linked financially. The United States lent money to Germany so that Germany could pay reparations to England and France. England and France then repaid war debts to the United States.

Interdependent Banking American bank and business loans enabled Europeans to pay war debts to the U.S. government. This arrangement sustained prosperity as long as U.S. banks had enough money to make foreign loans. With the collapse of the stock market, the worldwide cycle of debt payments ended.

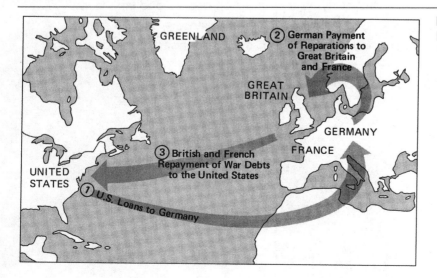

How U.S. Loans Financed International Prosperity, 1924–1929

International Trade The lifeblood of the international economy was trade. Protective tariffs hurt all nations, including the United States. Nevertheless, in 1930, many in Congress hoped to protect domestic industries from foreign competition with the *Hawley-Smoot Tariff*, which increased import taxes on more than a thousand items. European nations, in turn, raised their own tariffs, and U.S.-European trade dropped by half. Partly because of the tariff war, the worldwide depression deepened.

Political Repercussions

Hoover's Response Herbert Hoover was president during the worst years of the *Great Depression*, 1930–1932. His attempts to revive the economy included the following:

★ cutting taxes to encourage consumerism

★ greatly increasing government expenditure on public projects—dams, highways, harbors, and so forth

★ persuading Congress to establish the *Federal Farm Board* (1929) to buy farm goods and keep up prices

★ persuading Congress to establish the *Reconstruction Finance Corporation* (1932) to fund banks, railroads, and insurance companies threatened with bankruptcy (Hoover's most successful program)

★ declaring a **debt moratorium** (temporary halt on the payment of war debts) to fight the worldwide spread of the depression.

"Rugged Individualism" Hoover did not believe that government should directly aid the poor. His creed was "rugged individualism"—decisions by businesses and individuals on how best to help themselves. Moreover, he felt that when businesses succeed, everyone benefits indirectly from profits that "trickle down" to wage earners.

IMPACT OF THE DEPRESSION

Unemployment

In 1932, 12 million workers—25 percent of the labor force—were unemployed. The employed worked for much lower wages than in the 1920s. Prices paid to farmers were desperately low. Factories produced only half of their 1929 output. About 5,000 banks had closed their doors, forever cutting off depositors from their savings.

"Bonus Army" In the summer of 1932, 17,000 unemployed veterans of World War I marched to Washington, D.C. They wanted the government to pay them immediately bonuses owed to them at a later time. The *"Bonus Army"* set up shacks near the Capitol. When the protesters ignored Hoover's order to leave, he sent federal troops to break up their encampment.

Desperate Conditions Jobless people who became homeless slept in tents and shacks clustered in areas called **"Hoovervilles."** They also hid in railroad boxcars and traveled in search of jobs or handouts. Men and women sold apples on city street corners.

Women and Minorities

As the depression deprived women of job opportunities, they again concentrated on family needs.

African Americans suffered the full impact of the depression. Last to be hired, they were usually first to be fired.

Falling Prices and Rising Unemployment, 1929–1932

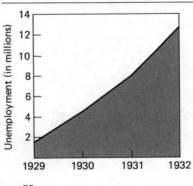

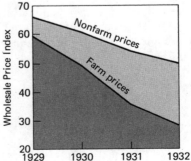

New York City depression scenes: "Hooverville" in Central Park and (inset) people receiving mission handouts of bread and coffee, 1930

Native Americans continued to live in poverty on reservations.

Nativist distrust of immigrants and opposition to immigration continued as jobs became scarce.

The land of Great Plains farmers turned into a *Dust Bowl*, for several reasons—poor farming practices, long drought, and high winds that pulled moisture from the soil. As they lost income and land, they took to the open road looking for work as migrant farmworkers. So many came from Oklahoma that all of them became known as "Okies."

★ In Review

1. Summarize basic economic weaknesses that contributed to the stock market crash and the Great Depression.
2. Explain how Hoover responded to the depression.
3. Identify the following: "rugged individualism," "trickle-down" economics, Reconstruction Finance Corporation, "Bonus Army," and "Hoovervilles."

FRANKLIN D. ROOSEVELT'S NEW DEAL

In 1932, Hoover lost by a huge margin to his Democratic presidential challenger, Franklin D.

Roosevelt. Roosevelt's plan was to help people directly by giving them government jobs. Federal paychecks would give them hope and purchasing power, which would put money back into the economy.

Roosevelt tried out many ideas for solving the economic crisis. During his first and part of his second term (1933–1938), he favored programs that came to be known as the *New Deal*.

Roosevelt and his advisers—the "brain trust"—had three main goals—*relief, recovery, and reform*: Relieve the misery of the poor and unemployed, bring about the recovery of business, and reform the economic system to prevent mistakes in the future like those that had caused the depression.

Relief of Suffering

In Roosevelt's first three months in office—almost one hundred days—more important laws were enacted than during all of the 1920s. The times called for bold measures, and the Democratic majority in Congress gave the president almost all that he asked for. The laws passed during these *Hundred Days* had a long-lasting effect on the country.

"Bank Holiday"   After the stock market crash, many lost faith in banks and withdrew their money. Banks could not produce all the cash called for and failed. In 1933, Roosevelt declared

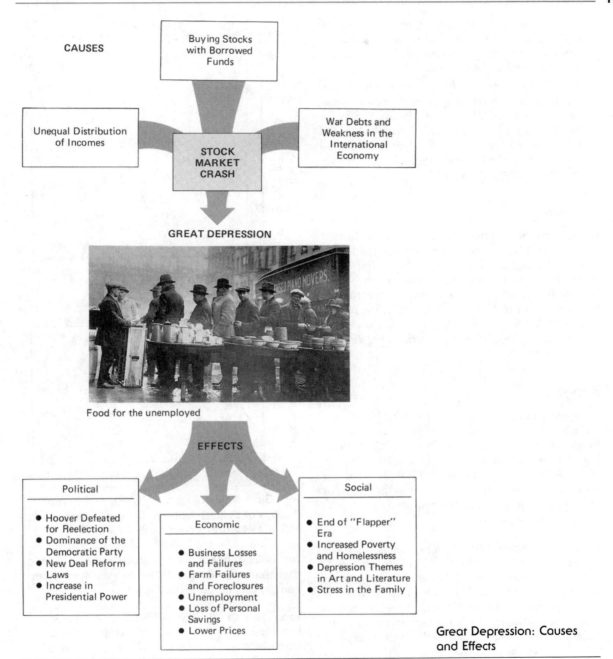

Food for the unemployed

Great Depression: Causes and Effects

a nationwide *"bank holiday."* Congress passed the *Emergency Banking Act*, which allowed sound banks to reopen. The drain on banks stopped and public confidence was restored.

Federal Emergency Relief Act The *Federal Emergency Relief Act* (1933) created the *Federal Emergency Relief Administration (FERA)*. It gave fed-eral money to the states to set up projects that gave people jobs.

Strategies Against Unemployment

★ The *Public Works Administration (PWA)*, set up in 1933, put people to work building roads, bridges, libraries, hospitals, schools, court-houses, and other public projects.

★ *The Civilian Conservation Corps (CCC),* set up in 1933, employed men between 18 and 25 in flood control, soil conservation, forest replanting, and park construction.

★ *The Works Progress Administration (WPA),* set up in 1935, organized public projects and paid workers to do them. Only the head of a family—usually a man—could qualify. Women who headed families were given less skilled jobs. Workers who had been offered private employment were ineligible.

Recovery

Fair Competition The *National Recovery Administration (NRA),* set up in 1933, encouraged business and labor to draw up codes of fair practices—maximum work hours, minimum wages, productivity, and prices. The codes were to help businesses control production and raise prices, and help labor by putting people to work and raising wages. The NRA gave workers the right to form unions.

Relief

Mortgages For homeowners who could not meet mortgage payments, Congress created the *Home Owners Loan Corporation (HOLC)* in 1933. The *Federal Housing Administration (FHA),* which followed in 1934, insured bank loans for the construction of new housing and the repair of old homes, and reduced the required down payment for buying homes.

Scarcity and Parity The *Agricultural Adjustment Act (AAA)* of 1933 paid farmers to limit production and raise farm prices. The money came from a "processing tax" on the industries that made raw products into finished goods. Farmers had to destroy a portion of their crops and livestock to raise real income to **parity** (the higher prewar price level for farm products).

Search for Effective Reform

Banking The *Glass Steagall Act* (1933) created the *Federal Deposit Insurance Corporation (FDIC),* which backed and insured bank deposits up to a certain amount, thus making them risk-free.

Stock Market The *Securities and Exchange Commission (SEC)* of 1934 regulated the pricing of

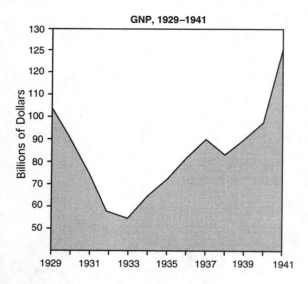

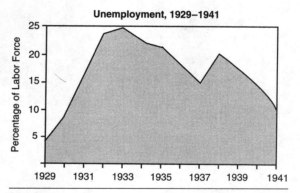

Top: Gross National Product (GNP), 1929–1941 (billions of dollars); bottom: Unemployment, 1929–1941 (percent of labor force)

stocks and bonds and required publication of basic data about them. A major goal was to curb margin buying and speculation.

Social Security The *Social Security Act* (1935) established old-age insurance through a joint tax on employers and employees. Workers thus received a monthly income at age 65. The act also gave laid-off workers compensation while they job-hunted and provided grants to the states for the care of the disabled, the blind, and dependent children.

Labor and Unions The *Wagner Act* (1935) guaranteed workers the right to unionize and engage in **collective bargaining** (process by which workers and employers work out differences about wages, hours, and working conditions). The *National Labor Relations Board* could force employers to deal fairly with a union representing the majority of workers. Firing anyone for joining a union was illegal. From 1935 to 1940, more than five million workers joined unions, doubling total union membership.

The *Fair Labor Standards Act* (1938) set minimum wages (increased from 25 to 40 cents an hour) and maximum hours (reduced from 44 to 40 hours a week) in industries engaged in interstate commerce. Time and a half was to be paid for overtime. Children under 16 were prohibited from working in such industries.

In 1935, the most powerful union within the A.F. of L. was the *United Mine Workers*. Its leader, John L. Lewis, objected to A.F. of L policy of favoring skilled crafts workers over the less skilled workers. He favored the creation of one industrial union, which represented all American workers (black and white, skilled and unskilled). In 1938, it became a separate union, the C.I.O. (Congress of Industrial Organizations).

Unions in the C.I.O. devised "sitdown strikes," in which workers occupy a factory and refuse to work or leave until demands are met. One such strike shut down General Motors automobile factories in the winter of 1936 and 1937. The company yielded to most of the union's demands.

Model Yardstick

The lands watered by the Tennessee River were often flooded. Farmers had no electric power and were desperately poor. In 1933, Congress created the *Tennessee Valley Authority (TVA)* to accomplish the following goals:

★ build dams to control floods

★ build power plants and provide electricity

★ charge fair prices for TVA-generated electricity

★ build reservoirs to hold needed water.

Many viewed TVA as a model for Roosevelt's plan of relief, recovery, and reform. Throughout the region, people experienced relief in the form of TVA jobs, recovery in the form of electric power, and reform through flood control and water conservation.

NEW DEAL CONTROVERSIES

Constitutional Issues

Supreme Court and the NRA In *Schechter Poultry Corp. v. United States* (1935), a chicken-raising company challenged the law that had created the *National Recovery Administration* (see page 168) by arguing that industry codes under this law gave legislative power to the executive branch. The Court agreed and declared the act unconstitutional.

Supreme Court and the AAA In 1936, the Court considered whether a processing tax could be collected to pay farmers under the Agricultural Adjustment Act of 1933 (see page 168). When the Court ruled against the tax and the law, Congress passed a new Agricultural Adjustment Act (1938). It (1) replaced the tax with direct federal payments to farmers, (2) tried to stabilize farm prices by storing surplus produce and releasing it in times of scarcity, (3) provided for soil conservation, (4) allowed marketing quotas for certain crops, and (5) insured wheat crops against natural disasters.

Election "Mandate"

Before the 1930s, Republicans had usually been in the majority. Democrats had relied on Southerners for support—and they were usually conservative in everything except anti-Republicanism. The New Deal, however, appealed to many Northerners—industrial workers, immigrants, African Americans, ethnic Americans, and liberals. It also appealed to the farmers it had helped. These groups formed a majority, and Roosevelt was reelected in 1936 by a landslide.

"Court-Packing" Proposal Angered by the Supreme Court's anti–New Deal decisions, Roosevelt proposed increasing the number of justices from 9 to 15—in effect, enabling him to appoint six politically sympathetic justices. The president was accused by many of trying to "pack" the court, and Congress defeated his plan in 1937.

Third-Term Controversy In 1940, Roosevelt was elected to a third term and in 1944, to a fourth. Republicans accused him of breaking the two-term tradition. After Roosevelt's death in 1945, Congress proposed the Twenty-second Amendment limiting future presidents to two full terms. It was adopted in 1951.

Opposition to the New Deal

Conservative business leaders and politicians in both parties criticized Roosevelt. Such New Deal

"The Spirit of '37": FDR berating the Supreme Court for opposing the New Deal

programs as the TVA, they complained, undermined free enterprise. "Creeping socialism" was being substituted for the "rugged individualism" that had made the United States great.

While conservatives voiced strong opposition to Roosevelt and his programs, radical groups who wanted to do away with free enterprise in part or altogether also targeted him:

★ *Alfred E. Smith*. Alfred Smith was a Roman Catholic Democrat who had run for president against Herbert Hoover. At first, he supported Roosevelt. By 1934, however, Smith turned against the president and his New Deal and helped form the Liberty League, a conservative antilabor organization.

★ *Huey Long*. The most serious challenge to Roosevelt's leadership came from Huey Long, governor of Louisiana. Long called for the rich to give up their fortunes to provide every American family with $5,000. Through this "Share Our Wealth" program, each family would also be guaranteed an annual income of $2,500. (These were considerable sums at the time.) Long was assassinated in 1935.

★ *Father Charles Coughlin*. Father Coughlin, a Roman Catholic priest, used **racism** (preju-

dice and discrimination based on the supposed superiority of some groups over others) to attack the New Deal on national radio. He accused Jews of controlling banks worldwide and causing the depression. Though false, such charges gained Coughlin some popularity until the Catholic Church removed him from the radio.

★ *Dr. Francis Townsend*. Dr. Townsend, a California physician, won a following by proposing to provide $200 monthly to each unemployed citizen over 60. The recipients would have to spend the money within the same month. Although impractical, Dr. Townsend's plan was a forerunner of Social Security.

★ *Radical Reformers*. Norman Thomas, a Socialist, ran for president in 1928, 1932, and 1936. Thomas wanted changes more radical than New Deal reforms, and he thought that such changes could be achieved peacefully, through elections.

Communists, who were more extreme, felt that only a violent revolt of the working class would bring about reform.

Support for the New Deal

Defenders of the New Deal argued that Roosevelt had saved democracy and free enterprise. His programs of economic relief had prevented extremists from tearing the nation apart. Moreover, New Deal reforms (Social Security, regulated banking, minimum wages) extended reforms of the Progressive Era. They were intended to avoid some bad effects of capitalism (bank failures, economic insecurity, possible depressions) while preserving good effects (freedom of choice, inventiveness, economic growth).

THE ROOSEVELTS: KEEPING THE PEOPLE IN MIND

FDR as Communicator

In 1920, Roosevelt had become crippled by infantile paralysis. Nevertheless, he seemed a pillar of strength to many Americans, who drew confidence from his statement (in the first inaugural address) that ". . . the only thing we have to fear is fear itself. . . ." To explain his New Deal programs to as many as possible and calm their anxieties, he gave regular radio "fireside chats."

Eleanor Roosevelt

FDR's wife, Eleanor Roosevelt, championed liberal causes. Acting as the president's eyes and ears, she visited areas hard-hit by the depression. Speaking out boldly on public issues, she came to symbolize the "new woman"—active in national and world affairs.

New Deal and Women

Women of the 1930s achieved fame in various fields. Amelia Earhart was the first woman to fly a plane across the Atlantic. As secretary of labor, Frances Perkins became the first woman in the cabinet, administered many New Deal relief programs, and helped abolish child labor.

New Deal and African Americans

"Among American citizens there should be no forgotten man and no forgotten races." Thus, Roosevelt expressed his awareness of how the government had long neglected blacks. New Deal programs provided African Americans with what they most needed—jobs.

Roosevelt organized a "Black Cabinet" of distinguished African American leaders, such as Robert Weaver, an expert on urban housing, and Mary McLeod Bethune, an expert in education.

When African American opera singer Marian Anderson was denied the right to perform in a concert space in Washington, D.C., Eleanor Roosevelt invited Anderson to sing at the Lincoln Memorial. Such gestures led thousands of African Americans to become Democrats.

The Roosevelts' personal sympathies did not wipe out racism and discrimination. The industrial codes of the NRA allowed white workers higher wages than blacks. Moreover, TVA administrators were far more likely to hire whites than African Americans.

Indian Reorganization Act

In 1934, Congress passed the *Indian Reorganization Act* in an effort to improve the status of Native Americans. The government stressed tribal over individual ownership of reservation land and encouraged the preservation of Native American culture. Reservation schools began to stress scientific farming. Nevertheless, Native Americans were still desperately poor and had few job opportunities on or away from the reservations.

CULTURE OF THE DEPRESSION

Literature, Drama, and Music

During the 1930s and 1940s, novelist William Faulkner created characters who exemplified social tensions in Southern society. So did playwright Lillian Hellman, who, in addition, treated both domestic and international social issues of the time.

The Great Depression inspired John Steinbeck to depict American people's struggles against hardship. His novel *The Grapes of Wrath* (1939) creates an unforgettable picture of Oklahoma sharecroppers ("Okies"), who set out for the fruit orchards of California. Steinbeck's novel shows these people pitted against cruel and impersonal economic forces.

The WPA hired writers, artists, actors, and musicians to write, paint, and perform. One historical WPA project involved interviews with former slaves and the children of slaves in order to better document slavery in America.

The "hot jazz" of the Roaring Twenties gave way to the "swing" of the 1930s. Band leaders such as Glenn Miller led white musicians playing music mostly by white composers. Benny Goodman's band included such great African American musicians as vibraphonist Lionel Hampton and pianist Teddy Wilson.

During this period, however, most bands were segregated. The bands of Cab Calloway, Duke Ellington, and Count Basie played music by African American composers.

Popular Culture

During the depression, movies became more popular than ever. For a few cents, people could escape from their troubles and watch stars such as Shirley Temple, Clark Gable, James Stewart, and Judy Garland perform in a make-believe world of romance and opulence. Such hits as *The Wizard of Oz* (1939) satisfied people's needs for both fantasy and fun. Other classics of the time treated serious social themes.

Comic books first appeared in the United States in the 1930s. *Superman* paved the way for *Batman*, *Captain Marvel*, *Wonder Woman*, and *Spiderman*.

★ In Review

1. Explain how each of the following New Deal acts or programs contributed to re-

lief, recovery, or reform: (a) Emergency Banking Act, (b) Federal Emergency Relief Act, (c) Works Progress Administration, (d) Public Works Administration, (e) Civilian Conservation Corps, (f) National Recovery Administration, (g) Home Owners Loan Corporation, (h) Federal Housing Administration, (i) Agricultural Adjustment acts, (j) Federal Deposit Insurance Corporation, (k) Securities and Exchange Commission, (l) Social Security Act, (m) National Labor Relations Board, (n) Fair Labor Standards Act, and (o) Tennessee Valley Authority.

2. Summarize the effects of the Great Depression and the New Deal on (a) labor unions, (b) women, (c) African Americans, and (d) Native Americans.

3. Describe the programs of three opponents of the New Deal. Why were these ideas popular?

Chapter Review

MULTIPLE-CHOICE QUESTIONS

Refer to the graphs on page 168 to answer question 1.

1. The graphs illustrate that, between 1929 and 1941, (1) the GNP and unemployment were unrelated (2) as the GNP increased, so did unemployment (3) when people found jobs, they were able to afford more goods and services (4) the Great Depression was aggravated because of industry's high productivity in the face of high unemployment.

Use the map on page 164 to answer questions 2 and 3.

2. Which of the following conclusions can be drawn from the map? (1) Loans from the United States prevented a stock market crash before 1929. (2) The payment cycle helped to make the Great Depression worldwide. (3) Credit was tight and hard to get during the late 1920s. (4) U.S. banks granted preferential loan rates to Germany.

3. Which component is missing from the cycle on the map? (1) reparation payments to France (2) reparation payments to Germany (3) loans to Germany (4) repayments of war debts to the United States.

Use the chart on page 167 to answer questions 4 and 5.

4. The belief that the 1920s were a decade of great wealth was (1) false (2) untrue for many people (3) true for rural areas (4) partially true for skilled workers.

5. The chart shows that the (1) stock market crash was the most important cause of the Great Depression (2) Great Depression was mainly a result of global economic weakness (3) ease of obtaining loans coupled with "get rich quick" stock schemes were the true causes of the Great Depression (4) Great Depression was generated by international and domestic economic weaknesses.

6. The New Deal (1) successfully used laissez-faire to combat the Great Depression (2) endorsed a large degree of government action (3) was a compromise between Democratic and Republican leaders (4) immediately solved the problems of the Great Depression.

Read the following debate about the New Deal and then answer questions 7 and 8.

Speaker A: Our economy has been ruined by costly government programs that destroy free enterprise and individual initiative.

Speaker B: Our economy will be helped by public works projects, unemployment insurance, and retirement insurance. The New Deal is a peaceful and necessary revolution.

Speaker C: This is no revolution but simply the evolution of an idea that began with populism and progressivism.

Speaker D: It doesn't matter whether these changes are revolutionary or evolutionary. The important thing is to conserve resources through the democratic process.

7. Speaker C is referring to (1) a regulatory government role (2) free and unlimited coinage of silver (3) civil rights for minorities (4) an income tax amendment.

8. Speaker A is most likely a (1) farmer (2) corporate executive (3) union member (4) African American.

Refer to the cartoon on page 170 and answer question 9.

9. What viewpoint is expressed by the cartoon? (1) The New Deal was a military as well as political force. (2) Congress accepted most of Roosevelt's plans for dealing with the depression. (3) Roosevelt strictly observed checks and balances. (4) The judicial branch in the 1930s was controlled by the executive branch.

THEMATIC ESSAYS

1. **Theme:** Causes of the Great Depression. The 1920s business boom masked weaknesses in the economy that ultimately helped trigger the Great Depression.

   Task

   ★ Choose two areas of economic weakness during the 1920s. Show how each weakness helped lead the United States into the Great Depression.
   ★ Describe how developing world interdependence after World War I helped make the Great Depression a global crisis.

   You may wish to select economic weaknesses such as overproduction, easy credit, and the unequal distribution of wealth.

   A discussion of international trade and banking may help illustrate how the Great Depression grew to worldwide proportions.

2. **Theme:** New Deal. Roosevelt's New Deal was marked by dramatic action by the federal government to fight the ravages of depression.

   Task: Select two New Deal programs. For each one:

   ★ describe the problem that it was designed to correct
   ★ evaluate its effectiveness.

   You may include programs dealing with banking, labor, the stock market, or any other aspect of the economy.

3. **Theme:** New Deal and Constitutional Issues. Although the New Deal did much to counter effects of the Great Depression, it was constitutionally controversial.

   Task: Choose two ways in which the New Deal caused controversy. For each one:

   ★ describe the controversy
   ★ explain how it was resolved.

   Areas to consider may involve checks and balances, federalism, presidential power, and the proper role of government.

DOCUMENT-BASED QUESTIONS

*Study each document and answer the question that follows it. Then read the **Task** and write your essay. Include references to most of the documents and additional information you retain about U.S. history and government.*

Historical Context: The 1932 presidential election entailed a fundamental disagreement over the degree of federal involvement proper to solve the severe problems of the depression.

Document 1: From a speech by President Hoover at Madison Square Garden, New York City, October 31, 1932:

> . . . you can not extend the master of government over the daily lives of a people . . . making it master of . . . souls and thoughts.
>
> Expansion of government in business means that . . . to protect itself from the political consequences of its errors [government] is driven . . . to greater and greater control of . . . press and platform. Free speech does not live many hours after free industry and free commerce die. . . .

Even if [government's] conduct of business could give us . . . maximum . . . instead of least efficiency, it would be purchased at the cost of freedom.

Question: Why did Hoover choose to avoid most direct federal involvement with private business during the depression?

Document 2: Refer to the larger photograph on page 166 and answer the question.

Question: Why did people call the settlement shown in the photo a "Hooverville"?

Document 3: From President Roosevelt's first inaugural address, March 4, 1933:

. . . Plenty is at our doorsteps, but a generous use of it languishes in the very sight of the supply. . . .

. . . Our greatest primary task is to put people to work. . . . It can be accomplished in part by direct recruiting by the government itself, treating the test as we would treat the emergency of a war, but at the same time, through this employment, accomplishing greatly needed projects to stimulate and reorganize the use of our national resources.

Question: How did Roosevelt propose to fight the unemployment caused by the depression.

Task

★ Describe the differing philosophies of President Herbert Hoover and his presidential challenger, Franklin D. Roosevelt.
★ Explain why Roosevelt won the election of 1932 by an overwhelming majority of the popular vote.

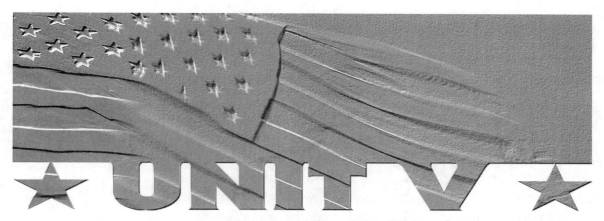

★ UNIT V ★

The United States in an Age of Global Crisis

Chapter 14
Peace in Peril: 1933–1950

★ Documents and Laws	★ Events	★ People
U.S. Neutrality Acts (1935–1939)	Japanese invasions of Manchuria and China (1931–1937)	Winston Churchill
Destroyer-for-Bases Agreement (1940)	Italian invasion of Ethiopia (1935–1936)	Thomas E. Dewey
Atlantic Charter (1941)	German invasion of Rhineland (1936)	Albert Einstein
Lend-Lease Act (1941)	Spanish Civil War (1936–1939)	Dwight D. Eisenhower
Executive Order 9066 (1942)	German annexation of Austria,Czechoslovakia, and Poland (1938–1939)	Adolf Hitler
Korematsu v. *United States* (1944)	Holocaust (1941–1945)	Douglas MacArthur
	Japanese attack on Pearl Harbor (1941)	Benito Mussolini
	Allied invasion of Normandy (1944)	Franklin D. Roosevelt
	Germany's unconditional surrender (1945)	Hideki Tojo
	Atomic bombings of Hiroshima and Nagasaki (1945)	Harry S. Truman
	Nuremberg Trials (1945–1946)	Strom Thurmond
		Henry Wallace

★ **Objectives**

★ To review U.S. isolationism and assess its impact on foreign policy in the 1930s.

★ To recognize how military aggression increasingly threatened U.S. security before 1941.

★ To examine the impact of World War II on various groups.

★ To summarize U.S. military participation in World War II.

★ To analyze the impact of World War II on domestic policy.

ISOLATIONISM AND NEUTRALITY

Traditional U.S. policy toward Europe had been isolationism and neutrality. When World War I began in 1914, Wilson's first move was to proclaim U.S. neutrality. Only German submarine attacks on American shipping forced him—reluctantly—to ask for a declaration of war. Wilson became an internationalist in the effort to win public approval for the League of Nations.

The Senate, however, reverted to a policy of isolationism and rejected the League. Tired of international politics and disillusioned with war, most Americans in the 1920s agreed. **Pacifists**, in particular, disapproved of military buildups and support for **belligerents** (nations involved in war).

Rise of Dictatorships

A type of government called **fascism** glorifies war, preaches extreme nationalism, and calls for obedience to an all-powerful dictator. In Italy, the Fascist party, led by Benito Mussolini, seized power in 1922. Anyone who criticized Mussolini's regime was at risk.

The Treaty of Versailles imposed crushing reparations on Germany, took from it the Saar Valley with its profitable coal mines, and made it accept complete responsibility for World War I. Germany, its pride wounded, faced economic ruin.

Adolf Hitler, leader of the fascistic Nazi party, turned German rage and frustration against the Jews. In 1933, Hitler seized absolute power as chancellor (prime minister).

Hitler (left) and Nazi troops in Berlin

Neutrality Acts of 1935–1937

Congress enacted the Neutrality acts, as follows:

★ no sale or shipment of arms to belligerents

★ no loans or credits to belligerents

★ no travel by U.S. citizens on belligerents' ships

★ purchase of nonmilitary goods by belligerents to be paid in cash and transported in their ships—the **cash-and–carry principle**.

Spanish Civil War

Beginning in 1936, Fascists in Spain tried to overthrow the Republican government. The Soviet Union sent military support to the Republicans, and Germany and Italy aided the Fascists.

For Germany and Italy, the civil war as a testing ground for new weapons—tanks and airplanes. The Republicans, including some Communists and Socialists, also looked to Western democracies for help. An American volunteer unit, the Abraham Lincoln Brigade, answered the call. Soviet assistance and volunteer fighters, however, were no match for new German-supplied weapons. In 1939, Spain fell to fascism.

FDR's "Quarantine" Speech

President Roosevelt was concerned about aggression by Germany, Italy, Fascist Spain, and Japan. When Japan invaded China in 1937, Roosevelt gave the "Quarantine" speech, proposing that democratic nations "quarantine" aggressors to "protect the health of the [international] community against the spread of the disease." Isolationists warned about possible American involvement in war. Polls showed that most Americans agreed with them, and Roosevelt gave no direct assistance to Europe's democracies.

Triumph of Aggression

The timid policies of the democracies led to the triumph of aggression and the failure of peace efforts.

Germany, Japan, Italy (1932–1940) Hitler violated the Treaty of Versailles by ordering German troops into the neutral Rhineland (1936). In 1938, Germany invaded Austria, and Hitler announced his intention of seizing Czechoslovakia's Sudetenland, where many Germans lived.

Meanwhile, Mussolini sent Italian troops to conquer Ethiopia in Africa. It fell in 1936.

The military leaders dominating Japan's government used similar methods. Japanese troops marched into Manchuria in 1931 and invaded China's heartland in 1937.

Munich Conference **Appeasement** is the policy of yielding to an aggressor's demands in order to avoid armed conflict. In 1938, British and French leaders applied this policy at the Munich Conference, where they gave in to Hitler's annexation of the Sudetenland. Hitler claimed that this was the last act of expansionism he would make.

A few months later, Germany occupied all of Czechoslovakia and threatened Poland. By 1939, it was clear that Hitler could be stopped only by force.

Start of World War II

In September 1939, Germany invaded Poland in a swift advance of troops, tanks, and planes called **blitzkrieg**. Britain and France declared war on Germany.

During the first two years of World War II

"Come on in. I'll treat you right. I used to know your Daddy": 1936 pro-isolation reminder of what happened to Americans in World War I

"The Other Road"

from *Straight Herblock* (Simon & Schuster, 1964)

(1939–1941), Britain, France, and their allies suffered a series of defeats. Germany forced the surrender of Poland in 30 days. Its armies then swept over Denmark and Norway. France fell to the Nazis in June 1940.

In 1939, Soviet leader Joseph Stalin had signed a prewar nonaggression pact with Hitler—a pledge that if war broke out, the two countries would not attack each other. With France beaten and the Soviet Union uninvolved, Britain alone had to try and stop Germany and Italy from conquering all of Europe. Planning an invasion of England in September 1940, Hitler ordered the heavy bombing of British cities to weaken them. The British RAF (air force) downed so many German planes that Hitler called off the invasion.

Gradual U.S. Involvement

With the outbreak of war and early German successes, Americans began to understand that a German victory in Europe would threaten U.S. security.

Neutrality Act of 1939 In 1939, Roosevelt persuaded Congress to pass a new Neutrality Act. U.S. war supplies could now be sold to belligerents under the cash-and-carry principle.

Destroyers Deal/Lend-Lease Roosevelt gave Britain 50 U.S. destroyers to use against submarines. In exchange, Britain gave the United States eight naval and air bases in North and South America. The exchange was called the destroyers-for-bases deal.

But Britain needed more supplies than could be obtained by cash-and-carry. Roosevelt persuaded Congress to authorize the lending of war materials to Britain. The 1941 Lend-Lease Act ended U.S. neutrality. Although not yet at war, the United States had committed huge economic resources to fighting Germany and had become what Roosevelt called the "arsenal of democracy."

Atlantic Charter In August 1941, Roosevelt and the British prime minister, Winston Churchill, met aboard ship near Newfoundland to formulate the *Atlantic Charter*, with the following aims:

★ right of all nations to self-determination

★ understanding that neither the United States nor Britain would seek territory from the war

★ **disarmament** (removal of weapons) of aggressor nations

★ "permanent system of general security" in the future.

"Hands Across the Sea": FDR with a fist for Hitler and the helping hand of Lend-Lease for Britain

★ In Review

1. Define and explain isolationism, fascism, appeasement, Neutrality acts, "Quarantine" speech, Lend-Lease Act, and Atlantic Charter.
2. Give one example of aggression committed in the 1930s by (a) Germany, (b) Italy, and (c) Japan.
3. Describe the causes that led to a change in U.S. policy from isolationism in 1939 to involvement in 1940 and 1941.

UNITED STATES IN WORLD WAR II

Pearl Harbor

Throughout the 1930s, the United States viewed Japanese aggressions in China as violations of the Open Door Policy (see page 139). In 1940, the United States placed an embargo on U.S. exports to Japan that had helped it maintain its war machine—oil, aviation gasoline, scrap iron, and steel.

By 1941, Japanese leaders believed that U.S. entry into the war might block their planned invasion of Indonesia. They decided to launch a surprise attack on the U.S. Pacific fleet.

On December 7, 1941, Japanese planes bombed the U.S. naval base at Pearl Harbor, Hawaii, sinking 19 ships, destroying 150 planes, and killing 2,335 soldiers and sailors.

The next day, President Roosevelt, calling December 7 "a date which will live in infamy," asked a willing Congress to declare war on Japan. Germany and Italy then declared war on the United States. The American people abandoned isolationism and rallied to the war effort.

Human Dimensions

"Arsenal of Democracy" Allied hopes for victory depended largely on how fast U.S. factories could turn out war goods. Government officials encouraged every industry to stop production of consumer goods and retool for ships, planes, bombs, bullets, and other military supplies.

Role of Women As young men joined the armed forces, women became the chief producers of ships, aircraft, and other war supplies. The number of women in the labor force went from about 15 million in 1941 to about 19 million in 1945.

Women also enlisted in support (but not in combat) units of the armed services. Many re-

tired workers, too old for armed service, returned to industrial work.

Mobilization Congress enacted a draft (selective service) law in 1940. Every man between 21 and 35 was required to register for possible service. By 1945, 12.5 million men and women—about one out of three of those eligible—were in uniform.

More than a million African Americans served, about half of them overseas. Hopes for equal treatment were again dashed when they were placed in segregated units. Black civilians held relatively high-paying jobs in Northern defense plants. Such opportunities greatly increased African American migration from the South.

Financing the War As spending on the war effort rose to billions of dollars, government debt grew daily, and people were encouraged to buy war bonds. Hollywood stars promoted bond sales nationwide. Popular entertainers such as Bob Hope organized shows that took movie and recording stars around the globe to entertain U.S. soldiers.

"Rosie the Riveter Steps Out," in defiance of her traditional role as homemaker

Rationing As industry shifted from consumer to wartime production, many goods became scarce—clothing, sugar, meat, rubber, and gasoline—and were subject to **rationing**. Americans received coupon books that limited their purchases of a rationed item. The *Office of Price Administration* made sure that retail prices of scarce products did not exceed allowable limits and cause inflation.

Military Service Service people were sent far from home and often lived in regulated, sometimes harsh, conditions. Those in battle faced death at every turn. The death of friends and the obligation to kill an enemy often caused severe psychological problems. The wounded were often disabled for life. For some, adjustment to military life was difficult. Most in the services, however, understood that they were in a war to save democracy.

Allied Strategy and Leadership

Assistance to the Soviet Union In June 1941, Hitler broke his nonaggression pact with Stalin with a massive assault against the Soviet Union. In response, the United States provided military aid to the Soviets and followed it up with Lend-Lease assistance of U.S. military equipment.

Europe First Despite Japan's attack on Pearl Harbor, the Allies' strategy was to defeat Nazi Germany first. They took more than three years to win back the territories taken by Germany and Italy in the first two years of war.

After initial successes, the Germans in the Soviet Union suffered a crushing defeat at Stalingrad (1942–1943). In the North African desert, the British defeated the Germans at El Alamein (1942). In 1943, combined assaults by the British and Americans forced the surrender of Germany's North African army. From their African bases, the Allies invaded Sicily and began a long campaign to liberate Italy.

On June 6, 1944 (code name: *D-Day*), the Allies began the liberation of France. The largest amphibious (sea-to-land) force in history crossed the English Channel to secure beachheads on the

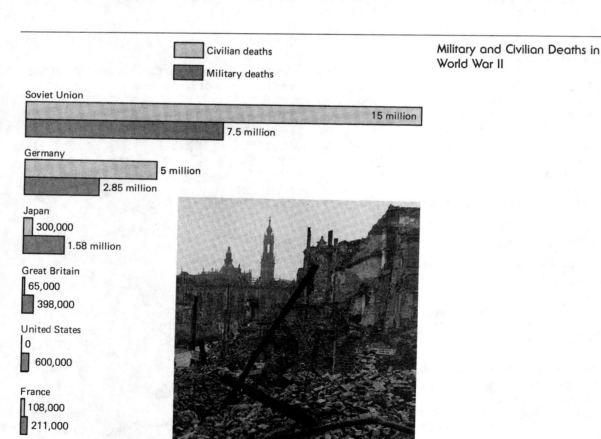

Military and Civilian Deaths in World War II

Civilian deaths

Military deaths

Soviet Union
15 million
7.5 million

Germany
5 million
2.85 million

Japan
300,000
1.58 million

Great Britain
65,000
398,000

United States
0
600,000

France
108,000
211,000

coast of Normandy (northern France). From these strongholds, General Dwight D. Eisenhower, Supreme Allied Commander in Western Europe, led the fight to control Normandy and then all of France. Paris was liberated in August and the push to Germany began.

Soviet troops also moved rapidly toward Germany and its capital, Berlin, from the other direction. In April 1945, U.S. and Soviet troops met on German soil. With the end near, Hitler committed suicide, and Germany surrendered unconditionally on May 7, 1945 (*V-E Day*), ending the war in Europe.

Two-Front War   By 1942, Japan occupied much of Asia and the islands of the South Pacific. Forced by Japan's successes to fight a two-front war, U.S. leaders developed a Pacific strategy known as "island hopping." U.S. forces concentrated on winning back only those islands that put them within striking distance of Japan. The Americans defeated the Japanese in several major battles. A turning point in the war at sea was the U.S. victory at Midway (1942).

Atomic Bomb

Manhattan Project   When Hitler initiated a program to exterminate Jewish citizens, the great German-Jewish scientist Albert Einstein, among others, fled to the United States. Einstein advised Roosevelt to develop an atomic bomb before Germany could do so. Roosevelt committed funds to the *Manhattan Project* (code name for the project to develop an atomic bomb) in Los Alamos, New Mexico.

Decision to Use the Bomb   President Roosevelt died in 1945. His successor, Harry S. Truman, planned on achieving final victory by invasion of Japan. Persuaded that an invasion might result in the deaths of hundreds of thousands of American soldiers, Truman chose another option—to save American lives by using the atomic bomb. His

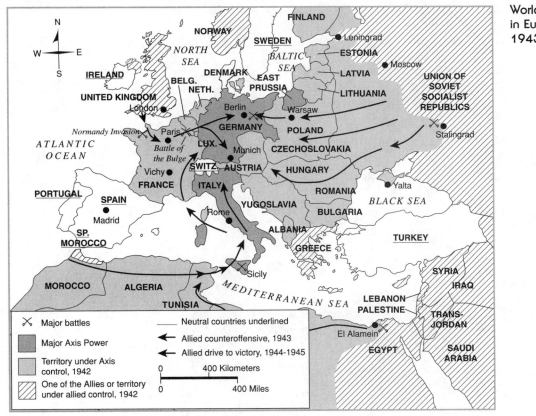

World War II in Europe, 1943–1945

decision knowingly condemned thousands of Japanese civilians to death, but he reasoned that the bomb's very destructiveness would force a Japanese surrender.

On August 6, 1945, a U.S. plane dropped an atomic bomb on Hiroshima. Three days later, a second bomb fell on Nagasaki. The two explosions instantly killed more than 100,000 Japanese. (Many thousands of others died later from effects of nuclear radiation.) Japan surrendered immediately. Thus ended the most destructive war in history. The total death toll for all nations was 17 million military deaths and probably more than twice that number in civilian deaths. The U.S. death toll was about 600,000.

Was the United States justified in dropping the bombs?

★ Although more than 100,000 people died from the atomic explosions, many times that number (including Japanese civilians and soldiers) might have died during a U.S. invasion.

★ Instead of dropping atomic bombs on civilian targets, the United States could have demonstrated the new weapon's power by dropping it over the ocean close to Japan.

★ The United States dropped a bomb on Nagasaki less than a week after the first drop on Hiroshima. It could have waited a little longer for a Japanese surrender.

U.S. Occupation of Japan

General Douglas MacArthur, Supreme Commander of the U.S. forces occupying Japan in 1945, was responsible for (1) demilitarizing the country (making it incapable of waging war) and (2) democratizing it. He supervised adoption of a new constitution (1947) that took all power from the emperor, guaranteed free elections and representative government, banned a Japanese army and navy, and declared Japan averse to war forever. Millions of dollars were spent rebuilding Japan's economy. By 1955, it was a prosperous nation closely allied with the Western democracies.

War's Impact on Minorities

Japanese Americans Thousands of Japanese Americans served loyally in the U.S. armed forces. Even so, Roosevelt yielded to nativist prejudice by signing *Executive Order 9066* (1942),

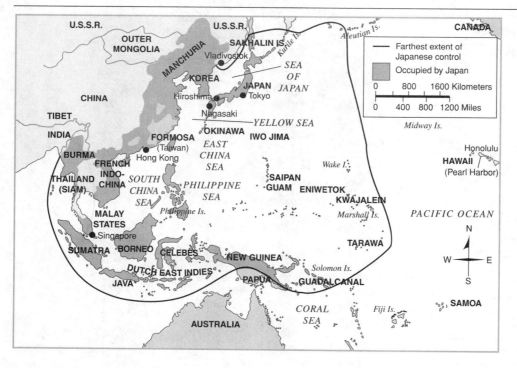

World War II in the Pacific, 1941–1945

which mandated the forced removal of 110,000 Japanese Americans from their homes in California and other Western states to barbed-wire "relocation centers." Most were released before war's end, but about 18,000 suspected of disloyalty were kept in a California relocation center until Japan surrendered.

In spite of this harsh violation of Japanese American civil rights, the Supreme Court, in *Korematsu* v. *United States* (1944), ruled that the removal was justified by military necessity. In recent years, Japanese Americans thus mistreated have received formal apologies from the government and some financial compensation

Segregation in the Military Segregation of African Americans in the armed forces did not end until after World War II.

Holocaust

As U.S. troops moved across Germany, they came upon concentration camps whose inmates, mainly European Jews, had barely survived Hitler's policy of **genocide** (extermination of an entire people). The Nazis had captured Jews in occupied European countries and murdered them or worked them to death in such camps. About six million Jews were killed in the **Holocaust**, the systematic Nazi slaughter of Jews.

Many Jews fleeing the Nazis tried to enter the United States. About 175,000 were accepted, but hundreds of thousands more were rejected although the immigration quota for Germany remained unfilled.

ADJUSTING TO PEACE

War Crimes Trials

From November 1945 to October 1946, a unique trial took place in Nuremberg, Germany. The defendants were former Nazi military and political leaders accused of war crimes, especially the mass murders of Jews. Judges at this first Nuremberg Trial represented the Allies. Of 24 defendants, 19 were convicted, and 10 executed. These decisions established the precedent that national leaders could be held responsible for "crimes against humanity."

Thus, at war crimes trials held in Japan, seven Japanese officers, including wartime leader Hideki Tojo, were sentenced to execution.

Demobilization

U.S. **demobilization** (reduction of armed forces in peacetime) proceeded rapidly. In just two years, 11 million soldiers were released from service.

Inflation and Strikes

During the war, the government had tried to prevent inflation by imposing price controls to regulate what businesses could charge for products. After the war, such goods as cars, gasoline, and rubber products were once more available, and consumers were eager to buy them. Most businesses wanted the controls removed. Reluctantly, President Truman complied. Without controls, prices increased by 25 percent from mid-1945 to mid-1946.

Businesses raised prices but not wages. One union after another struck for higher pay. Strikes in the steel, automobile, coal, and railroad industries threatened to cripple the economy. In response to a 1946 coal strike, Truman, a friend to labor; threatened to order U.S. troops to operate the mines, and he also proposed drafting striking railroad workers and ordering them to work the trains as soldiers. Both strikes were settled without these actions.

GI Bill of Rights

In 1944, Congress enacted a measure known as the *GI Bill of Rights*. It entitled veterans to free hospital care, grants and loans for college, and guaranteed loans for buying homes and investing in businesses. The law also gave a boost to colleges, universities, and the housing industry.

TRUMAN'S FAIR DEAL

As vice president, Truman succeeded Roosevelt, who died in 1945. Truman was elected president in his own right in 1948. Truman's domestic program, known as the *Fair Deal*, added to the reform ideas of the New Deal.

Partisan Problems With Congress

The war years had been characterized by **bipartisanship** (two parties acting together for the national good). During Truman's presidency, however, Republicans and Democrats were again at odds over almost every domestic issue.

Congress passed some parts of the Fair Deal while rejecting others. It approved the following measures:

★ increase in the minimum wage from 40 to 75 cents an hour

★ extension of Social Security benefits to 10 million people not originally covered

★ funds for low-income housing and slum clearance

★ increased funds for flood control, irrigation projects, and electrical-power projects.

Congress rejected the following measures:

★ national health insurance

★ federal aid to education

★ legal protection of African American civil rights.

Over Truman's veto, the Republican-controlled Congress enacted the *Taft-Hartley Act* (1947). Designed to limit the power of unions, it provided for the following:

★ Union leaders had to sign loyalty oaths that they were not Communists and did not advocate violent overthrow of the government.

★ A labor union could no longer demand a **closed shop** in which an employer can hire only dues-paying members of one union.

★ A labor union could not conduct a **secondary boycott**, by which strikers refuse to buy products from companies doing business with their employer.

★ An employer could sue a union for **breach of contract** (failure to carry out a contract's terms).

★ The president could call for an 80-day "cooling-off" period to delay a strike that threatened the economy or national security.

Upset Election of 1948

In the 1948 presidential election, Truman faced opposition within his own party. A liberal group of Democrats led by former vice president Henry Wallace thought Truman's foreign policy was too tough on the Soviets. The conservative "Dixie-crats," led by Governor Strom Thurmond of South Carolina, objected to Truman's support of civil rights for African Americans. Polls showed that the Republican candidate, Governor Thomas E. Dewey of New York, was far ahead of Truman. However, Truman's energetic campaign and the strong support of labor unions, farmers, and minorities carried him to victory in a close election.

Truman and Civil Rights

Continued Difficulties for Minorities Conditions remained difficult for African Americans. In the South, schools were segregated by law (***de jure* segregation**). In the North, housing patterns, not law, often imposed segregation in schools (***de facto* segregation**).

Truman's Policy Truman recognized that a democracy cannot deny fundamental rights to a large group of citizens. One of his first acts as president was to end segregation in the armed forces. He also established a *Fair Employment Board* to ensure African Americans equal opportunity to hold civil service jobs.

Truman urged Congress to enact laws to abolish poll taxes and punish those guilty of lynching African Americans. Congress refused to enact such laws, but Truman's stance paved the way for civil rights laws adopted later in the 1950s and 1960s.

★ In Review

1. Identify each of the following and give its significance: (a) Pearl Harbor, (b) "arsenal of democracy," (c) D-Day, (d) "island hopping," (e) Manhattan Project, (f) *Korematsu* v. *United States*, (g) Holocaust, (h) Nuremberg trials, (i) GI Bill, (j) Fair Deal, and (k) Taft-Hartley Act.

2. How did the need to wage total war alter the nature of American society?

3. Describe how each of the following were moral issues arising from the war experience: (a) integration of the armed forces, (b) nuclear warfare, (c) Japanese American civil rights, (d) Holocaust, and (e) war crimes trials.

Chapter Review

MULTIPLE-CHOICE QUESTIONS

Refer to the cartoon on the left of page 178 and answer questions 1 and 2.

1. The umbrella is a symbol of (1) war (2) an unsuccessful policy (3) resistance to Nazi Germany (4) international cooperation.

2. The statement most clearly implied by the cartoon is that (1) World War II could have been prevented by further appeasement (2) peaceful nations are usually exploited (3) appeasement did not prevent war (4) humans make progress despite war.

Refer to the cartoon on page 177 and answer questions 3 and 4.

3. Which of the following would the cartoonist most likely have supported at the outbreak of World War II? (1) Lend-Lease (2) immediate U.S. entry on the side of the Allies (3) special privileges for soldiers on leave (4) avoiding participation in the war.

4. The event that the cartoonist is referring to is (1) the Spanish-American War (2) the Boxer Rebellion (3) the Holocaust (4) World War I.

5. An immediate result of President Roosevelt's "Quarantine" speech was (1) isolationist criticism (2) rapid decline of isolationist feeling (3) increased military aid to the Allies (4) Japan's decision to withdraw from China.

Use the cartoon on page 179 to answer question 6.

6. The cartoon shows that, as a result of World War II, (1) fewer women became pregnant (2) traditional roles of women changed (3) divorces increased (4) men stopped working in factories.

Refer to the bar graph on page 180 to answer questions 7 and 8.

7. The graph shows that, in contrast to the rest of the listed nations, the Soviet Union and Germany suffered more (1) physical destruction (2) civilian but fewer military deaths (3) combined civilian and military deaths (4) military and fewer civilian deaths.

8. The graph shows that (1) France had more total losses than Britain (2) the United States had the fewest military losses of the Allies (3) Japan had more civilian losses than Germany (4) twice as many Soviet civilians were killed as Soviet military personnel.

9. Forced removal of Japanese Americans from their homes during World War II was closely related to (1) a labor shortage (2) racial prejudice (3) effects of the Great Depression (4) imperialism in Latin America.

10. A major goal of the Fair Deal was to (1) improve economic benefits for working people (2) extend postwar trading privileges to Germany and Japan (3) limit the power of labor unions (4) shift educational funding from state and local governments to the federal government.

THEMATIC ESSAYS

1. **Theme:** Fighting World War II: War Experience and Morality. The experience of fighting World War II made Americans face a number of moral issues.

   Task: Select two moral issues that World War II brought into focus. For each issue:

   ★ show how World War II made the issue a major moral question
   ★ describe the decision that was made to deal with the issue and the explanation given for reaching that decision.

   You may wish to consider use of atomic weapons, trying war criminals, and the conflict between national security and Japanese American rights.

2. **Theme:** The United States and the Coming of World War II. Necessity demanded that the

U.S. government under President Roosevelt practice neutrality while, in fact, assisting the British and preparing for its own entry into the war.

Task: *Specifically* describe how the U.S. government practiced neutrality while preparing itself for and becoming involved in World War II.

You may wish to include the Neutrality acts, Lend-Lease, public opinion, and the Atlantic Charter.

DOCUMENT-BASED QUESTION

*Study each document and answer the question that follows it. Then read the **Task** and write your essay. Include references to most of the documents and additional information you retain about U.S. history and government.*

Historical Context: Opening hostilities of World War II made the United States decide whether to aid the democratic nations fighting the forces of dictatorship, oppression, and militarism.

Document 1: From the agreement forming the Rome-Berlin-Tokyo Axis, 1940:

The governments of Germany, Italy, and Japan consider it a condition precedent of a lasting peace, that each nation of the world be given its own proper place. . . .
   ARTICLE 1. Japan recognizes and respects the leadership of Germany and Italy in the establishment of a new order in Europe.
   ARTICLE 2. Germany and Italy recognize and respect the leadership of Japan in the establishment of a new order in Greater East Asia.
   ARTICLE 3. Germany, Italy, and Japan agree to cooperate . . . on the aforesaid basis [and] assist one another with all political, economic, and social means, if one of the three Contracting Parties is attacked by a Power at present not involved in the European war or in the Chinese-Japanese conflict.

Question: Why was Roosevelt concerned about the German-Italian-Japanese agreement?

Document 2: From an address by President Roosevelt, 1941:

Suppose my neighbor's home catches fire, and I have a length of garden hose four or five hundred feet away. If he can take my garden hose and connect it up with his hydrant, I may help him to put out his fire. Now, what do I do? I don't say to him before that operation, "Neighbor, my garden hose cost me $15; you have got to pay me $15 for it". . . . I don't want $15—I want my garden hose back after the fire is over. . . . If it goes through the fire all right, . . . he gives it back to me. . . . But suppose it gets smashed up . . . . He says, "All right, I will replace it." Now, if I get a nice garden hose back, I am in pretty good shape.
   In other words, if you lend certain munitions and get [them] back . . . you are all right. If they have been damaged . . . it seems to me you come out pretty well if you have them replaced by the fellow to whom you have lent them.

Question: How was Roosevelt suggesting we help the British in their fight against the Nazis?

Document 3: Refer to the cartoon on the right of page 178.

Question: How does the cartoon show the influence of Roosevelt's Lend-Lease Act?

Document 4: Charles Lindbergh, as quoted in *The New York Times*, April 24, 1941:

We have weakened ourselves . . . [and] divided our own people, by this dabbling in Europe's wars. [Instead of] concentrating on American defense, we have been forced to argue over foreign quarrels. We must turn our eyes and our faith back to our own country [so that] a different vista opens before us.
   Practically every difficulty we would face in invading Europe becomes an asset to us in defending America. Our enemy, and not we, would then have the problems of transporting millions of troops across the ocean and landing them on a hostile shore. . . .

Question: Why did Charles Lindbergh feel that the United States should remain neutral?

Document 5: From an editorial in *The New York Times*, April 30, 1941, in answer to Charles Lindbergh:

. . . That conqueror [Hitler] does not need to attempt at once an invasion of continental United States in order to place this country in deadly danger. We shall be in deadly danger the moment British sea power fails; the moment the eastern gates of the Atlantic are open to the aggressor; the moment we are compelled to divide our one-ocean Navy between two oceans simultaneously. . . .

Question: Why did the editor of *The New York Times* disagree with Charles Lindbergh?

Task

★ Explain the arguments that supported and rejected U.S. neutrality during the opening years of World War II.
★ Describe how the United States participated in World War II before entering the war as a combatant.

Chapter 15
Peace With Problems: 1945–1960

★ Documents and Laws	★ Events	★ People
Smith Act (1940)	United Nations established (1945)	Winston Churchill
Truman Doctrine (1947)	Yalta and Potsdam conferences (1945)	Dwight D. Eisenhower
Point Four Program (1949)	"Iron curtain" speech (1946)	Jiang Jieshi
McCarran Act (1950)	Hiss case (1948)	George Kennan
Dennis et al. v. *United States* (1951)	Universal Declaration of Human Rights (1948)	Douglas MacArthur
Watkins v. *United States* (1957)	Berlin Airlift (1948–1949)	Joseph McCarthy
Yates v. *United States* (1957)	Marshall Plan (1948–1951)	Mao Zedong
	Chinese Communist defeat of Nationalists (1949)	Eleanor Roosevelt
	NATO established (1949)	Joseph Stalin
	Soviet Union A-bomb test (1949)	Harry S. Truman
	Rosenberg case (1950)	
	Korean War (1950–1953)	
	Oppenheimer case (1954)	
	European Economic Community (1957)	
	European Union (1994)	

★ Objectives

★ To understand how U.S. involvement with the UN ended U.S. isolationism.

★ To describe U.S. global commitments after World War II.

★ To explain the origins of the cold war.

★ To compare U.S. postwar policies toward Europe and Asia.

★ To describe cold-war conflicts in Berlin, China, and Korea.

★ To analyze how the cold war affected U.S. domestic policy.

INTERNATIONAL PEACE EFFORTS

United Nations

Representatives of the United States and its allies met in San Francisco in April 1945 to replace the League of Nations with the *United Nations (UN)*. In this new peacekeeping organization, representatives from member nations would meet to settle disputes and stop aggressions like those that had led to World War II.

According to the *UN Charter* (constitution), all members could vote in the *General Assembly*. The *Security Council* consisted of five permanent members—the Soviet Union, Britain, France, China, and the United States—and ten nonpermanent members serving two-year terms. In the event of an international crisis, a unanimous Security Council vote, along with four votes from nonpermanent members, would allow the UN to take military action.

An *Economic and Social Council* would attempt to reduce hunger and improve health care in poor countries. A *Trusteeship Council* would decide on the futures of former colonies of Japan and Germany. An *International Court of Justice* would hear legal cases involving disputes between nations.

In 1945, by a vote of 89 to 2, the Senate approved U.S. membership in the UN. Isolationism was at an end. As the world's mightiest nation and only atomic power, the United States prepared to play a leading role in international affairs.

Eleanor Roosevelt's Role In 1945, Eleanor Roosevelt was appointed U.S. representative to the UN, where she served until 1953. Elected chairperson of the Human Rights Commission in 1946, she was largely responsible for passage of the *Universal Declaration of Human Rights*.

Universal Declaration of Human Rights In 1948, the UN General Assembly approved the Universal Declaration of Human Rights, which cited such civil and political rights as freedom of speech and religion, freedom of movement and **asylum** (protection by a government of a person fleeing danger or mistreatment), equality before the law, and the rights to a fair trial, participation in government, and freedom from torture. It cited such economic, social, and cultural rights as the right to food, clothing, housing, medical care, education, social security, a decent standard of living, and work, as well as to form labor unions, marry and raise a family, and maintain one's culture.

Displaced Persons

The fascism of the 1930s and the widespread fighting of World War II created many **refugees** (people who flee life-threatening conditions or persecution in their own countries). In 1951, the UN General Assembly created the *United Nations High Commissioner for Refugees* to safeguard the well-being and rights of refugees, help them return to their countries or settle elsewhere, and coordinate international action to end refugee problems.

EXPANSION AND CONTAINMENT IN EUROPE

Summit Conferences

In 1945, Franklin Roosevelt, Winston Churchill, and Joseph Stalin—the "Big Three"—held a summit conference at Yalta in the Soviet Union. After Roosevelt's death in July of that year, President Truman represented the United States at a similar conference at Potsdam, Germany. The "Big Three" agreed to a number of principles about how to treat Germany and Japan in defeat:

★ Germany would be disarmed.

★ Germany—and its former capital, Berlin—would be divided into four zones of occupation (British, American, French, and Soviet).

★ War criminals in both countries would be put on trial.

★ Japan would be occupied chiefly by U.S. troops.

★ Polish territory would be granted to the Soviet Union.

The agreement about Poland was made at Yalta. Critics complain that Roosevelt had conceded too much to the Soviets by allowing the occupation of Poland, which led to the Soviet domination of Eastern Europe. Others point out that the Soviets also made an important concession—they agreed that after the defeat of Germany, they would fight Japan. Furthermore, Soviet troops were already in Eastern Europe at the time of Yalta; in effect, the region was already theirs.

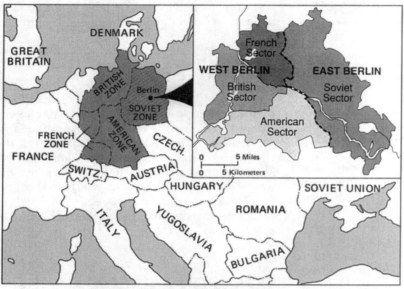

The division of Germany and Berlin, 1945

Division of Germany and
Berlin After World War II

Origins of the Cold War

Western leaders believed that the Soviet Union intended to gain control over other nations by supporting Communist revolutions.

The Soviet government feared the United States because (1) it uniquely possessed nuclear weapons and (2) it was part of a **coalition** (alliance for joint action) of Western capitalistic democracies.

The postwar U.S.-Soviet rivalry was based on opposing **ideologies** (belief systems). It was known as the **cold war** because the nations never fought each other, but rather showed their hostility in the following ways:

★ arms race to build the most powerful nuclear weapons

★ aid to rebel or government forces in local and regional wars, depending on which side leaned toward communism or democracy

★ **espionage** (spying)

★ propaganda to smear and condemn the opposition's way of life

★ space race to impress world public opinion with "firsts" in space exploration

★ mutual condemnation during meetings of the UN General Assembly and Security Council.

Soviet Satellites

At Yalta and Potsdam, Stalin had agreed that postwar governments in Eastern Europe should have free and fair elections. Instead, Communist parties supported by occupying Soviet armies took control of the police, newspapers, and radio stations. Communist candidates were voted for in rigged elections.

Communist parties controlling Eastern European countries took orders from the Soviet Union. The one exception was Yugoslavia. In effect, almost all Eastern European states were Soviet **satellites**; that is, their policies were dictated by the Soviet Union.

Each of the Allies was to occupy, briefly, one zone of Germany, after which the country would be united under a democratically elected government. Instead, Germany remained divided in two—a democratic West Germany and East Germany, a Soviet satellite.

"Iron Curtain" In a 1946 speech at Fulton, Missouri, Winston Churchill said that an "iron curtain" had descended across Europe. In other words, there would be little contact between the Soviet satellites, which were no longer free countries, and the democracies of Western Europe.

NORTH
SEA
GREAT
BRITAIN
SWEDEN
DENMARK
BALTIC SEA
NETH.
BELG.
LUX.
WEST GERMANY
FRANCE
SWITZ.
AUSTRIA
ITALY
EAST GERMANY (1945)
POLAND (1947)
SOVIET UNION
CZECHOSLOVAKIA (1948)
HUNGARY (1947)
ROMANIA (1946)
YUGOSLAVIA (1945)
BULGARIA (1946)
ALBANIA (1944)
BLACK SEA
GREECE
TURKEY

Nations under Soviet control (with the date Communists came to power)

Nation with Communist government but independent of Soviet control

Soviet Satellites in Eastern Europe After World War II

Postwar Uses of U.S. Power

Many Americans wanted Europe to resolve its own postwar problems. President Truman and congressional leaders, however, believed that a Europe weakened by war was open to Soviet domination. The administration therefore initiated a policy conceived by U.S. diplomat George Kennan and labeled **containment**. It called for U.S. military and economic efforts to prevent Soviet influence and expansion from spreading.

Truman Doctrine In 1947, Greece was in danger of being overthrown by Greek Communists. If it became a Soviet satellite, Turkey might follow. Truman asked Congress for $400 million in military aid for both nations. His statement, the *Truman Doctrine*, said in part: "The free peoples of the world look to us for support in maintaining their freedoms. If we falter in our leadership we may endanger the peace of the world—and we shall surely endanger the welfare of our own nation." Congress passed a foreign aid bill, the first of many during the cold war. Thus, Greece and Turkey turned back the Communist threat.

Marshall Plan In 1947, Western Europe was still in desperate economic shape. Communist parties in France and Italy won many supporters. Tru-

man's secretary of state, George Marshall, proposed an ambitious program designed to promote recovery and contain communism in Europe. Under this *Marshall Plan*, Congress approved $12 billion for economic assistance to Europe. By 1951, Communists had little hope of controlling France or Italy, although they remained strong. (The United States had offered Marshall Plan aid to all nations in Europe; the Soviet Union and its satellites refused.)

Berlin Airlift In Germany, the Soviets controlled the zone that surrounded Berlin. In 1948, they announced a closing of the land routes to West Berlin, the part of the city under British, French, and American control.

As commander in chief, Truman ordered the U.S. Air Force to deliver food and other vital supplies to West Berlin by air. The *Berlin Airlift* became a daily routine for almost a year. In 1949, the Soviets ended their ineffectual blockade.

Soviet A-Bomb and H-Bomb Tests

In 1949, the Soviet Union exploded its first atomic bomb (A-bomb). By 1952, the United States had developed the hydrogen bomb (H-bomb), which was thousands of times more destructive than the atomic bomb The next year, the

Soviet Union successfully tested an H-bomb. The world now witnessed an arms race as the two most powerful nations competed to produce more and more nuclear weapons.

Western European Organizations

Common Market / European Community / European Union After World War II, Western European countries gradually restored their economies. The most important factors were: (1) U.S. economic aid—the Marshall Plan; (2) Western Europe's skilled workforce; (3) strong demand for consumer goods such as new cars and appliances; and (4) the reduction of regional trade barriers.

In 1952, France, West Germany, the Netherlands, Belgium, Luxembourg, and Italy formed the *European Coal and Steel Community*. They hoped to increase prosperity by removing tariffs on coal, iron ore, and steel, and by regulating their production.

In 1957, the same six countries created the *Common Market* or *European Economic Community (EEC)* to eliminate all tariff barriers among members. Eventually, Britain, Greece, Portugal, Spain, Ireland, Denmark, Austria, Finland, and Sweden joined.

Member nations of the Common Market then set up the *European Community (EC)* to promote

Cartoon comment on the sorry state of the planet after an atomic war

the free flow of goods, services, people, and capital among members. In 1991, the EC met in Maastricht, the Netherlands, and agreed to launch a common currency (the euro), establish a European Parliament to set common foreign policies, and work toward a common defense policy. In 1994, the EC became known as the *European Union (EU)*. In 1998, the *European Central Bank* was established. As of May 2004 there are 25 European Union countries, and 12 have changed over completely to the euro. Most of the new members are from Eastern Europe and a number of other nations have applied to join the union. Widespread economic problems have caused a reevaluation by the member nations of the financial regulations and requirements for EU membership and adoption of the eruo.

North Atlantic Treaty Organization (NATO) The Soviet Union and its satellites posed a threat to Western Europe's security. For the first time, the United States joined a military alliance in peacetime. In 1949, Truman signed, and the Senate approved, a treaty with 11 nations (Britain, France, Italy, Belgium, the Netherlands, Denmark, Norway, Iceland, Portugal, Luxembourg, and Canada). It created the *North Atlantic Treaty Organization (NATO)*, whose purpose was to discourage Soviet aggression and thus avoid war. The allies agreed "that an armed attack against one or more of them . . . shall be considered an attack against all." NATO's strategy rested on a shield-and-sword concept: European and U.S. ground troops would be a "shield" against Soviet attack. U.S. nuclear weapons would be the "sword."

★ In Review

1. Explain the significance of Senate approval for U.S. membership in the UN.
2. Summarize the origins of the cold war.
3. Define and explain the significance of each of the following: UN Declaration of Human Rights, refugees, Yalta and Potsdam conferences, satellite nation, iron curtain, containment, Truman Doctrine, Marshall Plan, Common Market.

CONTAINMENT IN ASIA, AFRICA, AND LATIN AMERICA

In his 1949 inaugural address, Truman announced his *Point Four Program*, a foreign policy of economic aid to fight the cold war in underde-

Cartoonist's view of U.S. international alliances and commitments after World War II

veloped regions of the world. Congress thereafter voted for foreign aid to developing countries in Asia, Africa, and Latin America.

United States and China

After the defeat of Japan, U.S. policy makers hoped that China would become a strong and prosperous democracy. But China fell under control of a Communist government.

Rise of Mao Zedong During the 1920s and 1930s, a Communist army led by Mao Zedong fought against China's government army led by Jiang Jieshi, head of the Nationalist party. The fighting ceased when Japan attacked China during World War II but continued after the war.

Flight of Jiang Jieshi The United States gave economic and military aid to the Nationalists, and the Soviet Union did likewise for Mao's Communist forces. Mao attracted peasant recruits by the millions, and they defeated Jiang Jieshi and his Nationalists in 1949. They fled to the island of Taiwan.

"Hot War" in Korea At the close of World War II, the Japanese fled from Korea as Soviet armies moved in from the north and U.S. armies from the south. The two forces agreed on the 38th par-

allel of latitude as a temporary line between their zones of occupation. After the cold war began, the 38th parallel became a permanent border between North Korea with its Soviet-backed Communist government and South Korea with its U.S.-supported government.

In 1950, North Korean troops marched into South Korea. Truman ordered U.S. troops into South Korea and called on the UN to defend its government. (The Soviet Union had temporarily withdrawn its UN representative and thus lost veto power in the Security Council.)

As commander in chief, Truman pursued an undeclared war in Korea, calling it a "police action" (see map on page 194).

Chinese Involvement U.S. General Douglas MacArthur commanded the UN forces in Korea. After a series of defeats, his forces made a surprise attack behind enemy lines and pushed the North Koreans back toward the Yalu River on the Chinese border. When MacArthur pursued them, China sent thousands of soldiers across the Yalu River. Overwhelmed by this assault, UN South Korean forces retreated south of the 38th parallel.

Truman, MacArthur, and "Limited War" MacArthur urged Truman to let him bomb Chinese bases in Manchuria to stop the Chinese attack. Recognizing the danger of a larger war, Truman refused. MacArthur then tried to persuade congressional leaders to back the bombing of China. Truman, determined to keep to a "limited war," removed MacArthur as commander of UN forces.

COLD WAR AT HOME

Because of the postwar Communist takeover of Eastern Europe and China, many Americans feared that their own country might also be targeted by Communist spies and sympathizers.

During the presidencies of Harry S. Truman and Dwight D. Eisenhower, the government tried to determine the loyalty of its employees and others by measures that restricted free speech.

Truman and Loyalty Checks

In 1946, newspapers reported that Canadian government workers had given secrets about the American atomic bomb to the Soviet Union. In the United States, President Truman began a system of **loyalty checks** of federal employees: He

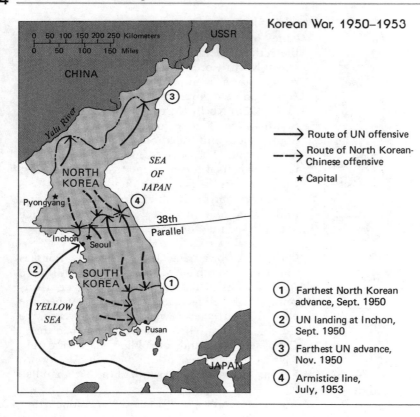

Korean War, 1950–1953

→ Route of UN offensive
--→ Route of North Korean-Chinese offensive
★ Capital

① Farthest North Korean advance, Sept. 1950
② UN landing at Inchon, Sept. 1950
③ Farthest UN advance, Nov. 1950
④ Armistice line, July, 1953

ordered the Federal Bureau of Investigation (FBI) and the Civil Service Commission to find out if such persons had ever belonged to a Communist or other **subversive** organization. (The U.S. government defined "subversive" as someone "seeking to overthrow [the government].") The U.S. attorney general listed 90 possibly subversive organizations, although, in many cases, he failed to prove the charge. Between 1947 and 1951, 3 million government workers were investigated. More than 200 lost their jobs as "security risks."

Anti-Communist Legislation

Smith Act Enacted before U.S. entry into World War II, the *Smith Act* prohibited any group from advocating or teaching violent overthrow of the government. It also prohibited anyone from belonging to such a group. In effect, since Communists advocated the overthrow of capitalist governments (not necessarily by violence), the Smith Act was used to make the Communist party illegal in the United States.

Several Supreme Court cases tested whether the act violated First Amendment guarantees of freedom of speech and association. Eugene Dennis and others were members of the Communist party in the 1940s. When they were arrested and convicted, under the Smith Act, of making speeches threatening national security, they appealed to the Supreme Court. In *Dennis et al.* v. *United States* (1951), the Court ruled that their First Amendment rights had not been violated because the speeches presented a clear and present danger of overthrowing the government by force.

In *Yates* v. *United States* (1957), the Court shifted position on the Smith Act. It decided that any idea could be advocated as long as the speaker did not urge people to commit dangerous acts.

McCarran Act In 1950, Congress passed the *McCarran Act (Internal Security Act)*. It was aimed at "Communist-front" organizations—groups that did not admit to Communist affiliations but were accused of receiving Communist support or harboring Communist members. The law required all Communist and Communist-front organizations to file membership lists and financial statements. It also prohibited (1) the employment of Communists or members of Communist-front organizations in defense plants and (2) the entry into the United States of Communists or former Communists.

House Un-American Activities Committee (HUAC)

In the 1940s, a special committee of the House of Representatives—the *House Un-American Activities Committee (HUAC)*—held hearings on disloyalty.

A labor organizer, John Watkins, was called before HUAC and answered questions about his own dealings with Communist groups. He refused, however, to give information about other persons on the grounds that it was not relevant to HUAC's work. Watkins was convicted of violating a federal law against refusing to answer a congressional committee's questions. In 1957, he appealed to the Supreme Court. In *Watkins* v. *United States*, the Court ruled that a witness at a congressional hearing may refuse to answer any question that does not relate to the committee's lawmaking task.

Hiss Case In 1945, Alger Hiss, a member of the State Department, accompanied Franklin Roosevelt to the Yalta conference. He then became director of a private world peace organization. In 1948, Whittaker Chambers, a former Communist, testified before HUAC that Hiss had been a Communist spy in the 1930s and had given Chambers secret government documents. Hiss denied the accusations but was convicted of **perjury** (lying under oath) and sentenced to five years in prison.

Rosenberg Case

The Soviet Union tested its first atomic bomb in 1949. In 1950, Julius and Ethel Rosenberg were charged with passing secrets about the bomb to the Soviets. Found guilty of conspiracy to commit espionage, the Rosenbergs maintained their innocence and appealed to the Supreme Court and President Eisenhower. Despite worldwide appeals on their behalf, they were executed in 1953.

Oppenheimer Case

Dr. J. Robert Oppenheimer was one of the physicists who built the atomic bomb in 1945. He later opposed U.S. development of a hydrogen bomb because he feared an uncontrolled arms race and the ultimate destruction of the world. Because of his public stand, the government accused Oppenheimer of being a Communist and a security risk. In 1954, it withdrew his security clearance.

McCarthyism

During the Korean War years (1950–1953), a Wisconsin senator, Joseph McCarthy, intensified American distrust of Communists and fear of subversion.

Portraying himself as a defender of U.S. security, McCarthy conducted Senate committee hearings in which he accused government officials, actors, writers, educators, and others of being "Communist sympathizers." Their constitutional rights were disregarded, and many lost their jobs. New jobs were difficult to find because businesses would **"blacklist"** (refuse to hire) those under investigation.

In 1954, McCarthy began to investigate the Army, which he demanded the right to question in committee. The hearings, unlike earlier ones, were televised.

Between April and June 1954, a TV audience of 20 million watched the Army-McCarthy hearings. Seeing the senator in action—interrupting and bullying witnesses and making reckless charges—many were offended. As the public turned against him, McCarthy lost both supporters and power. In December 1954, the Senate voted to **censure** (officially criticize) him for conduct damaging to the reputation of the Senate. The term "McCarthyism" has come to mean "the use of reckless and unfair accusations in the name of suppressing political disloyalty."

COLD-WAR POLITICS

Loss of China

China had two governments—Mao's Communists on the mainland (the People's Republic of China) and Jiang's Nationalists on Taiwan. Each claimed legitimacy. Through the 1950s and 1960s, the United States recognized only the Nationalists.

In the same period, the Nationalists represented China in the UN, despite Soviet attempts to unseat them in favor of Mao's Communists.

Truman's Loss of Popularity

As the 1952 election drew near, voters' complaints against the Truman administration grew:

★ Negotiations for a Korean armistice had been stalemated for more than a year.

★ Inflation, caused by war expenses and Truman's failure to settle a steelworkers' strike, was hurting the economy.

★ Communists controlled China.

★ According to Senator McCarthy, many Communists had infiltrated the government.

★ Some of Truman's political friends were suspected of corruption.

★ Truman had removed the popular General MacArthur from command in Korea.

All these problems led to the victory of the Republican presidential candidate, Dwight D. ("Ike") Eisenhower.

Stalemate and Truce in Korea

The war in Korea dragged on, with high casualties and no decisive victories. There was a stale- mate near the 38th parallel. In 1952, Republican presidential candidate Eisenhower had promised, if elected, to "go to Korea" and end the fighting. He did so in 1953, and soon afterward, a truce established the 38th parallel as the official line between North and South Korea. An armistice was signed in June 1953.

★ In Review

1. Describe one success and one failure of U.S. foreign policy in Asia between 1945 and 1955.
2. Explain how the United States responded to the Communist threat at home.
3. Identify and explain the significance of each of the following: Mao Zedong, Jiang Jieshi, Yalu River, Point Four Program, Smith Act, HUAC, *Watkins* v. *United States*, Alger Hiss case, Rosenberg trial, J. Robert Oppenheimer, McCarthyism.

Chapter Review

MULTIPLE-CHOICE QUESTIONS

Use the cartoon on page 192 to answer questions 1 and 2.

1. The cartoonist believes that the United States (1) must join the UN (2) should outlaw atomic weapons (3) should install an international "hot line" to prevent an accidental atomic war (4) can never depend on other nations to maintain peace.

2. The cartoonist's viewpoint is that (1) new weapons technologies will make warfare too horrible to wage (2) if World War II had continued, there would have been only one survivor (3) after the next war, the only technology will be the telephone (4) World War III will result in the end of humankind.

Refer to the map on page 190 and answer question 3.

3. The map shows that after World War II, (1) Germany became a joint Soviet-U.S. colony (2) Germany and Berlin were at first divided between the major Allies (3) France had the most control of Germany (4) U.S. policy toward Germany was opposed by three world powers.

Refer to the map on page 191 and answer questions 4 and 5.

4. The map shows that (1) the Soviet Union worried about attacks across its western borders (2) Yugoslavia became a democracy (3) the United States had an increasing influence among nations that were not Soviet satellites (4) the Soviet Union was clearly attempting to take over Europe.

5. A comparison of this map with the one on page 190 shows that (1) the British, French, and U.S. zones became West Germany while

the Soviet Union controlled East Germany (2) all of Berlin came under Soviet control (3) Germany was reunited shortly after the end of World War II (4) communism had little impact in France and Italy.

Use the cartoon on page 193 to answer questions 6 and 7.

6. The figure of "Americanism" stands for (1) isolationism (2) imperialism (3) anticommunism (4) internationalism.

7. The cartoonist is critical of (1) loyalty oaths (2) strikes by organized labor after World War II (3) the Marshall Plan (4) HUAC.

8. Korea was divided in 1945 as a result of (1) popular elections (2) a civil war (3) a political compromise reflecting cold-war realities (4) a dispute in the UN.

9. In the early 1950s, Americans were *most* divided over the issues of (1) nationalistic loyalty versus individual right to dissent (2) improving schools versus saving tax dollars (3) need for nuclear power versus fear of radiation (4) growth of big business versus its environmental impact.

10. Critics of McCarthyism stressed that (1) the government should be on guard against Communist subversion (2) fears of subversion can lead to erosion of constitutional liberties (3) loyalty oaths prevent espionage (4) communism is likely to gain influence in times of prosperity.

THEMATIC ESSAYS

1. **Theme:** Containment of Communism. After World War II, the United States under President Truman faced the new challenge of expanding communism.

   Task: Describe two methods by which the administration halted or contained the spread of communism in Europe and the rest of the world. For each method:

   ★ explain the program
   ★ illustrate the program as it applied to a specific area or nation
   ★ describe the ultimate impact of the program on limiting the spread of communism.

Consider the Truman Doctrine, Marshall Plan, Point Four Program, and formation of NATO as possible examples.

2. **Theme:** Security and Democracy During the Late 1940s and 1950s. The threat of global communism made many Americans fear that traitors were seriously undermining the interests and well-being of the United States.

   Task

   ★ Describe two examples ˄ federal involvement in a hunt for Communists within American society.
   ★ Show how, in at least one case, a constitutional value or individual right was sacrificed in pursuit of the Communist menace. (You may use an example already used in the first part or choose a new example.)

3. **Theme:** The Cold War. The cold war was an ideological contest that engaged the United States and the Soviet Union in conflicts mainly involving a third nation or area.

   Task

   ★ Discuss how U.S.-Soviet peace agreements helped create the cold war.
   ★ Demonstrate how two events during the post–World War II period helped increase U.S.-Soviet tension.

   The summit meetings at Yalta and Potsdam should be discussed in answer to the first section. For the second section, consider using the rise of Mao Zedong and Chinese communism, Soviet testing of an A-bomb, formation of NATO, and the outbreak of "hot war" in Korea.

DOCUMENT-BASED QUESTION

*Study each document and answer the question that follows it. Then read the **Task** and write your essay. Include references to most of the documents and additional information you retain about U.S. history and government.*

Historical Context: After World War II, two superpowers waged a cold war for global dominance. An early test of will was over Korea. The fighting there led to a dispute between President Truman and General MacArthur, the result of which was MacArthur's dismissal.

Document 1: President Truman, as quoted in *The New York Times*, April 12, 1951:

So far . . . a limited war in Korea [has] prevented aggression [leading to] general war. . . . We have taught the enemy a lesson. He has found out that aggression is not cheap or easy. . . .

We do not want . . . the conflict . . . extended. We are trying to prevent a world war—not start one. . . .

But you may ask: "Why can't we take other steps to punish the aggressor?". . .

If we were to [bomb Manchuria and China . . . assist Chinese Nationalist troops] . . . we would . . . risk . . . a general war . . . we would become entangled in a vast conflict . . . and our task would become immeasurably more difficult all over the world.

What would suit . . the Kremlin [Soviet Union] better than for our military forces to be committed to a full-scale war in Red China?

Question: Why did President Truman wish to fight a "limited" war in Korea?

Document 2: General MacArthur, as quoted in *The New York Times*, April 19, 1951:

. . .The Communist threat is a global one. Its successful advance in one sector threatens . . . every other sector. . . .

I made it clear that . . . not . . . to destroy the enemy build-up . . . [not] to utilize [the] friendly Chinese force . . . on Formosa . . . not . . . to blockade the China coast . . ., and [without] hope of major reinforcements, . . . the military standpoint forbade victory. . . .

War's very object is victory, not prolonged indecision.

In war there can be no substitute for victory.

Question: Why did General MacArthur disagree with President Truman's conduct of the Korean War?

Document 3: President Truman in the *Congressional Record*, April 10, 1951:

With deep regret I have concluded that General . . . MacArthur is unable to give this wholehearted support to the policies of the United States . . . and . . . United Nations . . . . I have, therefore, relieved [him] of his commands. . . .

Full and vigorous debate on matters of national policy is . . . vital [to] our free democracy. It is fundamental, however, that military commanders must be governed by the policies . . . issued to them [as] provided by our laws and Constitution. In time of crisis, this consideration is particularly compelling.

Question: Why did Truman remove MacArthur from his command in Korea?

Document 4: Refer to the map on page 194.

Question: What was the result of the Korean War?

Task

★ Describe the conflicting strategies of Truman and MacArthur regarding the Korean War.
★ Evaluate the wisdom of Truman's dismissal of MacArthur in light of the results of the war and the president's constitutional powers as commander in chief.

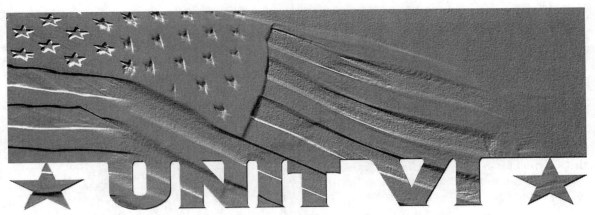

★ UNIT VI ★

The World in Uncertain Times

Chapter 16
Toward a Postindustrial World: Living in a Global Age

★ Events	★ People
Three Mile Island nuclear accident (1979)	Daniel Bell
Chernobyl nuclear accident (1986)	Rachel Carson
Exxon Valdez oil spill (1989)	Herman Hollerith

★ Objectives

★ To explain how the United States is changing from an industrial to a postindustrial nation.

★ To describe changes in technology and their impact on the United States and the rest of the world.

★ To recognize how the nations of the world are closely linked economically by trade and electronic communications.

The Industrial Revolution began about 1750 and, in a sense, persists today. By the 1950s, however, a revolutionary era of new technology and economic systems was underway. This era is called the *information age* or *postindustrial age*. As the world moves into the 21st century, it is undergoing rapid change.

CHANGES IN THE POSTINDUSTRIAL AGE

Manufacturing: Energy Sources, Materials, Automation

Nuclear Power The industrial age relied on burning coal and oil for energy. Scientists, however, predicted that people might use up all the oil sometime in the 21st century. They began to look for new sources of energy.

Energy and heat can be created by the splitting of uranium atoms. In the 1950s, the U.S. government and electric power companies hoped that nuclear power plants might produce cheap and efficient energy in the future without polluting the air with smoke. However, there was an inherent danger—accidents might release harmful substances into the atmosphere. An additional problem was getting rid of waste radioactive by-products.

New Sources of Energy Scientists have experimented with using the sun as an energy source. Trapping its rays to heat a home or run a small automobile would be environmentally safe. But would it be practical? So far, devices to harness

Early 20th-century cartoonist's view of the world of 2023

solar energy have had only limited use. The same is true of modern windmills and other technological applications for tapping the winds, tides, and underground heat.

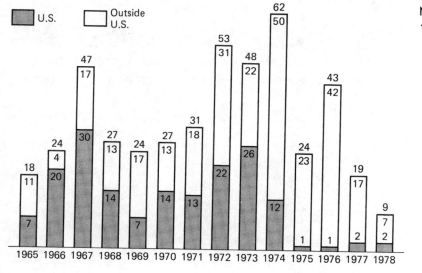

Nuclear Reactor Orders, 1965–1978

U.S. / Outside U.S.

Year	Outside U.S.	U.S.
1965	18	11 / 7
1966	24	4 / 20
1967	47	17 / 30
1968	27	13 / 14
1969	24	17 / 7
1970	27	13 / 14
1971	31	18 / 13
1972	53	31 / 22
1973	48	22 / 26
1974	62	50 / 12
1975	24	23 / 1
1976	43	42 / 1
1977	19	17 / 2
1978	9	7 / 2

Plastics and Light Metals In the postindustrial world, many items—calculators, computers, compact discs, wristwatch bands, car seats, cameras, radios, and carpets—are made entirely or in part of various plastics that did not exist before 1900.

The production of aluminum on a wide scale became practical in the early 1900s. Aluminum foil first appeared in 1947. Thereafter, manufacturers began to use aluminum to make many other things. Aluminum cans replaced glass bottles in the 1960s. In the 1970s, cars made from aluminum alloys were produced. Because of their lighter weight, they used less gas and were thus cheaper to run and less polluting to the environment.

Automation In the 1950s and 1960s, the U.S. economy made spectacular gains in productivity, largely because of **automation**—the manufacturing method in which one set of machines regulates other machines. Through automation, goods are assembled rapidly and with a minimum of human labor or error. Automation, however, has been a worry for factory workers because it reduces employment in jobs that require little education or skill.

Computerization

Electronic devices called **computers** helped make automation possible. The origin of the computer goes back to 1890, when an inventor named Herman Hollerith created a tabulating machine to speed the process of taking the census. To help the U.S. armed forces make rapid calculations during World War II, a 30-ton computer was put into operation in 1946. The Electronic Numerical Integrator and Calculator (ENIAC) consisted of 18,000 vacuum tubes. As an electric current flowed through the tubes, the machines made thousands of mathematical calculations in a few seconds.

This "first-generation" computer was replaced in the 1960s by a more powerful version. Instead of the vacuum tube, its basic electronic element was the transistor. Less than one-tenth the size of the vacuum tube, the transistor performed the same functions with greater speed and reliability.

In 1969, a smaller and more compact element—a thin square **microchip** of silicon imprinted with electronic circuits—replaced the transistor. Thus, smaller computers began to process and store more information at higher speeds and for less cost.

In the 1960s, a social scientist, Daniel Bell, observed that in a postindustrial society, "informa-tion is power. Control over communication services is a source of power. Access to communication is a condition of freedom." People now use computer discs to store **data** (information) that was formerly printed on paper. They can then transmit the data to other computers over telephone lines or through electronic signals bounced off space satellites.

The computer is the means to access the **Internet**, a network of computers that uses a system called the **World Wide Web** to provide information and resources on almost every available subject. The Internet has led to a new type of industry, as companies create **Web sites** on the Internet that enable a user to retrieve information and buy and sell products and services.

Widespread use of computers has led critics to point out a number of associated problems. How can computerized communications be kept private? Is there a limit to the amount of data a user needs or can absorb? Will commercial computer applications lead to a frenzy of overconsumerism? And how can computer programs be safeguarded against harmful electronic "viruses" that skilled but unethical users design and disseminate through the World Wide Web?

Corporate Structures

Such firms as General Motors (GM) and International Business Machines (IBM), which have plants and selling outlets in many countries, are known as **multinational corporations (MNCs)**. They maintain headquarters in American cities but open manufacturing plants in developing countries where labor is cheaper. By the 1990s, hundreds of U.S. companies operated in six or more countries.

The Internet and World Wide Web are contributing to **globalization**, the expanding ability of individuals and corporations everywhere to communicate and do business with one another. As a result of U.S. leadership on the Internet, English is becoming the world's language.

Multinational business has vastly increased world trade and opened world markets for U.S. goods and services. Unfortunately, it has also resulted in the closing of U.S. factories and the loss of manufacturing jobs at home.

Employment By the second half of the 20th century, most Americans were involved in delivering services of some kind rather than in making products. By 1993, only one out of five workers in

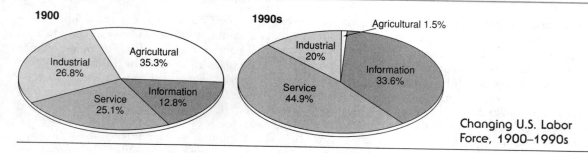

1900

Industrial 26.8%

Agricultural 35.3%

Service 25.1%

Information 12.8%

1990s

Agricultural 1.5%

Industrial 20%

Information 33.6%

Service 44.9%

Changing U.S. Labor Force, 1900–1990s

the labor force produced goods in a factory or on a farm. Four out of five workers either dealt with information (creating, transmitting, or storing it) or performed a service such as selling or transportation.

PROBLEMS OF THE POSTINDUSTRIAL ERA

Since the mid-1900s, technological and industrial growth has created environmental problems.

Pollution

Nuclear Waste Disposal and Accidents Waste materials from nuclear plants present special risks to the environment because they are radioactive. Moreover, there is the possibility that an accident might cause the nuclear core of a power plant to burn through its protective walls. In the event of such a "**meltdown**," the area for miles around could become radioactive. In 1979, a less serious accident occurred at the nuclear power plant at Three Mile Island, Pennsylvania. There was no "meltdown," but many people, frightened by the possibility, began to oppose building more nuclear plants. Opposition increased in 1986, when the nuclear power plant near the Soviet city of Chernobyl caught fire. Winds carried radioactive smoke across Europe.

Chemicals and Fossil Fuels In the 1960s, Americans became aware that industrial wastes and exhaust fumes were damaging the natural environment. In 1962, Rachel Carson published a book, *Silent Spring*, in which she identified the pesticide DDT, a chemical spray to kill insects, as the cause of the deaths of many birds and fish. She also explained that the extinction of wildlife would cause further damage to the entire envi-

ronment. In response to Carson's book, an environmental movement gained strength.

Sewage and factory waste polluted reservoirs of drinking water as well as such bodies of water as the Hudson River in New York and the Great Lakes. In 1989, the oil tanker *Exxon Valdez* spilled more than ten million gallons of oil off the Alaskan coast. Much of the marine- and wildlife there died. The cleanup took years.

Greenhouse Effect In the 1980s, scientists warned that forest fires, the burning of fossil fuels, and exhaust fumes from motor vehicles might cause the **greenhouse effect**. This occurs when carbon dioxide, along with water vapor, builds up in Earth's atmosphere and blocks infrared rays from escaping back into space. The resulting gradual increase in average temperatures may melt the polar ice caps, flood coastal cities, and harm plant and animal life.

Depletion of Ozone The **ozone layer**, a band of gas high above Earth, blocks the sun's ultraviolet light, which can cause skin cancer and other damage to human tissue. Aerosol sprays, Styrofoam materials, and chemicals used in refrigerators and air conditioners emit an ozone-destroying gas into the atmosphere. Canada, the United States, and all the nations of Western Europe have banned production of damaging substances.

Acid Rain **Acid rain** threatens the world's lakes and stream. It is caused mainly by factory chemicals and automobile exhaust fumes that enter the air as vapor and fall to Earth in acid-rich rain. In bodies of water thus polluted, fish die and plant growth is stunted. Wind currents carry this form of pollution hundreds and even thousands of miles. Half the acid rain that falls in Canada originates in the United States.

Reprinted with special permission of King Features Syndicate.

Energy Usage and Depletion of Resources

Between 1960 and the mid-1990s, energy usage in the United States increased by more than 100 percent. Increasing consumption spurred an increase in domestic production of crude oil as well as increased reliance on imported oil. As U.S. oil reserves ran low, the nation became ever more dependent on foreign petroleum. At the turn of the century, prices of imported oil rose significantly.

Waste Disposal

Plastic, glass, and aluminum items are not **biodegradable**; that is, they do not decompose readily when thrown away. Finding ways to dispose of them has become a nearly insoluble problem. Many communities recycle such items so that ma-

Hole in the Antarctic Ozone Layer, 1979–2002

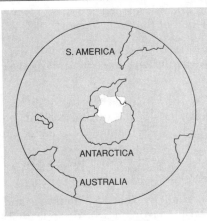

Southern Hemisphere
1979

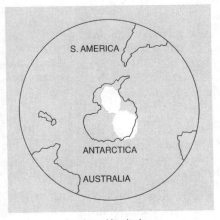

Southern Hemisphere
2002

The ozone layer

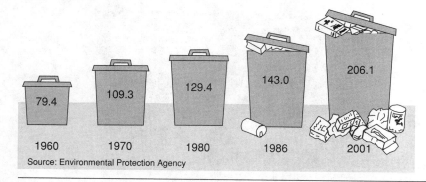

| 79.4 | 109.3 | 129.4 | 143.0 | 206.1 |
| 1960 | 1970 | 1980 | 1986 | 2001 |

Source: Environmental Protection Agency

U.S. Garbage Crisis (in millions of metric tons)

terials can be reused or turned into other products. Moreover, production of light metals such as aluminum consumes huge amounts of energy. To reduce these energy requirements, efforts are being made to reuse aluminum products.

★ In Review

1. Identify two characteristics of a postindustrial society that distinguish it from an industrial society.

2. Define multinational corporation and explain how it depends on modern technology.

3. Define and explain the significance of the following: greenhouse effect, ozone layer, and acid rain.

Chapter Review

MULTIPLE-CHOICE QUESTIONS

Use the cartoon on page 200 to answer question 1.

1. The cartoon shows that (1) cartoonists and writers will be replaced someday (2) technology had advanced only in the last several years (3) new ideas and inventions were important throughout the 1900s (4) someday there will be no need to work.

2. Which products are most crucial in the postindustrial world? (1) steel and iron (2) plastics and aluminum (3) steel and aluminum (4) plastics and iron.

3. A negative effect of new technologies on U.S. industry is a (1) decline in well-paid factory jobs (2) decline in service jobs (3) high failure rate among multinational corporations (4) consumer revolt against new technologies.

4. One consequence of multinational corporations is (1) increased risk of war (2) a decline in U.S. manufacturing jobs (3) increased poverty in underdeveloped countries (4) further depletion of the ozone layer.

Study the pie graphs on page 202 and answer questions 5–7.

5. The graphs show that during the 20th century, (1) demands of the workforce changed little (2) the need for manual labor increased (3) the skills most in demand changed (4) the workforce decreased most in the area of industrial labor.

6. The graphs indicate that (1) industrial and agricultural employment will disappear (2) service careers will give way to those dealing with information (3) the information sector is taking over industry, service, and agricul-

ture (4) preparation for a career today differs greatly from earlier times.

7. Which is the most accurate statement about the information in the graphs? (1) The computer has vastly changed the U.S. workforce. (2) Information industries have little to do with other sectors of the economy. (3) The computer will bring about a resurgence of the agricultural sector. (4) There will always be a demand for minimally skilled labor.

Refer to the bar graph on page 200 to answer questions 8 and 9.

8. A valid conclusion based on the graph's data is that (1) reactors are unsafe (2) orders for reactors peaked in the early 1970s (3) inflation is chiefly responsible for the varying numbers of reactors ordered (4) nations have become less dependent on reactors because of solar converters.

9. Which development would be most likely to help reverse the trend shown in the graph? (1) discovery of major new oil reserves in the Atlantic (2) an international agreement on nuclear arms limitation (3) expansion of solar energy applications (4) safer production of nuclear power and disposal of nuclear wastes.

Refer to the chart on page 204 and answer question 10.

10. The problem illustrated has been caused by (1) shorter hours for sanitation workers (2) increased purchasing power of U.S. citizens (3) introduction and increasing use of plastics and light metals (4) inadequate recycling by federal, state, and local governments.

THEMATIC ESSAYS

1. **Theme:** The Computer and Society. The development of the computer has changed how we live and work.

   Task

   ★ Show two ways in which the computer has changed U.S. society.
   ★ Describe *one* problem and *one* benefit resulting from the changes you described.

   You may use, but are not limited to, access to information, improved communication, and convenience.

Problems include privacy, information overload (access to more information than necessary), overconsumerism, and electronic "viruses."

2. **Theme:** Postindustrial World. An emerging postindustrial world has created new demands, opportunities, and challenges.

   Task

   ★ Describe *one* way in which a current problem can be solved in a postindustrial society.
   ★ Explain *one* problem in the transition from an industrial to a postindustrial society. (The problem may exist now or arise in the future.)

   You may cite, but are not limited to, energy and the development of new materials such as aluminum and plastic.

   Some problems to consider are waste management, pollution, and unemployment.

DOCUMENT-BASED QUESTION

*Study each document and answer the question that follows it. Then read the **Task** and write your essay. Include references to most of the documents and additional information you retain about U.S. history and government.*

Historical Context: Beginning around the 1950s, the United States and other industrial nations underwent changes that indicated the emergence of a postindustrial world. In the new millennium, the impact of postindustrialism is being felt worldwide. This new world will create demands on U.S. leadership and new problems for which leaders will have to find innovative solutions.

Document 1: From the magazine *L'Express*, Paris, France, May 17, 1976:

> The Russians depend on American agriculture in order to feed themselves and without American technology, Siberia would remain barren. The European leftists who demonstrated against the Vietnam War were dressed in jeans and listened to Bob Dylan every night.

Question: How has the new technology increased U.S. influence throughout Europe and the world?

Document 2: Babatunde Jose, Jr., as quoted in *Sunday Tide*, Port Harcourt, Nigeria, July 3, 1976:

Though [the United States] has not been a major participant in the African scene, she has nonetheless demonstrated her desire to help in the building up of the continent. American technological, scientific, educational, and cultural aid is what Africans want from America. We want the cooperation of [the United States] in the development of our friendships.

What we Africans do not want, however, is American imperialism and domination . . . .

Question: How can U.S. technological assistance be both helpful and harmful to many African nations?

Document 3: Refer to the cartoon on page 203.

Question: What does the cartoon say about the typical U.S. consumer's response to global warming?

Document 4: Refer to the maps on page 203.

Question: What is happening to the protective ozone layer above Antarctica?

Task

★ Explain how U.S. influence has expanded as the world has moved through the early stages of postindustrialism.

★ Describe *three* postindustrial problems facing the United States and the rest of the world. At least *one* problem should be different from those referred to in the documents.

★ Show how the United States can lead in solving a problem that you described.

Chapter 17
Containment and Consensus: 1945–1960

★ Documents and Laws	★ Events	★ People
Plessy v. *Ferguson* (1896)	Soviet A-bomb test (1949)	John Foster Dulles
Brown v. *Board of Education of Topeka* (1954)	Commonwealth status for Puerto Rico (1952)	Dwight D. Eisenhower
Interstate Highway Act (1956)	Korean War (1950–1953)	Orval Faubus
Civil Rights Act of 1957	Soviet H-bomb test (1953)	Martin Luther King, Jr.
Voting Rights laws (1957–1960)	Establishment of SEATO (1954)	Nikita Khrushchev
Eisenhower Doctrine (1958)	Bus boycott in Montgomery, Alabama (1955–1956)	Thurgood Marshall
	Suez Crisis (1956)	Gamal Abdel Nasser
	Polish and Hungarian uprisings (1956)	Rosa Parks
	Soviet launch of *Sputnik* (1957)	Jackie Robinson
	Desegregation of public schools, Little Rock, Arkansas (1957)	Adlai Stevenson
	Soviet downing of U-2 spy plane (1960)	Earl Warren

★ Objectives

★ To describe U.S. foreign policy of the postwar period under Eisenhower.

★ To understand how Eisenhower's domestic policies exemplified moderate conservatism.

★ To describe early victories in the African American struggle for civil rights.

★ To examine changes in American society in the 1950s.

EMERGING POWER RELATIONSHIPS

Beginning in the 1950s, the world was divided into three main political-economic groups:

★ *first world:* anti-Communist nations in the West

★ *second world:* the Soviet Union, its satellites, and allies

★ *third world:* underdeveloped, nonindustrial nations such as the newly independent nations of Asia and Africa and some Latin American nations.

The United States extended foreign aid to third-world countries to promote economic growth and thereby contain communism.

East/West

In 1949, after the Chinese Communists under Mao Zedong defeated the Chinese Nationalists led by Jiang Jieshi, the Western powers feared a Chinese-Soviet alliance. Given China's population and Soviet industrial and military strength, such an alliance would be formidable. The United States, which had historically allied itself with China against its Asian neighbors—in particular, Japan—now sought to enhance its relationship with Japan in order to contain China and the Soviet Union.

Moreover, with the formation of NATO in 1947, the United States and the Western European nations faced off against Soviet aggression. The Marshall Plan also aimed at resistance against Communist influence by helping countries in Western Europe rebuild their economies.

North/South

Except for Australia and New Zealand, the industrialized nations occupy the Northern Hemisphere. Most developing countries lie to the south, near the equator. A huge economic gap exists between the "have" nations (developed and industrialized) and the "have-not" nations (underdeveloped and still industrializing)—sometimes also known as the **third world**.

After World War II, the United States and other developed countries aided less developed countries with loans, grants, and technical assistance (expert advice). Multinational corporations have invested in poorer countries, opening factories and mines, and thus giving jobs to millions of third-world people. Corporations from developed countries can buy cheap raw materials and employ cheap labor to transform them into manufactures, and then sell the manufactured goods at competitively low prices.

On the other hand, developing countries have not benefited as much. Often unable to repay loans, they fall heavily in debt to industrialized nations. Increasingly, as the government budgets of third-world countries must be used to pay interest on international debt, regional resentment grows toward first-world creditors. In the United Nations, the poorer nations demand a change in policy that will relieve them of their crushing burdens of debt.

Growth in the world's population has only widened the gap between rich and poor nations. Populations in the poorer regions of the world grow much faster than elsewhere.

Eisenhower's Foreign Policy

End of the Korean War In 1953, six months after Dwight Eisenhower became president, North and South Korea agreed to a permanent truce. The war had been fought not for total victory but to contain Chinese and Soviet power. Today, the 38th parallel still separates South and North Korea.

Domino Theory and Massive Retaliation To impress upon the Soviet Union U.S. determination to stop the spread of communism, John Foster Dulles, Eisenhower's secretary of state, announced that any Soviet aggression would be met by **massive retaliation**. That is, the United States might resort to a policy of nuclear-weapons use called **brinkmanship**.

In the early 1950s, the cold war intensified as Chinese Communists took control of mainland China and North Korean Communists attempted a takeover of South Korea. As the French pulled out of French Indochina in 1954, Dulles developed the **domino theory**: Southeast Asia was a lineup of dominoes ready to topple; if Vietnam fell to communism, Cambodia, Laos, and Thailand would be likely to fall too.

"Atoms for Peace" By 1953, both the United States and the Soviet Union had A-bomb and H-bomb capabilities. Realizing that nuclear war would destroy the world, Eisenhower proposed an "atoms for peace" plan to the UN in 1953. Nations would pool their nuclear resources for

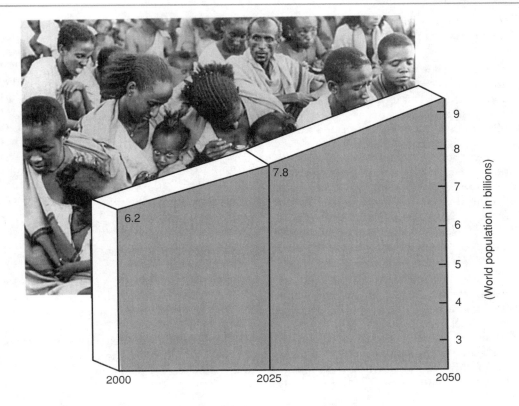

Projected World Population Growth, 2000–2050 (U.S. Census Bureau)

peaceful purposes, especially the production of electricity. Although the Soviet Union refused to participate, the United States, Canada, and their allies in Western Europe launched a limited version of the plan.

U-2 Incident In 1960, the Soviet Union shot down a U.S. spy plane, the U-2. After initial denials, Eisenhower admitted that U-2 planes were commonly used for spying. As a result of the U-2 incident, Soviet leader Nikita Khrushchev canceled a summit conference with Eisenhower, and cold-war tensions increased.

SEATO In 1954, the United States formed the *Southeast Asia Treaty Organization (SEATO)*, an alliance similar to NATO in Europe. Members were Britain, France, the United States, Australia, New Zealand, Pakistan, Thailand, and the Philippines (granted independence from the United States in 1946).

The U.S. alliances in Asia and Europe were based on the assumption that the Soviet Union masterminded Communist movements throughout the world. Thus, Americans viewed communism as a single force. In the 1960s and 1970s, however, U.S. policy makers realized that Chinese Communists and North Korean Communists differed in their goals from Soviet Communists.

Aswan Dam/Suez Canal In 1956, Egypt's leader, General Gamal Abdel Nasser, asked the United States for help in building the Aswan Dam along the Upper Nile River; its purpose was to generate electricity and irrigate the desert. When the United States refused, Nasser turned to the Soviets, who agreed to help. Nasser then proclaimed **nationalization** of the Suez Canal route through Egypt to the Red Sea. (Nationalization is the government takeover of property formerly owned by a colonial power or private company.) To regain the canal, Britain and France, its former owners—joined by Israel—launched an attack on Egypt. Eisenhower, worried that the Soviet Union might enter the conflict as Egypt's ally, condemned the attack. The invading forces withdrew, UN peacekeepers moved in, and the Suez Canal remained under Egyptian control.

Polish and Hungarian Uprisings In 1956, anti-Soviet riots broke out in Poland and Hungary. The Soviet Union agreed to a slight loosening of control in Poland. In Hungary, however, Soviet tanks rolled into the capital city of Budapest and crushed the uprising.

Eisenhower sent no military assistance to the Hungarian "freedom fighters." In response to NATO, the Soviets had formed a military alliance known as the *Warsaw Pact* with its satellites. To avoid war, Eisenhower chose not to challenge the pact by interfering in a Soviet sphere of influence. The Soviet Union was equally careful not to challenge NATO.

Eisenhower Doctrine The resentment felt by most Arab nations because of U.S. support of Israel led to growing Soviet influence in the Middle East. In 1957, Eisenhower—determined to contain this influence—stated that the United States would send troops to any Middle Eastern nation that asked for help against communism. This *Eisenhower*

Doctrine was first applied in Lebanon in 1958. The presence there of U.S. troops helped that country avert a Communist takeover.

Sputnik In 1957, the Soviet Union took the world by surprise by launching *Sputnik*, an artificial satellite that orbited Earth. Both Eisenhower and his successor, John F. Kennedy, wanted to show that U.S. space technology was superior to that of the Soviets. Under their leadership, Congress committed vast resources to the race for space. Between 1957 and 1963, the United States launched many satellites, began training astronauts for Earth-orbiting missions, and spent large sums on science education.

★ In Review

1. Define each of the following terms: "have" and "have-not" nations, domino theory, brinkmanship, nationalization, and Suez Crisis.
2. Explain how each of the following built on and extended the policy of containment: massive retaliation, SEATO, the Eisenhower Doctrine.

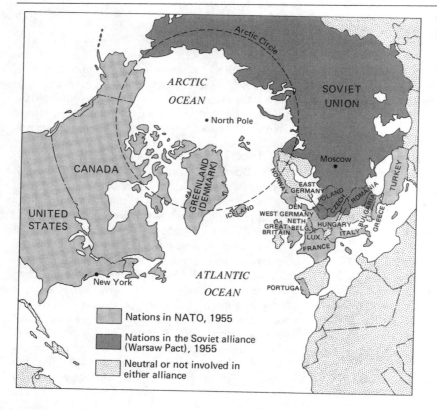

Cold-War Military Alliances—NATO and the Warsaw Pact

3. For each Soviet action listed, state how the United States responded: forcibly putting down a 1956 revolt in Hungary; launching *Sputnik* in 1957; shooting down a U-2 spy plane in 1960.

DOMESTIC POLITICS

In the 1952 presidential election, Eisenhower had easily defeated his Democratic opponent, Governor Adlai Stevenson of Illinois. In 1956, Eisenhower won a second term, defeating Stevenson by an even greater margin.

Eisenhower Peace

Peacetime Economy Eisenhower's domestic policies were mostly conservative—notably, laissez-faire for business and an increase in states' rights.

In the early 1950s, oil wells off the coasts of Texas, Louisiana, and California became very productive. The states claimed power to regulate and tax any oil drilled near their coastlines. President Truman had argued that such offshore oil rights were under the authority of the federal government. Eisenhower, however, sided with the states. In 1953, he gave them power to control oil rights within their territorial waters.

Eisenhower criticized the federal-run Tennessee Valley Authority power projects, which he called "creeping socialism."

While favoring business, Eisenhower disagreed with conservative Republicans who wished to cut back social programs begun by Democrats. To show his concern for people's welfare, Eisenhower persuaded Congress to enact the following laws and programs:

★ increase in the minimum wage from 75 cents to one dollar an hour

★ increase in Social Security benefits for retired persons and extension of coverage to more workers

★ creation of the cabinet-level Department of Health, Education, and Welfare, with a woman, Oveta Culp Hobby, as its secretary

★ government loans for students to attend college.

Interstate Highway Act In 1956, Eisenhower persuaded Congress to legislate the building of 42,000 miles of interstate highways linking major cities. (They would also be useful to the military in national emergencies.) The billions of federal dollars spent benefited the automobile, tourist, trucking, and housing industries, among others.

Suburbanization New highways increased the number of suburbs outside cities. Suburbanites drove between their homes and city jobs or became railroad commuters.

Warren Court President Eisenhower appointed Earl Warren, governor of California, as chief justice of the United States. Under Warren (1953–1969), the Supreme Court made controversial landmark decisions concerning the Bill of Rights. (See pages 228–229.)

CIVIL RIGHTS AND CONSTITUTIONAL CHANGE

Eisenhower, like Truman, found himself involved in the African American struggle for equal rights. Having fought to liberate peoples in Asia and Europe during World War II, African Americans felt that it was time for them to gain freedom from racial discrimination at home.

Cartoon criticizing President Eisenhower's apparent indifference to some U.S. problems

"The Helicopter Era"
from *Herblock: A Cartoonist's Life* (Times Books, 1998)

Challenges to Discrimination and Segregation

Jackie Robinson Jackie Robinson joined the Brooklyn Dodgers (now the Los Angeles Dodgers) in 1947. He was the first African American to play on a major league baseball team. At first, Robinson endured racial insults—from whites in the crowd, white teammates, and opposing ballplayers. He also had to stay in segregated motels and rooming houses when his team was playing out-of-town games.

His athletic talents and determination to keep calm won him the admiration of millions. In 1962, Robinson was the first of many African Americans elected to the Baseball Hall of Fame. His breaking of the color barrier in major league baseball quickly led to integration on other teams.

Brown v. Board of Education of Topeka The 1954 Supreme Court decision in *Brown* v. *Board of Education of Topeka* was a turning point in the civil rights movement. This landmark case came to the Court shortly after Earl Warren was appointed chief justice.

In *Plessy* v. *Ferguson* (1896), the Court had held that railroads, schools, hotels, and other facilities could be segregated if they were "separate but equal"—that is, if the facilities for whites and blacks were roughly the same.

In the early 1950s, public schools in Topeka, Kansas, were segregated. An African American student, Linda Brown, happened to live closer to a white elementary school than to the nearest black one. The white school rebuffed her father's attempt to enroll Linda there. Brown, aided by the NAACP, sued the Topeka Board of Education. A lower federal court rejected the suit on "separate but equal" grounds. Brown and the NAACP then appealed to the Supreme Court.

Thurgood Marshall, an African American lawyer employed by the NAACP, represented Brown. Marshall used legal arguments as well as psychological evidence uncovered by Kenneth

Former prisoners of war returning from Korea: The integrated U.S. Army of the 1950s

Jackie Robinson of the Brooklyn Dodgers—first African American in baseball's major leagues

Clark, an African American psychologist. Clark's studies had shown that African American children felt inferior because of segregation.

The Court, in a reversal, declared that segregated schools could not be equal because of the psychological damage that they inflicted on minority children. The justices unanimously agreed that segregation deprived children of equal educational opportunities and that Topeka's schools, and similar ones, violated the Fourteenth Amendment's guarantee of equal protection.

In announcing the unanimous verdict, Chief Justice Warren cited the following argument, among others:

> . . . Compulsory school attendance laws and the great expenditures for education both demonstrate . . . the importance of education to our democratic society. It is required in . . . our most basic public responsibilities, even . . . the armed forces. It is the very foundation of good citizenship . . . it [awakens] the child to cultural values . . . [prepares] for later professional training, and [helps in adjustment] to [the] environment. . . . it is doubtful that any child [can] succeed in life [without] the opportunity of an education. Such an opportunity . . . must be made available to all on equal terms.
>
> . . . Does segregation . . . in public schools . . . , even though the physical facilities . . . may be equal, deprive . . . the minority group of equal educational opportunities? We believe that it does.

Shortly afterward, the Court ruled that segregated school systems had to be desegregated. In 1967, Thurgood Marshall was appointed to the Supreme Court.

Launching the Civil Rights Movement

As the 1950s progressed, civil rights workers also challenged segregated buses, lunch counters, and movie theaters.

Montgomery Bus Boycott Montgomery, Alabama, was a typical Southern city in that it required African Americans to sit in the rear of a bus. In 1955, Rosa Parks, an NAACP official returning home from work, refused to give up her seat to a white passenger. She was arrested and charged with violating segregation laws. Martin Luther King, Jr., a young Baptist minister, organized an African American boycott of the city's buses. After more than a year, during which the boycott hurt the bus system and business in general, Montgomery agreed to desegregate its transportation system.

After *Brown* v. *Board of Education of Topeka* ended *de jure* segregation in education, many people wanted a similar ruling applied to transportation. The Montgomery bus boycott highlighted the issue nationally. In 1956, the Supreme Court ruled that segregation in transportation was unconstitutional.

Forceful School Desegregation By 1957, the Little Rock, Arkansas, Board of Education had a deseg-

Rosa Parks in the front of a Montgomery, Alabama, bus when Southern segregation laws required African Americans to sit in the back

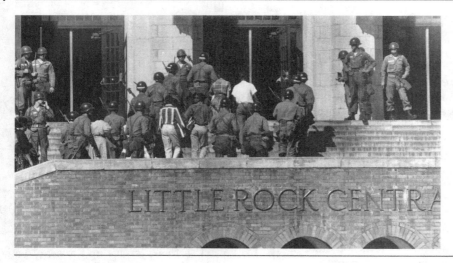

Little Rock, Arkansas: Federal troops protect African American students attending a formerly all-white high school.

regation plan and ordered a white high school to admit a few African Americans. Governor Orval Faubus, however, stated that troops were needed to keep order and then posted the Arkansas National Guard around the school to stop the African Americans from entering. A federal court reaffirmed their right to enter and prohibited the governor from interfering. Faubus removed the troops only after a white mob had stepped in to prevent African Americans from entering.

Faubus's actions challenged the authority of the federal government and the Supreme Court. Reluctantly, Eisenhower called the Arkansas National Guard into federal service and ordered it to protect African Americans as they entered the school. He also sent U.S. soldiers to keep order and prevent further trouble.

Strategy of Nonviolence Beginning in 1960, the *Student Nonviolent Coordinating Committee (SNCC)* organized sit-in demonstrations throughout the South. They would enter a segregated restaurant and sit at the counter. When refused service, they remained in their seats. Many were arrested, but sit-ins, combined with boycotts, led to desegregation in Dallas, Atlanta, and Nashville.

Civil Rights Act of 1957 African Americans in Southern states were often stopped from voting. Moreover, many African Americans knew that they risked their lives and property by appearing at a polling place.

In 1957, Congress enacted a civil rights law calling on the Justice Department to stop illegal practices that prevented African Americans from voting. In 1960, another civil rights law called for federal "referees" to intervene when voting rights

were denied. Although these laws—the first such laws since Reconstruction—were too weak to really protect African American voters, they paved the way for stronger legislation in the 1960s.

★ In Review

1. Identify and explain the significance of each of the following: Interstate Highway Act, Jackie Robinson, Rosa Parks, sit-ins, Civil Rights Act of 1957.
2. Summarize the background, facts, and Supreme Court decision in *Brown* v. *Board of Education of Topeka*. Explain its long-term significance.

Crowd of whites protest integration of Little Rock Central High School.

THE PEOPLE

Prosperity and Consumerism

After World War II, Americans spent a lot of money on the things they had lived without during the depression and World War II. These purchases marked a new kind of middle-class society. The urge to acquire more and more possessions became known as **consumerism**.

Postwar Consumption   In the postwar years, millions of Americans bought cars. Automobile sales spurred the growth of the steel, rubber, and glass industries. Spending on travel, restaurants, and motels increased. The gasoline required for auto trips was plentiful and cheap.

Since cars had enabled people to live in suburbs, suburban developments mushroomed. Middle-income families filled their roomy suburban homes with the latest appliances.

Television, developed in the 1920s, became widely available in the early 1950s. By 1953, more than half of U.S. households had at least one set. TV entertainment profoundly influenced American society.

For one thing, television intensified consumerism. Every show had a commercial "sponsor"—a company who paid for the show so as to advertise its products to a huge audience. TV was a visual medium, and its ads were more effective than radio ads in promoting sales. TV shows often carried the names of corporate sponsors—"The Kraft Television Theater," "The Palmolive Comedy Hour," and so on.

Television influenced American tastes and habits. Most people seemed to prefer light entertainment—sports, comedy shows, and adventure movies—to more serious educational programs. As people watched more and more TV, they spent less time doing such meaningful things as reading books or taking family outings. Critics of television believed (and still believe) that it had a negative effect on the values and habits of children and teenagers. On the other hand, for those who were interested, TV offered excellent cultural programs—plays, concerts, news commentary, and documentaries.

Baby Boom   The postwar prosperity influenced married couples to plan on larger families. Between 1945 and 1960, some 50 million babies were born. The dramatic increase in the birthrate was known as the **baby boom**. It increased sales of homes, cars, and appliances as well as toys, fad items, and teen clothing. Communities had to build more schools.

Migration and Immigration

As white middle-class Americans moved to the suburbs, African Americans from the South and new immigrants from Latin America moved into cities. By the 1950s, African Americans and Hispanics had become significant and growing minorities in the North.

Suburban Mass Production   Builders created entire suburban communities. One, established in Levittown, New York, used the same design for all of its houses so that they could be mass-produced. **Mass production** (manufacture of goods in large quantities by machine) meant lower costs. Thus, returning soldiers were able to buy affordable homes.

Cities in Decline   The increase in urban populations raised troubling issues for city governments. In general, the new populations were poorer than the middle-income groups that they were replacing. Inevitably, there was a decline in the tax base within the cities just as the need for greater services soared. By the 1970s, many cities were close to bankruptcy and desperately needed federal aid.

New Immigration Patterns   Most Latin American newcomers came from Mexico, Cuba, and Puerto Rico.

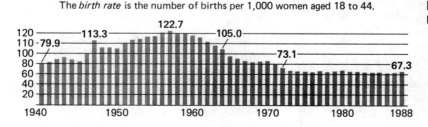

The *birth rate* is the number of births per 1,000 women aged 18 to 44.

Baby Boom—and Baby Bust: U.S. Birthrate, 1940–1988

Poor Mexicans sought economic opportunity in the United States. They came as *braceros* (laborers) to harvest crops in California, Texas, and other Southwestern states. While many entered in compliance with immigration laws, many others crossed the border illegally.

Puerto Rico had become a U.S. territory in 1898 as a result of the Spanish-American War. In 1917, Congress granted Puerto Ricans full U.S. citizenship. In 1952, their island was given commonwealth status; that is, Puerto Ricans elected their own governors and did not pay U.S. federal taxes. As U.S. citizens, Puerto Ricans may enter or leave the United States at will. After World War II, many of them settled in New York and other Northeastern cities in search of jobs, which were scarce back home.

Fidel Castro's Communist revolution in Cuba (1959) caused hundreds of thousands of Cubans to flee to the United States. They settled in Miami and other Florida cities. Most Cuban immigrants had middle- or upper-income backgrounds and readily found good employment in the United States.

★ In Review

1. Define consumerism, baby boom, Levittown, *bracero*.
2. Explain the significance of television as a force for change in American society.
3. Describe the new immigration patterns of the 1950s.

Chapter Review

MULTIPLE-CHOICE QUESTIONS

Refer to the graph on page 209 and answer questions 1 and 2.

1. The graph indicates that (1) the rest of the world has lagged behind the United States in birth control (2) Africa and the Middle East have the highest birthrates (3) between 1990 and 2050, world population is expected to double (4) development of urban areas worldwide has resulted in couples having more children.

2. The graph shows that (1) the world food supply should be adequate for only the next 25 years (2) demands on world resources will increase (3) the moon, Venus, and Mars will be colonized to support the growing population (4) sex education has been unsuccessful and should be eliminated.

Use the map on page 210 to answer question 3.

3. The map illustrates a situation similar to that (1) in Europe prior to World War I (2) before the Spanish-American War (3) in Asia at the time of the Boxer Rebellion (4) in Africa in 1900.

Refer to the cartoon on page 211 and answer question 4.

4. The cartoonist believed that (1) the public overwhelmingly supported Eisenhower's policies (2) Eisenhower appeared indifferent to many problems (3) Eisenhower personally solved the problems facing Americans (4) air travel was becoming more popular.

5. The significance of the civil rights laws of 1957 and 1960 was that they (1) ended discrimination in public facilities (2) were the first civil rights laws passed since Reconstruction (3) equalized employment opportunities (4) protected women as well as racial minorities.

Base your answer to questions 6 and 7 on the following song lyrics:

Little Boxes

Little boxes on the hillside, little
boxes made of ticky tacky,

Little boxes on the hillside, little
   boxes all the same,
There's a green one and a pink one,
   and a blue one and a yellow one.
And they're all made out of ticky tacky,
   and they all look just the same.
And the people in the houses
All went to the university,
Where they were put in boxes
And they came out all the same,
And there's doctors and lawyers,
And business executives,
And they're all made out of ticky tacky,
And they all look just the same.

           Malvina Reynolds,
         "Little Boxes," 1962

6. According to the song, during the postwar years, (1) homes were built with substandard materials (2) education was overemphasized (3) businessmen ignored workers' rights in spite of gains made by unions (4) there was an alarming degree of conformity among Americans.

7. The problems highlighted by the song were most likely alleviated by (1) a national school curriculum (2) an increase in inexpensive mass-produced goods (3) immigration from Asia, Latin America, and the West Indies (4) a decrease in new housing construction.

Use the graph on page 215 to answer questions 8 and 9.

8. An almost immediate result of the change in birthrate during the late 1940s and 1950s was (1) a rise in Social Security benefits (2) overcrowded classrooms (3) women entering the workforce (4) increasing cold-war tensions.

9. The probable cause for the birth statistics of the late 1940s and 1950s was that (1) there was little knowledge of birth control (2) the number of marriages and families increased after World War II (3) the marriage rate dropped after World War II (4) divorces increased during the 1950s.

10. Increased immigration from Mexico and migration from Puerto Rico after World War II were fueled primarily by (1) the desire for political freedom (2) the increase in bilingual education (3) the desire for economic opportunity (4) an appreciation for U.S. popular culture.

THEMATIC ESSAYS

1. **Theme:** U.S. Foreign Policy, 1945–1960. U.S. commitment to contain communism resulted in a period of peace with tension.

   Task

   ★ Describe *one* example of how the United States promoted peace or avoided potential conflict.
   ★ Describe *one* incident that increased cold-war tensions.

   Consider the end of the Korean War, the policies of John Foster Dulles, development of the H-bomb, "atoms for peace," the U-2 incident, new alliances such as NATO and SEATO, the Suez Crisis, the anti-Communist uprising in Hungary, the Eisenhower Doctrine, and the launching of *Sputnik* by the Soviet Union. You are not limited to these examples.

2. **Theme:** The United States in the 1950s: Conformity and Change. Some historians view Americans of the 1950s as conformists. Others view the period as a time of great change in U.S. society.

   Task

   ★ Describe *one* way in which Americans sought to conform.
   ★ Demonstrate *one* example of how change was taking place simultaneously with conformity.

   You may use, but are not limited to, the interstate highway system, suburban development, early civil rights actions, television, the automobile, consumerism, the baby boom, the decline of cities, and immigration patterns.

DOCUMENT-BASED QUESTION

*Study each document and answer the question that follows it. Then read the **Task** and write your essay. Include references to most of the documents and additional information you retain about U.S. history and government.*

Historical Context: In spite of some small gains by African Americans during the late 1940s and 1950s, implementation of equal rights for black people would be a long and difficult process.

Document 1: Refer to the upper photograph on page 212.

Question: What does the photo show about the armed services in the 1950s?

Document 2: Refer to the lower photograph on page 212.

Question: How did Jackie Robinson serve as a symbol of hope to many African Americans?

Document 3: Refer to the reading on page 213.

Question: What was the chief justice saying about segregated school facilities?

Document 4: Refer to the photograph on page 213.

Question: How did Rosa Parks help promote integration in Montgomery, Alabama?

Document 5: Refer to the photographs on page 214.

Question: Why was it difficult to integrate Central High School in Little Rock, Arkansas?

Task

★ Give *one* example of how hope for a better future was provided for African Americans during the late 1940s and 1950s.

★ Show how, in spite of the gains made, the average African American in the 1950s was still a second-class citizen.

Chapter 18
Decade of Change: The 1960s

★ Documents and Laws	★ Events	★ People
Vocational Rehabilitation Act (1920)	NASA created (1958)	Neil Armstrong
Mapp v. Ohio (1961)	Assassination of Medgar Evers (1963)	Stokely Carmichael
Gideon v. Wainwright (1963)	Assassination of President Kennedy (1963)	James Chaney
Civil Rights Act of 1964	Civil rights march in Birmingham, Alabama (1963)	Cesar Chavez
Twenty-fourth Amendment (1964)	March on Washington (1963)	Betty Friedan
Great Society legislation (1964–1968)	Assassination of Malcolm X (1965)	John Glenn
Voting Rights Act of 1965	Civil rights march from Selma to Montgomery, Alabama (1965)	Andrew Goodman
Miranda v. Arizona (1966)	National Organization for Women (NOW) founded (1966)	John F. Kennedy
Kaiser Aluminum and Chemical Corporation v. Weber (1979)	Assassination of Martin Luther King, Jr. (1968)	Robert Kennedy
P.A.R.C. v. Commonwealth of Pennsylvania (1971)	*Apollo 11* astronauts walk on moon (1969)	Nikita Khrushchev
Equal Employment Opportunity Act (1972)	AIM protest in Washington, D.C. (1972)	Lyndon B. Johnson
Mills v. Board of Education of District of Columbia (1972)	AIM protest at Wounded Knee (1973)	Martin Luther King, Jr.
Title IX (1972)	Defeat of Equal Rights Amendment (1982)	Malcolm X
Roe v. Wade (1973)		Thurgood Marshall
Vocational Rehabilitation Act, amended (1973)		James Meredith
Education for all Handicapped Children Act (1975)		Elijah Muhammad
Regents of the University of California v. Bakke (1978)		Ho Chi Minh
		Ngo Dinh Diem
		Michael Schwerner
		Alan Shepard
		Earl Warren

KENNEDY YEARS

The New Frontier

In his 1961 inaugural address, President Kennedy showed a determination to champion liberty against **totalitarianism** (all-controlling political dictatorship such as Soviet communism). He appealed to the idealism of American youth: "Ask not what your country can do for you. Ask what you can do for your country."

Kennedy's *New Frontier* program included proposals for federal aid to education, greater Social Security benefits, assistance to Appalachia (a poor rural region stretching from Pennsylvania to Alabama), protection of African American civil rights, and public health insurance for the elderly.

Domestic Policy Although both houses of Congress had Democratic majorities, Kennedy was able to pass only a few of his programs:

★ funds for urban renewal (rebuilding rundown city neighborhoods)

★ funds to aid the poor of Appalachia and other "distressed areas."

Other programs were rejected:

★ grants to states for school construction and teachers' salaries

★ Medicare (public health insurance) for elderly Americans

★ a new civil rights law enabling the government to act boldly against discrimination and segregation.

Such important programs were adopted during Lyndon Johnson's administration (1963–1968).

Desegregation

Interstate Buses   A new tactic in the civil rights movement was **freedom rides**. By crossing state lines on interstate buses, white and black freedom riders highlighted that segregation existed in interstate commerce (as defined in the Constitution) and, therefore, was not a matter of local law. Robert Kennedy, the president's brother and U.S. attorney general, persuaded the Interstate Commerce Commission (ICC) to desegregate the buses.

University of Mississippi   In 1962, a young African American, James Meredith, tried to enroll at the all-white University of Mississippi. Told by the governor not to enroll and threatened by a crowd of whites, Meredith stood firm. Kennedy ordered 400 federal marshals to the university to protect Meredith. He became the first African American to graduate from the University of Mississippi. Soon, other Southern colleges and universities began admitting African Americans.

Martin Luther King, Jr.   After the Montgomery bus boycott (see page 213), Martin Luther King, Jr., emerged as an African American leader.

King believed that nonviolent **civil disobedience** (refusal to obey unjust laws) would prevail against segregation. He effectively used this strategy to challenge segregation laws.

In 1963, King led a peaceful march through Birmingham, Alabama, to protest segregation there. The police attacked the marchers with dogs, water from fire hoses, and electric cattle prods. King and other marchers were arrested.

Writing from jail, King explained his action: "I submit that an individual who breaks [an unjust]

law . . . and who willingly accepts . . . imprisonment in order to arouse the conscience of the community . . . is . . . expressing the highest respect for law."

Medgar Evers   Medgar Evers was an NAACP leader who organized economic boycotts, marches, and picket lines. In 1963, Byron De La Beckwith, a white supremacist, assassinated Evers. In two trials, all-white juries could not reach a verdict. Finally, in 1994, Beckwith was sentenced to life in prison.

March on Washington   In 1963, King and other civil rights leaders organized the March on Washington to alert Congress to the need for stronger civil rights laws. More than 200,000 participated and heard King's powerful "I Have a Dream" speech, a portion of which follows:

> . . . I have a dream that one day this nation will rise up and live out the true meaning of its creed: "We hold these truths to be self-evident; that all men are created equal." I have a dream that one day on the red hills of Georgia the sons of former slaves and the sons of former slaveowners will be able to sit down together at the table of brotherhood.
>
> . . . I have a dream that my four little children will one day live in a nation where they will not be judged by the color of their skin but by the content of their character. . . .
>
> . . . With this faith we will be able to work together, to pray together, to struggle together,

to go to jail together, to stand up for freedom together, knowing that we will be free one day.

Cold War Crises

Kennedy continued the policy of containment.

Bay of Pigs   In 1959, Fidel Castro overthrew Cuba's military dictator, Fulgencio Batista. The United States approved the change until Castro seized American-owned properties in Cuba and established a Communist regime. Cuba was only 90 miles from the U.S. mainland and had fallen under Soviet influence.

Eisenhower had approved assistance to Cuban exiles who planned to invade Cuba and oust Castro. Kennedy also supported the plan. But he rejected supporting the invasion with U.S. air power. In April 1961, the invasion was launched in an area known as the *Bay of Pigs*. It was an embarrassing failure for the Kennedy administration.

Vienna Summit/Berlin Wall   In 1955, West Germany had joined NATO, and East Germany the Warsaw Pact. By 1961, West Germany had become more prosperous than Soviet-controlled East Germany, and many East Germans fled to West Germany. Shortly after Kennedy's inauguration, Nikita Khrushchev threatened to sign a Soviet treaty with East Germany allowing the East German Communists to cut off all the food shipped to West Berlin by land. Kennedy and Khrushchev met in a summit conference in Vienna, Austria, but came to no agreement.

Martin Luther King, Jr., in Washington, D.C., 1963, where he delivered his "I Have a Dream" speech

The Caribbean and Central America

In August 1961, the Soviets and East Germans built the *Berlin Wall* to prevent East Berliners from escaping to West Berlin. Kennedy traveled to West Berlin to assure the people that any threat against them would be a threat against the United States too.

Cuban Missile Crisis In October 1962, U.S. spy planes discovered Soviet nuclear missiles in Cuba. Kennedy sent U.S. ships into Cuban waters to intercept Soviet ships. He demanded that Soviet ships carrying missiles to Cuba turn around and that the missiles already in Cuba be removed. Many Americans feared nuclear war if Khrushchev disregarded Kennedy.

But Khrushchev complied. In return, Kennedy agreed never again to support an invasion of Cuba. The *Cuban missile crisis* was considered Kennedy's greatest success, as the Bay of Pigs invasion had been his greatest failure. Afterward, the Soviet Union and the United States became more cautious with each other.

Indochina

Vietnam Civil War Vietnam lies just south of China. After the Japanese occupiers left in 1945, nationalist leader Ho Chi Minh proclaimed independence from French colonial rule. But the French regained military control. Ho, a Communist, undertook **guerrilla warfare** (surprise attacks by small bands of raiders) from northern Vietnam. In such warfare, advanced technology has only limited effectiveness.

U.S. Involvement After a major defeat at Dien Bien Phu in 1954, the French withdrew from French Indochina (Cambodia, Laos, and Vietnam). In each country, Communists competed with other factions to win control.

In 1954, a conference about Indochina was held in Geneva, Switzerland. The United States attended only as an observer. French, Vietnamese, and other diplomats agreed to divide Vietnam at the 17th parallel of latitude into a Communist north and a non-Communist south. In two years, elections would be held to unite the country under one government.

A civil war, however, broke out in the south between supporters of Ho and those of South Vietnam's government led by Ngo Dinh Diem. To contain Ho's faction, Eisenhower increased U.S. support of South Vietnam by sending U.S. advisers to train South Vietnam's loyal soldiers.

Deeper Involvement Under Kennedy President Kennedy continued Eisenhower's policy of giving South Vietnam military aid and increased the advisers from 2,000 in 1961 to 16,000 in 1963. He hoped to fortify Diem against a Communist takeover and inspire him to fight poverty and make democratic reforms. Instead, Diem tried to crush Buddhist opposition with violence and provoked greater opposition. In 1963, Diem was assassinated by South Vietnamese military leaders.

Latin America

Kennedy developed a Marshall-like plan to promote economic growth in Latin America and contain the spread of communism from Cuba.

American and Soviet warships in showdown over Soviet missiles in Cuba

This *Alliance for Progress* gave Latin American nations, excepting Cuba, $20 billion over ten years. Latin America, however, lacked Western Europe's democratic tradition, and most of the aid funded the ruling classes rather than the poor. Congress allowed the program to die out.

Peace Corps

Another foreign aid program, the *Peace Corps*, sent volunteers to help people in Africa, Asia, and Latin America by teaching them literacy and modern methods of agriculture and health care. The Peace Corps tried to build goodwill for the United States through person-to-person contact in developing countries.

Race to the Moon

The Soviet launch of *Sputnik* in 1957 spurred Eisenhower to sign the *Space Act of 1958*, which created the *National Aeronautics and Space Administration (NASA)* to compete with the Soviets in space. In 1961, Soviet cosmonaut Yuri Gagarin became the first human to orbit Earth in outer space. Less than a month later, a NASA rocket lifted astronaut Alan Shepard into space but not into orbit. In 1962, astronaut John Glenn orbited Earth for five hours.

In 1961, Kennedy announced that the United States would be the first nation to land a human on the moon. In July 1969, *Apollo 11* carried Michael Collins, Neil Armstrong, and Edwin Aldrin, Jr., to the moon, as millions around the world watched on TV. As Neil Armstrong set foot on the lunar surface, he said: "That was one small step for a man, one giant leap for mankind." Kennedy's promise had been kept.

Nuclear Test-Ban Treaties

By 1963, U.S.-Soviet relations had improved. The superpowers signed a treaty agreeing to end nuclear-weapons testing in the atmosphere, outer space, and underwater. Underground tests were permitted. In 1967, another treaty banned putting nuclear weapons in orbit around Earth, on the moon, or on planets. The "hot line" established a direct telephone link between the U.S. president and Soviet premier so that they could communicate quickly in a crisis.

Kennedy Assassination

President Kennedy was shot and killed on November 22, 1963 in Dallas, Texas. The police arrested Lee Harvey Oswald, but another assassin killed Oswald two days later. A mystery still surrounds Kennedy's death.

RIGHTS OF DISABLED CITIZENS

Background

A disabled person is someone with a physical or mental impairment that substantially alters a major life activity. Popular attitudes toward disability were once characterized by ignorance, fear, and superstition.

In the 19th century, attitudes became more humane. Social reformer Thomas Hopkins Gallaudet, for instance, established a school for the hearing-impaired in Connecticut in 1817; John Dix Fischer began the New England Asylum for the Blind in 1829; and Dorothea Dix (active 1840–1860) argued that the mentally disabled should be put in humane mental hospitals. In 1865, President Lincoln established Gallaudet College for hearing-impaired students.

"Normalization"   In the early 20th century, a policy called "normalization" aimed to help the disabled enter mainstream society and lead more normal lives. The *Vocational Rehabilitation Act*

Astronaut Edwin E. Aldrin, Jr., walking on the moon, 1969

(1920) was the first major federal program to assist disabled veterans of World War I by counseling, guidance, job training, and placement. The *Social Security Act* (1935) made the law permanent and provided federal funds.

Activism (1966–1990)

Kennedy created a *President's Council on Mental Retardation* in 1962. It called attention to the job needs and capabilities of disabled persons and encouraged businesses to hire them.

During the Kennedy administration, a sports program, the "Special Olympics," was started for mentally retarded children and adults.

Litigation

★ *P.A.R.C.* v. *Commonwealth of Pennsylvania* (1971). The U.S. district court ruled that Pennsylvania could not prevent mentally retarded children from participating in free public education. Equal protection under the law required state programs for educating mentally retarded children.

★ *Mills* v. *Board of Education of District of Columbia* (1972). The Supreme Court established that children between 7 and 16, even if emotionally or mentally disabled, must be included in regular classes unless the school district provides a special program.

Legislation

★ *Education of the Handicapped Act* (1966). In 1965, the *Elementary and Secondary Education Act (ESEA)* set up special funding known as Title I to meet the needs of economically disadvantaged students. The 1966 amendment provided grants for "handicapped" children.

★ *Vocational Rehabilitation Act* (1973). This amendment to the original act of 1920 prohibited discrimination against the physically disabled in any federal program or state program supported by federal funds. It provided for ramp accesses in public buildings, specially equipped buses for passengers in wheelchairs, suitable bathroom facilities in public places, and sign-language interpretations of public television programs.

★ *Education for All Handicapped Children Act* (1975). This law provided for testing to identify handicaps, a list of rights for handicapped children and their parents, and funds to assist

state and local school districts in providing special education.

★ *Americans With Disabilities Act* (1990). This law protected 43 million mentally and physically impaired Americans against discrimination. It required businesses to facilitate employment of disabled persons by providing "reasonable accommodations"—restructuring jobs, changing workstation layouts, and altering equipment. All new public accommodations had to be accessible to the disabled. In existing facilities, barriers to services were to be removed if "readily achievable."

Dependence to Independence

Activism by Veterans   Veterans wounded in Vietnam held demonstrations to show that doors and stairs of courthouses, schools, and other public buildings made access difficult for people in wheelchairs. The federal government then required public buildings to have at least one entrance for wheelchairs, to make some telephone booths and toilets accessible to the handicapped, and to design buses so that passengers in wheelchairs could board.

Deinstitutionalization   The mentally ill were often kept in state mental hospitals for years with little or no treatment. In 1975, the Supreme Court ruled that such people who were not dangerous could not be confined against their will. New medicines and federal aid to local communities provided support for the mentally ill. Many of those released, however, lacked skills and could not find jobs. By the late 1980s, many of them were living on the streets.

Mainstreaming   Disabled children had often been placed in special schools. Many believed that such segregation damaged a child's self-image and ability to learn. A series of laws and court decisions during the 1970s mandated **mainstreaming**— providing special education services in regular classrooms so that disabled and nondisabled children could be educated together. Special classrooms or schools were to be used only if a child's disability was too severe for mainstreaming.

★ In Review

1. Summarize domestic policies during the Kennedy administration.

2. Explain how each of the following created a cold-war crisis for Kennedy: (a) Bay of Pigs invasion, (b) Berlin Wall, (c) Cuban missile crisis, and (d) Laos and Vietnam.

3. Define and evaluate the philosophy of Martin Luther King, Jr., as it has been used to protest unjust laws.

JOHNSON'S GREAT SOCIETY

Vice President Lyndon Johnson succeeded Kennedy as president. Johnson, a more experienced politician, shared Kennedy's belief in liberal reforms. To realize his domestic program, the *Great Society*, Johnson got Congress to pass more important legislation than any president since Franklin D. Roosevelt. Johnson was elected president in his own right in 1964.

Expanding Kennedy Social Programs

War on Poverty/VISTA During Johnson's first term, Congress enacted the Civil Rights Act of 1964 (see page 227). Johnson also announced an "unconditional" *War on Poverty*. As a first step, Congress passed the *Economic Opportunity Act* (1964), which authorized one billion dollars for antipoverty programs. He also established VISTA (Volunteers in Service to America). Modeled on the Peace Corps, VISTA sent volunteers to poor rural and urban areas of the country, including Native American reservations, to teach and lend technical support.

Medicare To help senior citizens pay for hospital care, doctor care, and other medical needs, Congress established *Medicare*, which became part of the Social Security system in 1964. People 65 or older were insured for much of the cost of health care. States also received *Medicaid*—federal grants to pay the medical bills of needy persons.

Education The *Elementary and Secondary Education Act* (1965) authorized $1.3 billion for educational programs such as Head Start—giving instruction to disadvantaged preschool children.

The *Higher Education Act* (1965) authorized scholarships to low-income students qualified for college.

Environmental Issues In response to the environmental movement inspired by Rachel Carson's *Silent Spring* (see page 202), Congress enacted several laws to control pollution and protect land, air, and water. The *Clean Air Act of 1963* funded state conferences to call attention to air quality and pollution. In 1965, the *Water Quality Act* attempted to establish clean-water standards. Also in 1965, the *Motor Vehicle Air Pollution Control Act* mandated the federal government to establish automobile emission standards.

CIVIL RIGHTS MOVEMENT

African Americans in High Positions

Without President Johnson's backing, the Civil Rights Act of 1964 and the Voting Rights Act of 1965 (see pages 227–228) might not have passed. In 1966, he appointed as secretary of Housing and Urban Development (HUD) Robert C. Weaver—the first African American to serve in a president's cabinet. In 1967, Johnson appointed Thurgood Marshall to the Supreme Court—the first African American to serve there.

Black Protest, Pride, and Power

Activism With Nonviolence The following organizations in the civil rights movement were moderate in their methods and goals. They achieved political and economic equality through nonviolence:

★ *National Association for the Advancement of Colored People (NAACP)*. (See page 129.)

★ *Urban League*. The Urban League sought to end discrimination in employment and hous-

1963 drawing of African Americans on a nonviolent civil rights march

ing and increase job opportunities for African Americans.

★ *Student Nonviolent Coordinating Committee (SNCC)*. Students who joined this organization participated in sit-ins and other peaceful demonstrations against Jim Crow laws in the South.

★ *Southern Christian Leadership Conference (SCLC)*. Founded in 1957 by Martin Luther King, Jr., SCLC coordinated African American efforts to end segregation in the South. Its nonviolent protests included boycotts, sit-ins, and marches.

★ *Congress of Racial Equality (CORE)*. Founded during World War II, CORE, under the leadership of James Farmer, conducted freedom rides in the 1960s. White and black Americans took long-distance bus trips to check that terminals in the South were not segregated. Though attacked by racist mobs, members responded with **passive resistance** (endurance of violence without retaliation).

Black Muslims/Black Panthers In the mid-1960s, more radical leaders—Eldridge Cleaver, Stokely Carmichael, and Angela Davis—were dissatisfied with the pace of progress. They called for "black power" and spoke of racial revolution. Two groups committed to black power were the *Black Muslims* and the *Black Panthers*.

Black Muslims are a group of African American followers of Islam. The founder, Elijah Muhammad, advocated (1) a separate African American state within the United States and (2) pride in being black. A leading Black Muslim,

Malcolm X, formed his own group in 1963. He told his followers to obey the law but also urged them to fight back against physical abuse.

Organized in 1966, the Black Panthers advocated force to achieve "black power." They formed a semi-military organization, wore uniforms, and carried rifles. They also demanded "better education, better medical care and better housing." Their chief spokesman and minister of information was Eldridge Cleaver.

Civil Unrest More than 30 African American churches were bombed during the 1960s. In 1963, the bombing of a Baptist church in Birmingham, Alabama, killed four African American girls.

In 1964, three young activists—James Chaney, a Southern black, and two white Jewish students from New York, Andrew Goodman and Michael Schwerner—tried to register African American voters in Mississippi and were killed by unknown assailants. The Ku Klux Klan was suspected, but the case was never solved.

To rally support for registering African Americans in Alabama, Martin Luther King, Jr., in 1965, organized a long-distance march from Selma to the state capital, Montgomery. The marchers were beaten by the police and harassed by a hostile crowd. Johnson sent federal troops to protect them, although one marcher, Viola Liuzzo, was killed shortly after reaching Birmingham.

In northern cities, African Americans living in poor, crowded neighborhoods, many of them unemployed, realized that civil rights laws would not immediately solve their problems. The bombing of black churches and murders of civil rights

CORE freedom riders faced attacks on their buses as well as other grave personal dangers.

Montgomery, Alabama, civil rights marcher attacked by police dog, 1965

workers fueled anger and distrust of whites, which erupted in riots. The 1965 Watts riot in Los Angeles lasted six days and resulted in 34 deaths and $200 million worth of property damage. In the summers of 1966 and 1967, similar outbreaks occurred in more than 167 cities, including Detroit, Michigan, and Newark, New Jersey.

Investigating the rioting, the Kerner Commission noted that the United States was becoming two "separate but unequal" societies, one black and one white. It recommended government programs to relieve urban poverty and increase job opportunities for African Americans.

Assassinations of Civil Rights Leaders Three African American leaders were assassinated during the 1960s. Medgar Evers was killed by white racists in 1963. In 1965, Malcolm X was killed by three Black Muslim opponents. Martin Luther King, Jr., was killed in 1968. News of King's death touched off riots in many cities. A Southern white, James Earl Ray, was believed to be the assassin, but in the 1990s, some questions about his guilt were raised.

Legislation

Civil Rights Act of 1964 This law authorized the U.S. attorney general to bring suit over civil rights violations and prohibited various forms of **racial discrimination** (denying equal rights because of race). It prohibited the following:

★ discrimination in restaurants, hotels, and gas stations

★ discrimination in government-operated facilities such as parks and pools

★ discrimination in federal projects such as urban renewal and antipoverty programs

★ discrimination by employers of 100 or more workers and by labor unions of 100 or more members (later reduced to 25).

White person protesting the speed of African Americans' civil rights gains

from *Straight Herblock* (Simon & Schuster, 1964)

In effect, the act abolished Jim Crow laws and practices.

In *Heart of Atlanta Motel, Inc.* v. *United States* (1964), a motel owner challenged Congress's right to outlaw discrimination in motels. The Court ruled that Congress had the right under the powers of the interstate commerce clause of the Constitution.

Twenty-fourth Amendment The Twenty-fourth Amendment (1964) prohibited a poll tax in federal elections (for president, vice president, and Congress). It especially benefited Southern African Americans, many of whom were too poor to pay poll taxes. Soon after ratification, many states abolished the poll tax in state and local elections too.

Voting Rights Act (1965) This law prohibited literacy tests as means of barring African Americans from voting and authorized federal registrars to help blacks register in areas where they had been afraid to do so. Within a year, the number of registered Southern blacks increased by about 50 percent.

Court Decisions (1950–1995)

Educational Equity In *Sweatt* v. *Painter* (1950), the Supreme Court had declared that a black student, Herman Sweatt, must be accepted by the University of Texas law school because the African American law school was unequal. In that same year, a black student at the University of Oklahoma challenged being seated apart from white students in classes and the cafeteria. The Court ruled in *McLaurin* v. *Oklahoma State Regents* that a state may not treat a student differently because of race.

Brown v. *Board of Education of Topeka* (1954) had ended *de jure* segregation in education. In 1964, the Court ruled that schools in Prince Edward County, Virginia, could not use public funds to support private schools for white students.

In the 1970s, the Supreme Court challenged *de facto* segregation in the North, stemming from housing patterns. In several cases, the Court ruled that busing should be used to desegregate neighborhood schools. This ruling led to some violence by whites.

Affirmative Action Under Johnson, the government adopted a policy of **affirmative action**. To ensure that past discrimination did not continue, the government encouraged businesses to increase job opportunities for women and minorities. It also cut off financial aid to colleges and universities without affirmative action programs. Businesses without such programs lost their government contracts.

One of the first affirmative-action-in-education decisions of the Court was *Regents of the University of California* v. *Bakke* (1978). The university had twice rejected the application of Allan Bakke, a white man, even though his entrance examination scores were higher than those of many who had been admitted. The university argued that it had set aside 16 out of 100 openings for minority students to fulfill affirmative action goals. Bakke sued the university for violating the equal-protection clause of the Fourteenth Amendment.

Ruling in favor of Bakke, the Court declared that the university's approach to affirmative action was unconstitutional because it involved racial quotas. It said, however, that race could be one factor—but only one—in deciding whom to admit.

Preferential Employment In 1971, the Court ruled against racial discrimination in employment. A power company in North Carolina required applicants without high school diplomas to take intelligence tests. The Court declared that such a requirement violated the Civil Rights Act of 1964 and the Fourteenth Amendment, which called for equality under law.

Kaiser Aluminum and Chemical Corporation v. *Weber* (1979) involved an affirmative action plan to correct racial imbalance in the workforce. The workers at Kaiser had been almost exclusively white. The steel workers' union and the company agreed to develop a training program in which half of the trainees would be African American. Brian Weber, a white worker, sued Kaiser because he had been rejected for the program even though he had more **seniority** (years of service) than the African Americans selected.

The Court ruled that Kaiser's affirmative action plan was reasonable because it was temporary and did not deprive white workers of their jobs.

In *Fullilove* v. *Klutznick* (1980), the Court, citing the equal-protection clause of the Fourteenth Amendment, voted in favor of the requirement that 10 percent of federal funds for local public works projects be used to acquire services from minority-owned businesses.

The Court did not always favor affirmative action. In a case involving the firefighters of Memphis, Tennessee, it ruled that African American workers hired to reduce racial imbalance could be laid off first if they had less seniority than white coworkers. In 1995, the Court ruled against favoritism toward women and minority businesspeople bidding on government contracts.

Equal Housing In *Jones* v. *Alfred H. Mayer Co.* (1968), the Court voted in favor of equal housing by ruling that the Thirteenth Amendment, which ended slavery, implied equal treatment of all citizens with respect to ownership of private property.

Voting Rights/Legislative Reapportionment In *Baker* v. *Carr* (1962), the Supreme Court ruled that all legislative districts must have approximately the same number of persons ("one person, one vote"). Thus, voting districts in African American areas could no longer contain more people than voting districts in white areas. As a consequence of this decision, the number of representatives from urban areas increased, which improved minority representation in state legislatures.

Modern Women's Movement

The Nineteenth Amendment gave women the vote, but not equal rights in the workplace. After World War II, women left their jobs to make way for ex-servicemen returning to the workforce. During the 1950s, most middle-income women believed in staying at home and caring for their families while their husbands provided the family income. Such traditional views were challenged in the 1960s by **feminists** (those in favor of women's rights and opposed to political, economic, and social inequality between men and women).

Kennedy Commission/Civil Rights Act of 1964 In 1963, Kennedy established a commission to investigate and review the role of U.S. women, with Eleanor Roosevelt as first chairperson. One goal of the Civil Rights Act of 1964 was to ban job discrimination on the basis of sex.

Title IX (1972) Title IX, which aimed to promote equal treatment in schools for female staff and students, stated that "no person in the United States shall, on the basis of sex, be excluded from participation in, be denied the benefits of, or be subjected to discrimination under any education program or activity receiving federal financial assistance." One consequence was that schools and colleges greatly increased sports programs for females.

NOW (1966–Present) In 1966, feminist leaders formed the *National Organization for Women*

"How Come No Founding Mothers?" A cartoonist's view of women's complaints about their exclusion from history

Drawing by Dana Fradon; © 1972 The New Yorker Magazine, Inc.

(NOW). Its goals included equal pay for equal work, day-care centers for the children of working mothers, and the passage of antidiscrimination laws. It also aimed to increase awareness about how men unfairly dominate women's lives.

Many NOW members, experienced in the civil rights movement, organized marches and demonstrations. NOW also supported female candidates for office and lobbied for changes in law. Spokespersons such as Gloria Steinem and Bella Abzug became famous. In the 1970s, Abzug represented a New York City district in Congress. Steinem founded *Ms.*, a magazine focused on feminist issues.

NOW still works for equal pay for equal work and such issues as a woman's right to abortion. It is politically strong on both state and national levels.

Shifting Roles and Images In 1963, Betty Friedan wrote *The Feminine Mystique*, which questioned the assumption that women were happiest at home, and challenged women to redefine their roles. Friedan argued that women were not the "weaker sex" but as capable as men, and deserved equal opportunity to pursue high-level jobs.

Equal Rights Amendment In 1972, Congress proposed the *Equal Rights Amendment (ERA)* to the Constitution. It stated: "Equality of rights under the law shall not be denied or abridged by the United Sates or any state on account of sex." For ten years, NOW and other feminists campaigned for the ratification against strong opposition. The amendment failed to win support from the required 38 states.

Many NOW lawyers argued that discrimination against women violated the equal protection clause of the Fourteenth Amendment, according to which no state may "deny to any person within its jurisdiction the equal protection of the laws." Thus, government support of all-male schools such as Stuyvesant High School in New York City was successfully challenged.

Roe v. Wade (1973) A pregnant woman in Texas wanted an abortion, which was prohibited by state law. The Supreme Court ruled the law unconstitutional because it violated a woman's constitutional right to privacy. A woman could choose to have an abortion during the first six months of pregnancy. During the last three months, however, a state may prohibit an abortion to protect the fetus (unborn child)—considered a person at this stage.

Roe v. *Wade* has sparked an ongoing controversy. Supporters argue that the right to privacy applies to a woman's body. Opponents argue that a fetus is a person as pregnancy begins and has a right to life then.

Equality in the Workplace Friedan and other feminists charged that male employers tended to discriminate against female workers. Median (average) income for men in the mid-1960s was $7,500 a year, compared to $5,600 for women. Men were more likely to obtain high-level positions and gain admittance to professional schools.

The *Equal Employment Opportunity Act* (1972) required equal pay for equal work and banned discriminatory practices in hiring, firing, promotions, and working conditions.

Today, many women confront a "glass ceiling"—an invisible barrier of discrimination in private corporations—that limits their attaining the highest positions. Women who raise families part-time rather than work full-time rarely reach the high-level positions. In the year 2000, women still earned about 75 percent of the salary of men in the same fields.

Domestic Abuse In the last decades of the 20th century, many women turned to courts for protection against domestic abuse. Private foundations and women's shelters, which provide a place to seek help, have also reduced women's acceptance of domestic abuse.

Hispanic American Activism

"Brown Power" Hispanic (Spanish-speaking) Americans began to organize a movement for "brown power."

Organized Farm Labor Like thousands of Mexican Americans in the Southwest, Cesar Chavez had worked long hours for low pay as a migrant farm laborer. Employers often exploited such workers. Unfortunately, with no permanent residences, they were extremely difficult to organize until Chavez succeeded in establishing the *United Farm Workers*.

From 1965 to 1970, Chavez's union struggled for *La Causa*—better pay and greater respect from California's grape growers. The union struck employers and urged Americans to boycott California grapes. Chavez insisted on complete nonviolence. Eventually, his tactics won major concessions. In 1970, the largest grape growers in California signed a contract with Chavez's union.

Cuban and Haitian Immigration By the 1950s, the U.S. Hispanic population had become a significant and growing minority. Castro's 1959 revolution in Cuba made hundreds of thousands of Cubans flee to the United States, mainly to Florida cities. This immigration continued into the 1980s.

Throughout the 1960s, "Papa Doc" Duvalier ruled Haiti. He formed a private military force and brutally put down all opposition. As a result, there was a surge in immigration from Haiti, primarily to Florida and New York. Continuing oppression and poverty in the 1980s increased illegal immigration from Haiti.

Political Involvement Hispanic American involvement in politics has increased in states with large Hispanic minorities—Florida, Texas, California, and New York. In the 1980s, Miami elected its first Cuban-born mayor, Xavier Suarez, and Florida elected a Hispanic American governor, Bob Martinez. In 1988, President Reagan appointed Lauro Cavazos as secretary of the Department of Education. Hispanic Americans such as Nathan Quinones, Joseph Fernandez, and Ramon Cortines all served as chancellor (chief executive officer) of New York City's school system.

Native American Activism

Grievances and Goals Native Americans from various reservations joined forces to assert "red power." The *National Congress of American Indians* complained that the Bureau of Indian Affairs (BIA) had failed for decades to raise Indians' standard of living. According to a 1960 study, they had a life expectancy of only 46 years, compared with 70 years for the population as a whole. More than other ethnic minorities, Indians suffered from malnutrition and unemployment. Activists demanded the following rights:

★ greater freedom on reservations (less supervision by the BIA)

★ return of fishing and hunting rights that Native Americans once enjoyed—even if state game laws had to be changed

★ greater economic assistance against poverty

★ fulfillment of broken U.S. treaties guaranteeing Native American land claims.

Occupation of Alcatraz In 1969, a small group took control of Alcatraz Island in San Francisco Bay, site of a former federal prison. The occupiers believed that an 1860s treaty gave them the right to seize federal lands no longer in use. But the main purpose was to highlight injustice toward American Indians. In time, the occupiers numbered more than 600 Indians, who called themselves "Indians of All Nations." After two years, communications and electricity were cut and most of the Indians left. The federal government removed the rest. The Indians, however, had publicized their grievances.

Wounded Knee In 1972, the radical *American Indian Movement (AIM)* occupied the BIA offices in Washington, D.C., and demanded that the government honor historical treaties. In 1973, more than 200 armed members gained control of Wounded Knee, South Dakota (see page 121). During their two-month occupation, they demanded that old treaty rights be reinstated. They won no concessions, but they prepared the way for later court victories by several Native American tribes. In 1975, Congress passed the *Indian Self-Determination and Education Act*, designed to increase self-government by reservation inhabitants and their control over education.

Victories in Court Through the 1970s, Native Americans sued for lands promised them by treaties. One court granted the Narragansett Indians of Rhode Island the return of 1,800 acres. In another suit, the Penobscots of Maine won thousands of acres and millions of dollars. The Sioux of South Dakota won still another case, in which the court ruled that 7 million acres of land had been taken from their ancestors illegally.

Rights of the Accused

Conservatives accused the Supreme Court under Chief Justice Warren of interfering with state police powers. Liberals argued that fair police procedures are required by the Fourth, Fifth, and Sixth amendments.

***Mapp v. Ohio* (1961)** This case involved the Fourth Amendment's protection against "unreasonable searches and seizures." An Ohio court had convicted Dollree Mapp of a crime on the basis of evidence obtained without a search warrant. The Court ruled that wrongly obtained evidence cannot be admitted during a trial.

Gideon v. Wainwright (1963) This case involved the Sixth Amendments' guarantee that the accused shall "have the assistance of counsel for his defense." Accused of breaking into a Florida poolroom, Clarence Gideon could not afford a lawyer. Florida provided lawyers for defendants only in capital cases (punishable by death). The Court ruled that Gideon was tried unfairly because a state must provide lawyers to poor defendants in all criminal cases.

Escobedo v. Illinois (1964) This case also involved the right of an accused person to counsel. The Illinois police arrested Danny Escobedo as a murder suspect. During questioning, the police refused Escobedo's request for a lawyer. Statements that he made were later used at his trial to convict him. The Court ruled that Escobedo's right to counsel under the Sixth Amendment had been violated.

Miranda v. Arizona (1966) Ernesto Miranda did not ask to see a lawyer when questioned by the Arizona police. After two hours, he signed a written confession of kidnapping and rape. The Court's decision stated: "Prior to any questioning, the person must be warned that he has a right to remain silent, that any statement he makes may be used as evidence against him, and that he has a right to the presence of an attorney." The police now read "Miranda rights" to arrested suspects before they are questioned.

★ In Review

1. Identify the goals of reformers in each of the following movements: (a) women's rights, (b) rights of Hispanic Americans, and (c) rights of Native Americans.
2. How did the civil rights movement influence the demands for equality on the part of Hispanic Americans and Native Americans?
3. Select three landmark Supreme Court cases of the Warren Court, and for each case, (a) identify the constitutional issue involved and (b) summarize the Court's decision.

Chapter Review

MULTIPLE-CHOICE QUESTIONS

Base your answer to question 1 on the following excerpt from John F. Kennedy's inaugural address concerning the cold war:

Let every nation know, whether it wishes us well or ill, that we shall pay any price, bear any burden, meet any hardship, support any friend, oppose any foe, to assure the survival and the success of liberty.

1. Kennedy was declaring that the U.S. government would (1) actively support voting rights for African Americans (2) attack Cuba (3) work to prevent the spread of communism (4) support Israel against hostile neighbors.

Use the map on page 222 to answer questions 2 and 3.

2. The map illustrates that concern over communism in Cuba was intensified because of Cuba's (1) size (2) nearness to the United States (3) easy access to the Soviet Union (4) proximity to other Communist nations.

3. A key U.S. concern regarding the Cuban revolution was that (1) Cuba could become a base for spreading communism throughout Latin America (2) recent Cuban immigrants would leave the United States (3) Cuba provided a port where Soviet ships could compete with U.S. trade in Latin America (4) the lucrative U.S.-Cuban tourist trade would end abruptly.

4. The New Frontier and the Great Society shared the idea that (1) foreign trade should be cut to a minimum (2) the federal government should meet economic and social needs of the less fortunate (3) taxes should be raised

to stimulate consumer spending (4) key industries should be nationalized.

Refer to the cartoon on page 227 and answer question 5.

5. The cartoon shows that (1) the public was not ready for true civil rights (2) some whites complained that civil rights activists wanted too much too soon (3) equal opportunity was not as available in the professions as in industry (4) there will always be prejudice against African Americans.

Use the cartoon on page 229 to answer question 6.

6. A valid generalization to be drawn from the cartoon is that (1) women have not had an important role in U.S. history (2) women have become more appreciative of American art (3) women have become more conscious of their role in American society (4) women artists are demanding greater respect for their contributions.

7. In what respect was the civil rights movement of Native Americans similar to that of African Americans? (1) Both concerned treaty rights. (2) Both concerned unfair treatment of an ethnic minority. (3) Both were inspired by the women's movement of the 1800s. (4) Both were ignored by the white majority.

8. Informing suspects of their legal rights during an arrest is required as a result of (1) customs adopted from English common law (2) state law (3) a U.S. Supreme Court decision (4) a law passed by Congress.

THEMATIC ESSAYS

1. **Theme:** Federal Activism. From the 1950s through the 1970s, the U.S. government took an active role in creating change and reform, which benefited many people.

Task

★ Choose *one* example of federal legislation and *one* Supreme Court decision from the 1950s through the 1970s. Explain how each created positive change for a specific group.
★ Evaluate the degree of success of each of the examples selected.

Examples of federal legislation involve the handicapped, voting rights, health care, civil rights, and poverty.

Examples of Supreme Court decisions involve integration, rights of the accused, voting, and affirmative action.

You are not limited to these suggestions. Specific names of the federal law and Supreme Court case are not necessary so long as detailed descriptions are given.

2. **Theme:** Public Opinion and the Civil Rights Movement. In the 1960s, public opinion influenced the federal government to begin ensuring greater equality for African Americans.

Task

★ Describe *two* specific examples of how civil rights leaders used public opinion to promote greater equality for African Americans.
★ Describe how the media (television, radio, newspapers, etc.) helped promote or influence pubic opinion about civil rights or the antiwar movement.
★ Evaluate the degree of success of either example that you described.

You may use, but are not limited to, integration of facilities, voter registration, equality of educational opportunity, and the March on Washington.

DOCUMENT-BASED QUESTION

*Study each document and answer the question that follows it. Then read the **Task** and write your essay. Include references to most of the documents and additional information you retain about U.S. history and government.*

Historical Context: The civil rights movement utilized a variety of tactics to create a more equitable society.

Document 1: Martin Luther King, Jr., in a letter from a Birmingham jail, April 1963:

Nonviolent direct action seeks to create such a crisis and establish such creative tension [that] a community that has consistently refused to negotiate is forced to confront the issue. It seeks so to dramatize the issue that it can no longer be ignored. . . . [Creating tension] . . . may sound rather shocking. . . . I am not afraid of the word tension. I have earnestly worked and preached against violent tension, but . . . constructive nonviolent tension . . . is necessary for growth.

Question: Why did King recommend nonviolent direct action?

Document 2: Refer to the drawing on page 225.

Question: Why would the artist have agreed with the speech excerpted on page 221?

Document 3: Refer to the photographs on pages 226 and 227.

Question: What happened to many people in the South who demanded civil rights?

Document 4: Stokely Carmichael in "What We Want," 1966:

> But our vision is not merely of a society in which all black men have enough to buy the good things of life. When we urge that black money go into black pockets, we mean the communal pocket. . . . into the community . . . to benefit it. . . . We want to see black ghetto residents demand that an exploiting store keeper sell them, at minimal cost, a building or a shop that they will own and improve cooperatively . . . [by means of] a rent strike, or a boycott, and a community so unified . . . that no one else will move into the building or buy at the store. The society we seek . . . is not a capitalist one. It is a society in which . . . community and humanistic love prevail.

Question: What new tactics did Carmichael suggest that African Americans use?

Document 5: Statement by the minister of defense of the Black Panthers, May 2, 1967:

> The Black Panther Party . . . calls upon . . . people in general and . . . black people in particular to . . . note . . . the racist California Legislature which is . . . considering . . . keeping the black people disarmed and powerless [while] racist police agencies . . . are intensifying the terror, brutality, murder, and repression of black people.
>
> Black people have begged, prayed, petitioned, demonstrated, . . . to get the *racist* power structure . . . to right the wrongs . . . perpetrated against black people. . . . these efforts have been answered by . . . repression, deceit, and hypocrisy. As [U.S.] aggression . . . escalates in Vietnam, the police agencies [here] escalate the repression of black people . . . . Vicious police dogs, cattle prods, and increased patrols [are] familiar sights . . . . City Hall turns a deaf ear to the pleas of black people . . . .
>
> . . . the time has come for black people to arm themselves against this terror before it is too late.

Question: How did the Black Panther party feel African Americans should respond to conditions in the United States?

Task

★ Describe different tactics suggested by various civil rights activists as the 1960s progressed.
★ Explain why civil rights leaders changed strategies at various times during the 1960s.

Chapter 19
Limits of Power—Turmoil at Home and Abroad: 1965–1973

★ Documents and Laws	★ Events	★ People
Tonkin Gulf Resolution (1964) Pentagon Papers (1971)	Vietnam War (1965–1975) Assassination of Robert Kennedy (1968) Tet Offensive (1968) Democratic Convention of 1968 Election of 1968 War protest march in Washington, D.C. (1969) National Guard firing on students at Kent State University (1970) U.S. withdrawal from Vietnam (1973) North Vietnamese victory (1975)	Dwight D. Eisenhower Daniel Ellsberg Abbie Hoffman Hubert Humphrey Robert Kennedy Henry Kissinger Lyndon B. Johnson Eugene McCarthy Richard Nixon Bobby Seale George Wallace

★ Objectives

★ To understand various public pressures that affect the American political system.

★ To realize the limitations of modern war technology in dealing with nationalistic uprisings.

★ To explore the consequences of U.S. involvement in Vietnam.

★ To analyze the policies of Lyndon Johnson and Richard Nixon.

UNITED STATES AND COMMUNISM IN INDOCHINA

(*Notes:* (1) To review the domino theory and its application to French Indochina during the Eisenhower administration, see page 208. (2) To review the early stages of the Vietnam conflict, see page 222.

President Eisenhower believed that a U.S. failure to respond to the Communist challenge in Indochina would damage the credibility of U.S. commitments elsewhere in the world.

Johnson and "Americanization" of the War

In 1963, President Johnson promised "no wider war" in Vietnam, but in 1964, he concluded that South Vietnam was losing to the Vietcong (Communist guerrillas in South Vietnam). To counter North Vietnam's strong support of the Vietcong, Johnson began an "Americanization" of the war by sending in U.S. troops.

In August 1964, inaccurate reports of North Vietnamese gunboat attacks on two U.S. ships in the Gulf of Tonkin near North Vietnam provoked Johnson to ask Congress for increased military aid to South Vietnam. Congress responded with the *Tonkin Gulf Resolution*. It authorized the president "to take all necessary measures to repel any armed attack against the forces of the United States and to prevent further aggression." Johnson now had power to use armed force in Vietnam however he wanted to. Like the Korean War, the Vietnam War began and was fought without a formal declaration of war by Congress.

Escalation/Tet Offensive In 1965, Johnson sent combat troops to Vietnam and bombed targets in the north. The U.S. troop count rose from 184,000 in 1965 to 536,100 in 1968. This **escalation** (steady buildup of forces) was intended to lead to a quick U.S. victory. It was also meant to prevent a takeover of much of Asia by Communist China and the Soviet Union.

In January 1968, Communist forces made major gains in South Vietnam and were about to

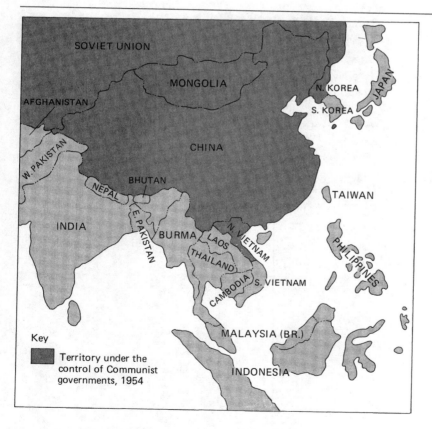

Asia in 1954

Key

Territory under the control of Communist governments, 1954

capture the capital, Saigon. Although this so-called Tet Offensive was pushed back, it demonstrated Communist strength and forced the Americans to anticipate a long war.

Debating the War

Arguments for the War To answer American doubts about U.S. involvement in Vietnam, Johnson, in a 1965 speech, offered the following reasons:

★ Since 1954, the United States had pledged to help South Vietnam.

★ To end U.S. commitments to South Vietnam would make U.S. commitments elsewhere untrustworthy.

★ A Communist victory in South Vietnam would threaten neighbors in Southeast Asia and foster Communist aggression throughout the region.

★ Communist China was supporting North Vietnam's war effort as part of "a wider pattern of aggressive purposes."

Arguments Against the War Opponents of U.S. involvement offered the following arguments:

★ Communist North Vietnam did not take orders from China or the Soviet Union, and Vietnam was a historic enemy of China. North Vietnam was really fighting for nationalistic reasons.

★ The distant war was not vital to U.S. security, and Vietnam's resources were not vital to the U.S. economy.

★ A long land war in Asia involving U.S. troops was too costly.

★ The South Vietnam government was corrupt and undemocratic.

★ South Vietnam's army was incapable of winning against the Vietcong guerrillas and the disciplined North Vietnamese troops.

★ Thousands of Americans were being killed and wounded.

Student Protests

Draft Protesters/Political Radicals Many people felt that the Vietnam War was not a worthwhile cause and that the enemy posed no threat to the United States.

College students adopted various protest strategies. They publicly set fire to their draft cards. Radical groups such as *Students for a Democratic Society (SDS)* occupied college buildings and chanted defiant slogans. Other students moved to Canada to escape the draft.

By 1966, the nation was sharply divided between "doves" (opposed to war) and "hawks" (for even greater use of military power in Vietnam).

Cultural Radicals As 1968 began, a new youth movement arose. Its members were against the war and preached love and nonviolence. Their lifestyle, known as the **counterculture**, placed a high value on personal honesty and creativity and generally opposed the norms of American culture—mar-

"Snow White and the Seven Experiments": 1970 cartoon targeting U.S. hypocrisy in supporting Asian military regimes

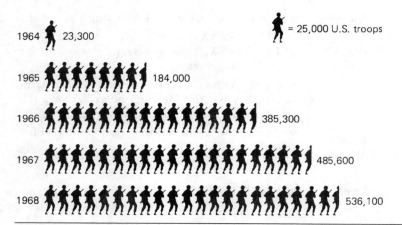

1964 23,300

= 25,000 U.S. troops

1965 184,000

1966 385,300

1967 485,600

1968 536,100

U.S. Troop Buildup in Vietnam, 1964–1968

riage, patriotism, and business. The more extreme members were known as "hippies" and "flower children." Some of them united as "families" and usually lived in rural **communes**.

1968: Year of Turmoil

The president and his advisers insisted that U.S. and South Vietnamese forces would eventually win. TV new reports, however, showed that most South Vietnam villages were still controlled by the Vietcong. Members of the press spoke of a "credibility gap" between the government's and the public's view. Opposition to the war increased.

"The Strategists," one for total commitment in Vietnam, the other for total noninvolvement—and both unrealistic

Johnson and Reelection In the presidential campaigns of 1968, young people supported an antiwar candidate, Senator Eugene McCarthy of Minnesota. John Kennedy's brother, Robert, also announced his candidacy for the Democratic nomination. In a television address to the American people, Johnson announced an end to the bombing of North Vietnam and the start of peace negotiations. To prevent politics from compromising the peace plan, he said that he would not seek or accept nomination for reelection.

Assassination of Robert Kennedy In June 1968, Robert Kennedy was killed by an Arab nationalist named Sirhan Sirhan. Many believed that, had he lived and won the presidency, he might have helped overcome social and political divisions—between young and old, and blacks and whites.

Democratic Convention The 1968 Democratic National Convention took place in Chicago. Hubert Humphrey, Johnson's vice president, beat out Eugene McCarthy for the nomination. The well-known radicals Abbie Hoffman and Bobby Seale led protests against the Democrats' choice. The Chicago police overreacted to the protests and verbal abuse, and their harsh treatment of the demonstrators was televised.

Election of Richard Nixon The violence associated with the Democratic convention and Humphrey's support of the war helped the Republicans and their candidate, Richard Nixon. A third-party candidate from Alabama, George Wallace, took away thousands of Southern votes from both major candidates. In one of the closest elections in U.S. history, Nixon won the presidency.

Social Impact of the Vietnam War The Vietnam War created deep divisions within American society. Many veterans of World War II felt that Americans should serve their country with pride; they reviled the actions of radical students and the counterculture. And returning Vietnam veterans were offended not to receive a traditional and enthusiastic welcome-home.

Opponents of the war felt a responsibility to protest against a war that they considered immoral and purposeless. They challenged the trustworthiness of elected officials and the U.S. policy of acting as "policeman of the world."

WAR IN VIETNAM: THE NIXON YEARS

As promised, Johnson sent diplomats to Paris to discuss peace with the North Vietnamese. The talks continued under Nixon, as did the war.

Nixon and his national security adviser, Henry Kissinger, proposed a pullout from South Vietnam by both North Vietnamese and American troops at the same time. The North Vietnamese rejected the proposal.

"Vietnamization" and Heavy Bombing

Nixon then announced a gradual withdrawal from Vietnam of U.S. troops while the South Vietnamese were trained to carry on the war alone. He called this strategy "Vietnamization." Meanwhile, he secretly ordered bombing raids over Cambodia to cut off Cambodian land routes used by the North Vietnamese to move troops and materials south.

More Protests As the war stretched on, many who had supported it joined the antiwar movement. On October 15, 1969, dissidents participated in a peaceful nationwide protest. One month later, more than 250,000 protesters marched from the Washington Monument to the White House.

In 1970, news of the bombing of Cambodia led to protests on many college campuses. At Kent State University in Ohio, four students were killed and several wounded when the National Guard opened fire to break up a peaceful demonstration.

Pentagon Papers In 1971, Daniel Ellsberg, an official in the Department of Defense, released to several newspapers, including *The New York*

Times, a secret Pentagon study of U.S. involvement in Vietnam. Feeling that the study would damage support at home for the war, Nixon demanded that *The Times* refrain from publishing it. In *New York Times* v. *United States*, the Supreme Court denied the claim that national security was at stake and ruled that, under the First Amendment's guarantee of freedom of the press, newspapers had the right to publish the Pentagon papers.

Withdrawal From Vietnam In 1972, as more U.S. troops left Vietnam, Nixon ordered the continuous bombing of North Vietnam, including, for the first time, its capital, Hanoi. In addition, the harbor of Haiphong was mined to cut off shipments of oil and other supplies. Still, South Vietnamese forces lost ground to the Communists.

Meanwhile, U.S.–North Vietnamese negotiations continued, and in early 1973, South Vietnam, North Vietnam, and the United States agreed on the following terms of cease-fire:

★ The last U.S. troops (fewer than 50,000) would leave Vietnam.

★ North Vietnamese forces in South Vietnam would remain there.

★ South Vietnam's government would remain in place until elections could be held.

"Middle Course"—State Department Vietnam policy of commitment, but not full commitment

★ The Vietcong would return all American prisoners of war (POWs) and fully account for Americans missing in action (MIAs).

U.S. involvement in Vietnam had ended, but the Vietnam War continued for almost two more years.

North Vietnamese Victory South Vietnam's government did not long survive on its own. In 1975, a combined force of Vietcong and North Vietnamese swept into Saigon and thus won control of all of Vietnam. Cambodia and Laos also fell to Communist forces. The defeat of South Vietnam, despite U.S. military aid and fighting power, demonstrated limitations on the U.S. presidency and on U.S. power.

Consequences of the Vietnam War

Casualties and Costs About 58,000 Americans died in the Vietnam War, and 365,000 were wounded. A memorial wall in Washington, D.C., lists the names of the dead.

Some soldiers who were imprisoned and tortured or overwhelmed by combat suffered from **post-traumatic stress disorder** (recurring flashbacks and nightmares). Others developed medical problems that were probably caused by Agent Orange, a chemical used to kill vegetation that gave cover to the Vietcong. Some veterans became dependent on drugs.

Government spending on the war was so great that it put a strain on the U.S. economy as the president would not raise taxes for political reasons. Simultaneous huge spending on domestic programs (Johnson's Great Society) forced the government to borrow billions more. The **national debt** (accumulation of debts owed to purchasers of government bonds) soared to record heights, and inflation increased during and after the war.

Impact on Foreign Policy Although active antiwar protesters were a minority, millions of Americans doubted the wisdom of U.S. involvement in a distant conflict. Distrust of government policies grew, and the policy of containment came in for sharp criticism. For many years both the American people and Congress would be reluctant to become involved in another foreign conflict.

War Powers Act Many members of Congress regretted enactment of the Tonkin Gulf Resolution.

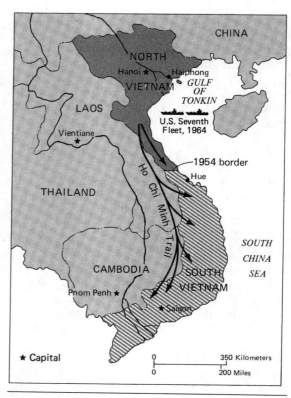

Vietnam War

To limit the president's power, Congress passed the 1973 *War Powers Act*, with the following major provisions:

★ Within 48 hours of sending troops into combat, the president must inform Congress of the reasons for the action.

★ If troops fight abroad for more than 90 days, the president must obtain Congress's approval for continued fighting or bring the troops home.

★ In Review

1. Identify the following and explain the significance of each: Tonkin Gulf Resolution, "Americanization," Tet Offensive, "doves," "hawks," "hippies," "credibility gap," "Vietnamization," Pentagon papers, and War Powers Act.
2. Summarize the arguments for and against the Vietnam War.
3. Evaluate the short-term and long-term effects of the Vietnam War on the United States.

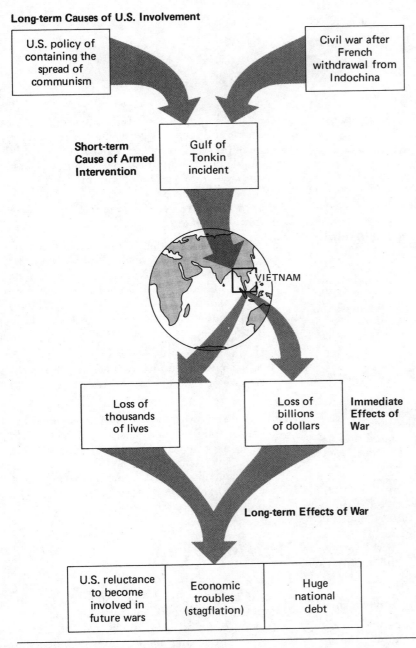

Long-term Causes of U.S. Involvement

U.S. policy of containing the spread of communism

Civil war after French withdrawal from Indochina

Short-term Cause of Armed Intervention

Gulf of Tonkin incident

VIETNAM

Loss of thousands of lives

Loss of billions of dollars

Immediate Effects of War

Long-term Effects of War

U.S. reluctance to become involved in future wars

Economic troubles (stagflation)

Huge national debt

Vietnam War: Causes and Effects

Chapter Review

MULTIPLE-CHOICE QUESTIONS

Use the cartoon on page 237 to answer questions 1–3.

1. The cartoon criticizes U.S. foreign policy (1) everywhere (1) in Latin America (3) in Asia (4) in Europe.

2. The cartoon accuses the United States of (1) imperialism (2) contradicting its ideals (3) poor leadership (4) starting wars.

3. The cartoonist probably feels that the situation was caused by (1) expansionists in Congress (2) paranoia about communism (3) resurgence of nazism and fascism (4) a rise in international terrorism.

Refer to the chart on page 241 and answer questions 4 and 5.

4. The chart shows that the Gulf of Tonkin incident (1) was the main cause of the war (2) resulted in containment (3) increased U.S. participation in the war (4) led to the French withdrawal from Vietnam.

5. A conclusion to be drawn from the chart is that the Vietnam War (1) affected the United States for only several years after it ended (2) was caused by a single incident (3) was the fault of the United States (4) had long- and short-term causes and long- and short-term effects.

Use the cartoon on page 238 to answer questions 6 and 7.

6. The cartoonist feels that (1) winning the war regardless of cost was the ladder to containing communism in Southeast Asia (2) the United States was more likely to contain communism in the Middle East than in Asia (3) the United States should have attacked communism within the Soviet Union (4) neither those supporting escalation or withdrawal truly understood the situation.

7. The cartoonist was probably most in favor of (1) gradual elimination of U.S. troops (2) gradual increase of U.S. involvement (3) more military advisers but fewer fighting men (4) continuing U.S. participation until a stable non-Communist government was able to prevent the spread of communism.

Refer to the cartoon on page 239 to answer questions 8 and 9.

8. The viewpoint of the cartoon is that the State Department (1) was having trouble resolving a North and South Vietnam border dispute (2) was conducting a limited war (3) was secretly supporting Johnson's opponents (4) was contemplating a military withdrawal in 1968.

9. During which other war might a similar cartoon have been drawn? (1) the Spanish-American War (2) World War I (3) World War II (4) the Korean War.

10. The War Powers Act of 1973 was passed because Johnson and Nixon (1) had made treaties without informing the Senate (2) were able to involve U.S. forces in combat without congressional approval (3) had failed to control antiwar protests (4) had refused to present military budgets to Congress.

THEMATIC ESSAYS

1. **Theme:** The United States Versus Communism in Asia. The United States, originally founded on the principle of achieving independence, found itself in the role of a great power attempting to prevent the independence of a colonial people.

   Task

   ★ Describe how the United States became involved in Vietnam after 1954.
   ★ Show how the development of communism in Asia led the United States to a great commitment in Vietnam.

   In answering the first part, you may refer to the rise of Vietnamese nationalism during

World War II, the war between Vietnamese nationalists and French imperialists, and the peace treaty signed at Geneva in 1954.

In answering the second part, you may show how the U.S. government was influenced by the rise of Mao Zedong, the Korean War, the domino theory, and the unpopularity of the South Vietnamese government.

2. **Theme:** The Vietnam War and U.S. Domestic Policies. The Vietnam War had an impact on the United States in ways not foreseen when it entered the conflict. As a result of extended U.S. participation in Vietnam, there were significant changes at home.

Task

★ Describe *two* ways in which the war changed the United States.

★ Show how *one* of the changes you discussed had a lasting impact on the United States.

You may discuss, but are not limited to, the effects of the war on the election of 1968; Johnson's Great Society program; and the attitude of (a) the American public toward government, (b) soldiers who fought in the war, and (c) high school and college students.

DOCUMENT-BASED QUESTION

*Study each document and answer the question that follows it. Then read the **Task** and write your essay. Include references to most of the documents and additional information you retain about U.S. history and government.*

Historical Context: Committing troops to the war in Vietnam became one of the most hotly protested federal actions in U.S. history. Many Americans, particularly high school and college students, questioned the wisdom of U.S. involvement.

Document 1: Refer to the map on page 236.

Question: Why were many Americans fearful of a Communist victory in Vietnam?

Document 2: Refer to the graph on page 238.

Question: How did the United States become further involved in Vietnam between 1964 and 1968?

Document 3: Refer to the map on page 240.

Question: What were the Communist North Vietnamese able to do throughout South Vietnam?

Document 4: From an undated handbill entitled "An Appeal to the Conscience of the American People":

Opponents of the administration's policies point out that the many Saigon governments have been military dictatorships.

None of [them] were elected by the Vietnamese people. The United States refused to permit the elections provided by the Geneva Agreement of 1954 and installed Ngo Diem. South Vietnam has been ruled by [U.S.-supported] military dictatorship . . . ever since. Opposed by the majority of the people of South Vietnam, it has changed 14 times since January 1964.

Question: Why did the writer oppose U.S. support of South Vietnam (Saigon)?

Document 5: President Johnson in his State of the Union message, January 12, 1966:

We will stay because a just nation cannot leave to the cruelties of enemies a people who have staked their lives and independence on America's solemn pledge [during three U.S. presidencies].

We will stay because in Asia—and around the world—are countries whose independence rests . . . on confidence in America's word and . . . protection. To yield to force . . . would weaken that confidence, . . . undermine the independence of many lands, and . . . [provoke] aggression. We would have to fight in one land, and then . . . in another—or abandon much of Asia to . . . Communists.

Question: Why did Johnson feel that the United States should maintain its commitments in Vietnam?

Task

★ Explain the arguments supporting and opposing U.S. involvement in Vietnam.

★ Give specific reasons why one of the two sides had the better argument.

Chapter 20
Trend Toward Conservatism: 1969–1980

★ Documents and Laws	★ Events	★ People
Twenty-sixth Amendment (1971) SALT I (1972) Seabed Agreement (1972) *United States* v. *Nixon* (1974) Panama Canal treaties (1977) Camp David Accords (1978)	Arab-Israeli wars (1948–1973) Environmental Protection Agency (EPA) established (1970) Watergate Affair (1972) First oil crisis (1973) Nixon's resignation (1974) Indian Self-determination and Educational Assistance Act (1975) U.S. diplomatic recognition of Communist China (1979) Second oil crisis (1979) Hostage crisis in Iran (1979–1981) Soviet invasion of Afghanistan (1979)	Edwin Aldrin, Jr. Neil Armstrong Menachem Begin Harry Blackmun Leonid Brezhnev Warren Burger Jimmy Carter Gerald Ford Ayatollah Khomeini Henry Kissinger Mao Zedong John Mitchell Mohammad Reza Pahlavi (Shah of Iran) Richard Nixon Lewis Powell William Rehnquist Anwar Sadat

★ Objectives

★ To assess the impact of the Watergate Affair on the presidency.

★ To understand that periods of upheaval often lead to conservative reactions.

★ To compare and contrast the domestic policies of presidents Nixon, Ford, and Carter.

★ To identify and evaluate presidential responses to foreign policy challenges.

★ To explain how global interdependence influences domestic policies.

NIXON AS PRESIDENT

Richard Nixon—Dwight Eisenhower's vice president—was elected president in 1968 in the midst of anti–Vietnam War protests and growing distrust of government policies. His popularity increased while in office, and he easily won reelection in 1972.

Domestic Policies and Events

Modified Great Society Programs Nixon's policies were more conservative than Kennedy's or Johnson's. Judging many Great Society programs to be wasteful and impractical, he reduced expenditures on education, housing, job training, and welfare assistance. He persuaded Congress, for example, to eliminate the *Office of Economic Opportunity*, which had administered many programs for aid to the poor.

In other ways, Nixon expanded the government's role. He established the *Occupational Safety and Health Administration (OSHA)* to inspect workplaces for acceptable safety and health standards.

He also set up the *Drug Enforcement Agency (DEA)* as part of the Justice Department. It still coordinates efforts to reduce domestic sales and use of illegal drugs. Its agents are sometimes assigned to foreign governments attempting to curb illegal drug exports into the United States.

In 1970, the Sierra Club and other environmental groups organized a nationwide "Earth Day" to raise Americans' consciousness and exert pressure for tougher antipollution laws. Nixon persuaded Congress to establish the 1970 *Environmental Protection Agency (EPA)*. This agency had the power to enforce 15 federal programs already enacted for protecting the environment. Under the *Clean Air Act of 1970*, the EPA could set standards for monitoring the quality of the air. Under the *Clean Water Act of 1972*, it could assist state and local government projects for cleaning polluted rivers and lakes. In addition, DDT, a pesticide fatal to wildlife, was banned.

Nixon expanded the 1964 food stamp program for providing the poor with coupons for food. This program of the Department of Agriculture also provides subsidized school lunches for poor children and meals for the elderly poor.

Nevertheless, Nixon's policies tended to be conservative. He proposed a *New Federalism* to give states greater freedom in using federal funds. In effect, he asked the federal government to "share" its revenues with state and local governments. In 1971, Congress approved bills for **revenue sharing** that permitted a state or community to use federal funds as it wished.

Chief Justice Warren announced his retirement in 1969. After two of Nixon's nominees to replace him had been rejected by the Senate, Nixon selected a conservative judge, Warren Burger, who was approved. When three new vacancies on the Court arose, the judges who won Senate approval were Harry Blackmun, a moderate from Minnesota, Lewis Powell, and William Rehnquist, who held conservative views.

Moon Landing In 1969, Neil Armstrong and Edwin Aldrin, Jr., walked on the moon. For President Nixon, their feat was a welcome change from demonstrations against the Vietnam War.

Native American Self-determination In an attempt to improve conditions for Native Americans, Nixon returned to the Taos people of New Mexico their traditional lands and increased the number of Native American employees in the Bureau of Indian Affairs. In 1975, after Nixon left office, Congress passed the *Indian Self-determination and Educational Assistance Act*, which increased Native Americans' control of their own education and government.

Twenty-sixth Amendment Beginning in the late 1960s, many young Americans argued that if they were old enough to fight in Vietnam, they were old enough to vote. In 1971, ratification of the Twenty-sixth Amendment gave U.S. citizens 18 years or older this right.

Title IX In 1972, Congress passed an education act that included a provision known as *Title IX*. Its purpose was to make gender discrimination in educational programs illegal. (See page 229.)

Nixon's Internationalism

As vice president, Nixon had expressed hostility for the Soviet Union, China, and other Communist nations. As president, however, he attempted to ease cold-war tensions and scale back U.S. military commitments. In forming foreign policy, Nixon was advised by Henry Kissinger, his chief national security adviser and, later, secretary of state.

Kissinger and *Realpolitik* Kissinger argued that U.S. foreign policies should support the national self-interest. This focus on international political realities rather than ideals is known as **realpolitik**. Nixon attempted to apply it so as to reshape U.S. relations with major Communist powers.

Nixon Doctrine

In 1969, as anti–Vietnam War protests grew, Nixon announced the *Nixon Doctrine*. To avoid U.S. involvement in future wars in Asia, the nations there would have to carry the main burden of their own defense. They could no longer rely on the United States for massive military aid or large numbers of ground forces.

U.S.–Chinese Relations

After Mao Zedong's Communist government took over the Chinese mainland in 1949, the United States continued to recognize the Nationalist government, which had fled to Taiwan (see page 193).

During the 1960s, Mao's government began denouncing the Soviet Union, an action that negated the American belief that all Communist countries followed identical policies and formed a **monolith** (single, undivided force). China's suspicions of the Soviet Union prompted Nixon and Kissinger to try and establish normal relations with the People's Republic of China.

In 1972, Nixon surprised the world by announcing his plan to visit China and seek an understanding with its leaders. There followed a major shift in U.S. policy: decreased support for Nationalist China, and increased trade and good relations with mainland China. China and the United States soon exchanged performing troupes and athletic teams. They did not, however, exchange ambassadors until 1979, when the United States formally recognized the People's Republic.

U.S.-Soviet Détente

Toward the Soviet Union, Nixon pursued a foreign policy of **détente** (relaxation of tensions). A major goal of détente was to limit production of nuclear weapons. During Nixon's first term, the U.S.-Soviet *Strategic Arms Limitations Talks (SALT I)* resulted in an arms race breakthrough—fixed limits on intercontinental (long-range) ballistic missiles, or ICBMs; and antiballistic (defensive) missiles, or ABMs.

In 1972, Nixon and Soviet Premier Leonid Brezhnev met in Moscow. They signed the SALT I agreement. Nixon also agreed to end a 1949 trade ban against shipping U.S. goods to the Soviet Union. To ease a severe Soviet food shortage, Nixon offered (and Congress later approved) the sale of $750 million worth of U.S. wheat. This "grain deal" pleased Soviet officials and American farmers alike. In 1972, the two nations joined 100 others in signing the *Seabed Agreement*, a pledge never to install nuclear weapons on the ocean floor.

Middle East Negotiations

In October 1973, Arab nations of the Middle East attacked Israel in an attempt to regain the territories lost during the Arab-Israeli war of 1967. The United States supported Israel, and the Soviet Union backed Syria. Kissinger then traveled to the Middle East to arrange a cease-fire. At stake was not only the security of Israel but also U.S.-Soviet relations. A cease-fire was arranged after Israeli troops had successfully invaded Egypt, but a new crisis arose. Angered by U.S. support of Israel, several Arab nations announced an embargo on oil shipments to the United States and its Western allies.

Chairman Mao and President Nixon meeting in China, 1972

In Moscow, National Security Adviser Henry Kissinger and President Nixon share a toast to détente, while Premier Brezhnev (center) chats with diplomats.

"Let's talk about not watering them": U.S. and Soviet diplomats negotiate nuclear arms reduction.

Presidency in Crisis

Watergate Affair During the campaign for the 1972 presidential election, the Democrats nominated Senator George McGovern of South Dakota. Democratic headquarters was in a Washington, D.C., office building known as the Watergate. To get information about Democratic campaign plans, five men tried to break into the Watergate office. A watchman called the police, and the burglars were arrested.

President Nixon won reelection by a huge margin, but, as his second term began, the Watergate crisis broke. Throughout 1973, news reports suggested that the break-in had been planned by the White House staff and, perhaps, even the president. The *Federal Bureau of Investigation (FBI)* began to investigate, and two reporters from the *Washington Post* revealed that certain officials close to the president might have planned the break-in. Most dramatic was a Senate committee's televised investigation of members of the president's White House staff.

Meanwhile, Nixon repeatedly stated that he had no previous knowledge of the break-in and had attempted no cover-up.

United States* v. *Nixon The Senate committee then learned that the president had taped every conversation in his White House office. It re-

quested the tapes as evidence. Nixon released some and offered summaries and transcripts of others. He refused, however, to turn over certain tapes, claiming **executive privilege**. He argued that he would violate the separation of powers if he gave the tapes to a Senate committee or a special prosecutor.

In *United States* v. *Nixon* (1974), the Supreme Court ruled that due process of law is more important than executive privilege. The president then released the tapes, which revealed that, shortly after the break-in, Nixon had tried to protect those responsible for the crime. Since it is illegal to cover up a crime, Nixon's actions, if proved in court, would also be crimes.

Impeachment Process and Resignation Impeachment is a two-part process. First, a majority of the House of Representatives must charge a federal official, including the president, with misconduct. Second, two-thirds of the Senate must find the accused guilty, after which dismissal from office is automatic. The Chief Justice of the United States presides during the Senate trial.

In 1974, a committee of the House of Representatives voted to recommend Nixon's impeachment. At the urging of Republican advisers, Nixon appeared on television on August 8 and announced that he would turn over the presidency to Gerald Ford, whose appointment as vice president had been approved by Congress shortly before the Watergate Affair began. Ford's appointment had been the first time that the Twenty-fifth Amendment (1967) had been used to fill a vice presidential vacancy (see the section "Ford Presidency," which follows).

President Nixon, weighed down by Watergate, leaves foreign policy to Secretary of State Kissinger.

Assessment Beginning with Franklin Roosevelt, presidential power had grown significantly, especially in time of war (World War II, Korean War, Vietnam War). In 1973, historian Arthur Schlesinger, Jr., warned about this growth in power, noting that Johnson and Nixon seemed to ignore the concerns of both Congress and the American people.

The Watergate Affair and Nixon's resignation brought an end to the "imperial presidency," as Schlesinger had called abuse of executive power. Congress, the Supreme Court, and an independent press had checked Nixon, and Americans were relieved to see that the system of checks and balances was working well. Nixon served as an example to subsequent presidents not to overstep the limits of their constitutional power.

★ In Review

1. Identify and explain the significance of the following: OSHA, DEA, EPA, revenue sharing, Twenty-sixth Amendment, realpolitik, détente, SALT I.
2. Describe how Nixon changed U.S. foreign policy with regard to China and the Soviet Union.
3. Explain how the system of checks and balances applied to the Watergate Affair.

FORD PRESIDENCY

Gerald Ford was in an unusual situation when he took the oath of office as the new president. He had not been elected to either the vice presidency or the presidency. Rather, he had been appointed to replace Spiro Agnew, who had resigned the vice presidency as part of a plea agreement for bribe-taking while serving as governor of Maryland and as vice president.

In his inaugural address, Ford promised to restore trust in the government. He selected former governor of New York Nelson Rockefeller as vice president. A Senate committee conducted a long and probing investigation of Rockefeller before recommending his approval.

While in office, Ford followed moderately conservative policies.

Domestic Policy Issues

Pardon for Nixon A month after becoming president, Ford pardoned Nixon for any crime committed in the Watergate Affair. (Article II, Section 2, of the Constitution gives the president power to pardon wrongdoers and release them from punishment.) Others on Nixon's staff were less fortunate. Former Attorney General John Mitchell and key White House aides were convicted and imprisoned for the cover-up and perjury.

First Energy Crisis Between 1973 and 1974, the price of a barrel of oil jumped from $3 to $11 as a result of the oil embargo by Arab nations. Because factory machines cannot operate without oil, the increase affected the price of almost all manufactured products. In addition, the U.S. automobile industry suffered as consumers turned to smaller, fuel-efficient imports from Japan and Europe.

The embargo made Americans realize how dependent they had become on oil from the Middle East, where price and output were controlled by the *Organization of Petroleum Exporting Countries (OPEC)*. Japan and Western Europe were also almost totally dependent on OPEC oil. Worldwide, oil prices soared. This first **energy crisis** also led to long lines at gas stations.

OPEC lifted the embargo in 1974 but continued to limit production to keep prices high. The

"You're like a bunch of . . . of . . . of . . . CAPITALISTS!": Uncle Sam outraged at OPEC's control of the oil market

government urged Americans to conserve energy at home and on the road. After the crisis, however, the nation became even more dependent on foreign oil.

CARTER PRESIDENCY

The 1976 presidential election pitted President Ford against Jimmy Carter, a former governor of Georgia. In a close election, Carter emerged with 297 electoral votes to Ford's 240.

Carter proved to be a hardworking and honest president, dedicated to human rights. But his leadership disappointed many people. While urgently pressing Congress to pass certain laws, he was unable to inspire the Democratic majority to vote for them. Two other major issues, however, speeded the decline in his popularity: ineffectual response to a second energy crisis in 1979, and failure to win release of American hostages in Iran.

Domestic Policy Issues

Amnesty In 1977, Carter extended **amnesty** (general pardon) to Vietnam War draft evaders, many of whom had fled to Canada. Many Americans who had lost a loved one in the war were opposed. Nevertheless, Carter's move brought to a close the issue of how draft evaders should be treated.

Second Oil Crisis In 1979, a revolution in Iran caused a major cutback in its oil production. Oil prices climbed from about $11 to $40 a barrel and shocked the global economy. Again, there were long lines at gas stations, and motorists had to pay more than a dollar a gallon (compared to 80 cents before the shortage). In 1980, Congress voted $20 billion to develop synthetic fuels whose availability would not be affected by OPEC policies or upheavals in the Middle East.

Environmental Concerns Environmental concerns increased during the 1970s. In 1979, partial meltdown of a nuclear power plant at Three Mile Island, Pennsylvania, reminded Americans that even peaceful use of nuclear energy could release dangerous amounts of radioactive materials into the atmosphere. Pollutants that caused acid rain and radioactive wastes were also placing the environment at hazard.

Foreign Policy Issues

Middle East in Turmoil After World War II, constant unrest in the Middle East challenged U.S. policy makers to balance three main interests:

★ support for democratic Israel
★ support for Arab states to ensure a steady flow of oil to the West
★ containment of Soviet influence in the region.

Arab-Israeli Conflict Israel fought four wars with its Arab neighbors. First, from 1948 to 1949, Arab states attacked Israel but failed to crush it. Second, in the Suez Crisis of 1956, Israel, France, and Great Britain attacked Egypt. U.S. condemnation halted the attack, and Israel withdrew its forces. Third, in 1967, Israel defeated Jordan, Syria, and Egypt in six days and occupied the neighboring territories of the Golan Heights (taken from Syria), the Sinai Peninsula and Gaza Strip (taken from Egypt), and the West Bank of the Jordan River (taken from Jordan). Israel refused to return these territories, which served as buffer zones against future attacks.

Finally, the Yom Kippur War broke out in October, 1973. The Arab nations, seeking to win back territories lost in 1967, attacked Israel on the Jewish holy day of Yom Kippur. Israel soon drove back the enemy, and the United States, fearful of Soviet intervention, negotiated a cease-fire.

Middle East Mediation In 1978, Carter persuaded Egypt's president, Anwar Sadat, and Israel's prime minister, Menachem Begin, to discuss peace at Camp David, Maryland. The leaders then announced an agreement—the *Camp David Accords*—resolving the problems dividing their countries. In 1979, Egypt and Israel signed a treaty providing for the following:

★ Israel's return of the Sinai Peninsula to Egypt
★ Egypt's formal recognition of Israel as an independent nation
★ A pledge by Israel and Egypt to respect the border between them.

Sadat was condemned by fellow-Arabs, and Begin came in for harsh Israeli criticism. Nevertheless, Sadat and Begin both received the Nobel Peace Prize in 1978. Sadat's peace policy was to cost him his life; in 1981, he was assassinated by Muslim extremists.

Soviet Invasion of Afghanistan In 1979, the Soviet Union invaded Afghanistan, a Muslim nation located on its southern border. The invasion was an attempt to crush a rebellion against the Soviet-backed Communist government there.

Carter immediately suspended the U.S.-Soviet détente that had existed since 1972. Fearing that the Soviets might use Afghanistan as a base to seize oil fields in the Persian Gulf, Carter retaliated by cutting back U.S. grain shipments to the Soviet Union. He also announced that U.S. athletes would not participate in the 1980 Summer Olympics in Moscow.

Iranian Hostage Crisis Since 1953, the United States had supported Iran's monarch, Shah Mohammad Reza Pahlavi. In return for U.S. military aid, the United States used Iran as a base for spying on the Soviet Union. Meanwhile, the shah angered fundamentalist Muslims by modernizing the country in opposition to strict Muslim laws and customs. He also employed secret police to suppress this opposition.

In 1979, an important fundamentalist leader, Ayatollah (high-ranking religious scholar) Khomeini led a successful revolution, and the shah went into exile. Carter angered Iranian revolutionaries by allowing the ailing shah to enter the United States for medical treatment. In violation of international law, some of the revolutionaries invaded the U.S. Embassy in Iran's capital, Teheran, seized 62 Americans, and took 52 of them as **hostages** (persons held until ransom is paid or demands met). The revolutionaries demanded the return of the shah for trial. Carter refused and, in turn, demanded the hostages' release.

In April 1980, Carter ordered a military rescue. Unfortunately, helicopters carrying U.S. troops broke down, and the rescue effort failed.

Changing Relations With Panama Ever since Panama gained its independence in 1903, it had a special relationship with the United States. The United States owned and operated the Panama Canal as well as the bordering Canal Zone.

In the late 1970s, Carter recognized that nationalism in Panama required changes in the U.S. presence. He negotiated two treaties with Panama. The first transferred ownership of the canal and bordering zone to Panama in the year 2000. In the second, Panama and the United States agreed that the canal would always be neutral territory, and that the United States could defend it by military force, if necessary.

Carter and Human Rights During his presidency (1977–1981), Carter insisted that the United States use its influence to stop other governments from abusing their citizens and denying them their rights as humans. For Carter, friend and foe alike should respect these basic rights.

Military regimes in Argentina and Chile arrested thousands of people suspected of being dissidents. They were either imprisoned without trial or killed. El Salvador's friendly government and Nicaragua's hostile Communist regime both mistreated dissenting citizens. At Carter's urging,

Bindfolded American hostages being held in Iran, 1979

T. R. "I took Panama" Roosevelt does a double take in outrage at President Carter's Panama Canal "give-away."

Congress reduced or eliminated economic aid to these and other oppressive countries.

Oppressed peoples were best helped by being admitted into the United States as refugees from tyranny. From the end of the Vietnam War in 1975 into the 1990s, a steady stream of refugees fled reprisals by the Communist government in Vietnam. During Carter's presidency, thousand of Cubans fled Castro's dictatorship and thousands of Haitians escaped from the harsh laws and extreme poverty in their country. Many Americans wanted to turn these "boat people" away, but Carter let them stay.

Pessimism as the Carter Administration Ends

Carter lost the 1980 election, in part because of the situation in Iran. On January 20, 1981—the day when Carter left office—Iran announced release of the hostages. The hostage crisis, which took place only a few years after the Vietnam War, was a second blow to American prestige. Many Americans wondered whether the United States was declining as a world power.

★ In Review

1. Explain the significance of the Ford presidency.
2. How did Carter respond to each of the following issues: Soviet invasion of Afghanistan, Iranian hostage crisis, relations with Panama?
3. Evaluate the appropriateness of President Carter's emphasis on human rights in the conduct of U.S. foreign policy.

Vietnamese boat people, fleeing their homeland, arrive in Hong Kong.

Chapter Review

MULTIPLE-CHOICE QUESTIONS

Base your answers to questions 1 and 2 on the cartoon on the top of page 247.

1. The main idea is that the United States and Soviet Union could best preserve world peace by (1) maintaining a balance of terror (2) agreeing to stop the arms race (3) adopting isolationist policies (4) forming a military alliance.

2. The cartoon was most likely drawn to comment on the (1) Vietnam conflict (2) negotiation of a SALT agreement (3) U.S.-Soviet grain deal (4) outbreak of war in the Middle East.

Read the following headline and answer question 3.

NIXON MUST SURRENDER TAPES, SUPREME COURT RULES, 8 TO 0; HE PLEDGES FULL COMPLIANCE

3. Which feature of the U.S. constitutional system is best illustrated by the headline? (1) checks and balances (2) executive privilege (3) power to grant pardons (4) federalism.

Use the cartoon on page 248 to answer question 4.

4. The cartoon shows that in 1974 (1) the United States demanded a drastic cut in oil production (2) OPEC was born (3) oil-producing nations were able to manipulate oil prices (4) the United States ignored the rise in petroleum prices and produced more of its own oil.

5. A major goal of U.S. foreign policy in the Middle East has been (1) a peaceful settlement of Arab-Israeli issues (2) an end to U.S. cooperation with Arab nations (3) ownership of oil resources by Western nations (4) permanent UN control of disputed territories.

Use the photograph on page 250 to answer questions 6 and 7.

6. The photo shows that (1) U.S. citizenship does not guarantee safety overseas (2) American interference in foreign countries endangers its citizens abroad (3) by the end of the 1970s, U.S. policies were unpopular worldwide (4) Americans were advised to avoid overseas travel during 1979–1980.

7. The situation depicted resulted from (1) U.S. support of Israel (2) U.S. refusal to turn over the shah to the new Iranian government (3) Carter's negotiation of the Camp David Accords (4) Vietnamese support for the Iranian Revolution.

Use the cartoon on page 251 to answer questions 8 and 9.

8. The cartoonist felt that (1) there was historical precedent for the U.S. return of the canal (2) the return of the canal would result in better U.S.-Panamanian relations (3) Carter should have rethought the return of the canal (4) the return of the canal would prevent a revolution in Panama.

9. The cartoonist felt that Theodore Roosevelt would have (1) been upset over the return of the canal (2) approved of the return of the canal (3) negotiated a better treaty before returning the canal (4) invoked the Roosevelt Corollary before returning the canal.

Refer to the photograph on page 251 and answer question 10.

10. Which problem does the photo most anticipate for the United States? (1) training Vietnamese refugees for a new assault on Communist Vietnam (2) immigration and resettlement of Vietnamese refugees in U.S. society (3) relocating Vietnamese refugees in other nations (4) negotiating a peaceful return of Vietnamese refugees to their homeland.

THEMATIC ESSAYS

1. **Theme:** "Stagflation" during the 1970s. The end of U.S. participation in the Vietnam War,

coupled with an oil embargo by OPEC members, led to a unique economic hardship in the United States called "stagflation" (persistent inflation combined with stagnant consumer demand and relatively high unemployment).

Task

★ Describe how the end of U.S. involvement in Vietnam resulted in a decline in production and employment that caused economic recession.
★ Explain why the OPEC oil embargo took place.
★ Demonstrate why the oil embargo resulted in rising prices (inflation).
★ Show why "stagflation" was unusual and extremely difficult to solve.

Consider the relationship of the Vietnam War to production (law of supply and demand), the 1973 Yom Kippur War between Israel and its Arab neighbors, and the relationship between prices and production (another application of supply and demand).

2. **Theme:** The United States in an Interdependent World. Events of the 1970s showed that nations were becoming increasingly interdependent. This meant that after years of trying to be neutral or isolationist, the United States would have to adopt new strategies for existing in a constantly changing global environment.

Task

★ Describe *two* examples from the 1970s of the federal government being forced to respond to events in other parts of the world.
★ Show how both examples illustrate that the United States must adapt to a new interdependent world.
★ Suggest *one* strategy that the federal government can adopt to coexist in a world that is more interdependent than ever before.

You may discuss, but are not limited to, the Iranian Revolution, OPEC oil embargo, end of the Vietnam War, Soviet invasion of Afghanistan, and economic and political conditions of neighbors in Latin America and the Caribbean.

DOCUMENT-BASED QUESTION

*Study each document and answer the question that follows it. Then read the **Task** and write your essay.*

Include references to most of the documents and additional information you retain about U.S. history and government.

Historical Context: In spite of diplomatic successes, President Nixon's second term was plagued by the Watergate scandal, which erupted during the 1972 presidential election campaign.

Document 1: From Article I of the impeachment against Richard Nixon, 1974:

. . . Richard M. Nixon, in violation of his constitutional oath faithfully to execute the office of President . . . and . . . preserve, protect, and defend the Constitution . . . , and in violation of his constitutional duty to take care that the laws be faithfully executed, has prevented, obstructed, and impeded the administration of justice, in that:

On June 17, 1972, and prior thereto, agents of the Committee for the Re-election of the President committed unlawful entry of the headquarters of the Democratic National Committee . . . [to secure] political intelligence. Subsequent thereto, Richard M. Nixon . . . engaged personally and through his subordinates and agents, in [conduct] designed to delay, impede, and obstruct the investigation of such unlawful entry; to cover up, conceal and protect those responsible; and to conceal the existence and scope of other unlawful covert activities.

Question: Why was the House Judiciary Committee recommending that Nixon be impeached?

Document 2: From President Nixon's address to the nation, January 23, 1973:

Good evening. I have asked for this radio and television time tonight for the purpose of announcing that we today have concluded an agreement to end the war and bring peace with honor in Vietnam and in Southeast Asia. . . .

We must recognize that [this] is only the first step toward . . . peace. All parties must now see to it that this is a peace that lasts, and . . . heals, and a peace that not only ends the war . . . but contributes to the prospects of peace in the whole world. . . .

Question: What announcement did Nixon make to the nation on January 23, 1973?

Document 3: Refer to the photographs on page 246.

Question: Why did Nixon travel to Communist China and the Soviet Union?

Document 4: Refer to the cartoon on the bottom of page 247.

Question: What does the cartoon say about Nixon's ability to carry out foreign affairs (the other figure is Secretary of State Henry Kissinger)?

Task

★ Describe *two* examples of the conduct of foreign affairs during the Nixon administration.
★ Describe how Nixon increasingly had to concern himself with the Watergate scandal.
★ Evaluate the effect that Watergate had on Nixon's conduct of foreign affairs.

Chapter 21
New Outlook of the Reagan Years: 1981–1988

★ Documents and Laws	★ Events	★ People
Engel v. *Vitale* (1962)	GATT conferences (1947–1995)	Leonid Brezhnev
Abington School District v. *Schempp* (1963)	Civil war in El Salvador (1979–1991)	Jimmy Carter
Immigration Act of 1965	Civil war in Nicaragua (1979–1990)	F. W. de Klerk
Tinker v. *Des Moines School District* (1969)	Election of 1980	Sir Alexander Fleming
SALT II (1979)	Terrorist attack on U.S. marines in Lebanon (1983)	Gerald Ford
SDI (1983–1993)	Invasion of Grenada (1983)	Mikhail Gorbachev
Economic Recovery Tax Act (1981)	Iran-Contra Affair (1984–1992)	Jesse Jackson
Social Security Reform Act (1983)	U.S. embargo of South Africa (1986–1991)	Nelson Mandela
New Jersey v. *TLO* (1985)	Collapse of Soviet Union (1991)	Walter Mondale
Immigration Reform and Control Act (1986)	First nonapartheid elections in South Africa (1994)	Oliver North
Tax Reform Act (1986)		Ronald Reagan
INF Treaty (1987)		Desmond Tutu
Vernonia School District v. *Acton* (1995)		

★ Objectives

★ To assess the impact of Reagan's conservatism on domestic policies.

★ To understand the impact of Supreme Court decisions on schools.

★ To evaluate how the government responded to problems of farmers, the poor, "new new immigrants," and the elderly.

★ To explain the effects of U.S. foreign policy in the Caribbean, Central America, and Soviet Union.

Ronald Reagan, former movie star and two-term governor of California, defeated Jimmy Carter in the 1980 presidential election. Reagan was an extremely popular president. An experienced entertainer, he could use television to project a pleasing personality. He believed in reducing taxes and spending on social programs, and increasing spending on defense. His policies had a positive effect on business and a negative effect on the poor. In the election of 1984, Reagan overwhelmingly defeated Democratic challenger Walter Mondale, Carter's former vice president.

REAGAN AND THE GROWTH OF CONSERVATISM

A major issue during the Reagan presidency was whether the federal government or the state governments had prime responsibility for combating crime, improving schools, and providing for the general welfare. The Republican presidents (Nixon, Ford, Reagan, and, later, George H. Bush) believed that the chief responsibility lay with state and local authorities. Reagan adopted Nixon's New Federalism (see page 245) and urged states to take more responsibility for social and economic problems.

Throughout the 1980s, as the federal government trimmed its budget and cut back social programs, the states increased spending on everything from police salaries to hospital beds. Citizens raised objections, however, to paying higher taxes for improved public services. Candidates for election added to the public outcry by promising not to raise taxes at the federal or state level.

Supply-side Economics

In 1974, when Ford replaced Nixon, the U.S. inflation rate climbed to a frightening 11 percent. Under Carter, it increased to 13 percent. Government spending on the Vietnam War and high oil prices caused by the Arab oil embargo were largely responsible. The failure of Ford and Carter to control inflation was a big reason why neither won a second term.

Reagan's solution for inflation was called **supply-side economics**. According to this conservative theory, the economy would benefit if the government spent less and businesses spent more. Cuts in federal taxes would leave business with more money to invest, and consumers with more income to buy goods and services. At the same

Cartoonist's view of Washington's "new look" in the 1980s: The White House and Capitol have only right wings (they are very conservative).

time, there would be major cuts in welfare programs, which Reagan considered wasteful.

In 1981, Reagan persuaded Congress to enact the largest income tax cut in history. The *Economic Recovery Tax Act (ERTA)* reduced personal income taxes by 25 percent over three years and gave corporations generous tax credits.

The Federal Reserve's anti-inflation policy of high interest rates caused inflation to drop to 6 percent in 1982 and less than 4 percent in 1983. A severe business recession also lowered inflation. By late 1982, about 11 percent of the labor force were out of work. Prosperity returned in 1984, and low inflation continued for the remainder of the decade. But a new problem arose—staggering **budget deficits** (gaps when expenditures exceed revenues).

"Wall Flowers": Social programs are slighted by the government's budget—but not defense.

Tax Policy In 1986, Reagan urged Congress to pass the *Tax Reform Act*. Previous tax laws had divided taxpayers into several brackets according to earned income. The higher the taxable income, the higher the percentage of income paid in taxes. The new law created only two tax brackets. Lower-income people were taxed at 15 percent of taxable income and upper-income people at 28 percent.

Instead of being taxed at 50 percent, as formerly, people with very high incomes paid just 28 percent. Thus, a millionaire, who was in the same tax bracket as a person earning $30,000 a year, benefited most. The new law closed a few "loopholes" in the old tax code so that the wealthy could not deduct as much from their taxable income as before.

Budget Deficits The executive branch submits an annual budget to Congress, which lists what the government expects to spend and what it expects to receive as income from taxes. When spending exceeds income, there is a deficit. In the opposite case, there is a surplus.

Beginning with the depression years, the government usually ended its **fiscal year** (budget year) with a deficit. It made up the difference by borrowing millions, even billions, of dollars annually. This debt was manageable through the early 1960s. After the Vietnam War, however, the accumulation of yearly budget deficits amounted to a **national debt** exceeding $500 billion. It had climbed to nearly $1 trillion when Reagan submitted his first budget in 1981.

Effects of "Reaganomics" Critics called Reagan's economic policy "Reaganomics." The 1981 tax cuts meant lower revenues, and increased spending for defense meant higher expenditures. Record deficits occurred eight years in a row, and the national debt rose above $2 trillion by the end of the 1980s. By 1990, interest payments on the national debt cost the government about $150 billion annually. Partly because of the debt burden, the government was unable to adequately fund national needs such as highway repair and health care.

Business Deregulation

During the Progressive Era in the early 1900s, regulatory agencies were established to protect consumers. Carter and Reagan deregulated the economy by getting rid of government rules that controlled business competition.

★ National Debt, 1970–1998 ★
(billions of dollars)

Year	Debt	As Percent of Gross Domestic Product
1970	$ 380.9	38.7
1975	541.9	35.9
1980	909.0	34.4
1982	1,137.3	36.4
1984	1,564.6	42.3
1986	2,120.6	50.3
1988	2,601.3	54.1
1990	3,206.5	58.5
1992	4,002.1	67.6
1994	4,643.7	70.0
1996	5,181.9	68.0
1998	5,478.7	65.2

Carter deregulated four industries: oil, natural gas, airlines, and trucking. Government controls had kept the prices of oil and natural gas low for consumers. Carter phased out such price controls to encourage the search for new sources of oil and natural gas. He also persuaded Congress to eliminate the *Civil Aeronautics Board (CAB)*, which had regulated airline routes and rates for 40 years. Thus, U.S. airlines began to compete free of all restrictions except those imposed by federal safety standards. Rapid change marked the airline industry as profits fell, along with ticket prices, and more people flew.

Reagan ordered regulatory agencies in the executive branch to grant businesses greater freedom. He weakened some agencies by appointing opponents of regulation to head them. Business mergers increased during the Reagan years because antitrust laws were not enforced. Reagan also speeded up deregulation of the oil industry.

Reduced Federal Involvement in the Environment and Civil Rights

Reagan reduced support for environmental measures because he believed that environmental laws meant high costs for business and high prices for consumers. **Strip mining**—ground-level mining of minerals that leaves the landscape scarred and ridden with debris—increased as a method for extracting coal. Laws protecting wildlife were enforced only laxly.

Reagan's policy of reduced federal involvement and increased support of "states' rights" also weakened civil rights legislation. Federal support for busing and affirmative action decreased. Reagan did, however, establish Martin Luther King, Jr., Day as a national holiday.

Effect on Minorities A disproportionate share of the poor are from minority groups. Reagan's cuts in social programs meant that such groups as African Americans and Hispanic Americans did not benefit economically from the so-called Reagan Revolution. The income gap between white and black Americans increased.

Nevertheless, African Americans and Hispanic Americans made political progress. African Americans were elected as mayors in Atlanta, Detroit, Chicago, Los Angeles, and Philadelphia. Hispanic Americans were elected as mayors in San Antonio and Miami, and as governors in New Mexico and Florida.

In the 1990s, the Reverend Jesse Jackson, a civil rights activist, won a strong following as an African American leader. He also reached out to other minorities, women, and discontented farmers and workers, referring to this multiracial, multicultural blend of people as the "Rainbow Coalition." In 1984 and 1988, Jackson campaigned for the Democratic presidential nomination and came closer to being a presidential candidate than any other nonwhite American ever had.

Supreme Court and the Schools

The following cases focus on the extent to which the Bill of Rights applies to students in school:

Engel v. *Vitale* (1962) The parents of several pupils in New York schools objected to a prayer composed by the New York State Board of Regents and meant to be **nondenominational** (favoring no religious group in particular). The board had recommended that students voluntarily recite the prayer in classrooms at the beginning of each day. The Supreme Court ruled that the practice violated separation of church and state.

Abington School District v. *Schempp* (1963) Pennsylvania required that at least ten Bible verses be read in public schools each day. The Schempp family sued the Abington School District in Pennsylvania, claiming that Bible readings were against their religious beliefs. The Court ruled that Bible readings in public school violated the

"Trickle-Down Economics"—Reagan's tax reforms are generous to the rich but leave little for the poor.

First Amendment's guarantee against establishment of religion.

Tinker v. *Des Moines School District* (1969) The Supreme Court decided that students could not be penalized for wearing black armbands to school in protest against the Vietnam War. Students do not "shed their Constitutional rights to freedom of speech or expression at the schoolhouse gate."

New Jersey v. *TLO* (1985) A high school freshman, found smoking in the school bathroom, was made to open her purse. School officials found wrapping paper for cigarettes or marijuana, a list of students who owed her money, and a large amount of cash. The freshman was sentenced to one year of probation. The Court ruled that the school acted reasonably to maintain discipline; reasonable suspicion for searches and seizures in school need not be based on the "probable cause" provision of the Fourth Amendment.

Vernonia School District v. *Acton* (1995) The Court ruled that a school district can conduct random testing of urine for drugs. The Fourth Amendment right to privacy is not violated. Since student athletes are required to take medical tests, a drug test need not be based on suspicion of drug use among individual students. The state may exercise a greater degree of supervision over public school students than over adults.

★ In Review

1. Identify the following: supply-side economics, Tax Reform Act of 1986, budget deficits, national debt, deregulation.
2. Summarize Reagan's economic policies. Why are they also known as the Reagan Revolution?
3. According to the Supreme Court ruling in *Vernonia School District* v. *Acton*, how does the Bill of Rights apply to students in school and to adult citizens elsewhere?

NEW APPROACHES TO OLD PROBLEMS

Many problems of the 1980s and 1990s had their roots in the past. But the new conservatism proposed new solutions.

Feast and Famine for Farmers

Between 1940 and 1970, farmers doubled wheat production per acre and increased production of all crops per acre by 66 percent. At the same time, the number of farms and farmers declined. In 1994, about 2.5 percent of Americans were farmers, compared to 38 percent in 1900. The decline of the small family farm was closely linked to mechanization. Expensive equipment increased productivity on large and medium farms. But owners of small farms were unable to buy such equipment and could not compete. By 1995, most farm acreage was controlled by large agricultural corporations.

Farm Subsidies A **subsidy** is a grant of government money to a private enterprise. Since the Great Depression, the government had paid subsidies to farmers during years when crop prices were low. Laws enacted in 1973 and 1977 established **target prices** for such crops as wheat, corn, and cotton. If the market price fell below the target price, the government paid farmers the difference. This policy encouraged farmers to produce more crops. The government also paid farmers for using less of their land to raise crops. By the mid-1990s, many in Congress complained that farm price supports were too expensive.

Feast in the 1970s Farming is a business of feast (high demand, high prices) or famine (low demand, low prices). In the 1970s, prices for farm products were high, partly because of increased exports to the Soviet Union and other nations. Encouraged by the government, farmers borrowed money to modernize farms and increase production. Gains in productivity were spectacular.

Famine in the 1980s World demand for American crops declined in the 1980s. Farmers received low prices for what they could sell and were left with millions of tons of unsold grain. Carter's embargo on the sale of grain to the Soviet Union contributed to the problem (see page 250). With high debts and declining income, thousands of family farms went bankrupt.

In the 1980s, Reagan initiated two programs to help farmers. The first was "Payment in Kind" (PIK). To reduce the oversupply that had led to reduced prices, farmers who did not plant on their land were paid in surplus crops held by the government. A second program also entailed government payments to farmers for not planting. These programs helped farmers but increased the deficit. In the 1990s, grain exports again helped increase farm income.

Poverty in an Affluent Society

After World War II, most Americans had incomes high enough to sustain an affluent (prosperous) lifestyle. During the 1960s, however, millions of Americans still lived in poverty. Between 1960 and 1969, the number of poor Americans dropped from 40 million to 24 million, largely because of Johnson's War on Poverty.

In the 1970s, **stagflation** (unemployment and economic recession coupled with rising inflation) led to renewed increases in poverty. In the 1980s, larger numbers of homeless people appeared on city streets. The poorest Americans included children, single women with dependent children, African Americans, Native Americans, Latinos, migrant farm workers, and unemployed factory and mine workers. Increased poverty helped raise the crime and school dropout rates, as did the wide availability of crack, a new illegal drug that was inexpensive and highly addictive.

As social scientists pointed out, the wealthiest fifth of the population commanded an ever greater share of total national income. The widening income gap between rich and poor was viewed as a serious danger to American democracy.

In 1981, Reagan argued that financial aid to all except the "truly needy" made the poor become permanently dependent on the government.

The escalating defense budget reduces social programs to beggar status.

Many Americans, concerned about high taxes and budget deficits, supported his efforts to cut back federal poverty programs. Critics blamed the cuts in welfare programs for the increasing number of homeless. Others argued that the poor might represent a new and permanent "underclass" in American society that no amount of government aid could rescue.

"New New Immigrants"

In the 1980s, as in the 1880s, a new wave of immigrants rapidly changed the U.S. population. The "new new immigrants" came not from western Europe but from Latin America, the Soviet Union, Eastern Europe, the Middle East, and Asia.

Immigration Act of 1965   Between 1921 and 1965, U.S. immigration laws had favored western European nationalities. The *Immigration Act of 1965* ended the old quota system and set the following criteria for yearly admission of immigrants:

★ no more than 20,000 from one country

★ no more than 120,000 from Canada and Latin America

★ no more than 170,000 from Asia, Africa, Europe, and Australia

★ preference given to skilled workers, professionals, and those with family ties to U.S. citizens.

A 1953 law gave the president authority to admit refugees from political oppression. Ford used it to admit hundreds of thousands of Vietnamese, Laotians, and Cambodians after their countries fell to communism.

Illegal Immigrants   In addition to the millions of legal "new new immigrants," millions crossed the Mexico-U.S. border illegally. American employers were often glad to hire them because, having fled from extreme poverty, they were willing to work for lower wages than U.S. citizens. Labor unions feared that they would work for less than the minimum wage.

Members of Congress who wanted to curb illegal immigration used two arguments: (1) illegal aliens paid no taxes, placed a strain on city services, and increased the cost of city government; (2) tolerance of illegal aliens was unfair to immigrants who had waited years to enter the United States legally.

Immigration Reform   In 1986, with Reagan's approval, Congress enacted the *Immigration Reform and Control Act*, or *Simpson-Mazzoli Act*. It placed heavy fines on employers who knowingly hired illegal aliens. Illegal aliens who had arrived before 1982 were allowed to remain as legal residents.

Opponents of the law argued that employers would fear to hire Hispanic American legal residents because absolute proof of legality might be hard to obtain. In reality, the act has failed to stop the flow of illegal immigrants across the Mexican-U.S. border.

Encouraging Immigration   Social scientists point out some benefits of increased immigration:

★ Immigrants buy goods and services.

★ They pay taxes.

★ They may create jobs rather than take them away.

★ In the event that a decrease in the native birthrate creates a labor shortage, skilled workers from abroad will be needed.

★ The diverse backgrounds of immigrants enrich U.S. culture.

Changing Demographic Patterns

In 2004, people aged 65 and over (the elderly or "senior citizens") represented 12.4 percent of the

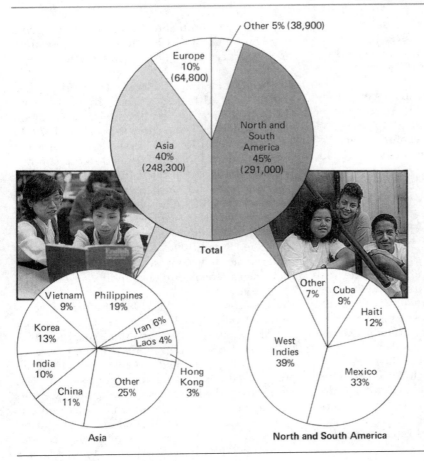

Sources of Legal Immigration to the United States, 1989

population, compared with only 5.5 percent in 1930.

Increased Life Expectancy In 1900, such common diseases as tuberculosis, influenza, and polio had no cures. Over the next 60 years, medical science brought them under control. In 1928, Sir Alexander Fleming discovered penicillin. This antibiotic and many other drugs developed since have accounted for major gains in **life expectancy**. Americans born in 1928 could expect to live to their mid-50s. In contrast, those born in 2005 can expect to live into their late 70s and early 80s.

As the number of elderly increased, so did their political influence. For millions of senior citizens of the 1970s and 1980s, the most important political issue was the future of Social Security. They organized pressure groups such as the *American Association of Retired Persons (AARP)* and the *Gray Panthers*. They pressured Congress for higher monthly checks that kept pace with inflation and for improved benefits under Medicare, which pays hospital and doctor bills for people 65 and over. In 1975, Congress passed a law linking Social Security benefits to the cost of living. The new provision was known as a **cost-of-living adjustment (COLA)**.

Increased Social Security Taxes The increased benefits were extremely expensive. Congress, therefore, passed two laws:

★ In 1977, the Social Security tax was raised. This tax, collected from workers' paychecks and from employers, goes into a fund that pays benefits to retired workers.

★ The *Social Security Reform Act* (1983) saved the system from financial collapse by speeding up planned increases in Social Security taxes. Also the age when recipients receive benefits will gradually rise from 65 to 67. Benefits for some higher income retirees will also be subject to partial taxation.

Since 1983, money coming into the Social Security system has paid benefits to the elderly. But social scientists predict trouble in this century, when huge numbers of baby boomers (born in the late 1940s and 1950s) retire.

★ In Review

1. How did Reagan attempt to solve (a) the farmers' dilemma and (b) poverty in an affluent society?
2. Why were some Americans opposed to illegal immigrants and others in favor of them?
3. What are the political, economic, and social implications of an increasingly elderly population?

UNITED STATES: GLOBAL POWER BROKER

Presidents of the Progressive Era (Theodore Roosevelt, Woodrow Wilson, and William H. Taft) intervened in the political affairs of the Dominican Republic, Haiti, and Nicaragua. These interventions caused a lasting resentment among Latin Americans. In the 1930s, Franklin Roosevelt adopted the *Good Neighbor Policy* of nonintervention in Latin America's internal affairs. After World War II, U.S. leaders followed both the interventionist and "good neighbor" paths at the same time. While they offered Latin America economic assistance as a means of thwarting Soviet influence there, they did not hesitate to intervene militarily at times.

Central America and the Caribbean

Reagan chose to oppose communism through containment. He believed that U.S. military intervention was warranted when U.S. interests were threatened, even if such intervention meant the loss of Latin American goodwill.

Grenada Invasion Grenada, an island nation in the Caribbean, has a population of 94,000. A few hundred Americans were attending medical school there in 1983 when Communist forces overthrew Grenada's democratic government. Believing that the students were in danger, Reagan sent in U.S. troops, who quickly defeated the Cuba-backed Communists and restored democratic rule.

Aid to El Salvador During the 1980s, civil war raged in the Central American nation of El Salvador. Fearing that the rebels might set up a Communist state, Reagan persuaded Congress to vote more than $600 million in military aid for El

Salvador's government. Nevertheless, the civil war continued until 1991, when UN negotiators arranged a cease-fire and peace settlement.

Aid to Nicaraguan "Contras" In nearby Nicaragua, U.S. aid helped a rebel group, the "*contras*," fight Nicaragua's Communist government, the "*Sandinistas*," who came to power in 1979. In 1982 and 1983, Reagan persuaded Congress to supply financial and military aid to the contras. In 1984, Congress granted financial aid but rejected military aid, only to reverse itself in 1986 and approve $160 million in military aid.

The civil war ended in 1990 when the Sandinistas permitted a free election, which they lost. The United States then provided aid to the new, moderately conservative government, and the contras returned to civilian life.

The Iran-Contra Affair In 1986, the press discovered that U.S. officials had broken a law banning sale of U.S. weapons to Iran. Many suspected that the arms sale was in exchange for the release of American hostages held in Lebanon. Indeed, the press called it the "arms-for-hostages deal." The money from the illegal arms sale secretly went to Nicaraguan contras in an operation carried out by Oliver North, a presidential aide and Marine lieutenant colonel. Questioned by a congressional committee, North testified that the president knew nothing about this Iran-Contra Affair. Some Americans, however, compared the scandal to Watergate.

Marines in Lebanon

Lebanon, a country north of Israel, is inhabited by various Christian and Muslim groups. During the 1970s, Muslims outnumbered Christians, and Palestinians in Lebanon's refugee camps began to protest the government's pro-Western policies. In 1975, a civil war erupted between the Christians and the allied Palestinians and Muslims.

Neighboring Syria supported radical, pro-Communist Palestinians of the PLO (see page 277). Israel sent troops to retaliate for PLO terrorist attacks on Israel. Israel bombarded the Lebanese capital, Beirut, and won a Palestinian withdrawal. In 1982, Reagan sent U.S. troops in to help keep peace. The next year, a terrorist bomb killed 241 marines near Beirut. Reagan then removed all U.S. troops.

Syria took control of much of Lebanon, while Israeli troops occupied a southern strip as a se-

Poor Contra goes to bed hungry every night.

CONTRA ALSO HAS NO BULLETS FOR HIS GUN, NO ROCKETS, NO GRENADES AND NO FUN AT ALL.
BUT WITH YOUR HELP, THERE IS HOPE. FOR JUST 100 MILLION BUCKS, YOU CAN ADOPT A CONTRA OF YOUR VERY OWN. AND REMEMBER, YOU'LL NOT ONLY BE NOURISHING A FRAIL LITTLE BODY — YOU'LL BE OVERTHROWING A GOVERNMENT!

WRITE YOUR CONGRESMAN & ASK HOW YOU CAN ADOPT-A-CONTRA

"Adopt a Contra"—critical view of undercover U.S. aid for military insurgents trying to overthrow Nicaragua's government

curity zone against attacks on northern Israel. During the 1980s and 1990s, militant groups in Lebanon launched rocket attacks and suicide raids against Israel, which retaliated with commando raids.

Economic Competition, Cooperation, Boycott

Beginning in the 1970s, the United States became less concerned with Communist expansion in Asia and more so with economic competition from Japan.

Japan By the early 1970s, Americans were buying many Japanese goods—automobiles, motorcycles, cameras, TVs, and radios. Consumers benefited from these high-quality imports, but U.S. manufacturers and labor unions worried about losing business and jobs.

After World War I, the United States became a creditor nation, but by the 1980s, it had become the world's largest debtor. The widest trade imbalance between U.S. exports and imports was with Japan.

After 1947, most nations, including the United States, had participated in conferences called the *General Agreement on Tariffs and Trade (GATT)*, which worked toward lowering tariffs between member nations. Reagan favored low U.S. tariffs too. High protective tariffs might trigger tariff wars that would hurt both the U.S. and the global economies. At the same time, the United States had to continually pressure Japan to change its trade policies, which placed quotas on the number of foreign goods that Japanese businesses could buy.

South Africa

During the Carter administration, U.S. policy toward Africa shifted from containment of communism to opposition to racial injustice, specifically in South Africa.

The British had taken control of South Africa after defeating the Afrikaners (Dutch settlers) in the *Boer War* (1899–1902). The Afrikaners, however, outnumbered the British, won control of the government in 1948, and broke ties with Britain in 1961.

The Afrikaner government practiced **apartheid** (strict racial segregation), which separated South Africa into four racial groups: whites, blacks, Asians, and "coloreds" (those of mixed ancestry). Blacks had to live apart from the other races, could not vote, and could work only in the lowest-paying occupations. They were required to carry identification passes and could enter white areas only for a limited time. Many blacks were even moved to "tribal homelands"–regions where, in fact, they had never lived before.

The populations of most nations are nonwhite. They viewed South African apartheid as an insulting carryover from when white Europeans ruled much of Africa and Asia. Third world members of the UN voted for resolutions condemning apartheid and calling on UN members to stop trading with South Africa.

Until the 1980s, many U.S. businesses and universities invested in South Africa's gold, diamond, and uranium mines. However, as its ruthless methods to enforce apartheid were increasingly reported on TV and dramatized in movies, many U.S. college students demonstrated against this injustice. South Africa's Episcopal archbishop, Desmond Tutu, visited U.S. cities to urge the ban on trade. In 1986, Congress passed an embargo over Reagan's veto.

South Africa began to change its policies in 1990. A new president, F. W. de Klerk, promised to integrate parks and beaches and to permit blacks to vote. In 1990, the black leader Nelson Mandela, imprisoned for 27 years for opposing apartheid, was released. On a U.S. tour, Mandela urged Americans to continue the embargo until apartheid ended. In 1991, however, President George H. Bush, Reagan's successor, persuaded Congress to lift the embargo, noting that progress had been made toward ending apartheid.

In 1994, the first South African elections were held in which all races could vote. Mandela's party—the *African National Congress (ANC)*—won a majority of seats in the legislature, and Mandela become the first black president. This transition to multiracial democracy ended U.S. boycotts of South Africa and increased cooperation between the two nations.

U.S.-Soviet Relations

From 1974 to 1989, the cold war went through three phases. First, Ford and Carter tried to improve U.S.-Soviet relations by continuing Nixon's détente. Second, during Reagan's first term as president (1981–1985), relations between the superpowers grew hostile again. Third, Mikhail Gorbachev became the Soviet leader in 1985 and eventually permitted Eastern European countries to shake off Soviet control. In the Soviet Union as well as in Eastern Europe, many aspects of communism were abandoned as unworkable.

Arms Limitation Efforts The 1972 SALT I agreement applied to defensive missiles (see page 246). In 1979, President Carter and Soviet Premier Brezhnev signed SALT II. This treaty limited offensive missiles by establishing a ceiling on how many long-range (low-flying) missiles could be launched from airplanes and submarines. Early in 1980, Carter withdrew the treaty because of the Soviet invasion of Afghanistan.

"Star Wars" Reagan, in his 1980 campaign for the presidency, promised to increase military spending. In his first year in office, he asked Congress for huge increases in the defense budget—$1.5 trillion over five years—for new bombers, submarines, and missiles. Congress approved most of the president's program.

Reagan's most ambitious proposal, set forth in a 1983 speech, was for a "space shield"—the *Strategic Defense Initiative (SDI)*. To critics, it sounded like something out of the popular movie *Star Wars*. The weapons would orbit Earth and shoot down Soviet missiles before they could reach U.S. targets. Though skeptical, Congress voted funds to explore the idea. Then, U.S.-Soviet relations improved, and in 1991, the Soviet Union collapsed. In 1993, after ten years of research and an outlay of $30 billion, President Clinton, George H. Bush's successor, eliminated the SDI program. However, President George W. Bush renewed the program as of 2001–2002.

Gorbachev and Soviet Relations In 1985, the Soviet Communist party selected a new leader, Mikhail Gorbachev. Relatively young and energetic, he proposed sweeping reforms to revitalize the Soviet system.

First, he told the people not to fear speaking their minds about public issues. This **glasnost** (openness) reversed years of an opposite policy of state arrests and imprisonment for frankness.

Perestroika (restructuring), a policy for economic reform, encouraged local bureaucrats and factory managers to make their own decisions rather than relying on orders from the government. Gorbachev also wanted to develop privately owned businesses run for profit. In reality, perestroika was a mixture of private enterprise and government welfare.

Gorbachev realized that the Soviet economy could not improve while a large percentage of the nation's resources went for the armed forces. Reagan's arms buildup was putting the United States far ahead in the arms race, and the Soviet Union could no longer afford to compete. Gorbachev and Reagan met three times to discuss arms control and other issues. In 1987, at their third

"Star Wars": Reagan's planned missile-defense shield seen as a costly computer game

The average Soviet shopper in the 1980s faced severe shortages of food and consumer goods.

What were Gorbachev and Reagan really thinking when they met to discuss arms reduction?

meeting, they signed the *Intermediate-range Nuclear Forces Treaty (INF Treaty)*. (Intermediate-range missiles can travel hundreds of miles, compared with longer-range ICBMs, which can cross oceans.) The treaty provided that all intermediate-range missiles in Europe be removed and dismantled by 1990.

★ In Revew

1. Identify and explain each of the following: Grenada, Sandinistas, contras, Iran-Contra Affair, tariff war, apartheid, Nelson Mandela, SALT II, SDI, Mikhail Gorbachev, glasnost, perestroika, INF Treaty.
2. Explain how each of the following posed a challenge to U.S. foreign policy: El Salvador, Nicaragua, civil war in Lebanon, South Africa.
3. To what extent did Reagan's foreign policy represent a return to traditional themes of cold-war and power politics?

Chapter Review

MULTIPLE-CHOICE QUESTIONS

Use the cartoon at the top of page 256 to answer questions 1 and 2.

1. The cartoon shows that after the 1980 election (1) there were no liberals or progressives in the federal government (2) the executive branch was liberal while the legislative branch was more conservative (3) conservatives captured the presidency and much of Congress (4) the Supreme Court made more conservative decisions to appease Reagan.

2. The likeliest explanation for the situation depicted was (1) greater public sympathy for affirmative action (2) the desire of Americans to return to isolationism (3) narrowed economic opportunities during the 1970s (4) a more youthful electorate.

Base your answers to questions 3 and 4 on the following excerpt from President Reagan's first inaugural address:

> . . . it is not my intention to do away with the government. It is rather to make it work—work with us, not over us; to stand by our side, not ride on our back. . . .

3. Reagan was applying a philosophy that would have been most approved by (1) Thomas Jefferson (2) John Kennedy (3) Franklin Roosevelt (4) Lyndon Johnson.

4. Reagan was appealing to the American tradition of (1) equality (2) democracy (3) individual freedom (4) big government.

Refer to the cartoon on page 258 and answer questions 5 and 6.

5. The cartoon refers to Reagan's (1) stand against government regulation of business (2) position on affirmative action (3) opposition to the Sandinistas (4) economic policy.

6. The cartoonist felt that (1) benefits for the wealthy would eventually benefit the middle class and poor (2) Reagan's economic policy would most benefit the middle class (3) the poor would get adequate benefits from Reagan's economic policy (4) Reagan's economic philosophy would benefit the rich and have progressively smaller benefits for the middle class and poor.

Base your answers to questions 7 and 8 on the cartoon on page 263.

7. The cartoon deals with U.S. foreign policy toward (1) Eastern Europe (2) the Far East (3) Latin America (4) Africa.

8. The cartoonist was suggesting that the United States (1) attempt to overthrow foreign governments (2) submit international disputes to the UN (3) provide foreign nations with military aid (4) not interfere with another nation's internal affairs.

Use the cartoon on page 264 to answer questions 9 and 10.

9. The cartoon depicts SDI ("Star Wars") as (1) realistic (2) impractical (3) in need of more research (4) easy to accomplish.

10. The taxpayer is (1) enthusiastic (2) in need of more information (3) concerned over the potential cost (4) demanding that SDI be abandoned to safeguard Social Security funds.

THEMATIC ESSAYS

1. Theme: "Reaganomics," a Conservative Revolution. Ronald Reagan's presidency marked a change in federal economic policy that has been called a "conservative revolution."

Task

★ Describe *two* aspects of Reaganomics.
★ Describe *two* specific examples of how Reagan applied Reaganomics to the U.S. economy.
★ Show a specific effect of *one* of the applications on a specific group.

You may use, but are not limited to, various federal social programs, taxation, federal regulation of business and industry, and relations with organized labor.

2. Theme: President Reagan and Military Spending. In spite of a conservative economic policy, the Reagan administration significantly increased the defense budget.

Task

★ Describe *one* reason why Reagan increased the defense budget at the same time as reducing spending in most other areas.
★ Discuss *one* specific economic effect of additional defense spending on the economy.
★ Evaluate the wisdom of increased defense spending in light of the specific impact it had on other aspects of the economy.

For the first part, you may use, but are not limited to, SDI ("Star Wars") and Reagan's foreign policy.

In answering the second part, you may discuss the national debt or how costs of increased military spending affected other specific segments of the national budget.

DOCUMENT-BASED QUESTION

*Study each document and answer the question that follows it. Then read the **Task** and write your essay. Include references to most of the documents and additional information you retain about U.S. history and government.*

Historical Context: Many people credit or blame Reagan for changing the nature of the United States and the world.

Document 1: Refer to the cartoon on the bottom of page 256.

Question: What does the cartoon say about Reagan's budget priorities?

Document 2: From a 1982 address by President Reagan concerning political developments in Central America:

> My fellow Americans, I must speak to you tonight about a mounting danger in Central America that . . . will grow worse . . . if we fail to take action now.
> . . . With over a billion dollars in Soviet-bloc aid, the Communist Government of Nicaragua has launched a campaign to subvert and topple its democratic neighbors.
> Using Nicaragua as a base, the Soviets and Cubans can . . . threaten the Panama Canal, interdict our vital Caribbean sea lanes, and, ultimately, move against Mexico. Should that happen, [millions of Latins] would begin fleeing north into the cities of the southern United States, or to wherever some hope for freedom remained.
> The United States Congress has before it . . . an aid package of $100 million for the more than 20,000 freedom fighters struggling to . . . eliminate this Communist menace at its source. . . . We are not asking for a single dime in new money. We are asking only to be permitted to switch a small part of our present defense budget—to the defense of our own southern frontier. . . .

Question: What was Reagan asking Congress and the American people to do regarding the Sandinista government in Nicaragua?

Document 3: Refer to the cartoon on page 265.

Question: What difficulties were going on at the Reagan-Gorbachev summit meeting?

Document 4: Refer to the cartoon on page 260.

Question: What was the cartoonist saying about spending priorities of the Reagan administration?

Document 5: Refer to the table on page 257.

Question: What happened to the national debt during the Reagan years (1981–1989)?

Document 6: Refer to the photo on page 265.

Question: What does the photo show about the economy of the Soviet Union prior to its collapse?

Task

★ Describe and evaluate the success of Reagan's foreign and domestic policies.
★ Explain what the long-term results of Reagan's foreign and domestic policies are on the United States of today.

Chapter 22
Entering a New Century: 1989–2005

★ Documents and Laws	★ Events	★ People
Supreme Court Decisions: *Texas v. Johnson* (1989) *Cruzan v. Director, Missouri Department of Health* (1990) *Planned Parenthood of Southeastern Pennsylvania, et al. v. Casey* (1992) Brady Bill (1993) North American Free Trade Agreement (NAFTA) (1994) U.S.-Cuban agreement raising quota of Cuban immigrants (1994) USA Patriot Act (2001)	Iran-Iraq War (1980–1988) Bull market (1987–2000) Berlin Wall dismantled (1989) Eastern European nations hold free elections (1989) Massacre in Tiananmen Square, Beijing (1989) U.S. invasion of Panama (1989) Reunification of East and West Germany (1990) Persian Gulf War (1990–1991) Dissolution of Soviet Union (1991) Civil war in Bosnia (1991–1995) Midterm elections of 1994 U.S. invasion of Haiti (1994) Russian-Chechnya wars (1994–1996, 1999–2000) Kosovo war for independence (1996) Comprehensive Test Ban Treaty (CTBT) (1996) Impeachment and trial of Bill Clinton (1998–1999) Decoding of human genome (2000) Election of 2000 September 11, 2001 attacks Afghanistan invasion (2001) Second Iraq War (2003) Election of 2004	Mahmond Abbas Al Qaeda Madeleine K. Albright Yasir Arafat Osama bin Laden Barbara Boxer George H. Bush George W. Bush Bill Clinton Hillary Rodham Clinton Dianne Feinstein Ruth Bader Ginsburg Mikhail Gorbachev Albert Gore, Jr. Alan Greenspan Saddam Hussein Kim Jong Il Slobodan Milosevic Carol Moseley-Braun Patty Murray Vladimir Putin Janet Reno Ariel Sharon Taliban Boris Yeltsin

★ Objectives

★ To examine domestic issues during the G. H. Bush, Bill Clinton, and G. W. Bush presidencies.

★ To identify forces and events leading to the end of the cold war and dissolution of the Soviet Union.

★ To analyze the U.S. role in the global economy.

★ To evaluate presidential responses to challenges in the Persian Gulf, Somalia, Haiti, the Middle East, Bosnia, Yugoslavia, Iraq, North Korea, and Russia.

GEORGE H. BUSH PRESIDENCY

When George H. Bush succeeded Reagan as president, he continued his predecessor's conservative policies into the 1990s.

Election of 1988

Demographics   Bush's election demonstrated the political importance of suburbanites. As the more affluent moved to the suburbs, they identified with Republican issues such as lowering taxes, reducing spending, and curbing crime and the sale and use of illegal drugs. Bush won over many former Democrats by promising to address these issues. He depicted his Democratic opponent, Michael Dukakis, as being soft on crime, and easily defeated him.

Political Action Committees   Political action committees (PACs) representing such special interests as farmers, senior citizens, labor unions, tobacco companies, gun lobbies, and oil companies contribute indirectly to the campaigns of like-minded candidates. Federal law forbids PACs to donate directly to candidates, so they spend money to get out the vote and promote issues that their candidates favor. Buying television time, for instance, is expensive, and political parties rely on PACs to pay for such promotions.

Domestic Issues

Bush, like Reagan, called for states to assume a larger role in domestic programs.

Environment   Many environmentalists made complaints at how slow the federal government was to clean up the 1989 *Exxon Valdez* oil spill (see page 202). Because of the ongoing policy of deregulation to make American businesses more competitive with foreign ones, enforcement of

such environmental measures as the Clean Air Act was weakened as well.

Economy   A 1980s business boom was marked by heavy consumer spending, high interest rates, and low savings. In 1991, however, the economy slipped into recession, and unemployment rose to 7 percent. Hoping to increase consumer and business borrowing, the Federal Reserve Board reduced the **discount rate** (interest charged to member banks).

Tax Increases/ Deficit Reduction   The federal deficit continued to rise. The 1985 *Gramm-Rudman-Hollings Act* mandated that the federal budget had to be balanced by the early 1990s. If Congress failed to reduce deficits to zero, the law provided for automatic budget cuts in all executive departments.

In 1990, Bush broke his 1988 campaign promise by raising taxes. He and Congress also worked out cuts in federal spending. The income tax rate for the wealthy was raised from 28 to 31 percent. Federal excise taxes on cigarettes, alcoholic beverages, and gasoline went up. Cuts were made in military and social programs.

Savings and Loan Bailout   The failure of hundreds of **savings and loan associations (S & Ls)** further burdened the economy. S & L owners had made unwise and, perhaps, illegal investment and loan decisions. The government had insured savings in such bankrupt businesses and was obligated to pay back depositors. To recover its losses, the government took over and tried to sell S & L property. The bailout cost taxpayers more than $300 billion.

Social Concerns

★ *Texas* v. *Johnson* (1989). A citizen had burned a U.S. flag in public as an act of protest. The Supreme Court ruled that the First Amend-

President George H. Bush

ment right to freedom of speech applied to this act, and, therefore, Texas's law against desecrating (harming) the flag was unconstitutional. In 2000, the U.S. Senate failed to pass a proposed constitutional amendment outlawing the burning of the flag.

★ *Cruzan* v. *Director, Missouri Department of Health* (1990). Nancy Cruzan had been injured in an automobile accident and was lying in a Missouri hospital with no evidence of brain function. Her parents wanted to terminate her life-support system, but the hospital refused. The Court ruled that a state may require clear evidence—for example, a living will—that a person did not wish to be sustained by life support in such an extreme situation.

★ *Planned Parenthood of Southeastern Pennsylvania, et al.* v. *Casey* (1992). Five Pennsylvania abortion clinics challenged state law requiring teenagers to obtain parental consent for an abortion. Upholding the law as constitutional, the Court empowered the state to limit (but not ban) abortions.

Family in Crisis In 1966, the divorce rate was twice as high as in 1950. Two out of every five 16-year-olds born during the 1970s saw their parents break up. By the 1990s, half of all marriages ended in divorce.

As single parents, divorced women suffered income loss and emotional strain. Some children also suffered emotionally from parental separations. Most lived with their mothers and shared their economic plight, which grew worse when fathers withheld child support. Government at all levels tried to make fathers pay court-awarded child support.

In the 1970s and 1980s, married women sought outside employment in record numbers. Sixty percent of them were in the labor force by 1990, compared with 25 percent in 1950. Thousands of single mothers also held jobs. Some worked to make full use of their talents. Growing numbers, though, worked because one income did not pay family expenses.

Drug Abuse Illegal drugs have been a domestic problem since the late 1940s. In the 1960s, increasing numbers of college students smoked marijuana. Teenagers and even preteens were used by organized crime to buy and sell illegal drugs. The use of crack in the 1980s only aggravated the problem.

Increasingly, law enforcement officials devoted time and resources to arresting and prosecuting drug "pushers" (sellers). But the demand among people of every class made it nearly impossible to stop or even reduce drug sales in major cities. In 1989, Bush declared a "war on drugs" that entailed spending more than $7 billion a year.

Drug addiction was partly responsible for increases in violent crime and property crime (burglary, larceny, and auto theft). In the 1980s, the rate of violent crime went up by nearly 30 percent.

Unknown in the United States before 1981, **AIDS (acquired immunodeficiency syndrome)** caused more than 200,000 deaths by the mid-1990s. The two most common causes of infection were sharing of needles to inject a drug into the bloodstream and sexual contact.

Foreign Policy Issues

Invasion of Panama In the late 1980s, Manuel Noriega came to power in Panama. Two U.S. grand juries indicted him for involvement in smuggling illegal drugs into the United States. In December 1989, Bush ordered a surprise invasion of Panama to drive Noriega from power and prevent his taking control of the Panama Canal. Noriega was captured, brought to the United States for trial, convicted in a federal court, and sentenced to imprisonment.

Free elections established a new Panamanian government friendly to the United States, which gave it aid. Other Latin American countries condemned the U.S. invasion as an act of aggression.

Berliners celebrating the fall of the Berlin Wall, 1989

Collapse of Communism In June 1989, Poland held free elections, and the Communists lost. Soviet leader Mikhail Gorbachev accepted the result.

The people of Hungary, Czechoslovakia, and Romania demanded free elections. Eventually in all of Eastern Europe the people voted to replace communism with democratically elected governments.

Fall of the Berlin Wall/German Reunification In November 1989, both East and West Germans tore down the Berlin Wall. Germany was officially reunited in October 1990. The new government pledged never again to take military action against its European neighbors.

End of the Cold War Bush and Gorbachev held their first summit conference in 1989, a major step toward ending the cold war. The United States promised food and economic aid to the Soviet Union, nuclear weapons systems in Europe were dismantled, and the Soviets agreed to support U.S. policy against Iraq.

Dissolution of Soviet Union In December 1991, the Soviet Union ceased to exist as a single nation for the following reasons:

★ *Economic failure*. Burdened by large military costs, the Soviet economy had steadily declined. Fewer goods reached the marketplace. Long lines formed to buy whatever goods were available. Critics called for an end to the old system.

★ *Yeltsin's rise to power*. In 1987, a radical reformer, Boris Yeltsin, broke with Gorbachev and resigned from the Communist party (the only legal one). In 1991, Yeltsin was elected president of the Russian Republic. In August 1991, Communist conservatives tried to oust Gorbachev and seize control. The **coup** (seizure of power) failed when Moscow's citizens, led by Yeltsin, blocked the path of Soviet troops, who refused to attack the crowd.

★ *Independence for the republics*. In 1991, all 15 republics in the Soviet Union demanded independence. In December, the presidents of Russia, Ukraine, and Belarus declared that the Soviet Union was "dead" and formed the *Commonwealth of Independent States (CIS)*, open to all republics. Shortly afterward, Gorbachev resigned.

Effects on U.S. Foreign Policy

The cold war ended officially in February 1992 when Bush and Yeltsin met to work out deep cuts in their arsenals of long-range missiles. Yeltsin gave assurances that nuclear missiles of the former Soviet Union would remain under central control. The United States and other Western nations pledged emergency aid for the Russian economy.

Crisis in Bosnia Founded after World War I, Yugoslavia consisted of six republics, of which Serbia was the most powerful. In 1991, the republic of Bosnia declared independence, which the United States recognized in 1992. Bosnia's population was made up of Bosnian Muslims, Serbian Orthodox Christians, and Croatian Roman Catholics.

Serbs felt that their dominance of Yugoslavia was threatened. Many Bosnian Serbs, unwilling to be a minority within the new state, opposed independence. As civil war broke out among the three groups, Serbs engaged in **ethnic cleansing** (expulsion or massacre of Muslims and non-Serbs from areas under Bosnian Serb control).

Persian Gulf Crisis/Operation Desert Storm In the 1980s, the four major producers of Middle Eastern oil were Saudi Arabia, Kuwait, Iran, and Iraq—all located on the Persian Gulf. Between 1980 and 1988, Iraq won small gains in territory during the Iran-Iraq War.

Shortly after the war, Iraq's military dictator, Saddam Hussein, accused Kuwait of taking an unfair share of oil revenues. In August 1990, Hussein claimed that Kuwait was part of Iraq and invaded and occupied it. The price of gasoline and heating oil soared. To pressure an Iraqi withdrawal, the UN voted to place an embargo on

Iraqi oil. This drop in the oil supply led to even higher fuel prices.

The Iraqi invasion of Kuwait alarmed world leaders. An act of aggression by a strong nation against a weak one, it opened the way for an Iraqi conquest of Saudi Arabia and, possibly, domination of the other Middle Eastern countries.

Bush announced a defensive effort called *Operation Desert Shield* and sent U.S. troops to Saudi Arabia. They were joined by forces from a UN-supported coalition of 28 nations, including Britain, France, Saudi Arabia, Syria, Turkey, and Egypt.

Members of the Security Council voted a series of resolutions: Iraq's unconditional withdrawal from Kuwait, an international embargo on trade with Iraq, and the use of force if Iraqi troops did not leave Kuwait by January 15, 1991. Both houses of Congress authorized Bush to send troops into combat in the Persian Gulf.

After the deadline expired, *Operation Desert Storm* went into effect, as thousands of planes from allied bases in Saudi Arabia made massive air strikes against military targets in Iraq and Kuwait. After more than a month of bombing attacks, U.S. and allied tanks swept across the desert toward Kuwait City and into Iraq and overwhelmed Iraqi forces. Hussein withdrew from Kuwait, and Bush announced victory.

As part of the cease-fire agreement, Iraq agreed to eliminate all poison gas and germ warfare capabilities and let UN observers inspect the sites. To enforce the agreement, the UN imposed trade **sanctions** (penalties) until Iraq complied with all terms. To prevent Hussein from ordering air attacks on Iraq's minority Kurdish population in the north, the United States created safe havens for the Kurds inside Iraq and established a "no-fly" zone in the north.

The Persian Gulf War liberated Kuwait and prevented Hussein from controlling the region's oil prices and supplies. It also demonstrated military cooperation between the nations of Western Europe and the United States. Even Russia had supported U.S. resolutions in the UN. Criticized for not removing Hussein, President Bush stated that the goal had been to liberate Kuwait.

Cartoon showing that rising oil prices cause pain and hardship for many consumers

★ In Review

1. Identify each of the following and explain its significance: savings and loan bailout, ethnic cleansing, Operation Desert Storm.

2. For each of the following Supreme Court cases, identify the constitutional issue involved and summarize the decision: (a) *Texas* v. *Johnson*; (b) *Cruzan* v. *Director, Missouri Department of Health*; and (c) *Planned Parenthood of Southeastern Pennsylvania, et al.* v. *Casey*.

3. Discuss the role of economics and political leadership in bringing about an end to the cold war.

CLINTON PRESIDENCY

Citing the Gulf War victory and the end of the cold war as achievements and blaming the Democratic majority in Congress for stalling his economic programs, Bush sought reelection in 1992. Arkansas governor Bill Clinton and running mate Senator Albert Gore, Jr., blamed economic ills on Bush and promised a change. Clinton was elected and won reelection in 1996 over Senator Robert Dole.

Domestic Issues

Social Concerns The election of a Democratic president, which ended 12 years of Republican leadership, marked a shift from Reagan-Bush conservatism. In his first term, Clinton worked with Democratic majorities in both houses to achieve a family and medical leave bill. It granted employees 12 weeks of unpaid leave to care for newborn infants and unwell family members. Clinton won approval for a program called *Americorps*, which enlisted young people in community service projects. With varying degrees of success, he also dealt with the following domestic issues:

Health Care Clinton's wife, Hillary Rodham Clinton, headed a task force to reform the health care system. The plan had two main objectives: to guarantee insurance coverage for all Americans and to prevent the costs of medical care from consuming increasingly more of the national wealth. Small businesses and the insurance industry vigorously opposed the plan and gained the strong support of Congress. By mid-1994, it was clear that health care reform would be indefinitely delayed.

Education Since the early 1970s, educators have reported low levels of student performance on

President Clinton presents his proposals for a national health plan at a town meeting.

standardized tests. Conservatives urged a "back to basics" approach (more math, reading, and writing). Liberals proposed restructuring schools so that teachers, parents, and students could take part in decision making. In the mid-1990s, setting improved national standards in education was widely debated. Clinton favored them and increased federal aid to schools. Influenced by the president's proposals, states began to increase local standards too.

Welfare Reform In 1996, Clinton signed into law a reform bill that sharply cut federal spending on welfare programs. Instead, it provided states with **block grants** (financial aid with few guidelines on their use) and required welfare recipients to work. The now-Republican-led Congress (see pages 275–276) strongly supported the bill while liberal Democrats objected strongly. As the program was implemented, welfare costs dropped.

Stability of Social Security Ever since the reform of 1983, money coming into the Social Security system has covered benefits paid out to the elderly. But social scientists predict trouble for the system by the 2030s, when the number of senior citizens has increased and the number of younger workers to fund the system has decreased. COLA increases are a further drain on Social Security funds.

Cartoon contrasting American students' poor skills with the highly developed ones of students in other lands

By permission of Chuck Assay and Creators Syndicate, Inc.

Gays in the Military Early in his presidency, Clinton removed the long-standing ban against homosexuals serving in the armed forces. To make the military more comfortable with the change, he stipulated that gays must remain silent about their sexual preferences ("don't ask, don't tell"). The policy stirred up controversy in both the military and civilian sectors.

Women in Government Clinton appointed a number of women to top posts. For example, in 1993, Janet Reno became the attorney general and Ruth Bader Ginsburg was appointed to the Supreme Court. In 1997, Madeleine K. Albright was appointed secretary of state.

Barbara Boxer and Dianne Feinstein of California, Carol Moseley-Braun of Illinois, and Patty Murray of Washington won Senate seats. The number of women in the House increased from 28 to 47.

Economy

New Technology By 1990, the personal computer was used as a tool of classroom instruction, a word processor, a record keeper, a calculator and problem solver, and a means for accessing **data bases** (information files). Speculative business entrepreneurs, eager to profit from the new technology, were attracted to the Internet (see page 201). Consumers began to use this network to purchase all types of goods and services. To a large extent, e-mail replaced letter writing and telephone calls. By the year 2000, companies producing new technological products and services were surpassing older corporations in market value.

One problem with computerized applications was the possibility for businesses and government to invade personal privacy. For a small user fee, almost anyone can access a data base listing people who had, for example, been arrested or failed to pay a debt.

Great strides were made in **genetics** (science of the heredity of living organisms). By the late 1990s, scientists were able to **clone** (reproduce from one parent without fertilization) such animals as sheep. They could also produce new forms of genetically altered soybeans and corn. In 2000, scientists researching **genomes** (genetic makeup of organisms) were able to identify the complete sequence of human DNA. They could thus detect genes that may cause such diseases as cancer and Alzheimer's.

Impact of Baby Boomers Because of the looming impact of the baby boom on the Social Security system, legislation was passed to gradually raise the age for collecting full Social Security benefits from 65 years of age to 67. Other effects of the aging baby boom generation have been the growth of retirement facilities and an increased sale of prescription drugs and vitamins.

"I never tire of looking at them"

from *Herblock On All Fronts* (New American Library, 1980)

Budget Deficits The national debt doubled from $1 trillion to $2 trillion during the Reagan presidency and remained a problem for Bush. One of Clinton's first acts was to submit to Congress a plan for reducing the deficit. Although opposed by every Republican and many Democrats, it passed by one vote each in the Senate and House. The measure increased the top income tax rate to 36 percent, increased the federal tax on gasoline slightly, cut spending, and thus provided for a deficit reduction of $496 billion over five years.

By 1994, a significant decline in unemployment signaled the recession's end. Economic upturn occurred despite layoffs by major corporations and several anti-inflation interest hikes by the Federal Reserve Board. By 1995, the economy appeared to be healthy. Though reduced, the national debt still exceeded $4 trillion. Clinton reduced both federal spending and federal employment.

Republican Midterm Victories For some Americans, Clinton was too liberal on social issues. For others, his failed national health plan was a sign of weak leadership. As a result, midterm elections of 1994 gave Republicans control of both the House and the Senate for the first time in 40 years.

The Republican platform, known as the *Contract With America*, included a balanced budget amendment, term limits for Congress, and welfare reform. It also outlined a smaller central government, with many functions and powers transferred to the states. Republicans hoped to cut spending by eliminating federal guidelines and reducing federal bureaucracy. Clinton opposed major portions of the Contract With America for fear that they would hurt the poor and the middle class.

Stock Market Trends From 1987 through the end of the 1990s, the stock market surged forward in a strong bull market. In 1987, the Dow Jones average (a grouping of 30 major companies) stood at 2,000. By 1999, it had increased to more than 10,000. A major reason for the increase was the growth in new technology businesses.

As wealth increased in the late 1990s, Alan Greenspan, chairman of the Federal Reserve, gradually raised interest rates in an attempt to slow the economy and stock market trading and thus prevent inflation. Reassured by the lowest unemployment rate in 40 years, the public kept up the economic boom by spending for all types of products.

Politics

Whitewater Investigations As governor of Arkansas, Clinton and his wife had taken loans from an Arkansas bank and purchased land in the Whitewater region. The value of this land was expected to increase greatly. Questions, however, arose regarding the loans and land purchase. A special Whitewater committee was established to determine if Clinton had acted improperly and violated the law.

After more than a year, the committee reached no specific conclusions about the president's conduct. The committee chairman, Senator Alfonse D'Amato, a New York Republican, felt that Clinton had "misused his power" and "attempted to manipulate the truth." Christopher Dodd, a Democratic senator, called the hearing "the most partisan and politicized hearing in the history of the Senate." Attorney General Janet Reno appointed a special prosecutor to investigate further. After several years the investigation ended without charges.

Gun Control Those opposed to gun control cite the Second Amendment's provision that "the right of the people to keep and bear arms shall not be infringed." Proponents of gun control note that the amendment specifies that the right to bear arms refers to a "well regulated militia." In 1993, Congress passed the *Brady Bill*, which called for a five-day waiting period and a background check by local officials before a handgun could be sold. (James Brady had been wounded in an assassination attempt on President Reagan in 1981.) In 1996, however, the Supreme Court, citing the division of powers between the federal and state governments, ruled that Congress could not require local officials to conduct background checks.

As violence involving guns increased, the gun control issue became more controversial. In April 1999, for instance, two teenagers shot and killed 12 fellow students and a teacher and wounded 30 others at Columbine High School, Littleton, Colorado. The *National Rifle Association (NRA)*, the main lobbying group opposed to gun control, argued that people rather than guns kill people. Others argued that guns must be made more difficult to obtain. An assault weapons bill, signed by President Clinton in 1994, was not renewed by Congress in 2004.

Campaign Finance Reform Americans have long been concerned about how much the two major parties spend on elections. In 1974, a federal law established disclosure requirements for campaign contributions and set specific limits on donations to individual candidates. However, it allowed unlimited contributions to political parties or organizations for party-building and issue education. Such contributions are called **"soft money."** In spite of restrictions, soft money is often used to benefit specific candidates. The 1974 law also began public financing of presidential elections and created a *Federal Election Commission*. In 1976, however, the Supreme Court, in *Buckley* v. *Valeo*, declared that mandatory spending limits on federal candidates and on those who support federal candidates reduces (1) freedom of expression as guaranteed in the First Amendment and (2) the ability to communicate political ideas. The ruling pointed out that "every means of communicating ideas in today's mass society requires the expenditure of money."

The high cost of television advertising is one reason why campaigns are expensive. And during the months-long campaign process, expenses for polling, travel, and staff mount up. A new campaign finance law limiting some "soft money" contributions was passed by Congress in 2002 and upheld by the Supreme Court in 2004. Concerns remain, because of record spending and fund raising during the 2004 presidential election.

Impeachment, Trial, and Acquittal In 1998, the special prosecutor turned from Whitewater to Clinton's sexual involvement with a young woman on the White House staff. At the same time, an Arkansas woman brought a sexual harassment lawsuit against him for an incident dating back to his time as governor. The special prosecutor accepted testimony by the president on videotape rather than in court. The president denied involvement with either the White House intern or the Arkansas woman. Evidence, however, was uncovered that Clinton was involved sexually with the intern; thus, his denial under oath led to a call for impeachment.

In November 1998, Clinton settled the harassment lawsuit but continued to deny wrongdoing. In December, the Republican-controlled House of Representatives voted for impeachment. The accusations, which focused not on the sexual affair but on the president's testimony, led to charges of perjury and **obstruction of justice** (attempting to influence others to conceal the truth). The proceeding then moved to the Senate for trial, with Chief Justice Rehnquist presiding. On February 12, 1999, the Senate, by a narrow margin, acquitted Clinton, and he remained in office.

U.S.-Middle East Relations

Palestinian Problem After Israel's 1948 and 1967 victories, Palestinian refugees were resettled in camps in Syria, Lebanon, and Jordan. Their poverty and nationalism gave rise to the *Palestine Liberation Organization (PLO)*, which aimed to eliminate Israel and make a Palestinian homeland there. Its main weapon was **terrorism** (systematic use of violence to achieve political goals). The PLO attacked Israeli settlements, buses, beaches, and airplanes, and even made anti-Israeli assaults elsewhere.

Intifadah More than a million Palestinians lived in the Israeli-occupied Gaza Strip and West Bank. Beginning in 1987, youths protested by throwing rocks, and Israeli troops sometimes retaliated with gunfire. This **intifadah**, or uprising, attracted international attention.

Changing Relations In a 1993 breakthrough, Israel's prime minister, Yitzhak Rabin, and PLO

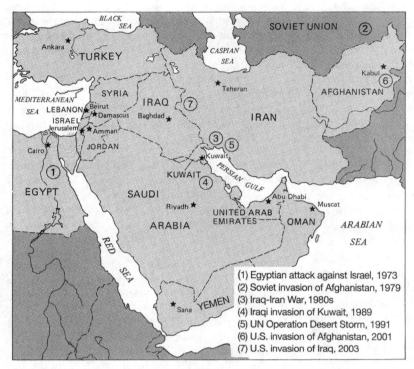

(1) Egyptian attack against Israel, 1973
(2) Soviet invasion of Afghanistan, 1979
(3) Iraq-Iran War, 1980s
(4) Iraqi invasion of Kuwait, 1989
(5) UN Operation Desert Storm, 1991
(6) U.S. invasion of Afghanistan, 2001
(7) U.S. invasion of Iraq, 2003

Invasions in the Middle East, 1973–2003

leader Yasir Arafat signed a "land for peace agreement":

★ Palestinians gained self-rule in the Gaza Strip and the West Bank town of Jericho.

★ The PLO recognized Israel and pledged to end terrorism.

In 1994, Jordan and Israel officially ended five years of war. In 1995, Israel agreed to expand Palestinian self-rule in the West Bank. The PLO reconfirmed Israel's right to exist and undertook to strengthen Palestinian antiterrorism measures.

Jewish and Arab extremists challenged this peace process. In 1995, an Israeli shot and killed Rabin. A new Palestinian resistance movement, Hamas, used terror bombing and suicide attacks against Israelis to disrupt peace efforts. The difficult movement toward peace continued with Presidents Clinton and George W. Bush working with different Israeli prime ministers and moderate Palestinian leaders.

United States in the Global Economy

NAFTA In 1994, Clinton completed negotiations begun by Bush for the *North American Free Trade Agreement (NAFTA)* with Mexico and Canada. This treaty immediately eliminated tariffs on some goods and phased out others. Thus, U.S., Canadian, and Mexican businesses gained a market of 380 million potential customers. This expanded market, it was hoped, would increase production and create jobs. Moreover, better economic conditions in Mexico might reduce illegal immigration to the United States. Many Canadian and U.S. workers, however, feared that if businesses moved to Mexico, where wages were lower, they would lose their jobs. Meanwhile, other Latin American countries expressed interest in joining the group in the future.

GATT After World War II, the major economic powers set up the *General Agreement on Tariffs and Trade (GATT)* to reduce and limit trade barriers and settle trade disputes. Periodic negotiations had further lowered tariffs among GATT members. In 1995, GATT changed its name to the *World Trade Organization (WTO)*. Now with 149 members, it is the major body overseeing international trade.

In 1999, the WTO met in Seattle, Washington, to promote increased global trade. Thousands of protesters, however, demonstrated against it for, in their view, promoting unrestricted trade among large multinational corporations at the expense of workers' rights and the environment.

In response, Clinton asked the WTO to include in its agenda protection of labor rights and the environment. But most developing countries feared that linking trade with labor and environmental standards would burden their economies or be used by others as an excuse to boycott their goods.

Critics of the WTO also said that it infringed on national sovereignties because it was empowered to settle trade disputes and impose sanctions on countries found in violation of the group's agreements. Supporters maintained that free trade led to greater global prosperity.

Farm Subsidies For many years, developing countries had been critical of United States subsidies to its farmers. These subsidies kept farm product prices low and prevented developing nations from profitably selling their agricultural goods in the United States. In the United States large-scale farmers and agribusinesses lobbied the government to maintain the subsidies. In 2004 the United States along with other developed countries reached a tentative agreement with the developing nations to reduce farm subsidies, particularly to cotton farmers. However, in 2005, negotiations for further reductions slowed.

Trade With China China, with its 1.3 billion people, is the greatest potential market in the world for American goods. Its violations of human rights, however, have been a stumbling-block to full-scale U.S.-Chinese trade.

Between 1978 and 1989, China's Communist leaders adopted several economic reforms:

★ People were encouraged to set up small businesses.

★ The country was opened to Western tourists and businesses.

★ Advice from the West on improving the economy was welcomed.

In the spring of 1989, Chinese troops fired on some hundred thousand student demonstrators gathered in Tiananmen Square in the capital of Beijing. They had been peacefully urging the government to make democratic reforms. The massacre and arrest of thousands of students were telecast around the world. President George H.

Bush criticized the massacre but did not carry out economic sanctions voted by Congress. He argued that the United States could best help the Chinese by keeping on good terms with their government.

Clinton continued Bush's policy while Chinese leaders ordered the arrest of more Chinese dissidents. He, too, believed that increased trade with a prospering China would lead to a better human rights policy there.

Trade With Japan In 1992, Bush and American business leaders urged the Japanese to accept more U.S. imports. They agreed only to "targets" rather than specific increases. President Clinton continued the campaign to get Japan to buy more American goods. He had limited success.

Trade With the Pacific Rim During the 1980s and 1990s, trade and industry grew rapidly in the Pacific Rim countries—South Korea, Taiwan, Thailand, Singapore, Malaysia, and Taiwan. Their clothing, shoes, electric appliances, and steel sold well in foreign markets. In the late 1990s, an economic downturn in the Pacific Rim made their products cheaper for Americans to buy. At the same time, American products became too costly for Asians, and their imports slowed.

Problems With Latin America Traditional Latin American imports to the United States have been coffee, bananas, copper, and tin. More recently, televisions, videocassette recorders, textiles, and automobiles have been added to the list. In 1999, the United States trade deficit with all of South and Central America was $13 billion.

The United States does not trade with Cuba. To damage Fidel Castro's Communist government, the United States imposed a trade embargo in 1962. Because Cuba's trading partners were Communist nations, the Soviet collapse in 1991 badly damaged its economy. Thousands of Cubans fled poverty and dictatorship by attempting to enter the United States illegally. As the number of "boat people" rose, the United States decided to intercept and turn back boats leaving Cuba. In 1994, a U.S.-Cuban agreement ended the exodus and raised the yearly quota of Cubans allowed to enter the United States.

U.S. Interventionism

Somalia During the last year of the George H. Bush presidency, the United States provided humanitarian aid to Somalia, an African nation suffering from famine and civil war. U.S. forces joined a UN force trying to end the civil war. In 1994, after significant multinational casualties, the United States withdrew. By 1995, all UN troops had left Somalia, where war and famine continued.

Haiti In 1990, Father Jean-Bertrand Aristide was elected president of Haiti. Less than a year later, a military coup ousted Aristide, who fled to the United States. In 1993, the UN imposed an oil and arms embargo on Haiti. Large numbers of Haitians tried to reach the United States by boat. Officials returned some to Haiti, held others in detention centers, and allowed still others to emigrate to welcoming countries.

Haiti's harsh military government refused to welcome Aristide back. In 1994, the UN authorized a multinational invasion, which was only averted when the Haitian military agreed to recognize Aristide. U.S. troops restored order, and Aristide resumed the presidency in October 1994. Haiti's democracy and its economy remained unsettled.

Bosnia In 1994, Bosnian Muslims and Croatians created a Muslim-Croat confederation while heavy Muslim-Serb fighting continued. Bosnian Serbs controlled more than 70 percent of the country. In 1995, the balance of power shifted, NATO launched heavy air strikes at Bosnian Serb targets, and a Croat-Muslim offensive recaptured significant territory. In 1995, after nearly four years of civil war, the leaders of Bosnia, Croatia,

and Serbia signed a peace treaty in Dayton, Ohio. It divided Bosnia into two autonomous (self-governing) regions: a Muslim-Croat federation controlling 51 percent of the country and a Serb republic holding 49 percent. About 60,000 NATO troops, including a large American force, stayed on as peacekeepers. A UN tribunal brought charges against suspected war criminals.

Yugoslavia Ethnic and religious conflicts also led to war in Kosovo, a Yugoslavian province with a population of roughly 90 percent Albanian Muslims and 10 percent Serbian Orthodox Christians. Until 1989, Kosovo had its own elected officials and Albanian language schools. Then, Slobodan Milosevic, the Yugoslavian president, forced Kosovo's elected officials to step down and reinstated Serbo-Croatian as the official language. When Albanians demanded full independence, Serbian officials countered with violence. Ethnic Albanians formed the Kosovo Liberation Army (KLA) in 1996 and conducted a guerrilla war for Kosovo's independence. Milosevic authorized dozens of executions of ethnic Albanians in Kosovo and burned thousands of their homes. Full-scale war erupted.

Fearful of Serbian "ethnic cleansing" in Kosovo, as earlier in Bosnia, the UN called for an immediate cease-fire as an alternative to air strikes. The Albanians signed the peace plan, but the Serbs rejected the provision calling for a NATO peacekeeping force in Kosovo. NATO then launched a massive air war against Yugoslavia and Serbian forces in Kosovo between March and

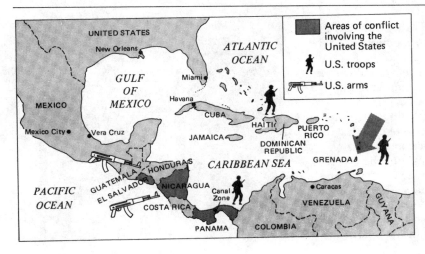

U.S. Interventions in Latin America in the 1980s and 1990s

June 1999. In retaliation, the Serbs terrorized Albanians, thousands of whom fled to Albania and Macedonia. In May 1999, the UN war crimes tribunal indicted Milosevic for "crimes against humanity." In June, he accepted a peace plan that included NATO occupation. A 50,000-member multinational force entered Kosovo, and refugees began returning home.

Iraq   After Iraq's 1991 defeat in the Persian Gulf War, UN inspection teams were to monitor Iraq's destruction of missiles and chemical and biological weapons. Iraq, however, refused access to some sites. In 1998, Iraq ordered the inspectors to leave, and the U.S. and Britain bombarded Iraqi military targets.

North Korean Nuclear Capability   In North Korea, the Communist regime of Kim Il Sung and his son and successor, Kim Jong Il, survived the collapse of communism elsewhere. In the early 1990s, North Korea was suspected of developing nuclear weapons. It denied the charge but refused UN inspection of its nuclear power plants. Under threat of UN economic sanctions, North Korea froze its nuclear program in exchange for two light-water reactors and economic and diplomatic concessions. (Light-water reactors are difficult to use in the production of nuclear weapons.) U.S.-North Korean relations remain clouded by suspicions that North Korea is secretly building nuclear weapons

U.S.-Russian Relations   Russia became an independent state in 1991. The United States and other Western nations pledged emergency economic aid to Russia, which began a series of economic reforms.

In 1996, the United States ratified START II, which aimed at a two-thirds reduction in each side's strategic nuclear weapons, and the Russian parliament ratified it in 2000. The United Sates is also working with Russia to dismantle hundreds of stockpiled Russian nuclear weapons.

Russia and the United States differ on a number of issues, however. The United States objected to Russia's use of force among its own people. In 1994, Russia sent troops into the Muslim region of Chechnya when it declared its independence. After almost two years of heavy fighting, Russian and Chechen leaders signed a peace accord in 1996. But in 1999, a series of explosions in Russia were blamed on Chechen terrorists,

which heated up the conflict again. Russia invaded Chechnya, causing more than 100,000 civilians to flee to neighboring regions. By February 2000, the Russian army claimed victory.

Meanwhile, on December 31, 1999, Boris Yeltsin resigned as president, naming Vladimir Putin as his successor. Putin, who had been largely responsible for Russia's defeat of Chechnya, won the 2000 presidential election.

In 2003 Russia agreed to build a nuclear power plant for Iran, which would produce electricity for domestic use. The U.S. and other Western powers objected, because they feared that sensitive nuclear and weapons technology would be transferred to Iran. In 2005, Russia proposed a plan whereby Iran would send uranium to Russia for enrichment into nuclear fuel, which would then be returned to Iran to produce electricity. Britain, France, Germany, and the U.S. endorsed the Russian proposal.

Other areas of disagreement have included Russia's opposition to including Eastern European countries in NATO, Russia's desire to end sanctions against Iraq, and Russia's objection to NATO's bombing of its traditional ally, Yugoslavia.

Chechen women protest the killing of their leader by a Russian missile.

Economic and Military Organizations

European Union The European Union (EU) originated in the 1950s from an effort by six Western European nations to reduce trade barriers. In 2004 the EU added 10 nations from Eastern and Southern Europe, for a total of 25. Many of its members now use a common currency, the euro, and a central bank coordinates monetary policy. Plans for political union have been controversial, as some nations fear a loss of national sovereignty. In 2005 a proposed EU constitution, which required unanimous consent by all members, was accepted by some members but rejected by voters in other nations. The rejection of the constitution means the next vote on ratification would not come until 2007. Although the question of political union remains unanswered, the economic power of the EU makes it a strong rival to the United States.

North Atlantic Treaty Organization With the collapse of the Soviet Union in 1991 and the end of the cold war in 1992, NATO members created a rapid deployment force to react to local crises. By the mid-1990s, 27 nations, including Russia and other former Soviet republics, established a working relationship with NATO known as the "Partnership for Peace." It provided for limited joint military exercises, peacekeeping missions, and the exchange of information. A multinational NATO force was deployed in Bosnia in 1995 and in Kosovo in 1999.

In 1997, NATO and Russia concluded the "Foundling Act," which increased Russian cooperation with NATO and paved the way for NATO to admit East European states. In March 1999, the Czech Republic, Hungary, and Poland officially joined NATO, the first former members of the Warsaw Pact to do so. Seven more nations in Eastern Europe were added in 2004.

Election of 2000

In the presidential election of 2000, the Democratic candidate, Vice President Albert Gore, Jr., faced Republican rival George W. Bush, governor of Texas and son of ex-President George H. Bush. There was no clear winner, owing to the close race in Florida, whose 25 electoral votes proved to be decisive. An automatic machine recount of ballots there was triggered, as required by state law.

For weeks the results of the election remained in doubt. The election was finally decided by an appeal to the U.S. Supreme Court. The Court, in a controversial decision, *Bush* v. *Gore*, ruled 5-4 that the Florida recount had to stop in order to meet the state schedule to select electoral college members, and that the recounting was violating the equal-protection clause of the 14th amendment. Gore then conceded the race.

★ In Review

1. Describe (a) three social concerns, (b) three economic concerns, and (c) two political concerns that arose during the Clinton administration.
2. Summarize the issues involved in the (a) movement for campaign finance reform and (b) the impeachment of Clinton.
3. Explain how each of the following posed a challenge to U.S. foreign policy during the 1990s: (a) Middle East, (b) Somalia, (c) Haiti, (d) Bosnia, (e) Yugoslavia, (f) Iraq, and (g) Russia.

GEORGE W. BUSH PRESIDENCY

Terrorism: Attacks and Responses

Shock quickly spread on the morning of September 11, 2001, as pictures of terrorist attacks on America were viewed across the nation. Islamic extremists had hijacked four large passenger airplanes. Two of the planes were flown into the World Trade Center in New York City, killing nearly 3,000 people, including several hundred heroic police officers and firefighters trying to rescue those trapped in the collapsing towers. A third plane was flown into the Pentagon, the nation's military headquarters, killing nearly 200 people, while the fourth plane, bound for Washington, D.C., crashed in a field in Pennsylvania after its passengers fought with the terrorists on board.

The 19 hijackers were followers of Osama bin Laden, a wealthy Saudi, who directed a terrorist network called Al Qaeda ("the Base"). Al Qaeda members were thought to have previously bombed U.S. embassies in East Africa in 1998 and in 2000 attacked the U.S.S. *Cole* in Yemen.

War on Terrorism Speaking after September 11, President George W. Bush said that the nation would search out Al Qaeda, Osama bin Laden, and terrorists across the globe and hold any nation protecting them accountable. He asked Congress to enact antiterrorist legislation and to provide funds to aid the reconstruction of New York City.

In October the U.S. government demanded that the fundamentalist Taliban government of Afghanistan end its protection of Al Qaeda members and their leader, Osama bin Laden. When the Taliban rejected the U.S. demand, U.S. air strikes were launched. An alliance was formed with Afghans fighting against the Taliban, and American troops were deployed in the country. By December the Taliban's control was ended but bin Laden remained at large. In 2004 a new constitution was written and elections were held, but Afghanistan remains an unsettled nation with regional warlords and fundamentalists opposed to democracy.

Congress passed the USA Patriot Act in October 2001, giving the government greater power and suspending the civil liberties of accused terrorists. Some aspects of the act were questioned by civil libertarians; it requires Congressional renewal in 2006. To coordinate government efforts against terrorism, an Office of Homeland Security was established and made a Cabinet department in 2003.

9/11 Commission Report President George W. Bush appointed a bipartisan commission to investigate the events that led to the September 11 attacks. The commission concluded that government agencies had missed or ignored terrorist activities in the U.S. The report called for greater coordination of intelligence and the appointment of a new Cabinet officer to bring together the work of all intelligence agencies, including the FBI and CIA.

Foreign Policy

President George W. Bush in his 2002 State of the Union address referred to an "axis of evil": Iraq, Iran, and North Korea, which were believed to have been developing nuclear weapons.

War Against Iraq After September 11, U.S. government officials became concerned that Iraq's possible possession of "weapons of mass destruction" (nuclear, biological, and chemical) could lead to their use in support of global terrorism. The U.S. plan for a preemptive attack on Iraq was opposed by many, including France, Germany, and Russia. Without a U.N. resolution of support, a U.S.-led coalition launched *Operation Iraqi Freedom* in March 2003. Within three months, direct military action was ended with the defeat of the Iraqi military forces. Later in the year, Iraqi dictator Saddam Hussein was captured.

President George W. Bush speaks to firefighters, police officers, and rescue workers at Ground Zero in New York City, September 14, 2001.

After the War The efforts of the U.S. and its coalition partners to rebuild Iraq and develop a democratic system immediately came under constant attack by guerrilla and terrorist forces representing the old regime and religious fundamentalists. By November 2005 over 2,000 U.S. soldiers had died in Iraq, most since the official end of the war.

United States policies in Iraq were subject to much controversy. After the war the U.S. conducted extensive searches for weapons of mass destruction but found no evidence of such weapons. Photographs of American soldiers mistreating Iraqis at the Abu Ghraib prison lead to an investigation that showed official neglect.

Some success was achieved in developing a democratic government based on Islamic law in Iraq. The work of an interim government resulted in the election in 2005 of a national assembly, which was to draft a constitution and appoint a president and prime minister. The challenge remained to avoid civil war and get the major religious and ethnic groups—Shiites, Sunnis, and Kurds—to work together.

With the unrelenting postwar violence in Iraq, opposition grew in the U.S. to continued involvement. While recognizing the good in ending the Iraqi dictatorship and efforts to establish a democratic society, opponents protested the escalating human, financial, and political costs to the United States.

Iran There has been hostility between the United States and Iran since the establishment of an Islamic state there and the U.S. hostage crisis of 1979–1980. The Iranians oppose the U.S. involvement in the Middle East, and the U.S. is concerned about Iranian efforts to develop nuclear weapons. In 2003 an investigation by the International Atomic Energy Agency revealed a secret Iranian nuclear program which, the Iranians claimed, was for peaceful purposes.

North Korea The Communist government led by dictator Kim Jong Il announced in 2002 that North Korea would restart its nuclear weapons program. In 2005 North Korea claimed that it had nuclear weapons and would soon test them. The U.S. feared that poor economic conditions would cause North Korea either to use the weapons against its neighbors or sell the weapons to terrorists. Unsuccessful efforts have been made by the United States, China, Russia, South Korea, and Japan to get North Korea to stop its nuclear weapons program.

Middle East Conflict The search for a peaceful solution to the conflict between Israel and the Palestinians continued. In 2003 President George W. Bush proposed a "roadmap for peace" that called for the removal of Israeli settlements in the occupied territories and the Palestinian Authority ending the violence against Israel. Continued

U.S. troops in Baghdad take cover during a gun battle after a rocket attack in August 2003.

terrorist attacks resulted in Israel building a security barrier to keep out suicide bombers.

Renewed hope for peace has come from a combination of events. In April 2004 Israeli Prime Minister Ariel Sharon announced a unilateral withdrawal from the Gaza Strip. The death of Palestinian leader Yasir Arafat led to the first free elections for Palestinians. Their new president, Mahmoud Abbas, called for peace with Israel. In February 2005, Abbas and Sharon declared a cease-fire to halt acts of violence. Israel completed its withdrawal from Gaza in September 2005.

Caribbean A number of old problems with some of its neighbors still commanded U.S. attention. In Haiti the government of President Jean-Bertrand Aristide lost public and military support in 2004 because of continued high unemployment and poverty rates. After widespread rioting, U.S. troops took Aristide into exile, and a 15-nation U.N. peacekeeping force endeavored to maintain peace under an interim president and prime minister.

Questions have increased about the U.S. trade embargo on Cuba. Fidel Castro, Cuba's Communist leader, has resisted changes even though his nation's economy has weakened since the demise of the Soviet Union. Since the 1990s the U.S. has discouraged Cubans from sailing to the U.S. A policy change in 2004 limited the amount of money Cuban Americans can send to their families in Cuba. Some, including a number of Cuban Americans, believe that the U.S. trade embargo should be reviewed.

Domestic Issues and Natural Disasters

Congressional Elections of 2002 The Republicans increased their majority in the House and gained control of the Senate. For the first time since the early 1950s, both the Congress and presidency were controlled by the Republican Party.

Taxes, Deficits, and the Economy In 2001 George W. Bush requested and Congress passed a $1.35 trillion tax cut spread over the next ten years. It was hoped that this would stimulate an economy that had slowed down from the collapse of technology stocks and the closing or downsizing of many companies. In 2002 and 2003, further tax cuts were made in the face of a weak economy. Capital gains taxes were cut and the childcare tax credit was increased.

Opposition to the tax cuts was based on a belief that they favored the wealthy, caused increased federal budget deficits, and added to the national debt. But a 2004 bipartisan study showed that all taxpayers received some tax relief. One-third of all tax cuts went to those in the top 1 percent tax bracket, while the top 10 percent of earners paid two-thirds of all federal income taxes, and 30 million of the lowest earners paid no federal income tax.

The yearly federal budget deficit was $300 billion in 2005 because of a combination of factors. These were tax cuts, slow economic growth, and increased spending, particularly for the war in Iraq. The trade deficit (the difference between the amount the nation spent on imports versus the amount it earned from exports) for the first nine months of 2005 was nearly $530 billion, up 18 percent from 2004, and running at a record annual rate of $700 billion. The deficit was caused in part by all-time high oil prices, resulting from hurricanes that shut down Gulf Coast production, and by cheap imports, especially from China.

To stimulate the economy, the Federal Reserve Bank lowered the discount rate (interest charged to banks) to 1 percent by 2003. Mortgage rates fell to record lows, and home buying and consumer spending increased. By 2004, employment had risen, and the Federal Reserve began slowly to raise the discount rate to avoid inflation. By the end of 2005, the rate had risen to 4 percent.

Corporate Bankruptcies and Scandals A number of large companies were found to have engaged in unethical practices and falsified their records to show inflated sales and profits. Federal legal charges were brought against executives at a number of companies, including Enron (energy trading), WorldCom (telecommunications), and Tyco, a large conglomerate. Accounting firms also were investigated for their involvement in falsifying records. Many employees and stockholders lost their life savings when the illegal activities were exposed. The companies went bankrupt, making their stock worthless.

Education President George W. Bush stressed the importance of education and in 2002 signed the No Child Left Behind Act. The law mandated stricter education standards and new testing requirements. It also permitted students to transfer from a school with low test scores to one with a higher success rate. The Supreme Court made a key ruling affecting education when it approved spending taxpayers' money for vouchers to pay tuition at private or religious schools. President Bush supported this decision because it gave students more choices, but opponents believed it violated the principle of separation of church and state and would also weaken public education by diverting funds.

Supreme Court Decisions

In the first years of the 21st century, the Supreme Court made a number of significant decisions on a wide range of issues:

★ *Gutter* v. *Bollinger* reaffirmed the 1978 *Bakke* decision that racial quotas were illegal, but that race could be a factor in college admissions at the University of Michigan.

★ *Lawrence* v. *Texas* stated that gay men and women had the right to privacy as part of the guarantee of due process, and therefore a Texas law was unconstitutional.

★ The Child Online Protection Act was upheld as constitutional because it served to protect minors using public library computers.

★ *Virginia* v. *Black, et al.* (2003) ruled that acts such as cross burning could be viewed as free speech as long as there was no intent to threaten people's lives.

★ Mandatory sentencing guidelines, set by Congress, were viewed by the Court in 2005 to be only guidelines, and federal judges were free to use or ignore them.

Medicare and Prescription Drugs

The first major addition to Medicare benefits was made when President George W. Bush and Congress agreed on a program to provide prescription drugs at lower-than-retail prices for Medicare recipients. The program went fully into effect in 2006.

Environmental Issues

President George W. Bush's position on a number of environmental issues has been criticized by many environmental groups. The president called for:

★ Voluntary industrial compliance with the Kyoto agreement on greenhouse gases

★ "Clean skies" legislation to reduce factory pollution, but excluding carbon dioxide emissions

★ Increased logging in the national forests to reduce fire risks

★ Limited oil drilling in the Arctic National Wildlife Refuge in Alaska to reduce reliance on foreign oil.

Hurricanes Katrina and Rita

On the morning of August 29, 2005, 145-mph winds and torrential rains swept onto the U.S. mainland coast near Buras, Louisiana. Over the next several days the Gulf Coast of the United States was hit by the greatest natural disaster in the nation's history. The areas most affected by this category five hurricane (the highest and most severe category) were the coastal areas of Louisiana and Mississippi, including the major city of New Orleans. The city itself created a unique problem because much of it was below sea level. Levees had been built to control flood waters. All residents of New Orleans were ordered to evacuate before the storm hit, but the city's large low-income population lacked the means to leave. When the levees broke, major government efforts were needed for quick evacuation and rescue of people trapped in the flooded city. Relief was slow to arrive. The absence of swift relief efforts left many people wondering whether local, state, and federal governments would be able to cope with additional major disasters and terrorist attacks.

More than a million people were displaced from their homes and communities by Hurricane Katrina. Nearly a thousand people lost their lives. The cost of rebuilding was estimated at $200 billion. New Orleans for a time resembled a third world nation. Relief workers found a city in which many persons lacked shelter, food, water, and medical services. For weeks afterward, residents sought missing family members. Thousands of now-homeless persons were relocated in Louisiana and across the country. Four weeks after Katrina's impact, a second hurricane, Hurricane Rita crashed into eastern Texas and western Louisiana. Several million residents were ordered to evacuate the city of Houston before the storm hit, causing major traffic jams on highways out of the city. This second storm was not nearly as powerful as Katrina, and caused far less damage, although some communities were severely affected. But, once again the ability of all levels of government to deal quickly and effectively with the major threats and actual disasters was called into question.

Space Exploration

Following the *Columbia* space shuttle disaster in 2003, which killed seven astronauts, serious concerns were raised about the cost and safety of manned flights. In 2004 President George W. Bush proposed a manned flight to the moon by the year 2020 in preparation for a manned trip to Mars. While pictures of Mars taken by an unmanned spacecraft in early

2004 stimulated the nation's interest in space, there were still serious doubts about manned flight and the overall costs of space exploration. Concerns were laid to rest when the space shuttle *Discovery* successfully returned to earth in the summer of 2005. NASA then announced plans for a manned space flight to the moon in 2018.

2004 Election

In November 2004, President George W. Bush defeated Massachusetts Senator John Kerry after a bitter and costly campaign. President Bush called his Democratic opponent a "flip-flopper" on the issues and lacking the leadership to fight the war on terror. Senator Kerry said the president had mismanaged the war in Iraq and the battle against terrorism, and that the Bush tax cuts for the wealthy should be repealed. Other issues in the campaign included: health care, Social Security, jobs, the economy, and "moral" values and social issues such as funding stem-cell research and banning same-sex marriages.

From a record 122 million voters President George W. Bush won 62 million votes, the highest number ever given a presidential candidate, and this equaled 51 percent, a majority of the popular vote. With his narrow victory in Ohio, President Bush won the Electoral College with 286 votes, to 251 for Senator Kerry. The Republican Party also expanded its majorities in Congress with 55 seats in the Senate and 232 seats in the House.

★ In Review

1. Explain the significance of each of the following: *Bush* v. *Gore*; the 9/11 Commission; budget deficits; Enron scandal; "No Child Left Behind" Act; Child Online Protection Act.
2. Discuss how the September 11 attacks affected the first term of the George W. Bush presidency in each of the following areas: (a) foreign affairs, (b) homeland security, and (c) individual rights.
3. In what way was President Bush's economic plan for the nation in his first term of office similar to that of President Ronald Reagan in his first term of office?

Chapter Review

MULTIPLE-CHOICE QUESTIONS

1. Bill Clinton was able to defeat President Bush in the 1992 election primarily because of (1) the U.S. failure to oust Iraq's Saddam Hussein from power (2) discontent over an economic recession (3) the 1989 U.S. surprise invasion of Panama (4) the signing of START I.

2. Which is a conclusion that may be drawn about U.S. foreign policy in the 1990s and early 2000s? (1) The United States returned to a policy of neutrality. (2) With the end of the cold war, the United States played the dominant role in international affairs. (3) The United States was successful in stabilizing the Middle East. (4) President Clinton was more successful than President George H. Bush in maintaining world peace.

3. Which is an accurate description of the domestic programs of President Bill Clinton? (1) The federal government took a more active role in domestic affairs than it did under Presidents Reagan and George H. Bush. (2) The federal government decreased its spending on welfare benefits. (3) The president's national health care program was enthusiastically supported by small businesses. (4) The programs became an important extension of the New Deal and Great Society.

4. An overview of the second term of the Clinton presidency indicates that (1) the administration was plagued with numerous difficulties, including the Whitewater investigation and presidential impeachment (2) the administration was able to work effectively with a strongly Democratic Congress

(3) the administration took a "hands-off" stance toward ethnic cleansing in the former nation of Yugoslavia (4) the activities of Saddam Hussein were ignored.

5. The outcome of the presidential election of 2000 was finally determined by (1) recount of votes in various counties in Florida (2) vote in the U.S. House of Representatives (3) decision by the U.S. Supreme Court (4) changes in the procedures of the Electoral College.

6. Which is an undeniable conclusion that may be derived from the results of the presidential election of 2000? (1) The state of Florida will have to revise its election laws. (2) The voting population of the U.S. is almost evenly divided between Republicans and Democrats. (3) The Electoral College must be eliminated. (4) Democratic candidate Al Gore should have become the next president.

7. Following the September 11, 2001, terrorist attacks, U.S. armed forces invaded Afghanistan to (1) support the antiterrorist Taliban government (2) remove a government that was providing a base for terrorist activity (3) promote religious and gender equality, as well as democracy (4) warn Saddam Hussein in Iraq to halt the development of weapons of mass destruction.

8. Which is an accurate statement about the USA Patriot Act? (1) Civil liberties are not absolute. (2) The Bill of Rights is being eliminated. (3) The federal government will be able to guarantee the safety of its citizens against terrorism. (4) Suspected terrorists will be deported.

9. In his 2002 State of the Union address, President George W. Bush referred to three nations as an "axis of evil." Why did the president single out these nations? (1) They harbored members of international terrorist organizations. (2) They refused to admit international weapons inspectors. (3) They were believed to be developing nuclear weapons technology that was banned by international treaty. (4) They refused to join the World Trade Organization.

10. The devastating effects of hurricanes Katrina and Rita in 2005 on the Gulf Coast of the United States caused many people to (1) praise the swift response of governments to these disasters (2) question the ability of governments to meet large-scale disasters (3) call for civilian populations to abandon the affected areas (4) call for the building of large barriers to withstand future hurricanes.

THEMATIC ESSAYS

1. **Theme:** The Impeachment Process. During his second term, President Clinton became only the second president in U.S. history to be impeached.

Task

★ Describe the specific constitutional charges against President Clinton.
★ Compare and contrast the result of the impeachment of Andrew Johnson with that of Bill Clinton.

2. **Theme:** Presidential Decision Making in the 1990s and Beyond. The president of the United States must make decisions, often very quickly, regarding emergencies and issues that have serious implications for or are crucial to the well being and security of the United States or other nations.

Task

★ Describe one problem faced by President George H. Bush, another problem faced by President Bill Clinton, and a third problem faced by President George W. Bush.
★ For each problem, discuss the president's options and the final decision he made.
★ Evaluate the implications of each president's decision.

In your discussion of President George H. Bush, you may wish to use the crisis in Bosnia, the Persian Gulf crisis, and the collapse of communism in the Soviet Union and Eastern Europe.

In your discussion of President Bill Clinton, you may wish to use an example such as the North American Free Trade Agreement (NAFTA), national health care, and crises in such nations or regions as Somalia, Bosnia, Kosovo, and Haiti.

In your discussion of President George W. Bush, you may wish to use an example such as the attacks of September 11, 2001, the Home-land Security Department, the invasion of Afghanistan, and the invasion of Iraq.

You are *not* limited to these suggestions.

DOCUMENT-BASED QUESTION

*Read each document and answer the question that follows it. Then read the **Task** and write your essay. Essays should include references to most of the documents along with additional information based on your knowledge of United States history and government.*

Historical Context: In the early years of the 21st century, the United States faces, as it has in the past, a number of challenging problems whose solutions will affect it and the other nations of the world for many years to come.

Document 1: Refer to the photograph on page 283.

Question: What events led the United States to engage in wars in the Middle East in the early 21st century?

Document 2: Refer to the graph on page 261.

Question: How did the nature of immigration change in the 1980s?

Document 3: Refer to the cartoon on page 274.

Question: How does the cartoonist feel about education in the United States as compared with other nations?

Document 4: Refer to the map on page 279.

Question: What does the map illustrate about recent U.S. relations with Latin American and Caribbean neighbors?

Document 5: Refer to the cartoon on page 272.

Question: What does the cartoon say about the ability of the U.S. government to control oil prices?

Task

★ Describe *two* problems that the United States is currently facing.
★ Discuss the options for each problem and suggest a potential solution.
★ Explain the outcome that you anticipate from your suggested solutions to the problems.

Student's Study Guide

U.S. history and government is a two- or three-semester course. Therefore, it is important to develop a strategy for remembering key topics and details. In that way, you will minimize difficulties in taking the Regents examination given at the end of the course.

Basic Strategies for Study

1. Review Frequently

Review daily or several times a week the material covered in class, and do all your homework assignments. Such periodic review will help you understand the connections between the different events studied without the need for cramming the day before a test.

2. Identify Recurring Vocabulary Terms

Terms such **federalism**, **checks and balances**, **states' rights**, **neutrality**, **judicial review**, and **due process** come up again and again in U.S. history and government. Identify them as they are repeated throughout the course.

3. Write Identifications, Not Definitions

Be sure you can explain the significance or historical importance of terms, names, and phrases that you encounter in the course. This is called *identification*. If your teacher asks you to keep an identification list, limit each identification to three or fewer sentences.

4. Create Broad Questions That Focus on Key Themes

By recasting the material under study into questions or problems, you will create an outline for study and understanding. Here are several examples from Chapter 19, "Limits of Power—Turmoil at Home and Abroad: 1965-1973":

★ Why were President Eisenhower and Secretary of State Dulles concerned about the domino theory?

★ How did the Tonkin Gulf Resolution change the U.S. role in Vietnam?

★ Why were young people especially involved in the antiwar movement?

★ How did Nixon's Vietnam policy compare with Johnson's?

★ What effects did the Vietnam War have on the United States for years afterward?

Learning to write such probing questions will teach you to arrange the material into smaller units of study and help you anticipate possible test questions.

5. Review Graphics Provided in Class and Your Textbook

Illustrations will be included in the Regents examination. Familiarity with graphs, maps, tables, charts, drawings, paintings, cartoons, and photographs will help you interpret and analyze them. (Specific suggestions for developing skill with graphics are given on pages 289–290.)

6. Review "In Review" and "Chapter Review" Questions

"In Review" questions reinforce your understanding of the key topics, section by section. "Chapter Review" questions simulate questions on the Regents examination. As you answer them, you become familiar with the Regents format.

7. Determine Cause-and-Effect Relationships

When you understand chronology—the order of historical events—you will better understand why events have taken place. This is called the *cause-and-effect relationship*.

Consider the following statements:

★ The issues of nullification, states' rights, and slavery resulted in the Civil War.

★ Jim Crow laws developed in the South as a result of the failure of Reconstruction.

Each statement contains a *cause* and *effect*. The first statement says that nullification, states' rights, and slavery were causes of the Civil war; in other words, the Civil War was an effect of these causes.

The second statement says that Jim Crow laws were the effect of the failure of Reconstruction; in other words, that failure helped cause Jim Crow laws.

Ask yourself (a) what past events caused the event you are studying to take place and (b) what were the later effects of that event. Thus, you will realize that history appears to flow from one topic to another, and that no event occurs in isolation.

Regents Examination, Part I: Multiple Choice

The Regents examination is a three-hour test consisting of three parts: 50 multiple-choice questions, worth 55 percent of the score; one thematic essay, worth 15 percent; and one document-based question (DBQ), worth 30 percent.

Standard Multiple Choice Most multiple-choice questions are like those you have regularly answered in high school. A question or statement requires completion. There are four possible choices. Here are strategies for answering standard multiple-choice questions:

★ Read all the choices. There are often one or more "decoy" choices. That is, they seem correct but, in fact, are not. A decoy often precedes the correct answer, and the careless student will be tempted to choose quickly and incorrectly.

★ Note such words as "all," "none," "always," and "never," which often signal an incorrect choice. Such words allow for no exceptions.

★ Note key terms that often point to the correct answer.

★ Weed out incorrect choices by the process of elimination.

★ Do not get stalled by a particular question. First answer the questions you know. Then attack questions that you can narrow down to two choices. Tackle the rest of the questions last.

Now put these strategies to work by answering the following multiple-choice questions from past Regents examinations:

Question 1: The framers of the U.S. Constitution showed the strongest commitment to democratic principles in regard to the (1) method for choosing cabinet members (2) election of members of the House (3) election of senators (4) selection of Supreme Court justices.

The key work is "democratic." To evaluate the best choice, determine which one gave the most power to citizens.

In choice 1, the president chooses cabinet members with the "advice and consent" of the Senate. This may appear to be correct because it reflects checks and balances, but remember that the question asks for the *strongest commitment to democratic principles*. (Also keep in mind that the founders did not foresee that the president would form a cabinet.)

Choice 2 refers to the election of members of the House, which is a democratic process.

Choice 3 refers to the election of senators as the *framers of the U.S. Constitution* designed it. This is not a good choice because state legislatures, not the people, originally elected senators.

Concerning choice 4, Supreme Court justices, like cabinet members, are appointed by the president and approved by the Senate.

Careful thought will convince you that choice 2 answers the question best.

Question 2: What is the most frequent criticism of the electoral college system? (1) An excessive number of third-party candidates are encouraged to run for office. (2) Electors frequently ignore the vote of the people. (3) The person who wins the popular vote is not always elected president. (4) the electors are not chosen by political parties.

The electoral college resulted from the founders' fear of the mob, or ordinary citizens—that the majority of voters could not select the best person as president.

Choice 1 deals with third-party candidates and has no relationship to the electoral college.

Choice 2 can be eliminated because each elector in each state is pledged to a particular candidate.

Choice 4 is incorrect because, although the voters determine who will be electors, the major political parties choose who runs for the electoral college.

Choice 3 is the correct answer. The electoral college's choice of president did not reflect the popular vote in three elections—Hayes-Tilden (1876), B. Harrison-Cleveland (1888), and Bush-Gore (2000).

Multiple Choice and Interpreting Graphics Some multiple-choice questions ask you to interpret an illustration, graph, or chart. This requires the development of special skills, such as identifying the meaning of symbols, the artist's point of view, and the underlying significance of the figures in a scene. The following political cartoon and question are from the January 1999 Regents examination:

Question 3: Base your answer on the following cartoon and on your knowledge of U.S. history and government.

The cartoon makes the point that Supreme Court decisions (1) sometimes do not resolve controversial issues (2) are usually accepted by both sides in a controversy (3) avoid dealing with controversial issues (4) ignore public opinion.

This cartoon provides several hints to the answer. Both women disagree with a Supreme Court decision on abortion, but their beliefs about what is the proper decision are opposite.

Choice 2 is incorrect because neither woman is satisfied.

The cartoon also shows that Choice 3 is incorrect because the abortion issue is shown to be very controversial.

Your decision is thus narrowed to choice 1 or 4. The cartoon shows that the decision has not resolved a controversial issue (choice 1). It also shows that the Court apparently did not take into account public opinion (choice 4). Therefore, you must decide which choice best reflects the cartoonist's point of view.

Obviously, this controversial abortion issue has not been resolved; it is so sensitive that there is no clear-cut public opinion. Choice 4, it turns out, is a decoy after the correct answer. The cartoon's main point is best illustrated by choice 1.

Some questions call for interpreting a table or chart. Consider the following chart and question from the January 1999 Regents examination:

Question 4: Base your answer to the question on the following table and on your knowledge of U.S. history and government.

★ Life Expectancy of U.S. Men and Women ★		
Year	Men	Women
1900	46.3	48.3
1950	65.6	71.1
1960	66.6	73.1
1970	67.1	74.7
1980	70.0	77.4
1990	71.8	78.8
1998	73.9	79.4

A valid conclusion based on the data in the table is that (1) men have received better medical attention than women (2) Americans are healthier than people in any other country (3) the average life expectancy increased steadily during the 20th century (4) most of the change in the average life span for men and women has occurred since 1950.

It is not the purpose of this type of question to require sophisticated mathematical calculations. Rather it tests the ability to understand and interpret information in a table, chart, or graph. Therefore, search for trends within the table. This table shows two trends taking place between 1900 and 1998:

★ Life expectancy increased during the 20th century.

★ Women tend to live longer than men.

The first trend is the subject of choice 3.

Choice 1 must be incorrect because (a) American men have tended not to live as long as American women and (b) the table provides no information on medical care.

Choice 2 should be eliminated because the table gives no information about people living outside of the United States.

Choice 4 is incorrect because the table gives no information for the years 1901 to 1949.

The best answer is choice 3.

Question 5: A correct conclusion based on the map is that (1) territorial boundaries were maintained as new states were created (2) all territories were acquired through wars and other conflicts (3) U.S. expansion generally occurred in a westerly direction (4) Southern territories were the last areas to be acquired.

The map shows that present-day state boundaries (the gray lines) do not always match territorial boundaries (the black lines). Thus, choice 1 must be eliminated.

Choice 2 is suspicious because it contains the world "all." A choice containing "all," "never," "none," or "always" might be correct, but even one exception would make the choice incorrect. And, in fact, choice 2 is incorrect because the map gives no information about how territories were acquired. (The statement is also historically inaccurate, as shown by the labels "Louisiana Purchase" and "Gadsden Purchase.")

Choice 4 is incorrect because the map shows that territories in the South (Florida and Texas) were acquired before 1853 when the final acquisition (the Gadsden Purchase) was made.

The map supports choice 3 because it shows that most territories were acquired in chronological order from left to right, or east to west—Treaty of Paris (1783), Louisiana Purchase (1803), and Annexation of Texas (1845). There are, however, some exceptions: the Oregon Territory was acquired two years before the Mexican Cession, the Gadsden Purchase was made after the Mexican Cession, and Florida was acquired in no apparent chronological pattern. But because choice 3 includes the word "generally," allowing for a few exceptions, it is still correct.

Regents Examination, Part II: Thematic Essay

The thematic essay focuses on a theme spanning several periods or linking several events in U.S. history and government. It asks you to show how well you understand the theme's importance and its role in the course. Examples of themes include nationalism, sectionalism, imperialism, geography, technology, warfare, peacekeeping, equality, checks and balances, and federalism.

In developing your answers to the essays in parts II and III B, keep the following definitions in mind:

★ **Discuss** means "to make observations about something, using facts, reasoning, and argument; to present in some detail."

★ **Describe** means "to illustrate something in words or tell about it."

★ **Evaluate** means "to examine and judge the significance, worth, or condition of; to determine the value of."

The following thematic essay might appear on the Regents examination:

Directions: Write a well-organized essay that includes an introduction, several paragraphs addressing the task, and a conclusion.

Theme: Presidential Decisions. During the last 100 years, U.S. presidents have made important decisions in an effort to solve crucial problems.

Task: From your study of U.S. history and government, identify two important presidential decisions made during the last 100 years. For each decision:

★ State *one* goal the president hoped to accomplish by the decision.

★ Discuss the historical circumstances surrounding the decision.

★ Discuss *one* immediate or *one* **long-term effect of the decision on U.S. history and government.**

You may use any important presidential decision in 20th-century U.S. history and government. Some suggestions include: (a) Woodrow Wilson seeks ratification of the Versailles Treaty (1918), (b) Franklin D. Roosevelt institutes the New Deal program (1933), (c) Harry S. Truman decides to drop atomic bombs on Japan (1945), (d) Dwight D. Eisenhower sends federal troops to Little Rock, Arkansas (1957), (e) John F. Kennedy places a naval blockade around Cuba (1962), (f) Lyndon Johnson proposes the Great Society program (1965), and (g) Jimmy Carter meets with Anwar Sadat and Menachem Begin at Camp David (1978).

Essay Guidelines: Be sure to:

★ Address all aspects of the task.

★ Analyze, evaluate, or compare and/or contrast issues and events whenever possible.

★ Fully support the theme with relevant facts, examples, and details.

★ Write a well-developed essay that is consistently logical and clearly organized.

★ Establish an initial framework that is more than a restatement of the task.

★ Conclude with a strong summation of the theme.

Key words and phrases in the task are (a) *identify* two *important presidential decisions*; (b) *for each decision*; *goal*; (c) *historical circumstances*; (d) one *immediate* or one *long-term effect*. By jotting them down, you create a checklist for organizing the thematic essay.

Observe the following seven additional guidelines:

1. Analyze the Question: Be sure you understand the theme and directions—the key words and phrases.

2. Organize the Information: Add the general information you plan to write about to your checklist to create an *instant outline*. For the sample thematic essay, you might include:

Two Presidential Decisions

1: Truman drops A-bombs on Japan (1945)

Goal: Force quick Japanese surrender

Historical Circumstances: Western European war over. Long war in Pacific continues; many casualties

Extent of Goal Achieved: Immediate Japanese surrender

Immediate/Long-Term Effect: Nuclear arms race begins

2: Eisenhower sends federal troops to Little Rock, Ark. (1957)

Goal: Desegregate Central High School

Historical Circumstances: Enforce *Brown* v. *Board of Education* (1954) on separate educational facilities

Extent of Goal Achieved: Black students admitted to school

Immediate/Long-Term Effect: Federal enforcement gives impetus to civil rights movement

Notice how you have expanded your checklist with ideas to flesh out your essay. The outline should take only five minutes.

3. Develop the Thesis: Use the theme or task to create an original thesis, such as the following thought-provoking one: "The president of the United States must often make difficult and controversial decisions that will have major effects on the nation both at the time the decision is made and for many years into the future."

4. Write the Introductory Paragraph: The introductory paragraph should include the thesis statement and background of your essay. Introduce examples taken from the instant outline and to be used in the essay. Include the decision by Truman to drop atomic bombs on Japanese cities and the decision by Eisenhower to enforce *Brown* v. *Board of Education* (1954) by sending federal troops to Little Rock, Arkansas.

5. Write the Supporting Paragraphs: These paragraphs *explain* your answer with facts, details, and examples. Elaborate on the facts from your instant outline. Be as specific as possible. *Do not* use meaningless facts or information unrelated to your theme.

6. Write the Concluding Paragraph: The concluding paragraph should restate the thesis in a fresh, interesting manner and briefly summarize the essay. A good concluding paragraph to the sample essay would be: "Both presidents Truman and Eisenhower made decisions that had an enormous impact on our nation's 20th-century history. Truman's decision to drop atomic bombs on Hiroshima and Nagasaki in 1945 ended World War II, but at the cost of many civilian lives and the start of a nuclear arms race. Eisenhower's decision to use federal troops to desegregate Central High School in Little Rock, Arkansas, in 1957 gave hope to African Americans and helped foster the growing civil rights movement."

7. Check the Essay: If time permits, reread your essay to correct grammar, spelling, punctuation, sentence structure, and errors in fact. Does your essay read clearly and make sense? Rereading the essay can improve your grade for the thematic essay portion of the Regents examination.

GENERIC THEMATIC ESSAY RUBRICS Those who score your thematic essay will use the following guidelines, or scoring scale:

5 Thoroughly develops all aspects of the task evenly and in depth

Is more analytical than descriptive (analyzes, evaluates, and/or creates information)

Richly supports the theme with many relevant facts, examples, and details

Demonstrates a logical and clear plan of organization; includes an introduction and a conclusion that are beyond a restatement of the theme

4 Develops all aspects of the task but may do so somewhat unevenly

Is both descriptive and analytical (applies, analyzes, evaluates, and/or creates information)

Supports the theme with relevant facts, examples, and details

Demonstrates a logical and clear plan of organization; includes an introduction and a conclusion that are beyond a restatement of the theme

3 Develops all aspects of the task with little depth or develops most aspects of the task in some depth

Is more descriptive than analytical (applies, may analyze, and/or evaluate information)

Includes some relevant facts, examples, and details; may include some minor inaccuracies

Demonstrates a satisfactory plan of organization; includes an introduction and a conclusion that may be a restatement of the theme

2 Minimally develops all aspects of the task or develops some aspects of the task in some depth

Is primarily descriptive; may include faulty, weak, or isolated application or analysis

Includes few relevant facts, examples, and details; may include some inaccuracies

Demonstrates a general plan of organization; may lack focus; may contain digressions; may not clearly identify which aspect of the task is being addressed; may lack an introduction and/or a conclusion

1 Minimally develops some aspects of the task

Is descriptive; may lack understanding, application, or analysis

Includes few relevant facts, examples, or details; may include inaccuracies

May demonstrate a weakness in organization; may lack focus; may contain digressions; may not clearly identify which aspect of the task is being addressed; may lack an introduction and/or a conclusion

0 Fails to develop the task or may only refer to the theme in a general way; *OR* includes no relevant facts, examples, or details; *OR* includes only the theme, task, or suggestions as copied from the test booklet; *OR* is illegible; *OR* is a blank paper

Regents Examination, Part III: Document-Based Questions And Essay (DBQ)

This essay calls for you to write a general essay after interpreting a variety of documents about the topic (maps, pictures, cartoons, graphs, charts). One or more questions on each document test your understanding of it. Here is a sample DBQ:

Directions: This document-based question consists of Part A and Part B. In Part A, you are to read each document and answer the question or questions that follow it. In Part B, you are to write an essay based on the information in the documents and your knowledge of U.S. history and government.

Historical Context: After the Civil War, the United States became much more industrialized. Between 1865 and 1910, industrialization improved life in many ways. Industrialization, however, also created social problems.

Part A

Document 1 (see table on page 295)
1a. Identify one aspect of American life shown in the chart that improved between 1870 and 1910.
1b. Identify one aspect of American life shown in the chart that worsened between 1870 and 1910.

Document 2
The groundwork principle of America's labor movement has been to recognize that first things must come first, ... Our mission has

Impact of Industrialization (1870-1910) ★

Year	GNP per Capita	Employed Children Under 15 Years of Age (millions)	% of U.S. Population		Infant Mortality Rate (deaths) Under 1 Year of Age per 1,000	High School Graduates (% of 17-year-olds with diplomas)	Telephone Usage (number of telephones per 1,000)	Steel Prod. (1,000 (short tons)
			Rural (%)	Urban (%)				
1870	$ 531	0.70	74	26	170	2.0	0	77
1880	744	1.10	72	28	161	2.5	1	1,400
1890	836	1.50	65	35	163	3.5	4	4,780
1900	1,011	1.75	60	40	141	6.5	18	11,220
1910	1,299	1.63	54	46	117	9.0	82	28,330

been the protection of the wage-worker, now, to increase his wages; to cut hours off the long workday, which was killing him; to improve the safety and the sanitary conditions of the workshop; to free him from the tyrannies, petty or otherwise . . . .

—Samuel Gompers

2. According to Samuel Gompers, why should workers organize into unions?

Document 3

The houses of the ward, for the most part wooden, were originally built for one family and are now occupied by several. Many houses have no water supply save [except] the faucet in the back yard, there are no fire escapes, the garbage and ashes are placed in wooden boxes. . . . The streets are inexpressibly dirty, the number of schools inadequate, sanitary legislation unenforced, the street lighting bad, the paving miserable and altogether lacking in the alleys and small streets, and the stables foul beyond description.

—Jane Addams, *Twenty Years at Hull House*

3. How was the life of the poor affected by the conditions described by Jane Addams?

Document 4

The sweatshop is a place where, . . . a "sweater" assembles journeymen tailors and needlewomen, to work under his supervision. He takes a cheap room outside the . . . crowded business center and within the neighborhood where the workpeople live. This is rent saved to the employer, and time and travel to the employed. The men can work more hours than

was possible under the centralized system, and their wives and children can help, ... For this service, . . . they cannot earn more than from 25 to 40 cents a day, ... In one such place there were fifteen men and women in one room, which contained also a pile of mattresses on which some of the men sleep at night. . . .

—Joseph Kirkland, *Among the Poor of Chicago*, 1895

4. According to Joseph Kirkland, what were conditions like in a sweatshop?

Document 5

AFTER THE FEAST, THE WORKING MAN GETS WHAT IS LEFT!

5a. According to the cartoon, what is one way in which the rich treated the workingman?
5b. What is one way in which such cartoons influenced public opinion toward the rich?

Document 6 From John D. Rockefeller's testimony before a congressional commission investigating industrial combinations, 1899:

Q: What are . . . the chief advantages from industrial combinations [trusts, monopolies, and so on] . . . to the public?

A: . . . Much that one man cannot do alone two can do together, . . . [Industrial combinations] are a necessity . . . if Americans are to have the privilege of extending their business in all the States of the Union, and into foreign countries as well. . . . Their chief advantages are: . . .

- Improvements and economies which are derived from knowledge of many interested persons of wide experience.

- Power to give the public improved products at less prices and still make profit for stockholders.

- Permanent work and good wages for laborers. . . .

—U.S. Industrial Commission,
Preliminary Report on Trusts and Industrial Combinations

6a. According to John D. Rockefeller's testimony, what did he believe was an advantage of industrial combinations?

6b. What was one reason why John D. Rockefeller would testify in favor of industrial combinations?

Document 7

7. According to the cartoon, what did Andrew Carnegie do with much of his wealth?

Part B

Task: Using information from the documents and your knowledge of U.S. history and government, write an essay in which you discuss the advantages and disadvantages of industrialization to American society between 1865 and 1910. In your essay, include a discussion of how industrialization affected different groups in American society.

Essay Guidelines: Approach the DBQ as you would any other essay question. Use the same guidelines as for the thematic essay (page 291), with one addition: Add references from *most* of the documents.

Look again at the seven documents in the sample DBQ. (Most DBQs have between six and nine documents.) Notice that there are two cartoons. The DBQ usually includes two or more graphic documents—cartoons, tables, charts, graphs, or pictures. Note that the documents contain a variety of ideas and perspectives on the topic—in this case, the advantages and disadvantages of American industrialization, and industrialization's effects on different groups. Some documents may be contradictory. This is not done to confuse you but to assess how well you analyze different points of view. (When you prepare your essay response, you will need to account for some of the differences of opinion.)

Now look at the questions following the documents. They test your understanding of the main idea of each document. All questions must be answered. Your answers may help you organize your essay response.

GENERIC DOCUMENT-BASED QUESTION RUBRIC
Those who score your document-based questions and essay will use the following guidelines, or scoring scale:

5 Thoroughly develops all aspects of the task evenly and in depth

Is more analytical than descriptive (analyzes, evaluates, and/or creates information)

Incorporates relevant information from at least xxx documents

Incorporates substantial relevant outside information

Richly supports the theme with many relevant facts, examples, and details

Demonstrates a logical and clear plan of organization; includes an introduction and a conclusion that are beyond a restatement of the theme

4 Develops all aspects of the task but may do so somewhat unevenly

Is both descriptive and analytical (applies, analyzes, evaluates, and/or creates information)

Incorporates relevant information from at least xxx documents

Incorporates relevant outside information

Supports the theme with relevant facts, examples, and details

Demonstrates a logical and clear plan of organization; includes an introduction and a conclusion that are beyond a restatement of the theme

3 Develops all aspects of the task with little depth or develops most aspects of the task in some depth

Is more descriptive than analytical (applies, may analyze, and/or evaluate information)

Incorporates some relevant information from some of the documents

Incorporates limited relevant outside information

Includes some relevant facts, examples, and details; may include some minor inaccuracies

Demonstrates a satisfactory plan of organization; includes an introduction and a conclusion that may be a restatement of the theme

2 Minimally develops all aspects of the task or develops some aspects of the task in some depth

Is primarily descriptive; may include faulty, weak, or isolated application or analysis

Incorporates limited relevant information from the documents or consists primarily of relevant information copied from the documents

Presents little or no relevant outside information

Includes few relevant facts, examples, and details; may include some inaccuracies

Demonstrates a general plan of organization; may lack focus; may contain digressions; may not clearly identify which aspect of the task is being addressed; may lack an introduction and/or a conclusion

1 Minimally develops some aspect of the task

Is descriptive; may lack understanding, application, or analysis

Makes vague, unclear references to the documents or consists primarily of relevant and irrelevant information copied from the documents

Presents no relevant outside information

Includes few relevant facts, examples, or details; may include inaccuracies

May demonstrate a weakness in organization; may lack focus; may contain digressions; may not clearly identify which aspect of the task is being addressed; may lack an introduction and/or a conclusion

0 Fails to develop the task or may only refer to the theme in a general way; OR includes no relevant facts, examples, or details; OR includes only the historical context and/or task as copied from the test booklet; OR includes only entire documents copied from the test booklet; OR is illegible; OR is a blank paper

Note the requirements for category 5. All aspects of the task must be developed, the essay must be more analytical than descriptive, and incorporate substantial, relevant outside information. The theme must be supported with many relevant facts, examples, and details.

Practical Plan For Success On The Regents Examination

Initial Preparation

There is no substitute for adequate, regular preparation. You teacher will probably review highlights of your two- or three-semester study of U.S. history and government. But this is not enough. In-class review merely suggests what you need to study and know.

Allow yourself four to six weeks of study time. It is better to study half an hour daily over this period than to cram for many hours several days before the examination. To review effectively, try the following suggestions:

★ Separate your studying into separate historical sections or periods. On average, two to four days should be spent on each one.

★ Plan a daily study schedule. This will help you adequately cover the entire U.S. history and government course.

★ Spend a short time reviewing the previous day's work to reinforce what you have already covered.

★ Study when you are alert rather than after exercise or a big meal.

★ Avoid distractions (television, radio, telephone, the Internet).

★ Take a five-minute break each study hour to help you stay fresh and retain what you have learned.

Knowing How and What to Study

Take a practice Regents examination before you begin your course of study. This will help you identify areas of study that need special attention. After reviewing for several weeks, take a different Regents examination. How far have you progressed, and what material still needs more review? (Your teacher should be able to supply you with past Regents examinations.)

Knowing the Examination Format

Use the practice Regents examinations to familiarize yourself with how each part of the test is structured. Understanding the form of each group of questions and how best to answer each one will help you maximize your score.

Knowing Important Vocabulary Terms and Names

You will not remember every term and name discussed during the course, but you should be familiar with important terms that apply to all periods of U.S. history and government, as well as terms and names related to particular historical eras. As you proceed through your course of study, make a list of these terms and names for periodic review.

Here are some tips for identifying such terms and names:

★ **Check off familiar terms.** The number of them that you already know will boost your confidence.

★ **Review eras for which you know the fewest terms.** Your check-off will identify areas in which you need more help. The glossary that follows will give you basic definitions.

★ **Make appropriate connections.** Linking related words, names, and terms is an effective way to reinforce the details in a large amount of material.

★ **Do not try to learn every term.** Trying to memorize everything is frustrating and practically impossible. Build a list designed to reacquaint you with key terms in U.S. history and government. The concepts they represent will be likely test subjects.

★ **Identifications are more important than definitions.** A definition gives you only the meaning of a term. An identification of a term's historical significance is a building block that will help you link one important concept with another.

Final Preparation

You have done everything possible to prepare for the Regents examination. Now get a good night's sleep. Arriving well rested at the testing room is the best preparation at this point. Last-minute cramming will be of little or no help and will prove harmful if it makes you too tired to perform well.

Glossary

abolition pre–Civil War reformers' goal of ending slavery

abolitionist person opposed to slavery

acid rain pollution caused when industrial and exhaust fumes in air dissolve in water vapor and fall as precipitation

acquired immunodeficiency syndrome (AIDS) fatal disease transmitted by a virus entering a person's body, as when drug users share needles or through sexual contact

affirmative action increased educational and job opportunities for women and minorities to make up for past discrimination

agriculture farming

alcohol substance produced from corn and burned alone or with gasoline (gasohol) to run car engines

alternative energy power from sources other than fossil fuels, nuclear reaction, or hydroelectricity

altitude elevation of a landform above sea level or other surface, such as the ocean floor

American System early 1800s legislation to encourage Western settlement by building roads and canals and placing high tariffs on imports

amnesty general pardon granted to a large group

anarchist one who believes in abolishing all government

animism religion in which humans seek security and prosperity by pleasing nature spirits

annexation takeover by one nation of another nation or territory

apartheid strict racial segregation formerly enforced by South Africa's white minority government against blacks and other racial groups

appeasement yielding to an aggressor's demands to avoid armed conflict

appellate jurisdiction higher court's authority to review a case tried in a lower court

arbitration impartial judgment in a dispute between labor and management

archipelago chain of islands

arctic climate long, dark, cold winter and summer of several weeks

area measure of how much of Earth's surface one place covers

assembly line arrangement of workers and machines in which products being manufactured pass on a moving belt from one operation to the next

asylum government protection of a person fleeing danger or mistreatment elsewhere

Australian ballot voting method in which a state-printed ballot is marked in secret

automation manufacturing method in which one set of machines regulates other machines

baby boom dramatic increase in the U.S. birthrate between 1945 and 1960

bail money or credit allowing an arrested person's release from jail pending trial

basin dry lowland surrounded by higher land; area drained by a river

belligerent nation involved in war

bicameral having two houses, as a legislature

bill of rights written list of personal liberties expressed as actions that a government may not take

biodegradable subject to natural decomposition

bipartisanship two major political parties acting together for the national good

Black Codes post–Civil War laws by Southern state conventions to limit the civil rights of African Americans; suspended as Reconstruction began

"blacklist" beginning in the early 1950s, organized refusal by businesses to hire persons suspected of being Communist sympathizers

blitzkrieg violent surprise German offensive during World War II, characterized by speed and mobility

block grant government financial aid given with few guidelines on its use

blockade   attempt by a nation's forces, usually a navy, to cut off access to another nation's ports, coastline, or other vital area

bootlegger   supplier of illegal alcoholic beverages

boycott   refusal to buy or sell goods or services in order to change a policy

breach of contract   failure to carry out terms formally agreed to

brinkmanship   pushing a dangerous confrontation to the limit of safety in order to achieve a desired outcome

broadleaf forest zone   area where deciduous trees, such as oaks and maples, predominate

budget   taxing and spending plan

budget deficit   gap when expenditures exceed revenues

"bull market"   economic condition when public confidence in stocks causes their prices to soar

cabinet   presidential advisory group composed of heads of executive departments

capital   buildings and equipment for producing goods and services; money to buy such buildings and equipment

capitalism   economic system marked by privately owned businesses competing for profits

carpetbagger   during Reconstruction, Northerner in the South seeking private gain

cash-and-carry principle   method of purchase by which a buyer pays in full and is responsible for transporting the goods; in particular, purchase by World War II belligerents of nonmilitary goods from the United States during its neutral period

caucus   meeting of party leaders to select candidates for office

censure   official reprimand of a member of Congress

census   official count of population, taken in U.S. every ten years

checks and balances   system by which one government branch may obstruct or defeat policies and decisions of other branches

chief executive   head of the executive branch

circuit court   group of courts with jurisdiction to review district court decisions

civil disobedience   purposeful refusal to obey laws regarded as unjust

climate   year-to-year weather conditions prevailing in a region over a long period

clone   living organism reproduced from one parent without fertilization

closed shop   workplace in which an employer must hire only dues-paying union members

coalition   alliance for joint action

cold war   period of U.S.-Soviet rivalry from 1945 to 1991, marked by espionage, hostile propaganda, the arms race, and the race in space

collective bargaining   process by which workers and employers work out differences about wages, hours, and working conditions

commune   rural community of counterculture "families"

company town   settlement near the site of a large company whose workers depend on it for employment

computer   high-speed electronic processor of data

concurrent powers   powers exercised jointly by the federal and state governments

conference committee   group of senators and representatives meeting to achieve a compromise between similar but differing bills

confirmation   Senate approval of a chief executive's appointment

coniferous forest zone   area where evergreen trees predominate

conservation   wise management and careful use of the natural environment

consolidation   combining of several businesses into one large company

conspicuous consumption   lavish spending habits to indicate social prestige

constituency   district of voters represented by an elected legislator

constitution   written plan of government

consumerism   tendency of the general public to buy more and more products in prosperous times

containment   U.S. cold-war policy of preventing Soviet power and influence from spreading to non-Communist nations

continental drift   slow movement of large land masses as Earth's plates slowly shift

cooperative   business owned and operated by those who buy its products or services

corporation   business chartered by a state and owned by shareholders who invest in it

cost-of-living adjustment (COLA)   automatic increase in Social Security benefits when inflation increases the costs of goods and services

cotton gin   device that separates seeds from cotton mechanically

counterculture   beginning in the late 1960s, lifestyle of young Americans that emphasized honesty and creativity and was opposed to such cultural norms as marriage, patriotism, and business

coup   small group's sudden violent overthrow of a government

craft worker   laborer with a trade skill

credit   time allowed for payment for goods or services sold on trust

czar   absolute monarch of Russia

data   information

data base   computerized information file

de facto **segregation**   separation of races that exists because of circumstances, such as housing patterns, rather than law

de jure **segregation**   separation of races authorized or required by law

debt moratorium   temporary halt on the payment of war debts

deciduous tree   tree that loses its broad, flat leaves seasonally

delegated powers   powers given to the federal government by the Constitution

demobilization   reduction of armed forces after war's end

democracy   government in which the people rule directly or through elected representatives

department store   retail business selling a wide variety of goods arranged in separate sections

depression   severe economic decline marked by business failures, high unemployment, and low production and prices

desert climate   heat, dryness, and scant vegetation

desert zone   dry area with scanty scrub vegetation

détente   relaxation of U.S.-Soviet tensions during the cold war

dictatorship   government in which all power is concentrated in one person or a small group

direct primary   state election to choose candidates by popular vote before the general election in November

disarmament   removal of weapons from aggressor nations

discount rate   interest charged by the Federal Reserve Board to member banks

disenfranchisement   cancellation of voting rights

dissenter   person opposed to a policy or cause supported by the majority

dissenting opinion   written explanation of why a minority of Supreme Court justices disagree with the majority's ruling

domino theory   in the 1950s, U.S. State Department belief that Southeast Asia's nations were like dominoes, ready to topple once any of them was taken over by communism

double jeopardy   being tried twice on the same charge

draft   compulsory enrollment for military service

earthquake   trembling ground caused by shifts within Earth's crust

elastic clause   grant by the Constitution to Congress of power not specifically stated to make "necessary and proper" laws

elector   member of a political group selected by voters to formally elect a president and vice president

electoral college   group of state officials casting ballots for a president and vice president

embargo   government order forbidding shipment of goods to another nation

energy crisis   acute shortage of oil leading to an increase in oil prices

entrepreneur   person who assumes the risk of organizing a business in hopes of profit

erosion   wearing away of Earth's surface by wind, rain, or ice

escalation   steady buildup of armed forces

espionage   spying

ethnic cleansing   use of force and terror to expel from an area a minority sharing a distinctive culture

ethnicity   common cultural bond uniting a large group of people

excise tax   tax on the sale of a domestic product

executive branch   part of government responsible for enforcing laws

executive privilege   argument that a president can withhold information from the legislative and judicial branches

extradition   return of a person accused of crime to the state where the crime was committed

fad   vivid, usually frivolous, form of social expression of short duration

fall line   boundary between elevated foothills and a coastal plain

fascism   government characterized by militarism, extreme nationalism, and a one-party dictatorship

federal system   system in which power is shared by central and state governments

federalism   principle by which political power is divided equally between central and state governments

feminist   person in favor of women's rights and opposed to political, economic, and social inequality between men and women

filibuster   attempt to stop passage of a Senate bill by talking indefinitely

fiscal year   budget year

foreclosure   repossession by a bank of property of a resident unable to repay a loan

fossil fuel   nonrenewable resource developed from ancient organisms; coal, petroleum, and natural gas

freedman   former slave

freedom ride   civil rights protest of the 1960s in which participants took interstate bus rides to spur desegregation of public transportation

frontier   imaginary dividing line between settlement and wilderness

gasohol   mixture of gasoline and alcohol from corn, used to run car engines

genetics   science of the heredity of living organisms

genocide   extermination of an entire national, ethnic, or religious group

genome   genetic makeup of an organism

geography   study of Earth's physical features, biology, and native cultures

geothermal energy   heat from within Earth, used to heat homes or generate electricity

gerrymandering   drawing voting districts so as to give a voting advantage to one political party

ghetto   urban neighborhood inhabited mostly by people of one nationality

glacier   ice-packed landform moving slowly across Earth's surface

glasnost Gorbachev policy to grant Soviet citizens more freedom of speech and the press

globalization expanding ability of people and corporations everywhere to communicate and do business with one another

graduated income tax income tax that takes proportionately more from high wage earners

"grandfather clause" in post–Civil War South, ruling that any male citizen could vote without restriction whose male ancestors could vote in 1867, when African Americans had not yet gained citizenship and the right to vote

grand jury citizen panel to determine whether enough evidence exists to indict a person for a crime

grassland zone area of low rainfall and only low-growing vegetation

greenhouse effect predicted warming of the world climate caused by excessive amounts of carbon dioxide building up in the atmosphere

growing season period between the last frost of spring and first frost of autumn

guerrilla warfare surprise attacks by small bands of raiders

habeas corpus order requiring a jailed person to be brought to court to determine whether detainment is lawful

highland climate cool to cold temperature with more moisture than in surrounding lowlands

holding company business combination owning a majority of stock in member companies and therefore able to dictate common policy

Holocaust systematic killing of Jews and other minorities by Nazi officials during World War II

"Hooverville" during the Great Depression, cluster of temporary dwellings for the homeless

hostage person held prisoner until ransom is paid or demands are met

humid continental climate high annual rainfall and widely varying summer and winter temperatures

humid subtropical climate hot, stormy summer and mild, moist winter

hydroelectric power energy generated when falling water turns turbines

ice age long period during which Earth's climate cools and glaciers spread

ideology belief system

impeachment accusation of wrongdoing against a government official

imperialism national policy of acquiring foreign territories or exercising control over them

implied powers federal powers derived from the elastic clause

impressment forcing people into military service, especially seamen of one country into another's navy

indemnity payment to cover damages and deaths

indentured servant person agreeing to work for a number of years in exchange for passage to a British colony

indictment formal statement by a grand jury charging a person with a criminal offense

Industrial Revolution period from about 1750 to the present marked by the invention of machines and systems to mass-produce goods

industrial union labor union representing all workers in an industry, regardless of skills, race, or other differences

industrial worker unskilled factory laborer

inflation constantly rising prices

initiative voters' power to propose ideas for new laws

injunction court order directing that an action be carried out or stopped

installment plan method of purchase by which partial payment is made immediately and the remainder paid out periodically

interchangeable parts separate elements of a manufactured product that are made exactly alike to ease assembly and repair

interlocking directorship placing of the same persons on executive boards of several companies as a means of limiting competition

Internet network of computers using the World Wide Web to provide information and resources on almost every subject

interstate commerce trade crossing state lines

interstate compact agreement between states for mutual assistance

intifadah widespread uprising by Palestinians living in Israeli-occupied territory

irrigation supplying of water for crops by artificial means

isolationism noninvolvement with foreign entanglements or organizations

Jim Crow laws in post–Civil War South, state and local laws denying African Americans free access to public facilities

joint-stock company organization in which merchants buy shares and the resulting capital is invested in business projects

judicial branch part of government responsible for applying laws in specific cases

judicial review Supreme Court's power to determine whether an act of Congress is constitutional

jurisdiction authority to hear and decide judicial cases

laissez-faire economic theory that business should not be regulated by government

landform natural feature of Earth's surface, including a part covered by water

landmark decision judicial ruling that marks a turning point or sets a precedent in law

latitude   measurement of how far a place is from the equator

lava   melted rock spewed out of a volcano

law of supply and demand   economic theory that when supply of an item is low, sellers can charge a high price, and that as supply increases, prices decrease as a result of competition

legislative branch   part of government responsible for making laws

libel   writing a false and unfavorable opinion about someone

life expectancy   average human life span in a particular population

literacy test   state requirement that a voter demonstrate the ability to read and write

lobbyist   professional advocate seeking to encourage a policy or influence a law favorable to a special interest group

loose construction   belief that the Constitution's elastic clause gives the federal government unstated powers

loyalty check   during Truman administration, FBI or Civil Service Commission search to uncover whether a person had ever belonged to a subversive organization

machine politics   organized control of elected officials by party leaders

magma   melted rock beneath Earth's surface

mainstreaming   education of disabled and nondisabled children together so as to provide special education services in regular classrooms

manifest destiny   early 19th-century belief that the United States was bound to expand westward to the Pacific and dominate North America

marine West Coast climate   cool summer, mild winter, and relatively high rainfall

mass production   manufacture of goods in large quantities by machine

massive retaliation   during the cold war, announced U.S. threat to meet Soviet aggression with a nuclear-weapons bombardment

Mediterranean climate   hot, dry summer and cool, rainy winter

Mediterranean scrub zone   area of hot, dry summer and wet winter, producing only low shrubs and small trees

"meltdown"   accident in which the nuclear core of a power plant burns through protective walls, allowing radioactive substances to escape into the environment

mercantilism   economic theory by which a colony supplies raw materials to the home country, which uses them to make goods to be sold in the colony for profit

merger   business combination in which two or more companies are united

methane   gas emitted from rotting organic matter and used as a heating fuel

microchip   tiny square of silicon imprinted with electronic circuits and their connections and capable of storing and processing data at high speed

militarism   nation's policy of glorifying its armed forces and aggressive spirit

mission   religious settlement to convert native people and offer humanitarian services

mixed forest zone   area of coniferous and broadleaf trees

mobilization   assembly of equipment and personnel in preparation for war duty

monolith   single undivided force

monopoly   exclusive control over the supply of a product or service

mortgage   money borrowed against the value of property

mountain   landform rising 1000 feet or more above nearby surfaces

muckraker   writer, especially in the Progressive Era, who exposed conditions needing reform

multinational corporation (MNC)   company operating plants, offices, or both in several countries

national debt   accumulation of debts owed to purchasers of government bonds

national guard   state force of citizen volunteers to serve in military or natural emergencies

nationalism   loyalty to one's nation and support of its interests; militant patriotism

nationalization   government takeover of property formerly owned by a colonial power or private company

nativist   one believing that foreigners are a threat to the majority culture and should be barred from entering the country

natural rights   theory that people are born with certain rights, such as of liberty and property

natural vegetation zone   band of land where natural conditions produce characteristic plants

navigable   capable of being used by ships, as a waterway

neutrality   policy of taking no sides in a war between other nations

nominating convention   meeting of party delegates to select candidates for office

nomination   party selection of a presidential candidate

nondenominational   favoring no religious group in particular

nonrenewable resource   mineral lacking organic matter and incapable of replicating itself

nuclear power   energy produced by using heat given off by radioactive substances

nullification   belief that a state can invalidate a federal law it considers unconstitutional

obstruction of justice   improper influence exerted on others to conceal the truth

ordinance regulation made by a city, county, or local government

original jurisdiction authority of a court to be first to hear and try a case

ozone layer band of gas high above Earth that blocks the sun's ultraviolet light and prevents it from damaging human tissue

pacifist opponent of war as a means of settling disputes or achieving national policy

pardon chief executive's power to forgive a convicted person's crime

parity equality, as of a nation's armed forces; price for farm products based on a price in an earlier base period

parliament advisory group; assembly of nobles, clergy, and commoners who make a nation's laws; (cap.) two-house British legislature

partnership multiple business ownership entailing liability for all debts

passive resistance endurance of violence without retaliation

patent government document giving the creator of a device or process exclusive right to market it

peaceable assembly nonviolent demonstration of the public will

perestroika Gorbachev policy for making the Soviet economy more efficient

perjury lying under oath

permafrost frozen underlayer of soil in the tundra

petit jury citizen panel that hears trial testimony and decides on a verdict

petition written request for a change in government policy

philanthropist person who uses wealth to fund humanitarian endeavors

plain large area of level or gently rolling land

plantation large farm with many workers

plateau flat or gently rolling expanse at high elevation

platform pre-election statement of a party's principles and policies

plurality number of votes cast for one of three or more candidates that is greater than the number cast for the others but not more than half

pocket veto automatic veto when a bill remains unsigned by the president and Congress adjourns fewer than ten days after passing it

pogrom sudden violent attack on a helpless minority community

political action committee (PAC) group funded by an organization to financially support political candidates favoring the organization's interests

poll tax payment formerly required for voting in some states; prohibited by the Twenty-fourth Amendment

polygamy having multiple marriage partners

pooling agreement between competing businesses to fix prices, share profits, and divide markets

popular sovereignty in pre–Civil War period, decision of voters in a territory to prohibit or allow slavery

popular vote ballots cast by the people

population density measure of concentration of people in a given area

post-traumatic stress disorder condition characterized by nightmares, irritability, depression, and guilt, caused by extreme stress; battle fatigue

power of the purse power to approve or reject a proposed tax

precipitation water that falls to Earth as rain, snow, sleet, or hail

predestination religious belief that every person's afterlife has been determined before birth

prevailing wind normal direction from which a high-altitude wind blows

primary election preliminary procedure by which voters choose between candidates for party nomination

productivity rate at which goods are manufactured

progressive late-1800s to early-1900s reformer dedicated to moderate political and social change through governmental action

propaganda facts, ideas, and rumors spread to help one cause and harm an opposing one

proprietorship single business ownership entailing liability for all debts

protectorate nation whose foreign policy is partly controlled by a foreign power

provisioning plantation large Northern farm producing food and lumber for West Indies sugar plantations

psychoanalysis treatment of mental or emotional problems through free association, reliving of troubling experiences, and recall of dreams; "talking cure"

racial discrimination denying someone equal opportunity because of race

racism prejudice and discrimination based on the supposed superiority of one group over others

ragtime music of the late 1800s and early 1900s marked by a lively, rhythmic style

railhead urban stopover on the cattle drive from Texas to Chicago

ratification formal approval

rationing government-imposed limits on food and other necessities for civilians during wartime

realpolitik foreign policy based on international political realities rather than ideology

reapportionment process by which a change in state population will result in a gain or loss of House seats

rebate former practice among competing railroads of refunding some of a large corporation's shipping charges

recall procedure by which voters can remove an elected official before expiration of the term

recession period of business decline

referendum voters' power to mark ballots for or against a proposed law

refugee person fleeing life-threatening conditions or persecution in the home country

regional agency official group administering operations crucial to neighboring states

renewable resource source of alternative energy that can be used without being diminished, such as solar power, wind power, alcohol, or methane

reprieve chief executive's power to postpone a convicted person's punishment

republic government in which the people elect representatives to make and execute laws

reservation land set aside for use by one or more Native American tribes

reserved powers under the Constitution, powers retained by the states

revenue sharing allowing state and local governments to decide how to spend federal grants

rules of succession procedure establishing the order in which government officials replace the chief executive in case of illness or death

salutary neglect pre–1763 British colonial policy of overlooking trade violations and allowing self-government

sanction action such as a trade restriction taken against a nation by one or more other nations to enforce adherence to international law

satellite in post–World War II period, country dominated by the Soviet Union

savings and loan association (S & L) cooperative that holds members' savings as dividend-bearing shares and invests in home mortgage loans

scalawag during Reconstruction, Southerner who cooperated with occupying Northerners

search warrant document authorizing a police search of a person or place for specified articles

secession state's separation of itself from previous ties and obligations to a federal union

secondary boycott refusal by strikers to buy products from companies doing business with their employer

sectionalism strong loyalty to one region within a nation

segregation separation of people on the basis of race

self-determination right of people with a common culture or nationality to form an independent nation

seniority privileges acquired by length of service

separation of powers division of governmental authority and duties among legislative, executive, and judicial branches

settlement house community center to aid city dwellers, especially poor immigrants

shale oil fossil fuel obtained by heating and crushing oil-bearing rock

share part-ownership in a business, based on the amount invested; stock

sharecropper farmer paying for use of a landlord's land with a portion of the annual crop

slum poor urban neighborhood of crowded streets and run-down buildings

social Darwinism theory that people, social groups, and businesses advance by means of free competition and that the stronger triumph over the weaker

socialism economic system based on public, rather than private, ownership of the means of production

"soft money" unlimited contribution to a political organization for party-building and issue education, sometimes misdirected to benefit a specific candidate

solar power energy derived directly from the sun

sovereignty independence

special interest group organization formed to exert pressure on lawmakers' decisions

speculator one making risky investments in hopes of high profits

sphere of influence area dominated by an imperialistic power

spoils system appointing people to government jobs on the basis of party loyalty rather than qualifications

stagflation unemployment and economic recession coupled with inflation

standing committee permanent House or Senate group specializing in a particular area of law

state militia group of volunteer soldiers for the common defense

steppe climate regular sunshine and little rainfall

steppe zone area with enough rainfall to support grass

stock part-ownership in a business, based on the amount invested; share

strict construction belief that federal powers are limited to those specified in the Constitution

strip mining ground-level mining of minerals that leaves the landscape scarred and ridden with debris

subarctic climate climate slightly more moderate than an arctic one, with a short summer warm enough for growing crops

subsidy government grant to a private enterprise

suburb residential community outside a city but near enough to allow residents to commute to city jobs

subversive person attempting to weaken or overthrow a government

suffragist one working to gain voting rights for women

summit conference meeting of heads of state to discuss affairs of mutual interest

supply-side economics policy of reducing federal taxes at the expense of benefit programs so as to give more money to businesses for investment and consumers for spending

supremacy clause part of U.S. Constitution stating that it and other U.S. laws take precedence over state and local laws

sweatshop   small manufacturing establishment with unsafe and unsanitary conditions

target price   farm goods price considered fair by the federal government; if the market price decreases, a farmer is paid a subsidy to make up the difference

tariff   tax on imports

temperance movement   organized effort to limit or ban sales of alcoholic beverages

tenant farmer   person working another's land and paying rent in cash or crops

tenement   multifamily urban dwelling with few amenities

terrorism   systematic use of violence to achieve political goals

third world   underdeveloped, nonindustrial nations of Asia, Africa, and Latin America

totalitarianism   political dictatorship that tries to control every aspect of citizen's lives

town meeting   meeting of self-governing village inhabitants, especially in New England

trade wind   mild northeast wind in the tropics

tributary   stream or small river feeding a larger stream, lake, or river

tropical climate   warm to hot summer and slightly cooler winter

tropical grassland zone   area of several dry seasons per year producing only scrub and scattered trees

tropical rain forest zone   area of year-round warmth and plentiful rain sustaining tall trees and thick undergrowth

trust   business combination of companies in the same field for the purpose of reducing competition or creating a monopoly

trust buster   progressive government executive dedicated to breaking up irresponsible monopolies

tundra zone   area of low temperature, little precipitation, and a short growing season of mosses, lichens, and stunted trees

ultimatum   final demand not subject to negotiation

unwritten constitution   traditions that have become part of the U.S. political system, such as political parties and the president's cabinet

veto   chief executive's power to refuse to sign a bill into law

vigilante   member of a self-appointed police force, especially on the Western frontier

volcano   mountain built up by lava and rock pouring out of a hole in Earth's crust

Web site   subject file on the World Wide Web

wind power   electricity generated by windmills

work ethic   traditional belief that hard work is morally good and will be rewarded with material success

World Wide Web   system that provides information and resources to the Internet

yellow journalism   newspaper's emphasis on scandals, crimes, and other shocking events to lure more readers

Yiddish   Germanic language of many central and eastern European Jews

zoning   local government regulations specifying business and home locations, land use, and allowable acreage for building sites

Index

UNITED STATES HISTORY AND GOVERNMENT
JANUARY 2006

Part I

Answer all questions in this part.

Directions (1–50): For each statement or question, write on the separate answer sheet the *number* of the word or expression that, of those given, best completes the statement or answers the question.

1 • Jamestown, founded in 1607
   • Plymouth colony, founded in 1620
   • New Amsterdam, founded in 1625

These early colonial settlements were similar in that each was located

(1) at the base of a mountain range
(2) near the coastline
(3) in an arid climate
(4) on offshore islands

2 During the early to mid-1700s, the British policy of salutary neglect toward the American colonies contributed to

(1) a decline in colonial manufacturing
(2) the decline of slavery in the northern colonies
(3) a decrease in French and Spanish influence in North America
(4) the development of independent colonial trade practices

3 In the Declaration of Independence, the argument for freedom from British rule is based primarily on the

(1) theory of divine right expressed by James I
(2) economic principles set forth by Adam Smith
(3) social contract theory of government developed by John Locke
(4) belief in a strong central government expressed by Alexander Hamilton

4 The constitutional basis for the separation of church and state is the

(1) establishment clause of the 1st Amendment
(2) double jeopardy provision of the 5th Amendment
(3) reserved powers of the 10th Amendment
(4) equal protection clause of the 14th Amendment

5 Which statement describes a characteristic of the government established by the Articles of Confederation?

(1) A Supreme Court had the authority to declare acts of Congress unconstitutional.
(2) The national government controlled interstate commerce.
(3) The president maintained exclusive control over foreign policy.
(4) A system was created where the states held the most power.

6 Which action during Washington's administration led to the Whiskey Rebellion in western Pennsylvania?

(1) passage of a new excise tax
(2) establishment of a presidential cabinet
(3) creation of the Bank of the United States
(4) ban on slavery in the Northwest Territory

7 The foreign policies of George Washington, Thomas Jefferson, and James Monroe were similar in that they each

(1) supported wars against England
(2) failed to acquire new territory
(3) attempted to avoid involvement in European affairs
(4) aided the French in return for their help during the Revolutionary War

8 Which action is considered part of the unwritten constitution?

(1) ratification of a treaty by the Senate
(2) formation of the first two political parties
(3) creation of a system of federal courts including the Supreme Court
(4) presidential veto of a bill passed by Congress

Base your answer to question 9 on the cartoon below and on your knowledge of social studies.

Good Morning, Doctor

Source: John Chase, *New Orleans Item*,
January 17, 1938 (adapted)

9 Which constitutional principle is best illustrated by the cartoon?

(1) federalism
(2) popular sovereignty
(3) judicial review
(4) checks and balances

10 "The enumeration [listing] in the Constitution, of certain rights, shall not be construed [interpreted] to deny or disparage [weaken] others retained by the people."

— 9th Amendment to the United States Constitution

The most likely reason this amendment was included in the Bill of Rights was to

(1) increase federal power over the people
(2) expand state control over individual citizens
(3) protect rights beyond those listed in the Constitution
(4) prevent Congress from granting additional rights to individuals

11 "The right of citizens of the United States to vote shall not be denied or abridged by the United States or by any State on account of race, color, or previous condition of servitude. . . ."

— 15th Amendment, Section 1, United States Constitution, 1870

Which actions did Southern States take to keep African Americans from exercising the rights guaranteed in this amendment?

(1) suspending habeas corpus and denying women the right to vote
(2) collecting poll taxes and requiring literacy tests
(3) establishing religious and property-holding requirements for voting
(4) passing Black Codes and establishing segregated schools

12 The Supreme Court decision in *Plessy* v. *Ferguson* (1896) had a major impact on the lives of African Americans because it ruled that

(1) segregation was illegal in educational institutions
(2) voting was a right guaranteed by the Constitution
(3) separate but equal public facilities were legal
(4) military occupation of the South was unconstitutional

13 Which action by the federal government during the late 1800s is an example of nativism?

(1) passage of the Chinese Exclusion Act
(2) creation of tribal reservations in the East
(3) grants of financial aid to western farmers
(4) support for the construction of trans-continental railroads

14 Which major population shift in the late 1800s occurred as a result of industrialization?

(1) northerners to the Sun Belt
(2) rural residents to urban areas
(3) working class people from the cities to the suburbs
(4) African Americans from the North to the South

Base your answers to questions 15 and 16 on the cartoon below and on your knowledge of social studies.

"The American Beauty Rose can be produced in all its splendor only by sacrificing the early buds that grow up around it."

— John D. Rockefeller, Jr.

Source: Guy R. Spencer, *The Literary Digest*, May 1905 (adapted)

15 Which idea of the late 1800s is most closely associated with this cartoon?

(1) regulated capitalism
(2) graduated income tax
(3) Social Darwinism
(4) the Gospel of Wealth

16 During the early 1890s, the federal government dealt with situations like the one shown in the cartoon by

(1) raising tariff rates on imported oil
(2) providing economic aid for small businesses
(3) prosecuting businessmen for graft and corruption
(4) passing the Sherman Antitrust Act

17 During the late 1800s, many farmers supported the idea that free and unlimited coinage of silver would

(1) end farm subsidies
(2) help farmers to repay their loans
(3) lead to lower prices for consumer goods
(4) decrease prices for farmland

18 Which term best describes Theodore Roosevelt, John Muir, and Gifford Pinchot?

(1) philanthropists
(2) conservationists
(3) yellow journalists
(4) captains of industry

19 During the Progressive Era, many state and local governments adopted initiative, referendum, and recall procedures that

(1) eliminated the need for the electoral college
(2) created political action committees (PACs)
(3) gave voters a more direct voice in government
(4) strengthened the role of the president's cabinet

20 The tragedy of the Triangle Shirtwaist Company fire of 1911 drew national attention to the need to

(1) restrict immigration from southern Europe
(2) establish full-time fire departments
(3) protect the safety of workers
(4) improve conditions for tenement dwellers

21 President Woodrow Wilson's Fourteen Points were proposed during World War I primarily to

(1) define postwar objectives for the United States
(2) outline military strategies for the United States
(3) convince other democratic nations to join the United Nations
(4) strengthen the United States policy of isolationism

22 To improve distribution of money and guarantee an adequate money supply, President Woodrow Wilson asked Congress to

(1) eliminate the gold standard
(2) limit foreign investment
(3) provide insurance for bank deposits
(4) establish the Federal Reserve System

23 The clear-and-present danger doctrine established in *Schenck* v. *United States* (1919) permits the government to

(1) declare war on any nation that attacks the United States
(2) limit speech that threatens the security of the nation
(3) break up monopolies that limit business competition
(4) outlaw organizations that threaten the civil rights of others

24 In 1920, women gained the right to vote as a result of a

(1) presidential order
(2) Supreme Court decision
(3) national election
(4) constitutional amendment

25 The Red Scare, the National Origins Acts of the 1920s, and the verdict in the Sacco and Vanzetti trial are examples of negative American attitudes toward

(1) immigrants
(2) business leaders
(3) African Americans
(4) labor union leaders

26 Improved mass-production techniques affected the American economy of the 1920s by

(1) reducing prices of consumer goods
(2) lowering the quality of most products
(3) causing higher unemployment
(4) decreasing the quantity of manufactured products

27 The Scopes Trial of 1925 is an example of

(1) the effects of assimilation on American culture
(2) a clash between scientific ideas and religious beliefs
(3) an increase in violence in American society
(4) government intervention in racial conflicts

Base your answer to question 28 on the map below and on your knowledge of social studies.

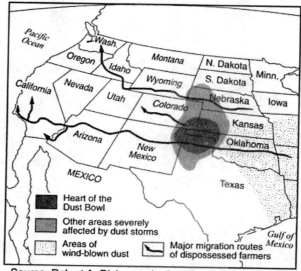

Source: Robert A. Divine et al., *America: Past and Present,* HarperCollins, 1995 (adapted)

28 Which region of the United States suffered most directly from the Dust Bowl?

(1) Southwest
(2) Pacific Northwest
(3) Rocky Mountains
(4) Great Plains

29 Which statement about Franklin D. Roosevelt's New Deal program is most accurate?

(1) Protective tariff rates increased.
(2) Social welfare programs were expanded.
(3) Government regulation of business was reduced.
(4) Government support of environmental conservation ended.

Base your answer to question 30 on the quotation below and on your knowledge of social studies.

". . . The people of Europe who are defending themselves do not ask us to do their fighting. They ask us for the implements of war, the planes, the tanks, the guns, the freighters which will enable them to fight for their liberty and for our security. Emphatically we must get these weapons to them, get them to them in sufficient volume and quickly enough, so that we and our children will be saved the agony and suffering of war which others have had to endure. . . ."

— President Franklin D. Roosevelt's "Fireside Chat," December 29, 1940

30 In this statement, President Franklin D. Roosevelt was asking the nation to

(1) support a declaration of war against Nazi Germany
(2) adopt a policy of containment
(3) join the League of Nations
(4) become the "arsenal of democracy"

31 Which factor contributed to the internment of Japanese Americans during World War II?

(1) labor shortage during the war
(2) influence of racial prejudice
(3) increase of terrorist activities on the West Coast
(4) fear of loss of jobs to Japanese workers

32 Following World War II, Eleanor Roosevelt was most noted for her

(1) support of racial segregation in the United States military
(2) role in creating the United Nations Universal Declaration of Human Rights
(3) opposition to the Truman Administration
(4) efforts to end the use of land mines

Base your answer to question 33 on the cartoon below and on your knowledge of social studies.

Eventually, Why Not Now?

Source: Jay Norwood "Ding" Darling, 1945

33 What is the main idea of this 1945 cartoon?

(1) The world community needs to stop the spread of nuclear weapons.
(2) Korea's development of atomic bombs has threatened world peace.
(3) The Treaty of Versailles was successful in preventing World War II.
(4) Germany should be criticized for using atomic bombs.

34 During the early 1950s, the tactics of Senator Joseph McCarthy were criticized because he

(1) violated important constitutional liberties
(2) displayed racial prejudice in his questions
(3) opposed the use of loyalty oaths
(4) ignored evidence of Soviet spying

Base your answer to question 35 on the graph below and on your knowledge of social studies.

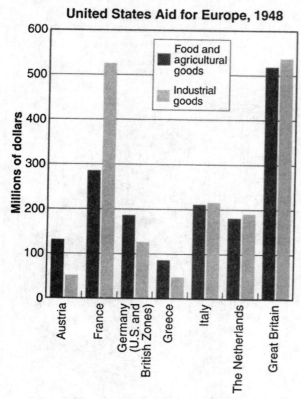

United States Aid for Europe, 1948

Legend:
- Food and agricultural goods
- Industrial goods

(Y-axis: Millions of dollars, 0 to 600)

(Countries: Austria, France, Germany (U.S. and British Zones), Greece, Italy, The Netherlands, Great Britain)

Source: *The Americans: In Depth Resources,* McDougal Littell, 1998 (adapted)

35 Information provided by the graph indicates that the Marshall Plan tried to prevent the spread of communism in Europe by

(1) providing military aid to France and Great Britain
(2) restoring economic stability throughout Western Europe
(3) encouraging domestic revolutions in Europe
(4) making European nations dependent on the United Nations

36 Which strategy did African-American students use when they refused to leave a "whites only" lunch counter in Greensboro, North Carolina, in 1960?

(1) economic boycott
(2) hunger strike
(3) petition drive
(4) civil disobedience

37 ". . . We choose to go to the moon. We choose to go to the moon in this decade and do the other things, not because they are easy, but because they are hard, because that goal will serve to organize and measure the best of our energies and skills, because that challenge is one that we are willing to accept, one we are unwilling to postpone, and one which we intend to win, and the others, too. . . ."

— President John F. Kennedy, speech at Rice University, September 12, 1962

The main purpose of this speech was to win public support for

(1) establishing a missile defense system on the Moon
(2) cooperating with communist countries in exploring space
(3) surpassing the Soviet Union in the space race
(4) controlling the spread of nuclear weapons

38 The requirement that all persons placed under arrest must be informed of their legal rights resulted from a

(1) custom adopted from English common law
(2) law enacted by Congress
(3) decision of the United States Supreme Court
(4) specific statement in the original Constitution of the United States

39 Which statement best describes an impact of the Watergate scandal on American society?

(1) The modern environmental movement began.
(2) Public trust in government declined.
(3) Voter turnout in elections increased.
(4) An economic recession ended.

40 United States involvement in the Vietnam War was based in part on a desire to

(1) prevent renewed Japanese expansionism in the Pacific
(2) assure access to an adequate supply of oil from the Middle East
(3) contain communism in Southeast Asia
(4) protect American business interests in China

Base your answers to questions 41 and 42 on the map below and on your knowledge of social studies. This map shows states where segregation in public schools was enforced by law until 1954.

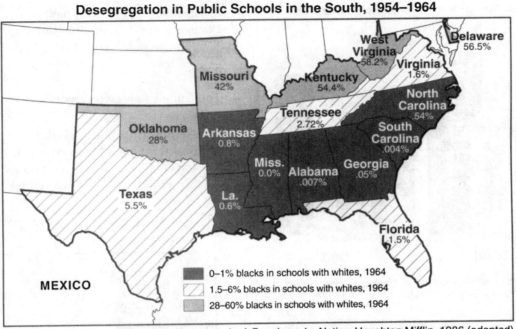

Desegregation in Public Schools in the South, 1954–1964

- ▓ 0–1% blacks in schools with whites, 1964
- ▨ 1.5–6% blacks in schools with whites, 1964
- ▒ 28–60% blacks in schools with whites, 1964

Source: Mary Beth Norton et al., *A People and a Nation*, Houghton Mifflin, 1986 (adapted)

41 Information provided by the map most clearly supports the conclusion that by 1964 racial desegregation of Southern schools was

(1) failing in Oklahoma, Missouri, Kentucky, and West Virginia
(2) supported by most voters in the South
(3) occurring at different rates in Southern states
(4) completed by the mid-1960s

42 The school desegregation that is shown on the map was most affected by the

(1) decline of the Ku Klux Klan
(2) passage of the equal rights amendment
(3) expansion of voting rights for African Americans
(4) decision of the Supreme Court in *Brown* v. *Board of Education of Topeka*

43 The Cuban missile crisis (1962) influenced President John F. Kennedy's decision to

(1) negotiate the limited Nuclear Test Ban Treaty with the Soviet Union
(2) reduce the nation's commitment to the North Atlantic Treaty Organization (NATO)
(3) forbid Americans to trade with and travel to Latin America
(4) send Peace Corps volunteers to aid developing countries

44 **"Gorbachev Proposes Nuclear Arms Reductions"**
"Berliners Travel Freely Between East and West"
"Russia Seeks To Join NATO"

These headlines are most closely associated with the

(1) military arms race
(2) decline of Cold War hostilities
(3) failures of the containment policy
(4) successes of communism in the Soviet Union

Base your answer to question 45 on the graph below and on your knowledge of social studies.

Percentage of Voters Who Say They Are:

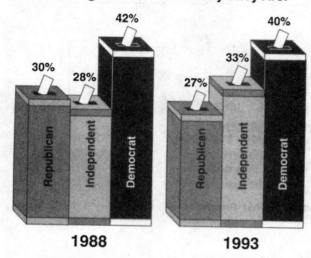

Source: The Gallup Organization. Bruce S. Glassman, ed., *Macmillan Visual Almanac*, Blackbirch Press, 1996 (adapted)

45 Information provided by the graph shows that between 1988 and 1993, there was an increased need for candidates of major political parties to win the support of

(1) ethnic minorities
(2) senior citizens
(3) independent voters
(4) the labor vote

46 *The Jungle* by Upton Sinclair and *Unsafe at Any Speed* by Ralph Nader were both intended to

(1) publicize the growing violence in American society
(2) suggest that a poor person could get rich with hard work
(3) encourage immigration reform
(4) make the public aware of the poor quality of certain products

47 The federal government enforced the antitrust laws in court cases against Northern Securities Company, AT&T, and Microsoft in an effort to

(1) increase business competition
(2) nationalize important industries
(3) improve public trust in corporate leaders
(4) generate more investment capital

48 The United States intervened in Haiti and Bosnia during the 1990s to

(1) gain access to new markets
(2) acquire colonies for an economic empire
(3) stop conflicts within those nations
(4) disrupt international drug trafficking

49 Which heading best completes the partial outline below?

I._____
  A. Berlin
  B. Germany
  C. Korea
  D. Vietnam

(1) Areas Divided as the Result of Wars
(2) Major Allies of the United States
(3) Original Signers of the League of Nations Charter
(4) Neutral Nations During World War II

50 Which statement about the impeachment trials of both President Andrew Johnson and President Bill Clinton is most accurate?

(1) The House of Representatives failed to vote for articles of impeachment.
(2) Only President Johnson was convicted and removed from office.
(3) Only President Clinton was convicted and removed from office.
(4) The Senate failed to convict either president.

Answers to the essay questions are to be written in the separate essay booklet.

In developing your answer to Part II, be sure to keep these general definitions in mind:

(a) <u>discuss</u> means "to make observations about something using facts, reasoning, and argument; to present in some detail"

(b) <u>explain</u> means "to make plain or understandable; to give reasons for or causes of; to show the logical development or relationships of"

PART II

THEMATIC ESSAY QUESTION

Directions: Write a well-organized essay that includes an introduction, several paragraphs addressing the task below, and a conclusion.

Theme: Individuals, Groups, and Institutions — Controversial Issues

> Many controversial *domestic* issues have divided the American people. The United States government has taken actions to address these issues.

Task:

> Identify *one* controversial *domestic* issue that has divided the American people and
> - Discuss the historical background of the controversy
> - Explain the point of view of those who supported this issue
> - Explain the point of view of those who opposed this issue
> - Discuss *one* United States government action that was taken to address this issue

You may use any controversial *domestic* issue that has divided the American people. Some suggestions you might wish to consider include placing Native American Indians on reservations, slavery, women's suffrage, Prohibition, the use of child labor, and the policy of unlimited immigration.

You are *not* limited to these suggestions.

Guidelines:

In your essay, be sure to
- Develop all aspects of the task
- Support the theme with relevant facts, examples, and details
- Use a logical and clear plan of organization, including an introduction and a conclusion that are beyond a restatement of the theme

In developing your answer to Part III, be sure to keep this general definition in mind:

>**discuss** means "to make observations about something using facts, reasoning, and argument; to present in some detail"

PART III

DOCUMENT-BASED QUESTION

This question is based on the accompanying documents. The question is designed to test your ability to work with historical documents. Some of the documents have been edited for the purposes of the question. As you analyze the documents, take into account the source of each document and any point of view that may be presented in the document.

Historical Context:

>During the 19th and 20th centuries, geography influenced many of the actions taken by the United States to expand its territory or to protect its national interests.

Task: Using information from the documents and your knowledge of United States history, answer the questions that follow each document in Part A. Your answers to the questions will help you write the Part B essay, in which you will be asked to

>• Discuss the influence of geography on actions that supported the territorial expansion **and/or** the protection of United States national interests during the 19th and 20th centuries

Part A
Short-Answer Questions

Directions: Analyze the documents and answer the questions that follow each document in the space provided.

Document 1a

> . . .The object of your mission is to explore the Missouri river; & such principal stream of it, as by its course & communication with the waters of the Pacific ocean, may offer the most direct & practicable water communication across this continent, for the purpose of commerce. . . .

— President Thomas Jefferson, Instructions to Meriwether Lewis, June 20, 1803;
Library of Congress Exhibition on Thomas Jefferson

Document 1b

The Louisiana Purchase and Western Exploration

Source: Joyce Appleby et al., *The American Journey*, Glencoe McGraw–Hill, 2003 (adapted)

1 Based on these documents, what was **one** goal of President Thomas Jefferson when he instructed Meriwether Lewis to explore the Missouri River? [1]

_____

_____

Score ☐

Document 2

... Besides the recovery of the country lost, or jeoparded [jeopardized] by our diplomacy of 1818, the settlers in Oregon will also recover and open for us *the North American road to India!* This road lies through the South Pass, and the mouth of the Oregon [River]; and as soon as the settlements are made, our portion of the North American continent will immediately commence its Asiatic trade on this new and national route. This great question I explored some years ago, and only refer to it now to give a glimpse of the brilliant destiny which awaits the population of the Oregon valley.

Twenty-two years ago, President Monroe, in a message to the two Houses of Congress, proclaimed the principle as fundamental in American policy, that no part of North America was open to European colonization, domination, interference, or influence of any kind [Monroe Doctrine]. That declaration had its reference to Great Britain and the Oregon [region], and it found its response in the hearts of all Americans. Time has not weakened that response, but confirmed it; and if any European power develops a design upon Texas, the response will apply to it also. ...

Source: Senator Thomas Hart Benton, Speech to the Senate on the Oregon Territory, June 3, 1844,
Congressional Globe, 28th Congress, 1st Session

2a According to this document, how would the United States benefit from control of Oregon? [1]

_____

_____

Score ☐

b According to Senator Benton, what feature of the Monroe Doctrine can be used to protect the United States national interest in the Oregon region? [1]

_____

_____

Score ☐

Document 3a

"On Our Way to Rio Grande"

> The Mexicans are on our soil
> In war they wish us to embroil
> They've tried their best and worst to vex [worry] us
> By murdering our brave men in Texas
> We're on our way to Rio Grande
> On our way to Rio Grande
> On our way to Rio Grande
> And with arms [guns] they'll find us handy. . . .

Source: George Washington Dixon, 1846 song about the
Mexican War; Erik Bruun and Jay Crosby, eds.
Our Nation's Archive, Black Dog & Leventhal Publishers, 1999

Document 3b

Prior to the Mexican War, President Polk sent John Slidell, a United States negotiator, to Mexico to offer to settle the disputes between the two nations.

> . . . And yet again, in his [President Polk's] message of December 7, 1847, that "the Mexican Government refused even to hear the terms of adjustment which he (our minister of peace) was authorized to propose, and finally, under wholly unjustifiable pretexts [reasons], involved the two countries in war, by invading the territory of the State of Texas, striking the first blow, and shedding the blood of our citizens on *our own soil*:"
> And whereas this House [of Representatives] is desirous to obtain a full knowledge of all the facts which go to establish whether the particular spot on which the blood of our citizens was so shed was or was not at that time *our own soil*: . . . .

Source: Abraham Lincoln, "Spot" Resolutions in the House of Representatives,
December 22, 1847; *Congressional Globe*, 30th Congress, 1st Session

3 According to these documents, what role did the Rio Grande play in the Mexican War? [1]

_____

_____

Score ▢

Document 4

I propose in this letter to present such considerations as seem to me pertinent [relevant] and feasible, in favor of the speedy construction of a railroad, connecting at some point our eastern network of railways with the waters of the Pacific ocean. . . .

6. We have already expended some scores of millions of dollars on fortifications, and are urgently required to expend as many more. Especially on the Pacific is their construction pressingly demanded. I do not decide how fast nor how far this demand may or should be responded to; but I do say that a Pacific railroad, whereby the riflemen of the mountains could be brought to the Pacific within three days, and those of the Missouri within ten, would afford more security to San Francisco than ever so many gigantic and costly fortifications. . . .

But enough on this head [topic].

The social, moral, and intellectual blessings of a Pacific railroad can hardly be glanced at within the limits of an article. Suffice it for the present that I merely suggest them.

1. Our mails are now carried to and from California by steamships, via Panama, in twenty to thirty days, starting once a fortnight. The average time of transit from writers throughout the Atlantic states to their correspondents on the Pacific exceeds thirty days. With a Pacific railroad, this would be reduced to ten; for the letters written in Illinois or Michigan would reach their destinations in the mining counties of California quicker than letters sent from New York or Philadelphia would reach San Francisco. With a daily mail by railroad from each of our Atlantic cities to and from California, it is hardly possible that the amount of both letters and printed matter transmitted, and consequently of postage, should not be speedily quadrupled. . . .

Source: Horace Greeley, *An Overland Journey from New York to San Francisco, in The Summer of 1859*, C. M. Saxton, Barker & Co., 1860

4 Based on this document, state **two** ways a railroad to the Pacific would help overcome the geographic obstacle of distance. [2]

(1)_____

_____

Score ☐

(2)_____

_____

Score ☐

Document 5

. . . It has come to be understood also by Senators and others that the great territory [Alaska] which Secretary Seward proposes to acquire has a far higher value, relative and intrinsic, than was at first represented by the opponents of the acquisition. We do not place very much importance upon the argument of a distinguished officer, that our national "virtue" would be strengthened by acquiring Russian-America; and we cannot give any weight to many other points that have been urged. But when it is made to appear that *coal* seams "strike the rugged fields of Sitka," and when Commodore Rodgers refers to the growth of *timber* which is particularly valuable on a coast so bare as that of the Pacific, and when we are told by high authority about the *fisheries,* whose wealth can scarcely be over-estimated, and which will probably become as important to us in the next generation as those of Newfoundland now are; and when further we are reminded by a Boston paper of the great *whale* fishery of the Northern Pacific and of Behrings Straits, in which Massachusetts is so deeply interested, we have things brought to our notice which are as easily appreciated here as upon the Pacific coast. And when in addition to all these considerations, we are reminded that in the opening trade with China and Japan— which we expect to see developed into such imposing proportions within a quarter of a century— the Aleutian islands which, being included in the proposed cession, stand almost as a half-way station—the route between the two Continents being carried far to the North by following the great circle and by currents; and that moreover these islands are likely to furnish the most commanding naval station in that part of the ocean—it must be admitted by all parties that the question is at any rate one of continental relations. We cannot doubt that points like these have been duly weighed by Senators during the past week, and will not be without power over their votes when they make their decision upon the treaty. . . .

Source: "The Russian Treaty Before the Senate", *The New York Times*, April 8, 1867 (adapted)

5 Based on this document, state *two* geographic benefits of acquiring Alaska. [2]

(1)_____

_____

Score ☐

(2)_____

_____

Score ☐

Document 6

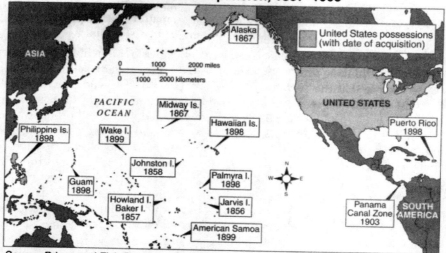

United States Expansion, 1857–1903

Source: Briggs and Fish-Petersen, *Brief Review in United States History and Government*, Prentice Hall, 2001 (adapted)

6 According to this map, how did the location of these possessions promote or protect United States interests? [1]

_____

_____

Score ☐

Document 7

... There are many among us who in the past closed their eyes to events abroad—because they believed in utter good faith what some of their fellow Americans told them—that what was taking place in Europe was none of our business; that no matter what happened over there, the United States could always pursue its peaceful and unique course in the world.

There are many among us who closed their eyes, from lack of interest or lack of knowledge; honestly and sincerely thinking that the many hundreds of miles of salt water made the American Hemisphere so remote that the people of North and Central and South America could go on living in the midst of their vast resources without reference to, or danger from, other Continents of the world.

There are some among us who were persuaded by minority groups that we could maintain our physical safety by retiring within our continental boundaries—the Atlantic on the east, the Pacific on the west, Canada on the north and Mexico on the south. I illustrated the futility—the impossibility—of that idea in my Message to the Congress last week. Obviously, a defense policy based on that is merely to invite future attack. . . .

— President Franklin D. Roosevelt,
Radio Address "On National Defense", May 26, 1940; FDR Library.

7 According to this document, why did some people believe that the United States was safe from foreign threats? [1]

_____

_____

Score [ ]

Document 8

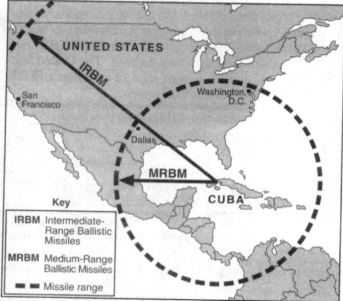

Ranges of Offensive Missiles in Cuba

Source: James H. Hansen, "Soviet Deception in the Cuban Missile Crisis,"
Studies in Intelligence: Journal of the American Intelligence Professional,
2002 (adapted)

8 According to this map, what was the role of geography in the Cuban missile crisis? [1]

_____

_____

Score ☐

Document 9

> U.S. interests in the Persian Gulf are vital to the national security. These interests include access to oil and the security and stability of key friendly states in the region. The United States will defend its vital interests in the area, through the use of U.S. military force if necessary and appropriate, against any power with interests inimical [unfriendly] to our own. The United States also will support the individual and collective self-defense of friendly countries in the area to enable them to play a more active role in their own defense. The United States will encourage the effective expressions of support and the participation of our allies and other friendly states to promote our mutual interests in the Persian Gulf region. . . .

Source: National Security Directive 45, "U.S. Policy in Response to the Iraqi Invasion of Kuwait,"
08/20/1990, George H. W. Bush Library

9 Based on this document, state **one** way that United States national interests in the Persian Gulf were affected by geography. [1]

_____

_____

Score ☐

Part B
Essay

Directions: Write a well-organized essay that includes an introduction, several paragraphs, and a conclusion. Use evidence from *at least five* documents in the body of the essay. Support your response with relevant facts, examples, and details. Include additional outside information.

Historical Context:

During the 19th and 20th centuries, geography influenced many of the actions taken by the United States to expand its territory or to protect its national interests.

Task: Using information from the documents and your knowledge of United States history, write an essay in which you

> • Discuss the influence of geography on actions that supported the territorial expansion *and/or* the protection of United States national interests during the 19th and 20th centuries

Guidelines:

In your essay, be sure to
- Develop all aspects of the task
- Incorporate information from *at least five* documents
- Incorporate relevant outside information
- Support the theme with relevant facts, examples, and details
- Use a logical and clear plan of organization, including an introduction and a conclusion that are beyond a restatement of the theme

UNITED STATES HISTORY AND GOVERNMENT

January 2006

Student . . . .

Teacher . . . .

School . . . .

Write your answers for Part I on this answer sheet, write your answers to Part III A in the test booklet, and write your answers for Parts II and III B in the separate essay booklet.

FOR TEACHER USE ONLY	
Part I Score	_____
Part III A Score	_____
Total Part I and III A Score	☐
Part II Essay Score	_____
Part III B Essay Score	_____
Total Essay Score	☐
Final Score (obtained from conversion chart)	☐

1 . . . .   26 . . . .
2 . . . .   27 . . . .
3 . . . .   28 . . . .
4 . . . .   29 . . . .
5 . . . .   30 . . . .
6 . . . .   31 . . . .
7 . . . .   32 . . . .
8 . . . .   33 . . . .
9 . . . .   34 . . . .
10 . . . .   35 . . . .
11 . . . .   36 . . . .
12 . . . .   37 . . . .
13 . . . .   38 . . . .
14 . . . .   39 . . . .
15 . . . .   40 . . . .
16 . . . .   41 . . . .
17 . . . .   42 . . . .
18 . . . .   43 . . . .
19 . . . .   44 . . . .
20 . . . .   45 . . . .
21 . . . .   46 . . . .
22 . . . .   47 . . . .
23 . . . .   48 . . . .
24 . . . .   49 . . . .
25 . . . .   50 . . . .

No. Right ☐

Part I

Answer all questions in this part.

Directions (1–50): For each statement or question, write on the separate answer sheet the *number* of the word or expression that, of those given, best completes the statement or answers the question.

1 Acquiring New Orleans as part of the Louisiana Purchase was considered important to the development of the Mississippi and Ohio River valleys because the city

(1) provided protection from attacks by the Spanish

(2) provided migrant workers for river valley farms

(3) served as a port for American agricultural goods

(4) served as the cultural center for the nation

2 During the colonial period, the British Parliament used the policy of mercantilism to

(1) limit manufacturing in America

(2) prevent criticism of royal policies

(3) deny representation to the colonists

(4) force colonists to worship in the Anglican Church

3 The Mayflower Compact and the Virginia House of Burgesses are examples of

(1) equal opportunities for women during the colonial period

(2) steps toward representative government

(3) economic agreements between the colonists and Native American Indians

(4) limitations placed on colonial Americans by the British government

4 One similarity between the Declaration of Independence and the Bill of Rights is that both documents

(1) provide for a government with three separate branches

(2) discuss colonial grievances against the monarchy

(3) stress the importance of individual liberty

(4) criticize the practice of slavery

5 Which heading best completes the partial outline below?

I._____
A. Representation
B. Slave trade
C. Taxation
D. Election of the president

(1) Causes of the Revolutionary War

(2) Provisions of the Treaty of Paris, 1783

(3) Protections under the 10th Amendment

(4) Compromises at the Constitutional Convention

6 French Enlightenment philosopher Baron De Montesquieu praised the British political system because it divided the power of government between the monarch and the two houses of Parliament.

Which principle included in the United States Constitution shows that the framers agreed with Montesquieu?

(1) separation of powers

(2) federal supremacy

(3) implied powers

(4) due process

7 Which headline illustrates the use of judicial review?

(1) "Congress Passes a Civil Rights Bill"

(2) "Conference Committee Meets to Finalize Budget"

(3) "New York State's Reapportionment Plan Ruled Unconstitutional"

(4) "President Signs SALT Agreement with Russia"

Base your answer to question 8 on the diagram below and on your knowledge of social studies.

Land Ordinance of 1785
Rectangular Land Survey System

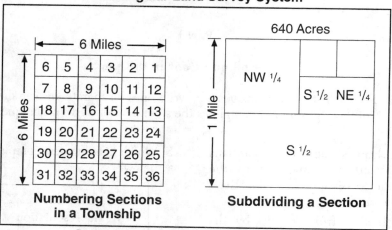

Numbering Sections in a Township

Subdividing a Section

Source: Edgar B. Wesley, *Our United States: Its History in Maps*, Denoyer-Geppert (adapted)

8 The system shown in the diagram was developed under the Articles of Confederation in order to

(1) divide lands seized from the Loyalists
(2) provide an orderly system of development for the Northwest Territory
(3) remove Native American Indians to areas west of the Appalachian Mountains
(4) extend slavery as the nation grew

---

9 Which statement is an example of the system of federalism?

(1) Cabinet members are appointed by the president.
(2) Revenue bills must begin in the House of Representatives.
(3) The national government coins money, but states cannot.
(4) The president can negotiate treaties, but the Senate has the power to ratify them.

10 The first amendment of the Constitution deals primarily with

(1) states' rights
(2) property rights
(3) rights of the accused
(4) rights of self-expression

11 One major reason that Alexander Hamilton proposed a national bank was to

(1) improve the economic position of the United States government
(2) help state governments collect taxes
(3) make loans available to owners of small farms
(4) reduce foreign investment in the United States

12 During the presidency of Andrew Jackson, the spoils system resulted in

(1) federal laws being nullified by the states
(2) elected officials rewarding their supporters with government jobs
(3) all free males being given the right to vote
(4) the end of political corruption in the federal government

13 The Seneca Falls Convention of 1848 was mainly concerned with

(1) ending slavery in all the states
(2) reducing consumption of alcoholic beverages
(3) improving treatment of the mentally ill
(4) expanding women's rights

14 The North's rapid economic growth during the Civil War was stimulated by

(1) the elimination of taxes on defense industries
(2) a reduction in the number of immigrants
(3) increased government demand for many products
(4) enslaved persons filling industrial jobs

15 Constitutional amendments adopted during Reconstruction were intended to

(1) provide legal and political rights for African Americans
(2) end property and religious qualifications for voting
(3) correct problems with the electoral college system
(4) limit the number of terms of the president

16 "The growth of a large business is merely survival of the fittest. The American beauty rose can be produced in the splendor and fragrance which bring cheer to its beholder only by sacrificing the early buds which grow up around it. This is not an evil tendency in business. It is merely the working out of a law of nature and a law of God. . . ."

— John D. Rockefeller, Jr.

Which concept is described by this passage?

(1) communism
(2) Populism
(3) utopian socialism
(4) Social Darwinism

17 In the South, the passage of Jim Crow laws in the 1870s and 1880s led directly to the

(1) racial integration of public schools
(2) decline of the Democratic party
(3) organization of the Ku Klux Klan
(4) segregation of public facilities

18 The growth of big business in the late 1800s resulted in

(1) a reduction in child labor
(2) the elimination of the middle class
(3) the widening of the economic gap between rich and poor
(4) a shift in transportation investment from railroads to canals

19 In the late 19th century, Congress tried to limit the power of monopolies by

(1) creating the Federal Trade Commission
(2) strengthening the Supreme Court
(3) adopting Granger laws
(4) passing the Sherman Antitrust Act

20 The main reason the United States implemented the Open Door policy in China was to

(1) promote immigration
(2) expand democratic reforms
(3) encourage religious freedom
(4) guarantee access to markets

21 Which United States policy is most closely associated with the annexation of Hawaii and the Philippines?

(1) neutrality
(2) isolationism
(3) imperialism
(4) international cooperation

22 In 1906, the publication of *The Jungle*, written by Upton Sinclair, led Congress to

(1) enact stronger prohibition laws
(2) support the national conservation movement
(3) establish a system for meat inspection
(4) legalize strikes and boycotts by labor unions

23 The Supreme Court decision in *Schenck* v. *United States* (1919) stated that

(1) immigrants have limited rights
(2) freedom of speech is not absolute
(3) rights of the accused may not be limited
(4) women should be granted suffrage

24 Progressive Era reforms such as the initiative, referendum, and recall attempted to

(1) increase the power of citizens in state and local government
(2) reestablish the system of checks and balances
(3) provide low-interest loans to farmers
(4) expand voting rights to Native Americans

25 What were two basic causes of the Dust Bowl during the early 1930s?

(1) strip mining and toxic waste dumping
(2) overfarming and severe drought
(3) clear-cutting of forests and construction of railroads
(4) overpopulation and urban sprawl

26 Which economic factor was a major cause of the Great Depression?

(1) purchase of stocks on credit
(2) increases in taxes on business
(3) reduction of tariffs on imports
(4) failure to produce enough consumer goods

27 During President Franklin D. Roosevelt's administration, the Federal Deposit Insurance Corporation (FDIC) and the Securities and Exchange Commission (SEC) were created as a way to

(1) provide jobs to those who were unemployed
(2) raise revenue for relief and recovery programs
(3) limit risks associated with savings and investments
(4) implement the new income tax amendment

28 **"Arms Sales to Warring Nations Banned"**

"Americans Forbidden to Travel on Ships of Warring Nations"

"Loans to Nations at War Forbidden"

"War Materials Sold Only on Cash-and-Carry Basis"

These headlines from the 1930s reflect the efforts of the United States to

(1) maintain freedom of the seas
(2) send military supplies to the League of Nations
(3) limit the spread of international communism
(4) avoid participation in European wars

29 A main purpose of government-ordered rationing during World War II was to

(1) increase foreign trade
(2) limit the growth of industry
(3) conserve raw materials for the war effort
(4) encourage women to enter the workforce

30 "... The Director of the War Relocation Authority is authorized and directed to formulate and effectuate [implement] a program for the removal, from the areas designated from time to time by the Secretary of War or appropriate military commander under the authority of Executive Order No. 9066 of February 19, 1942, of the persons or classes of persons designated under such Executive Order, and for their relocation, maintenance, and supervision. . . ."

— Executive Order 9102, March 18, 1942

Shortly after this executive order was signed, federal government authorities began to

(1) move Japanese Americans to internment camps
(2) deport German and Italian aliens
(3) detain and interrogate Chinese immigrants
(4) arrest the individuals who planned the attack on Pearl Harbor

31 In 1957, President Dwight D. Eisenhower sent federal troops to Little Rock, Arkansas, to

(1) protect civil rights marchers
(2) help African Americans register to vote
(3) enforce a Supreme Court decision to desegregate public schools
(4) end race riots resulting from a bus boycott

32 **"Batista Driven from Power"**

"Bay of Pigs Invasion Fails"

"U-2 Planes Reveal Soviet Missiles"

These headlines refer to the relationship between the United States and

(1) Canada
(2) Cuba
(3) Mexico
(4) Panama

Base your answer to question 33 on the photograph below and on your knowledge of social studies.

Source: James K. Martin et al.,
America and Its Peoples, 3rd edition,
Addison Wesley Longman

33 The protestors in the photograph are expressing their hatred for

(1) fascists   (3) immigrants
(2) communists   (4) police officers

34 One reason for the creation of the Peace Corps by President John F. Kennedy was to

(1) stop the spread of AIDS in Africa and Asia
(2) gain control of territory in Latin America
(3) provide workers for industrial nations
(4) give support to developing nations

35 A major goal of President Lyndon Johnson's Great Society program was to

(1) control economic inflation
(2) end poverty in the United States
(3) repeal several New Deal social programs
(4) return responsibility for welfare programs to the states

Base your answer to question 36 on the cartoon below and on your knowledge of social studies.

Source: Herblock, *The Washington Post*, June 18, 1963

36 The cartoonist is commenting on public reaction to the Supreme Court decision that

(1) restricted attendance in churches
(2) mandated home-based prayer
(3) declared school-sponsored prayer unconstitutional
(4) banned public observance of religious holidays

37 In *Gideon* v. *Wainwright* (1963) and *Miranda* v. *Arizona* (1966), the Supreme Court ruled that persons convicted of crimes had been

(1) denied due process of law
(2) denied a speedy and public trial
(3) victimized by illegal search and seizure
(4) sentenced to cruel and unusual punishment

38 The main goal of President Richard Nixon's foreign policy of détente was to

(1) assure American victory in Vietnam
(2) resolve conflicts in the Middle East
(3) abolish the North Atlantic Treaty Organization (NATO)
(4) improve relations with the Soviet Union

39 The Equal Pay Act, the Title IX education amendment, and the proposed Equal Rights amendment (ERA) were primarily efforts to improve the status of

(1) African Americans
(2) Native American Indians
(3) migrant workers
(4) women

40 A major policy of President Ronald Reagan's administration was to

(1) reduce defense spending
(2) lower federal income tax rates
(3) end desegregation of public facilities
(4) promote regulation of small businesses

41 The North American Free Trade Agreement (NAFTA) and the General Agreement on Trade and Tariffs (GATT) have encouraged countries to

(1) participate in the global economy
(2) create a uniform international currency
(3) accept similar wage and price controls
(4) regulate multinational corporations

42 "Influence of Political Action Committees Continues to Rise"

"Republicans and Democrats Spend over $100 Million in 2000 Presidential Election"

"Senate Passes Campaign Finance Reform Act"

What is the central issue of these headlines?

(1) Republicans and Democrats spend equal amounts of money.
(2) American citizens pay high taxes to support presidential campaigns.
(3) Money has a strong impact on the American political process.
(4) Candidates spend much of their own money on political campaigns.

Base your answer to question 43 on the cartoon below and on your knowledge of social studies.

Source: Scott Stantis, *The Birmingham News*, June 27, 2002
(adapted)

43 Which issue is the central focus of this cartoon drawn after September 11, 2001?

(1) Is there a need to give up some civil liberties to protect the nation?
(2) Should the United States reduce oil imports from the Middle East?
(3) Does the United States need fewer limits on immigration?
(4) Should the United States abandon the Constitution?

44 Which heading best completes the partial outline below?

> I. _____
>
>   A. Nullification crisis
>   B. Kansas-Nebraska Act
>   C. *Dred Scott v. Sanford*
>   D. Election of Lincoln (1860)

(1) Foreign Policies of the United States
(2) Government Policies Toward Native American Indians
(3) Consequences of Manifest Destiny
(4) Causes of Sectional Conflict

Base your answers to questions 45 and 46 on the graphs below and on your knowledge of social studies.

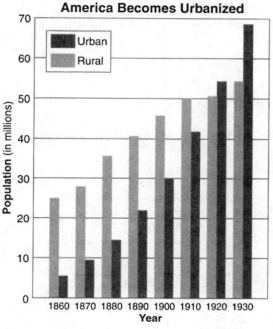

America Becomes Urbanized

Source: U. S. Census (adapted)

45 According to the graph, which was the first year in which more Americans lived in urban areas than in rural areas?

(1) 1860
(2) 1890
(3) 1920
(4) 1930

46 What was a major cause of the trend shown in the chart?

(1) availability of cheap farmland
(2) increased industrialization
(3) end of restrictions on immigration
(4) completion of the interstate highway system

47 What common problem did farmers of the 1890s and farmers of the 1920s face?

(1) failure to plant enough crops to meet local needs
(2) government overregulation of farming
(3) low tariffs on crops
(4) overproduction compared to consumer demand

48 The Panamanian revolt, the Russo-Japanese war, and the creation of the national parks system occurred during the presidency of

(1) William McKinley
(2) Woodrow Wilson
(3) Herbert Hoover
(4) Theodore Roosevelt

49 • Teapot Dome Scandal
• Harlem Renaissance
• Scopes trial

During which decade did these events occur?

(1) 1920s
(2) 1930s
(3) 1940s
(4) 1950s

50 One similarity in the presidential administrations of Abraham Lincoln, Franklin D. Roosevelt, and Lyndon Johnson is that each

(1) maintained a foreign policy of neutrality
(2) expanded the power of the presidency
(3) removed Supreme Court Justices from office
(4) decreased the size of the military

Answers to the essay questions are to be written in the separate essay booklet.

In developing your answer, be sure to keep these general definitions in mind:

(a) <u>describe</u> means "to illustrate something in words or tell about it"

(b) <u>discuss</u> means "to make observations about something using facts, reasoning, and argument; to present in some detail"

Part II

THEMATIC ESSAY QUESTION

Directions: Write a well-organized essay that includes an introduction, several paragraphs addressing the task below, and a conclusion.

Theme: Change — Turning Points

> Major historical events are often referred to as turning points because they have led to important political, social, and economic changes.

Task:

> Identify *two* major events in United States history that were important turning points and for *each*:
> * Describe the historical circumstances that led to the event
> * Discuss the political, social, *and/or* economic changes that resulted from the event.

You may use any major event from your study of United States history. Some suggestions you might wish to consider include the signing of the Declaration of Independence (1776), end of Reconstruction (1877), Henry Ford's use of the assembly line (1913), United States entry into World War I (1917), *Brown* v. *Board of Education of Topeka* (1954), passage of the Gulf of Tonkin Resolution (1964), and the fall of the Berlin Wall (1989).

You are *not* limited to these suggestions.

Guidelines

In your essay, be sure to
* Develop all aspects of the task
* Support the theme with many relevant facts, examples, and details
* Use a logical and clear plan of organization, including an introduction and a conclusion that are beyond a restatement of the theme

In developing your answer, be sure to keep this general definition in mind:

> <u>discuss</u> means "to make observations about something using facts, reasoning, and argument; to present in some detail"

Part III

DOCUMENT-BASED QUESTION

This question is based on the accompanying documents. The question is designed to test your ability to work with historical documents. Some of the documents have been edited for the purposes of the question. As you analyze the documents, take into account the source of each document and any point of view that may be presented in the document.

Historical Context:

> Since 1900, the mass media (newspapers, books, magazines, posters, photographs, newsreels, radio, films, and television) have had a significant influence on United States history and on American society.

Task: Using information from the documents and your knowledge of United States history, answer the questions that follow each document in Part A. Your answers to the questions will help you write the Part B essay, in which you will be asked to

> • Discuss the role that the mass media has played in influencing United States history ***and/or*** American society since 1900. Use historical examples to support your discussion.

Part A
Short-Answer Questions

Directions: Analyze the documents and answer the short-answer questions that follow each document in the space provided.

Document 1A

> . . . Meanwhile, radio network officials had agreed that the announcer of the presidential broadcast would be Robert Trout of the Columbia Broadcasting System's Washington station, whose manager was Harry C. Butcher. Two introductions were prepared; a formal one by Trout; a folksy one by Butcher. Both were submitted for review in the White House, whence word came promptly back that Roosevelt much preferred the folksy one. So it was that, at ten o'clock in the evening of March 12, Bob Trout's mellow voice told some 60 million people, seated before nearly 20 million radios, that "the President wants to come into your home and sit at your fireside for a little fireside chat."
>
> And Roosevelt did so.
>
> Riding his richly resonant tenor voice, he came as a smiling and reassuringly confident visitor into nearly 20 million homes to tell his friends there—a Buffalo shipping clerk, an elderly widow in Des Moines, a wheat farmer on the High Plains, a gas station operator in Birmingham, a secretary-typist in Memphis, an Oregon lumberman, a Chicago factory worker, a Kansas college professor, each in his or her own dwelling place—that they need have no fear. Everything that had gone wrong was being fixed up, and in a way that would keep things from going wrong again. . . .

Source: Kenneth S. Davis, *FDR: The New Deal Years, 1933–1937*, Random House, 1986 (adapted)

1a According to this document, how did President Franklin Delano Roosevelt use the fireside chats on the radio to influence the American people during the Depression? [1]

_____

_____

Score ☐

Document 1B

> . . . As a result we start tomorrow, Monday, with the opening of banks in the twelve Federal Reserve Bank cities — those banks which on first examination by the Treasury have already been found to be all right. This will be followed on Tuesday by the resumption of all their functions by banks already found to be sound in cities where there are recognized clearinghouses. That means about 250 cities of the United States. . . .

Source: Franklin D. Roosevelt, Fireside Chat, March 12, 1933

1b According to this document, what did the people learn about the banks during this fireside chat? [1]

_____

_____

Score ☐

Document 2

Veteran radio reporter, Robert Trout, speaking about radio news programs in the 1930s:

. . . It was a standard evening ritual in houses: people would gather round these rather large radio sets when the news came on, and nobody would talk very much until it was over. They listened to H. V. Kaltenborn bringing them coverage of the Spanish Civil War with the crackle of the rifles in the distance, and certainly nobody had ever heard real gunfire on the air before. Radio was bringing things right into people's homes, and it was beginning to affect the way people felt about what was going on in the world. So when something important happened in Europe, the country was prepared to listen. Americans had always been somewhat interested in Europe's affairs, but they just didn't feel that they were intimately affected by them. Now they were fascinated.

When Hitler annexed Austria, we did a full half hour of reports from Europe, with correspondents in Paris, Berlin, Washington, and London, and me in New York, acting as what would now be called an anchorman. Then in 1939 came the Czech crisis, which was a major radio event, and the country was enthralled by it all. They listened as much as they possibly could. We just took over the radio, doing minute-by-minute coverage, monopolizing the attention of the country. It was a great novelty then to be able to hear somebody like Hitler speaking, or to hear Neville Chamberlain coming back from Munich and waving the paper and saying, "This means peace in our time." To hear his actual words was amazing.

It's no exaggeration to say that radio brought the whole country together, all at the same instant, everyone listening to the same things. And the country liked being tied together that way. In the morning people would say, "Did you hear that last night? Did you hear Hitler speaking again? What was he talking about? Did you hear them all cheering, 'sieg heil'? What did you think?" It was on the tip of everybody's tongue. People didn't quite see, just yet, exactly how all these things overseas were ever going to intimately affect their daily lives. But it was the greatest show they'd ever been offered. . . .

Source: Peter Jennings and Todd Brewster, *The Century,* Doubleday, 1998

2 Based on this description by Robert Trout, state *two* impacts that radio had on Americans in the 1930s. [2]

(1)_____

_____

Score ☐

(2)_____

_____

Score ☐

Document 3

Source: U. S. Army, Adolph Treidler, artist, 1943

3 What was **one** purpose of this World War II poster? [1]

_____

_____

Score ☐

Document 4

Neal Shine, a reporter for *The Detroit Free Press*, writing of the newsreels shown in theaters during World War II:

> . . . We watched the newsreels, the Hollywood version of World War II, with scenes from the battlefields where we were always winning. There was a lot of censorship, as we found out in later years, because nobody wanted anybody to know how bad it really was. If there were any dead bodies, they were Japanese bodies. But Hollywood's version of the war suited us kids just fine. We fought that war in the East End Theater, the Plaza Theater, and the Lakewood Theater. We were on Guadalcanal, we were in *Thirty Seconds Over Tokyo*, we were carried away to these places. I remember something called *The Boy from Stalingrad*, an absolutely hyped propaganda film about a kid who stopped the entire German army by himself. We identified with him because he was a kid and we were kids, and we damned well would do what he did if we had to. If the Germans ever ended up on the east side of Detroit, we would draw the line somewhere around Market Street and defend our territory, just like the boy from Stalingrad. . . .

Source: Peter Jennings and Todd Brewster, *The Century*, Doubleday, 1998

4 According to Neal Shine, what impact did newsreels and movies have on children during World War II? [1]

_____

_____

Score ☐

Document 5

. . . Senator Joseph R. McCarthy, of Wisconsin, could not play upon the human emotions with the same skill as his friend, Richard Nixon. The trail that he [McCarthy] left on the face of my country will not soon fade, and there may be others who will try to follow in his footsteps. His weapon was fear. He was a politically unsophisticated man with a flair for publicity; and he was powerfully aided by the silence of timid men who feared to be the subject of his unfounded accusations. He polluted the channels of communication, and every radio and television network, every newspaper and magazine publisher who did not speak out against him, contributed to his evil work and must share part of the responsibility for what he did, not only to our fellow citizens but to our self-respect. He was in a real sense the creature of the mass media. They made him. They gave nation-wide circulation to his mouthings [opinions]. They defended their actions on the grounds that what he said was news, when they knew he lied. His initial appearances on television were in the role of a man whose sole desire was to oust communists from government and all responsible positions. That was his announced objective. The overwhelming majority of people undoubtedly sympathized with him. It has been said repeatedly that television caused his downfall. This is not precisely true. His prolonged exposure [on television] during the so-called Army-McCarthy Hearings, certainly did something to diminish [reduce] his stature. He became something of a bore. But his downfall really stemmed from the fact that he broke the rules of the club, the United States Senate, when he began attacking the integrity, the loyalty of fellow Senators, he was censured by that body, and was finished. The timidity of television in dealing with this man when he was spreading fear throughout the land, is not something to which this art of communication can ever point with pride, nor should it be allowed to forget it. . . .

Source: Edward R. Murrow, Guildhall Speech, London, 1959; Edward R. Murrow Papers

5 According to Edward R. Murrow, why was Joseph McCarthy a "creature of the mass media"? [1]

_____

_____

Score ☐

Document 6

> ... To keep things moving, Hewitt asked Kennedy: "Do you want makeup?" Kennedy had been campaigning in California and looked tanned, incredibly vigorous, and in full bloom. He promptly said, "No!" Nixon looked pale. He had made a vow to campaign in all fifty states and had been trying to carry it out. Besides, he had had a brief illness and has lost a few pounds; his collar looked loose around his neck. But after Kennedy's "no" he replied with an equally firm "no." Later his advisors, worried about his appearance, applied some Lazy-Shave, a product recommended for "five-o'clock shadow."
>
> The first debate was disastrous for Nixon. This had little to do with what was said, which on both sides consisted of almost ritualized [typical] campaign ploys and slogans. What television audiences noted chiefly was the air of confidence, the nimbleness of mind that exuded [came] from the young Kennedy. It emerged not only from crisp statements emphasized by sparse gestures, but also from glimpses of Kennedy not talking. Don Hewitt used occasional "reaction shots" showing each candidate listening to the other. A glimpse of the listening Kennedy showed him attentive, alert, with a suggestion of a smile on his lips. A Nixon glimpse showed him haggard; the lines on his face seemed like gashes and gave a fearful look. Toward the end, perspiration streaked the Lazy-Shave.
>
> Edward A. ("Ted") Rogers, principal television adviser to Nixon, protested the reaction shots. But Hewitt said they were a normal television technique and that viewers would feel cheated without them. Such elements may have played a decisive part in the Nixon catastrophe. Among those who heard the first debate on radio, Nixon apparently held his own. Only on television had he seemed to lose. . . .

Source: Erik Barnouw, *Tube of Plenty*, Oxford University Press, 1975

6 According to this document, how did John F. Kennedy benefit from his first televised campaign debate with Richard Nixon in 1960? [1]

_____

_____   Score ☐

Document 7

Martin Luther King, Jr., went to Birmingham in January 1963 to lead a campaign against segregation in public facilities, but his efforts there soon became a struggle against Jim Crow in all its insidious guises [subtle appearances]. In April King was arrested and jailed; on his release he and his aides began training children in techniques of nonviolent protest and sending them forth in orderly groups to be arrested. The strategy filled the city's jails with young blacks and provoked the city's pugnacious [combative] police commissioner, Bull Connor, into bringing police dogs and fire hoses into the fray. Charles Moore was there taking pictures for *Life* [magazine], and his unforgettable images of jets of water blasting demonstrators and of police dogs tearing into crowds helped put public opinion solidly behind the civil rights movement. Seldom, if ever, has a set of photographs had such an immediate impact on the course of history.

Source: Michael S. Durham, *Powerful Days: The Civil Rights Photography of Charles Moore*, Stewart, Tabori, and Chang

7 According to Michael S. Durham, how did photographs influence attitudes about the civil rights movement? [1]

_____

_____

Score ☐

Document 8

. . . A decade later, Vietnam was a different story. As journalist Arthur Lubow reminds us, "it was not a declared war and therefore the president could not impose military censorship." Also, it was the first war fought on television. In his book about American war correspondents, *Under Fire*, M. L. Stein sums up what that meant: "Television reporters and photographers brought the war in Vietnam home. . . . Night after night, in the comfort of their living rooms, Americans witnessed the agony of the wounded and dying, the physical destruction, and the unremitting brutality of war. There were complaints, some from the Pentagon, . . . [of] a distorted picture of the conflict. . . ."

Source: Ted Gottfried, *The American Media*, Grolier Publishing, 1997 (adapted)

8 According to this passage, how did television influence public opinion during the Vietnam War? [1]

_____

_____

Score ☐

Part B
Essay

Directions: Write a well-organized essay that includes an introduction, several paragraphs, and a conclusion. Use evidence from *at least five* documents in the body of the essay. Support your response with relevant facts, examples, and details. Include additional outside information.

Historical Context:

Since 1900, the mass media (newspapers, books, magazines, posters, photographs, newsreels, radio, films, and television) have had a significant influence on United States history and on American society.

Task: Using information from the documents and your knowledge of United States history, write an essay in which you

- Discuss the role that the mass media has played in influencing United States history **and/or** American society since 1900. Use historical examples to support your discussion.

Guidelines:

In your essay, be sure to
- Develop all aspects of the task
- Incorporate information from *at least five* documents
- Incorporate relevant outside information
- Support the theme with relevant facts, examples, and details
- Use a logical and clear plan of organization, including an introduction and a conclusion that are beyond a restatement of the theme

ANSWER SHEET

Student . . . .

Teacher . . . .

School . . . .

Write your answers for Part I on this answer sheet, write your answers to Part III A in the test booklet, and write your answers for Parts II and III B in the separate essay booklet.

```
┌─────────────────────────────────────────────┐
│              FOR TEACHER USE ONLY             │
│                                               │
│   Part I Score              _____          │
│                                               │
│   Part III A Score          _____          │
│                                               │
│                            ┌──────────┐       │
│   Total Part I and III A Score │      │       │
│                            └──────────┘       │
│                                               │
│   Part II Essay Score       _____          │
│                                               │
│   Part III B Essay Score    _____          │
│                                               │
│                            ┌──────────┐       │
│   Total Essay Score        │          │       │
│                            └──────────┘       │
│   Final Score                     ┌────────┐  │
│   (obtained from conversion chart)│        │  │
│                                   └────────┘  │
└─────────────────────────────────────────────┘
```

1........ 26........
2........ 27........
3........ 28........
4........ 29........
5........ 30........
6........ 31........
7........ 32........
8........ 33........
9........ 34........
10........ 35........
11........ 36........
12........ 37........
13........ 38........
14........ 39........
15........ 40........
16........ 41........
17........ 42........
18........ 43........
19........ 44........
20........ 45........
21........ 46........
22........ 47........
23........ 48........
24........ 49........
25........ 50........

No. Right ┌──────────┐
          └──────────┘

Part I

Answer all questions in this part.

Directions (1–50): For each statement or question, write on the separate answer sheet the *number* of the word or expression that, of those given, best completes the statement or answers the question.

Base your answer to question 1 on the map below and on your knowledge of social studies.

Slavery in the Colonies, 1775

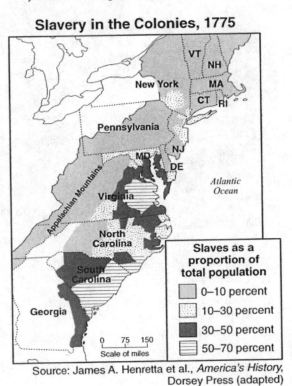

Source: James A. Henretta et al., *America's History,* Dorsey Press (adapted)

1 A conclusion supported by the information on the map is that slavery in the American colonies was

(1) declining by the start of the Revolutionary War
(2) concentrated in areas suitable for large plantations
(3) becoming illegal in the northern colonies
(4) growing fastest in the New England colonies

2 Judicial review, as practiced by the federal courts, resulted directly from

(1) the decisions of colonial governors
(2) the Articles of Confederation
(3) the Bill of Rights
(4) a Supreme Court decision

3 John Locke's theory of natural rights, as reflected in the Declaration of Independence, states that

(1) government is the source of all individual rights
(2) power should be concentrated in the monarchy
(3) power to govern belongs to the people
(4) individual liberties are best protected by a strong government

4 The Northwest Ordinance of 1787 set a precedent for other western territories by

(1) allowing slavery
(2) including voting rights for women
(3) providing a method for the creation of new states
(4) setting aside land for churches

5 The government created by the Articles of Confederation was unsuccessful at solving many major problems because

(1) unlimited power was given to the Supreme Court
(2) most power remained with the state governments
(3) members of Congress were elected according to each state's population
(4) political parties prevented the passage of legislation

6 The first amendment guarantee of freedom of speech was added to the United States Constitution primarily because its supporters believed it was essential to

(1) discourage criticism of government policies
(2) ensure the functioning of democracy
(3) limit political debate in Congress
(4) encourage more candidates to run for office

7 Which change within the federal government results from the census that is taken every ten years?

(1) The Supreme Court gains new justices.
(2) Members of Congress face new term limits.
(3) Large states gain additional seats in the Senate.
(4) Some states lose or gain members in the House of Representatives.

8 A major foreign policy success of President Thomas Jefferson's administration was the

(1) purchase of the Louisiana Territory
(2) support for the Alien and Sedition Acts
(3) victory in the war of 1812
(4) passage of the Embargo Act

9 *Federalism* is a term used to define the division of power between the

(1) president and the vice president
(2) Senate and the House of Representatives
(3) national and state levels of government
(4) three branches of the federal government

10 The major purpose of the Monroe Doctrine (1823) was to

(1) create a military alliance for the defense of North America
(2) guarantee democratic governments in Latin America
(3) secure new colonies in the Caribbean
(4) limit European influence in the Western Hemisphere

11 In the Compromise of 1850 and the Kansas-Nebraska Act of 1854, popular sovereignty was proposed as a way to

(1) allow northern states the power to ban slavery
(2) deny southern states the legal right to own slaves
(3) allow settlers in new territories to vote on the issue of slavery
(4) overturn previous Supreme Court decisions on slavery

Base your answers to questions 12 and 13 on the cartoon below and on your knowledge of social studies.

The "Strong" Government, 1869–1877

Source: J. A. Wales, *Puck*, May 12, 1880 (adapted)

12 What is the main idea of this cartoon from the Reconstruction Era?

(1) Southern society was oppressed by Radical Republican policies.
(2) Military force was necessary to stop Southern secession.
(3) United States soldiers forced women in the South to work in factories.
(4) Sharecropping was an economic burden for women after the Civil War.

13 Which congressional action led to the Southern viewpoint expressed in this cartoon?

(1) passage of the Homestead Act
(2) strengthening of the Fugitive Slave Laws
(3) military occupation of the former Confederate States
(4) ending the Freedmen's Bureau

14 In an effort to resolve conflicts with the frontier settlers in the 1870s, the federal government forced Native American Indians to

(1) move west of the Mississippi River
(2) live on reservations with definite boundaries
(3) relocate to urban industrial centers
(4) help build the transcontinental railroad

15 After 1880, a major new source of labor for American factories was

(1) western farmers who moved back to eastern cities
(2) young women who worked until they married
(3) formerly enslaved persons fleeing from the South
(4) immigrants from southern and eastern Europe

16 During the 19th century, the completion of the Erie Canal and the transcontinental railroads contributed to the industrial growth of the United States by

(1) making the movement of goods easier and cheaper
(2) protecting the United States from low-priced foreign imports
(3) encouraging subsistence farming
(4) connecting the United States to markets in Mexico and Canada

17 During the late 1800s, the principles of Social Darwinism were used to justify

(1) support for unlimited immigration
(2) desegregation of public facilities
(3) the use of strikes by organized labor
(4) the accumulation of great wealth by industrialists

18 What was the decision of the Supreme Court in *Plessy* v. *Ferguson* (1896)?

(1) Black Codes were unconstitutional.
(2) The citizenship principle established in *Dred Scott* v. *Sanford* was repealed.
(3) The 15th amendment failed to guarantee the right to vote to all males.
(4) Racial segregation did not violate the equal protection provision of the 14th amendment.

Base your answers to questions 19 and 20 on the cartoon below and on your knowledge of social studies.

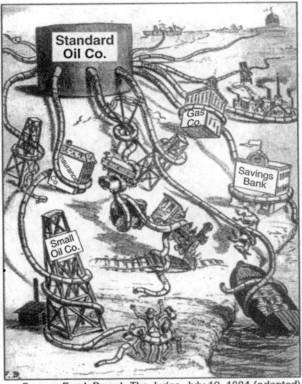

Source: Frank Beard, *The Judge*, July 19, 1884 (adapted)

19 Which type of business organization is being criticized in this cartoon?

(1) monopoly
(2) multinational corporation
(3) partnership
(4) proprietorship

20 Which government policy would this cartoonist most likely support?

(1) adopting antitrust laws
(2) easing regulations regarding mergers
(3) giving government subsidies to financial institutions
(4) encouraging large companies to relocate overseas

Base your answer to question 21 on the cartoon below and on your knowledge of social studies.

"A suggestion for the 53-cent dollar."

Source: Mark Sullivan, *Our Times, Vol. 1, The Turn of the Century* (adapted)

21 This cartoon from the 1896 presidential election campaign attacked William Jennings Bryan's proposal for

(1) free coinage of silver
(2) lower tariffs on farm goods
(3) strengthening the gold standard
(4) government regulation of the railroads

22 By proclaiming the Open Door policy in 1899, the United States was attempting to

(1) keep Japan from attacking and colonizing China
(2) increase trade between Russia and the United States
(3) ensure equal trading opportunities in China
(4) prevent European countries from colonizing the Western Hemisphere

Base your answer to question 23 on the speakers' statements below and on your knowledge of social studies.

Speaker A: It is more important now to focus on vocational training and economic opportunities than on removing obstacles to social equality for African Americans.

Speaker B: The Constitution is color-blind and recognizes no superior class in this country. All citizens are equal before the law.

Speaker C: The American Negro [African American] must focus on the achievement of three goals: higher education, full political participation, and continued support for civil rights.

Speaker D: African Americans should return home to Africa to establish their own independent nation free from white control.

23 During the early 1900s, reform leaders tried to advance the goals of *Speaker C* by

(1) supporting passage of Jim Crow laws
(2) forming the Tuskegee Institute in Alabama
(3) avoiding attempts to overturn racial segregation in the courts
(4) creating the National Association for the Advancement of Colored People (NAACP)

24 The photographs of Jacob Riis are most closely associated with the

(1) battlefields of the Civil War
(2) living conditions of the urban poor
(3) plight of sharecroppers in the South
(4) victims of the Dust Bowl on the Great Plains

25 In the 1920s, both Langston Hughes and Duke Ellington made major contributions to

(1) economic growth   (3) the creative arts
(2) educational reform   (4) political leadership

26 President Theodore Roosevelt's Big Stick policy was used by the United States to

(1) police the Western Hemisphere
(2) expand its colonial empire in Africa
(3) isolate itself from European conflicts
(4) settle a dispute between Russia and Japan

27 In the years before the United States entered World War I, President Woodrow Wilson violated his position of strict neutrality by

(1) secretly sending troops to fight for the democratic nations
(2) openly encouraging Mexico to send troops to support the Allies
(3) supporting economic policies that favored the Allied nations
(4) using United States warships to attack German submarines

28 Which Progressive Era political reform allows voters to choose party candidates to run for elected public offices?

(1) referendum   (3) initiative
(2) recall   (4) direct primary

29 In *Schenck* v. *United States* (1919), the Supreme Court upheld the right of government to protect national security during wartime by

(1) nationalizing important industries that supported the war effort
(2) limiting speech that presented a clear and present danger to the nation
(3) suspending the writ of habeas corpus for illegal aliens
(4) expelling enemy aliens who had favored the Central Powers

30 The changing image of women during the 1920s was symbolized by the

(1) passage of an equal pay act
(2) drafting of women into the army
(3) popularity of the flappers and their style of dress
(4) appointment of several women to President Calvin Coolidge's cabinet

Base your answer to question 31 on the graph below and on your knowledge of social studies.

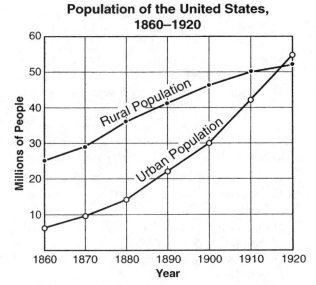

Population of the United States, 1860–1920

Source: United States Bureau of the Census (adapted)

31 Which statement about population distribution in the United States between 1860 and 1920 is best supported by the graph?

(1) Rural population declined after 1910.
(2) Many Americans migrated from urban to rural areas.
(3) Immigration played a limited role in urban growth.
(4) The population of cities grew at a faster rate than that of rural areas.

32 The economic prosperity of the 1920s was mainly the result of the

(1) adoption of lower tariff rates
(2) stricter enforcement of antitrust laws
(3) success of most United States farmers
(4) development of new industries for consumer goods

33 The Harlem Renaissance was important to American society because it

(1) highlighted the cultural achievements of African Americans

(2) isolated African Americans from mainstream society

(3) provided new political opportunities for African Americans

(4) brought an end to racial segregation in the North

34 The New Deal programs of President Franklin D. Roosevelt changed the United States economy by

(1) restoring the principle of a balanced budget

(2) expanding the trustbusting practices of Progressive Era presidents

(3) encouraging greater production of agricultural goods

(4) increasing government involvement with both business and labor

35 Which statement most accurately describes the foreign policy change made by the United States between the start of World War II (1939) and the attack on Pearl Harbor (1941)?

(1) The traditional isolationism of the United States was strengthened.

(2) The nation shifted from neutrality to military support for the Allies.

(3) War was declared on Germany but not on Japan.

(4) Financial aid was offered to both the Allied and Axis powers.

36 In 1948, President Harry Truman showed his support for civil rights by issuing an executive order to

(1) end the immigration quota system

(2) assure equal status for women in military service

(3) ban racial segregation in the military

(4) guarantee jobs for Native American Indians

Base your answer to question 37 on the poster below and on your knowledge social studies.

Source: Alfred T. Palmer, *Office of War Information*, 1943

37 During World War II, posters like this were used to

(1) prevent antiwar protests

(2) recruit more women workers

(3) convince women to enlist in the military services

(4) gain acceptance for wartime rationing programs

Base your answer to question 38 on the photograph below and on your knowledge of social studies.

Source: Bailey and Kennedy, *The American Pageant*, 9th edition, D.C. Heath and Co.

38 This photograph shows the post–World War II growth that was typical of

(1) tourist resorts
(2) suburban communities
(3) inner cities
(4) public housing projects

_____

39 The United States began a trade embargo against Cuba in the 1960s to

(1) encourage political change in Cuba
(2) promote domestic industries in Cuba
(3) motivate Cubans to immigrate to the United States
(4) end the domination of the banana industry by Cuba

40 One goal of President Lyndon Johnson's Great Society was to

(1) improve the quality of life for the poor
(2) privatize many government programs
(3) send additional troops to Vietnam
(4) reduce the number of nuclear weapons

41 The Civil Rights Act of 1964 was intended to end

(1) loyalty oaths for federal employees
(2) affirmative action programs in education
(3) unfair treatment of the elderly
(4) discrimination based on race or sex

Base your answers to questions 42 and 43 on the passage below and on your knowledge of social studies.

You have the right to remain silent. Anything you say can and will be used against you in a court of law. You have the right to speak to an attorney, and to have an attorney present during any questioning. If you cannot afford a lawyer, one will be provided for you at government expense.

— www.usconstitution.net

42 The requirements included in this passage are part of the Supreme Court's effort to protect the rights of

(1) individuals accused of crimes
(2) students from unreasonable searches
(3) defendants from double jeopardy
(4) criminals from cruel and unusual punishment

43 This passage resulted from which Supreme Court decision?

(1) *Mapp* v. *Ohio* (1961)
(2) *Gideon* v. *Wainwright* (1963)
(3) *Miranda* v. *Arizona* (1966)
(4) *Tinker* v. *Des Moines* (1969)

_____

44 • Announcement of Eisenhower Doctrine (1957)
• Operation Desert Storm (1991)
• Operation Iraqi Freedom (2003 – present)

These events involve attempts by the United States to

(1) protect human rights in Europe
(2) protect its interests in the Middle East
(3) deliver humanitarian aid to Africa
(4) contain the spread of communism in Asia

Base your answer to question 45 on the cartoon below and on your knowledge of social studies.

Teamwork

Source: Jim Morin, *The Miami Herald*,
King Features Syndicate, 1989

45 What is the main idea of this cartoon?

(1) The global economy is on the verge of collapse.

(2) Rich nations should help poor nations improve their economic conditions.

(3) One nation's economic problems affect many other nations.

(4) Each nation controls its own economic destiny.

46 During the 1990s, an increase in Mexican immigration to the United States was caused by the immigrants' desire for

(1) greater political freedom
(2) bilingual education
(3) better economic opportunities
(4) religious freedom

47 A major goal of the women's movement over the past twenty years has been to gain

(1) full property rights
(2) the right to vote
(3) equal economic opportunity
(4) better access to Social Security

48 A similarity between the Bank of the United States, created in 1791, and the present-day Federal Reserve System is that both were established to

(1) set tariff rates
(2) regulate the money supply
(3) achieve balanced budgets
(4) restrict the gold supply

49 The Supreme Court decisions in *Gibbons* v. *Ogden* and *Northern Securities Co.* v. *United States* were based on the federal government's power to

(1) issue patents
(2) control the stock market
(3) regulate interstate commerce
(4) encourage technological development

50 One similarity shared by President Andrew Johnson and President Bill Clinton is that both

(1) served only one term as president
(2) were impeached but not convicted
(3) had no vice president
(4) came to office after the death of a president

Answers to the essay questions are to be written in the separate essay booklet.

In developing your answer to Part II, be sure to keep this general definition in mind:

<u>discuss</u> **means "to make observations about something using facts, reasoning, and argument; to present in some detail"**

PART II

THEMATIC ESSAY QUESTION

Directions: Write a well-organized essay that includes an introduction, several paragraphs addressing the task below, and a conclusion.

Theme: Migration of Peoples

> Throughout our nation's history, important migrations or movements of people within the United States have occurred. These migrations have had a significant impact on both the people who moved and on American society.

Task:

> Identify *two* migrations or movements of people within the United States and for *each*
> - Discuss the historical circumstances that led to the migration of these people
> - Discuss the impact of the migration on the people who moved *and/or* on American society

You may use any important migration or movement of people from your study of United States history. Some suggestions you might wish to consider include the forced migration of Native American Indians (1800–1880), the westward movement (1840–1890), the migration of African Americans from the South to cities in the North (1900–1929), the Puerto Rican migration to the North after World War II (1945–1960), the westward migration from the Dust Bowl (1930s), suburbanization (1945–present), and the migration to the Sun Belt (1950–present).

You are *not* limited to these suggestions.

Guidelines:

In your essay, be sure to
- Develop all aspects of the task
- Support the theme with relevant facts, examples, and details
- Use a logical and clear plan of organization, including an introduction and a conclusion that are beyond a restatement of the theme

In developing your answer to Part III, be sure to keep this general definition in mind:

discuss means "to make observations about something using facts, reasoning, and argument; to present in some detail"

PART III

DOCUMENT-BASED QUESTION

This question is based on the accompanying documents. The question is designed to test your ability to work with historical documents. Some of the documents have been edited for the purposes of the question. As you analyze the documents, take into account the source of each document and any point of view that may be presented in the document.

Historical Context:

Following World War II, the United States and the Soviet Union emerged as rival superpowers. This rivalry led to a period known as the Cold War. During the first fifteen years of the Cold War (1945–1960), the threat of communism presented many different challenges to the United States.

Task: Using information from the documents and your knowledge of United States history, answer the questions that follow each document in Part A. Your answers to the questions will help you write the Part B essay, in which you will be asked to

> • Discuss how the threat of communism during the Cold War affected the United States in the period from 1945 to 1960

Part A
Short-Answer Questions

Directions: Analyze the documents and answer the questions that follow each document in the space provided.

Document 1

Source: Justus, *Minneapolis Star,* 1947 (adapted)

1 According to this cartoon, why was Congress rushing to the aid of Western Europe? [1]

_____

_____

Score ☐

Document 2a

This excerpt is from a telegram sent to the Soviet Ambassador to the United States from the Acting Secretary of State in September 1948. A copy of this telegram was sent to President Harry Truman on September 27, 1948.

1. The Governments of the United States, France and the United Kingdom, conscious of their obligations under the charter of the United Nations to settle disputes by peaceful means, took the initiative on July 30, 1948, in approaching the Soviet Government for informal discussions in Moscow in order to explore every possibility of adjusting a dangerous situation which had arisen by reason of measures taken by the Soviet Government directly challenging the rights of the other occupying powers in Berlin. These measures, persistently pursued, amounted to a blockade of land and water transport and communication between the Western Zones of Germany and Berlin which not only endangered the maintenance of the forces of occupation of the United States, France and the United Kingdom in that city but also jeopardized the discharge by those governments of their duties as occupying powers through the threat of starvation, disease and economic ruin for the population of Berlin. . . .

Source: Telegram from United States Department of State to President Truman, September 27, 1948

2a According to this passage, what action taken by the Soviet Union created tensions between the Soviet government and the governments of the United States and its Allies? [1]

_____

_____

Score ☐

Document 2b

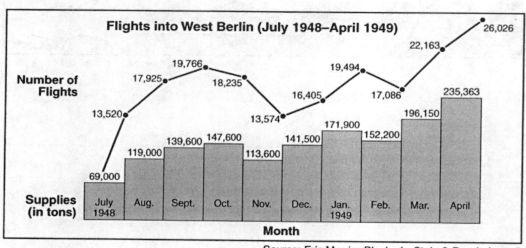

Source: Eric Morris, *Blockade*, Stein & Day (adapted)

2b According to this graph, what action was taken by the United States and its Allies in response to the events described in Document 2a? [1]

_____

_____

Score ☐

Document 3

> . . . NATO was simply a necessity. The developing situation with the Soviet Union demanded the participation of the United States in the defense of Western Europe. Any other solution would have opened the area to Soviet domination, contrary to the interests of the United States and contrary to any decent world order. At the time of the signing of the pact, April 4, 1949, I do not believe that anyone envisaged [imagined] the kind of military setup that NATO evolved into and from which de Gaulle withdrew French forces in 1966. It [NATO] was, rather, regarded as a traditional military alliance of like-minded countries. It was not regarded as a panacea [cure] for the problems besetting [affecting] Europe, but only as an elementary precaution against Communist aggression. . . .

Source: Charles E. Bohlen, *Witness to History, 1929–1969*, W. W. Norton & Company, 1973

3 According to this document, why was the North Atlantic Treaty Organization (NATO) necessary?   [1]

_____

_____

Score [ ]

Document 4

Initial newspaper stories concerning Senator McCarthy's speech in Wheeling, West Virginia, reported that the Senator said he knew of 205 communists in the State Department. Senator McCarthy later told the Senate he had used the number 57 in Wheeling. He placed this account of his Wheeling speech in the *Congressional Record*.

> . . . This, ladies and gentlemen, gives you somewhat of a picture of the type of individuals who have been helping to shape our foreign policy. In my opinion the State Department, which is one of the most important government departments, is thoroughly infested with Communists.
>
> I have in my hand 57 cases of individuals who would appear to be either card carrying members or certainly loyal to the Communist Party, but who nevertheless are still helping to shape our foreign policy.
>
> One thing to remember in discussing the Communists in our government is that we are not dealing with spies who get 30 pieces of silver to steal the blueprints of a new weapon. We are dealing with a far more sinister type of activity because it permits the enemy to guide and shape our policy. . . .

Source: Senator Joseph R. McCarthy, Speech, February 9, 1950, Wheeling, West Virginia, in *Congressional Record*, 81st Congress, 2nd Session

4 According to this document, what did Senator McCarthy suggest about communist influence in the United States government? [1]

_____

_____

Score ☐

Document 5

. . . The attack upon Korea makes it plain beyond all doubt that Communism has passed beyond the use of subversion to conquer independent nations and will now use armed invasion and war. It has defied the orders of the Security Council of the United Nations issued to preserve international peace and security. In these circumstances the occupation of Formosa [Taiwan] by Communist forces would be a direct threat to the security of the Pacific area and to United States forces performing their lawful and necessary functions in that area.

Accordingly I have ordered the Seventh Fleet to prevent any attack on Formosa. As a corollary of this action I am calling upon the Chinese Government on Formosa to cease all air and sea operations against the mainland. The Seventh Fleet will see that this is done. The determination of the future status of Formosa must await the restoration of security in the Pacific, a peace settlement with Japan, or consideration by the United Nations. . . .

— President Harry Truman, Press Release, June 27, 1950

5a Based on this document, state *one* reason given by President Truman to justify his concern about communism. [1]

.

_____

_____

Score ☐

b According to this document, state *one* action President Truman took after the attack on Korea. [1]

_____

_____

Score ☐

Document 6a

> . . . Our unity as a nation is sustained by free communication of thought and by easy transportation of people and goods. The ceaseless flow of information throughout the Republic is matched by individual and commercial movement over a vast system of inter-connected highways criss-crossing the Country and joining at our national borders with friendly neighbors to the north and south. . . .

Source: President Dwight D. Eisenhower, message to Congress, February 22, 1955

Document 6b

> . . . In case of an atomic attack on our key cities, the road net must permit quick evacuation of target areas, mobilization of defense forces and maintenance of every essential economic function. But the present system in critical areas would be the breeder [cause] of a deadly congestion within hours of an attack. . . .

Source: President Dwight D. Eisenhower, message to Congress, February 22, 1955 (adapted)

6 Based on these documents, state *two* reasons President Eisenhower believed that the Interstate Highway System was important to national defense. [2]

(1)_____

_____

Score ☐

(2)_____

_____

Score ☐

Document 7

. . . When the air-raid siren sounded, our teachers stopped talking and led us to the school basement. There the gym teachers lined us up against the cement walls and steel lockers, and showed us how to lean in and fold our arms over our heads. Our small school ran from kindergarten through twelfth grade. We had air-raid drills in small batches, four or five grades together, because there was no room for us all against the walls. The teachers had to stand in the middle of the basement rooms: those bright Pittsburgh women who taught Latin, science, and art, and those educated, beautifully mannered European women who taught French, history, and German, who had landed in Pittsburgh at the end of their respective flights from Hitler, and who had baffled us by their common insistence on tidiness, above all, in our written work.

The teachers stood in the middle of the room, not talking to each other. We tucked against the walls and lockers: dozens of clean girls wearing green jumpers, green knee socks, and pink-soled white bucks. We folded our skinny arms over our heads, and raised to the enemy a clatter of gold scarab bracelets and gold bangle bracelets. . . .

Source: Annie Dillard, *An American Childhood*, Harper & Row

7 According to this document, state *one* way schools were affected by the threat of communism. [1]

_____

_____

Score ☐

Document 8

> . . . Our safety, and that of the free world, demand, of course, effective systems for gathering information about the military capabilities of other powerful nations, especially those that make a fetish [obsessive habit] of secrecy. This involves many techniques and methods. In these times of vast military machines and nuclear-tipped missiles, the ferreting [finding] out of this information is indispensable to free world security.
>
> This has long been one of my most serious preoccupations. It is part of my grave responsibility, within the over-all problem of protecting the American people, to guard ourselves and our allies against surprise attack.
>
> During the period leading up to World War II we learned from bitter experience the imperative [absolute] necessity of a continuous gathering of intelligence information, the maintenance of military communications and contact, and alertness of command.
>
> An additional word seems appropriate about this matter of communications and command. While the Secretary of Defense and I were in Paris, we were, of course, away from our normal command posts. He recommended that under the circumstances we test the continuing readiness of our military communications. I personally approved. Such tests are valuable and will be frequently repeated in the future.
>
> Moreover, as President, charged by the Constitution with the conduct of America's foreign relations, and as Commander-in-Chief, charged with the direction of the operations and activities of our Armed Forces and their supporting services, I take full responsibility for approving all the various programs undertaken by our government to secure and evaluate military intelligence.
>
> It was in the prosecution [carrying out] of one of these intelligence programs that the widely publicized U-2 incident occurred.
>
> Aerial photography has been one of many methods we have used to keep ourselves and the free world abreast of major Soviet military developments. The usefulness of this work has been well established through four years of effort. The Soviets were well aware of it. Chairman Khrushchev has stated that he became aware of these flights several years ago. Only last week, in his Paris press conference, Chairman Khrushchev confirmed that he knew of these flights when he visited the United States last September. . . .

Source: President Dwight D. Eisenhower, Address, May 25, 1960,
Public Papers of the Presidents of the United States: Dwight D. Eisenhower 1960–1961

8 Based on this document, state *two* reasons given by President Eisenhower for gathering information about the Soviet military. [2]

(1)_____

_____

Score ☐

(2)_____

_____

Score ☐

Part B
Essay

Directions: Write a well-organized essay that includes an introduction, several paragraphs, and a conclusion. Use evidence from *at least five* documents in your essay. Support your response with relevant facts, examples, and details. Include additional outside information.

Historical Context:

Following World War II, the United States and the Soviet Union emerged as rival superpowers. This rivalry led to a period known as the Cold War. During the first fifteen years of the Cold War (1945–1960), the threat of communism presented many different challenges to the United States.

Task: Using information from the documents and your knowledge of United States history, write an essay in which you

- Discuss how the threat of communism during the Cold War affected the United States in the period from 1945 to 1960

Guidelines

In your essay, be sure to
- Develop all aspects of the task
- Incorporate information from *at least five* documents
- Incorporate relevant outside information
- Support the theme with relevant facts, examples, and details
- Use a logical and clear plan of organization, including an introduction and conclusion that are beyond a restatement of the theme

ANSWER SHEET

Student . . . .

Teacher . . . .

School . . . .

Write your answers for Part I on this answer sheet, write your answers to Part III A in the test booklet, and write your answers for Parts II and III B in the separate essay booklet.

FOR TEACHER USE ONLY	
Part I Score	_____
Part III A Score	_____
Total Part I and III A Score	☐
Part II Essay Score	_____
Part III B Essay Score	_____
Total Essay Score	☐
Final Score (obtained from conversion chart)	☐

1........	26........
2........	27........
3........	28........
4........	29........
5........	30........
6........	31........
7........	32........
8........	33........
9........	34........
10........	35........
11........	36........
12........	37........
13........	38........
14........	39........
15........	40........
16........	41........
17........	42........
18........	43........
19........	44........
20........	45........
21........	46........
22........	47........
23........	48........
24........	49........
25........	50........

No. Right ☐

UNITED STATES HISTORY
AND GOVERNMENT
JANUARY 2007

Part I

Answer all questions in this part.

Directions (1–50): For each statement or question, write on the separate answer sheet the *number* of the word or expression that, of those given, best completes the statement or answers the question.

Base your answers to questions 1 and 2 on the map below and on your knowledge of social studies.

North America, 1803

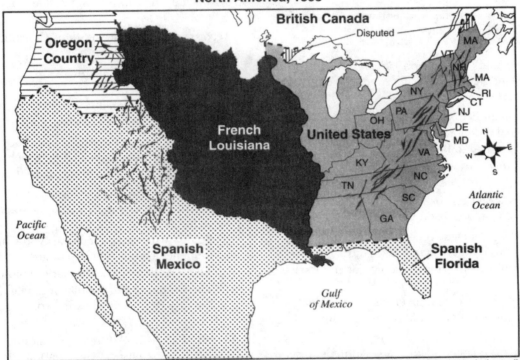

Source: *Exploring American History*, Globe Book Company (adapted)

1 Which geographic feature was the boundary line between the United States and French Louisiana in 1803?

   (1) Appalachian Mountains   (3) Mississippi River
   (2) Great Lakes   (4) Rocky Mountains

2 If the Great Plains were shown in this map, they would be located mostly in

   (1) French Louisiana   (3) the Oregon Country
   (2) Spanish Mexico   (4) the original thirteen states

3 Which document included John Locke's idea that people have the right to overthrow an oppressive government?

(1) Mayflower Compact
(2) Northwest Ordinance
(3) Declaration of Independence
(4) Bill of Rights

4 Many colonies objected to the Albany Plan of Union (1754) mainly because

(1) the colonies had just been given representation in Parliament
(2) the plan gave too much power to Native American Indians
(3) threats to colonial safety had ended
(4) colonial assemblies did not want to give up their individual power

5 Thomas Paine's publication *Common Sense* was most influential in persuading American colonists to support

(1) additional British taxes on the colonies
(2) colonial independence
(3) the Whiskey Rebellion
(4) continued ties with Great Britain

6 A major weakness of government under the Articles of Confederation was that

(1) the large states received more votes in Congress than the small states did
(2) the national government could not enforce its laws
(3) too much power was given to the president
(4) state governments could not coin money

7 To address the concerns of many Antifederalists during the debate over ratification of the Constitution, the Federalists agreed that

(1) political parties would be formed
(2) states would retain control of interstate commerce
(3) slavery would be eliminated by an amendment
(4) a bill of rights would be added

8 During the Constitutional Convention of 1787, the Great Compromise resolved a conflict over

(1) presidential power
(2) the issue of nullification
(3) representation in Congress
(4) taxes on imports

9 The United States Constitution requires that a national census be taken every ten years to

(1) provide the government with information about voter registration
(2) establish a standard for setting income tax rates
(3) determine the number of members each state has in the House of Representatives
(4) decide who can vote in presidential elections

10 According to the United States Constitution, the president has the power to

(1) nominate federal judges
(2) declare war
(3) grant titles of nobility
(4) reverse Supreme Court decisions

11 In the 2000 presidential election, which aspect of the electoral college system caused the most controversy?

(1) A state can divide its electoral votes among different candidates.
(2) States with few electoral votes have no influence on election outcomes.
(3) The selection of electors varies among states.
(4) The winner of the popular vote might not get the majority of the electoral vote.

12 In his Farewell Address, President George Washington advised the nation to avoid permanent alliances because he believed that the United States

(1) would risk its security by involvement in European affairs
(2) had no need for the products or markets of Europe
(3) possessed military power superior to any European nation
(4) needed to limit European immigration

13 The decision in *Marbury* v. *Madison* (1803) expanded the power of the Supreme Court by

(1) restricting the use of the elastic clause
(2) establishing the power of judicial review
(3) upholding the constitutionality of the National Bank
(4) interpreting the interstate commerce clause

14 Prior to 1850, what was a main reason the North developed an economy increasingly based on manufacturing while the South continued to rely on an economy based on agriculture?

(1) Protective tariffs applied only to northern seaports.
(2) Geographic conditions supported different types of economic activity.
(3) Slavery in the North promoted rapid economic growth.
(4) Manufacturers failed to make a profit in the South.

15 The *Declaration of Sentiments*, adopted during the Seneca Falls Convention in 1848, is most closely associated with the rights of

(1) immigrants
(2) enslaved persons
(3) Native American Indians
(4) women

16

> I. Actions Taken by President Abraham Lincoln During the Civil War
>
> A. Increased the size of the army without congressional authorization
>
> B. Arrested and jailed anti-Unionists without giving a reason
>
> C. Censored some anti-Union newspapers and had some editors and publishers arrested

Which statement is most clearly supported by these actions of President Lincoln?

(1) Wartime emergencies led President Lincoln to expand his presidential powers.
(2) President Lincoln was impeached for violating the Constitution.
(3) Checks and balances effectively limited President Lincoln's actions.
(4) President Lincoln wanted to abolish the Bill of Rights.

17 In the late 1800s, the creation of the Standard Oil Trust by John D. Rockefeller was intended to

(1) protect small, independent oil firms
(2) control prices and practices in the oil refining business
(3) increase competition among oil refining companies
(4) distribute donations to charitable causes

18 Passage of the Dawes Act of 1887 affected Native American Indians by

(1) supporting their cultural traditions
(2) attempting to assimilate them into mainstream American culture
(3) forcing their removal from areas east of the Mississippi River
(4) starting a series of Indian wars on the Great Plains

19 The changes in American agriculture during the late 1800s led farmers to

(1) grow fewer cash crops for export
(2) request an end to agricultural tariffs
(3) demand a reduced role for government in agriculture
(4) become more dependent on banks and railroads

20 The Supreme Court cases of *Wabash, St. Louis & Pacific R.R.* v. *Illinois* (1886) and *United States* v. *E. C. Knight Co.* (1895) were based on laws that were intended to

(1) limit the power of big business
(2) support farmers' efforts to increase the money supply
(3) maintain a laissez-faire approach to the economy
(4) improve working conditions for immigrants

21 The Spanish-American War (1898) marked a turning point in United States foreign policy because the United States

(1) developed a plan for peaceful coexistence
(2) emerged as a major world power
(3) pledged neutrality in future European conflicts
(4) refused to become a colonial power

Base your answers to questions 22 and 23 on the cartoon below and on your knowledge of social studies.

Woman's Holy War
Grand Charge on the Enemy's Works

Source: Currier and Ives,
Library of Congress (adapted)

22 The "Holy War" illustrated in the cartoon was an effort to

(1) recruit women soldiers
(2) promote world peace
(3) ban the sale of alcoholic beverages
(4) spread Christian religious beliefs

23 Women gained a victory in the "war" shown in the cartoon through the

(1) ratification of a constitutional amendment
(2) legalization of birth control
(3) expansion of missionary activities overseas
(4) repeal of national Prohibition

24 A primary reason for the establishment of the Open Door policy (1899) was to

(1) protect United States trade in the Far East
(2) gain control of the Panama Canal Zone
(3) encourage Chinese immigration to the United States
(4) improve relations with Russia

Base your answers to questions 25 and 26 on the statements below that discuss immigration laws in the early 20th century, and on your knowledge of social studies.

Speaker A: A literacy test as a requirement for immigration to the United States is reasonable. Great numbers of uneducated workers take jobs and good wages from our workers.

Speaker B: Requiring literacy of immigrants is unfair. It will keep people out because they lacked the opportunity to gain an education.

Speaker C: A literacy test will allow more people from northern and western Europe to enter. They are similar to the majority of the United States population.

Speaker D: Literacy is not an issue. The real purpose of this law is to discriminate against immigrants from certain parts of the world.

25 Supporters of literacy tests to restrict immigration would most likely favor the views of *Speakers*

(1) *A* and *C*   (3) *B* and *D*
(2) *B* and *C*   (4) *A* and *B*

26 The immigrants referred to by *Speaker D* were mainly from

(1) Canada and Mexico
(2) South America
(3) western Europe
(4) southern and eastern Europe

Base your answer to question 27 on the map below and on your knowledge of social studies.

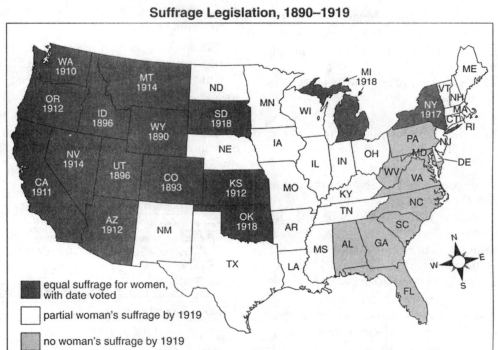

Suffrage Legislation, 1890–1919

Source: Sandra Opdycke, *The Routledge Historical Atlas of Women in America*, Routledge (adapted)

27 What does the map show about woman's suffrage legislation before ratification of the federal woman's suffrage amendment in 1920?

    (1) Opposition to woman's suffrage was strongest in the New England states.
    (2) New York was the first state to grant women the right to vote in state elections.
    (3) State legislatures never gave women the right to vote.
    (4) Many western states granted women suffrage before passage of the 19th amendment.

---

28 During the Progressive Era, public demands for direct consumer protection resulted in passage of the

    (1) Pure Food and Drug Act
    (2) Fair Labor Standards Act
    (3) Underwood Tariff
    (4) income tax amendment

29 The Federal Reserve System helps to regulate

    (1) the annual federal budget
    (2) state sales tax rates
    (3) Social Security payments
    (4) the nation's money supply

30 Which issue was the focus of the Supreme Court decision in *Schenck* v. *United States* (1919)?

    (1) freedom of speech for war protesters
    (2) relocation of ethnic minority groups
    (3) use of detention camps for enemy aliens
    (4) integration of military forces

31 During the Harlem Renaissance of the 1920s, African American authors and artists used literature and art to

    (1) end segregation of public facilities
    (2) promote affirmative action programs
    (3) celebrate the richness of their heritage
    (4) urge voters to elect more African Americans to political office

32 Which economic condition was a major cause of the Great Depression?

(1) high wages of industrial workers
(2) deficit spending by the federal government
(3) inability of industry to produce enough consumer goods
(4) uneven distribution of income between the rich and the poor

33 The march of the "Bonus Army" and referring to shantytowns as "Hoovervilles" in the early 1930s illustrate

(1) growing discontent with Republican efforts to deal with the Great Depression
(2) state projects that created jobs for the unemployed
(3) federal attempts to restore confidence in the American economy
(4) the president's success in solving social problems

Base your answer to question 34 on the cartoon below and on your knowledge of social studies.

The Galloping Snail

Source: Burt Thomas, *Detroit News* (adapted)

34 The cartoonist is commenting on President Franklin D. Roosevelt's efforts to

(1) veto several bills sent him by Congress
(2) end New Deal programs
(3) gain quick passage of his legislation
(4) slow down the legislative process

35 Critics of the New Deal claimed that the Tennessee Valley Authority (TVA) and the Social Security System threatened the United States economy by

(1) applying socialist principles
(2) imposing unfair working hours
(3) decreasing government spending
(4) eroding antitrust laws

Base your answer to question 36 on the ration card shown below and on your knowledge of social studies.

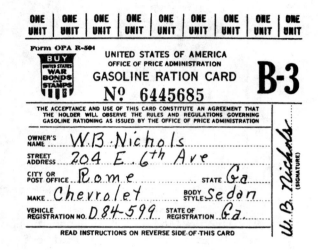

36 The use of this card, issued by the federal government, was intended to

(1) help the automobile industry
(2) support the troops in wartime
(3) increase the use of gasoline
(4) decrease the cost of automobiles

37 A goal of the Marshall Plan (1948) was to

(1) rebuild Japan after World War II
(2) provide military aid to the Warsaw Pact
(3) establish a Pan-American military alliance system
(4) provide economic aid to European nations threatened by communism

38 Which heading is most appropriate for the partial outline below?

I._____
   A. The House Un-American Activities Committee
   B. Loyalty review boards
   C. Bomb shelters
   D. *Watkins* v. *United States* (1957)

(1) Results of World War I
(2) The Cold War at Home
(3) Problems of Urbanization
(4) Reactions to Immigration

Base your answer to question 39 on the statement below and on your knowledge of social studies.

. . . Whenever normal agencies prove inadequate to the task and it becomes necessary for the Executive Branch of the Federal Government to use its powers and authority to uphold Federal Courts, the President's responsibility is inescapable.

In accordance with that responsibility, I have today issued an Executive Order directing the use of troops under Federal authority to aid in the execution of Federal law at Little Rock, Arkansas. This became necessary when my Proclamation of yesterday was not observed, and the obstruction of justice still continues. . . .

— President Dwight D. Eisenhower, September 24, 1957

39 The situation described in this statement grew out of efforts to

(1) uphold the Voting Rights Act
(2) pass a constitutional amendment ending poll taxes
(3) enforce the decision in *Brown* v. *Board of Education of Topeka*
(4) extend the Montgomery bus boycott to Little Rock

Base your answers to questions 40 and 41 on the cartoon below and on your knowledge of social studies.

Source: Herblock, *Washington Post*, 1974 (adapted)

40 The conflict that was the focus of the cartoon involved President Richard Nixon's attempt to

(1) increase the number of troops in Vietnam
(2) withhold evidence in the Watergate scandal
(3) impose mandatory wage and price controls
(4) improve relations with the People's Republic of China

41 The cartoon illustrates the constitutional principle of

(1) federalism
(2) checks and balances
(3) representative government
(4) civilian control of the military

42 Population increases that resulted from the baby boom of the 1950s and 1960s contributed to a

(1) housing surplus
(2) drop in immigration
(3) reduction in government services
(4) rise in demand for consumer goods

43 The 1961 Bay of Pigs invasion and the 1962 missile crisis are conflicts directly related to United States relations with which two nations?

(1) the Dominican Republic and Haiti
(2) Cuba and the Soviet Union
(3) China and Japan
(4) North Korea and South Korea

44 What was a central issue in the Supreme Court cases of *Gideon* v. *Wainwright* (1963) and *Miranda* v. *Arizona* (1966)?

(1) freedom of religion
(2) voting rights
(3) rights of the accused
(4) property rights

45 The economic policies of President Ronald Reagan (1981–1989) and President George W. Bush (2001–present) are similar in that both

(1) balanced the federal budget
(2) expanded welfare programs to end poverty
(3) used tax cuts to encourage economic growth
(4) decreased military spending

46 Since the 1990s, the primary issue concerning the health care system in the United States has been the

(1) increasing cost of medical care
(2) shortage of prescription drugs
(3) safety of medical procedures
(4) reorganization of hospitals

47 Books such as *Uncle Tom's Cabin*, *How the Other Half Lives*, and *The Feminine Mystique* all show that literature can sometimes

(1) expose government corruption
(2) cause violent revolution
(3) begin military conflict
(4) encourage social reform

48 The Progressive movement (1900–1920) was primarily a response to problems created by

(1) abolitionists   (3) industrialization
(2) nativists   (4) segregation

49 The term *Dust Bowl* is most closely associated with which historical circumstance?

(1) a major drought that occurred during the 1930s
(2) logging practices in the Pacific Northwest in the 1950s
(3) an increase in pollution during the 1960s
(4) the migration to the Sun Belt in the 1970s

50 The Camp David Accords and the Persian Gulf War both show the desire of the United States to

(1) create stability in the Middle East
(2) expand trade with Asian nations
(3) maintain friendly relations with Europe
(4) provide economic stability in Latin America

Answers to the essay questions are to be written in the separate essay booklet.

In developing your answer to Part II, be sure to keep these general definitions in mind:

  (a) <u>describe</u> means "to illustrate something in words or tell about it"

  (b) <u>discuss</u> means "to make observations about something using facts, reasoning, and argument; to present in some detail"

Part II

THEMATIC ESSAY QUESTION

Directions: Write a well-organized essay that includes an introduction, several paragraphs addressing the task below, and a conclusion.

Theme: Influence of Geographic Factors on Governmental Actions

> Actions taken by the United States government have often been influenced by geographic factors. Some of these factors include location, climate, natural resources, and physical features.

Task:

> Identify *two* actions taken by the United States government that have been influenced by geographic factors and for *each*
> - State *one* reason the United States took the action
> - Describe how a geographic factor influenced the action
> - Discuss the impact of the action on the United States

You may use any action taken by the United States government that was influenced by a geographic factor. Some suggestions you might wish to consider include the Lewis and Clark expedition (1804–1806), issuance of the Monroe Doctrine (1823), Mexican War (1846–1848), Commodore Perry's opening of Japan (1853), passage of the Homestead Act (1862), purchase of Alaska (1867), construction of the Panama Canal (1904–1914), entry into World War II (1941), passage of the Interstate Highway Act (1956), and involvement in the Persian Gulf War (1991).

You are *not* limited to these suggestions.

Guidelines:

  In your essay, be sure to:
  - Develop all aspects of the task
  - Support the theme with relevant facts, examples, and details
  - Use a logical and clear plan of organization, including an introduction and a conclusion that are beyond a restatement of the theme

In developing your answer to Part III, be sure to keep these general definitions in mind:

    (a) <u>explain</u> means "to make plain or understandable; to give reasons for or causes of; to show the logical development or relationships of "

    (b) <u>discuss</u> means "to make observations about something using facts, reasoning, and argument; to present in some detail"

Part III

DOCUMENT-BASED QUESTION

This question is based on the accompanying documents. It is designed to test your ability to work with historical documents. Some of the documents have been edited for the purposes of the question. As you analyze the documents, take into account the source of each document and any point of view that may be presented in the document.

Historical Context:

> Since World War II, conflicts in Asia have played a major role in the Cold War. One of these conflicts arose in Vietnam. United States involvement in this conflict was sometimes controversial. The decision to send troops to Vietnam had a major impact on American society and on United States foreign policy.

Task: Using information from the documents and your knowledge of United States history, answer the questions that follow each document in Part A. Your answers to the questions will help you write the Part B essay, in which you will be asked to

> - Explain the reasons for United States involvement in Vietnam
> - Discuss the impact of the Vietnam War on American society
> - Discuss the impact of the Vietnam War on United States foreign policy

Part A
Short-Answer Questions

Directions: Analyze the documents and answer the short-answer questions that follow each document in the space provided.

Document 1

. . . At the present moment in world history nearly every nation must choose between alternative ways of life. The choice is too often not a free one.

One way of life is based upon the will of the majority, and is distinguished by free institutions, representative government, free elections, guarantees of individual liberty, freedom of speech and religion, and freedom from political oppression.

The second way of life is based upon the will of a minority forcibly imposed upon the majority. It relies upon terror and oppression, a controlled press and radio, fixed elections, and the suppression of personal freedoms.

I believe that it must be the policy of the United States to support free peoples who are resisting attempted subjugation [control] by armed minorities or by outside pressures.

I believe that we must assist free peoples to work out their own destinies in their own way. . . .

Source: President Harry Truman, Address to Congress (Truman Doctrine), March 12, 1947

1a According to President Harry Truman, what is *one* problem when governments are controlled by the will of a minority? [1]

_____

_____

Score ☐

b According to President Truman, what policy must the United States support? [1]

_____

_____

Score ☐

Document 2a

> . . . Communist aggression in Korea is a part of the worldwide strategy of the Kremlin to destroy freedom. It has shown men all over the world that Communist imperialism may strike anywhere, anytime.
>
> The defense of Korea is part of the worldwide effort of all the free nations to maintain freedom. It has shown free men that if they stand together, and pool their strength, Communist aggression cannot succeed. . . .

Source: President Harry Truman, Address at a dinner of the Civil Defense Conference, May 7, 1951

2a According to President Harry Truman, why was it important for the United States to help defend Korea? [1]

_____

_____

Score ☐

Document 2b

Another Hole in the Dike

Source: Fred O. Seibel, *Richmond Times-Dispatch*, May 5, 1953 (adapted)

2b Based on this cartoon, what problem did the United States face in Asia by 1953? [1]

_____

_____

Score ☐

Document 3

THE NATURE OF THE CONFLICT

. . . The world as it is in Asia is not a serene or peaceful place.

The first reality is that North Viet-Nam has attacked the independent nation of South Viet-Nam. Its object is total conquest.

Of course, some of the people of South Viet-Nam are participating in attack on their own government. But trained men and supplies, orders and arms, flow in a constant stream from north to south.

This support is the heartbeat of the war. . . .

WHY ARE WE IN VIET-NAM?

Why are these realities our concern? Why are we in South Viet-Nam?

We are there because we have a promise to keep. Since 1954 every American President has offered support to the people of South Viet-Nam. We have helped to build, and we have helped to defend. Thus, over many years, we have made a national pledge to help South Viet-Nam defend its independence.

And I intend to keep that promise. . . .

Source: President Lyndon B. Johnson, Speech at Johns Hopkins University, April 7, 1965

3 According to President Lyndon B. Johnson, why was the United States involved in Vietnam? [1]

_____

_____

Score ☐

Document 4a

> . . . When the country looks to Lyndon Johnson these days, it gains the inescapable impression that Vietnam is America's top priority. Mr. Johnson uses the bully pulpit [power] of the Presidency (not to mention the Rose Garden) time and again to tell a painfully divided nation why it is fighting and must continue to fight in Southeast Asia. No amount of resistance—and it is growing—can blunt [lessen] his resolve. Few question his personal resolve on the Negro [African American] problem (he is, after all, the President who proclaimed "We Shall Overcome!" in a speech three years ago). But his public posture [position] here projects none of the sense of urgency that marks his Vietnam crusading. . . .

Source: "The Negro in America: What Must Be Done," *Newsweek*, November 20, 1967

Document 4b

Source: Charles Brooks,
Birmingham News (adapted)

4 According to these documents, what were *two* effects of the Vietnam War on American society? [2]

(1)_____

_____

Score ☐

(2)_____

_____

Score ☐

Document 5a

Anti-Vietnam War protesters march down Fifth Avenue in New York City on April 27, 1968. The demonstration attracted 87,000 people and led to 60 arrests. Also on the 27th, some 200,000 New York City students boycotted classes.

Source: *The Sixties Chronicle*, Legacy Publishing

Document 5b

This article appeared in the *New York Times* three days after the Kent State shootings.

Illinois Deploys Guard

More than 80 colleges across the country closed their doors yesterday for periods ranging from a day to the remainder of the academic year as thousands of students joined the growing nationwide campus protest against the war in Southeast Asia.

In California, Gov. Ronald Reagan, citing "emotional turmoil," closed down the entire state university and college system from midnight last night until next Monday. More than 280,000 students at 19 colleges and nine university campuses are involved.

Pennsylvania State University, with 18 campuses, was closed for an indeterminate [indefinite] period.

In the New York metropolitan area about 15 colleges closed, some for a day, some for the week, and some for the rest of the term.

A spokesman for the National Student Association said that students had been staying away from classes at almost 300 campuses in the country. . . .

Source: Frank J. Prial, *New York Times*, May 7, 1970

5 Based on these documents, state *two* ways the Vietnam War affected American society. [2]

(1)_____

_____

Score ☐

(2)_____

_____

Score ☐

Document 6

After the Vietnam War ended in 1975, large numbers of Vietnamese refugees settled in Westminster, California.

"Little Saigon" in Westminster, California

Source: Bailey and Kennedy, *The American Pageant*, D. C. Heath and Co., 1991

6 According to this photograph, how have Vietnamese immigrants contributed to American society? [1]

_____

_____

Score

Document 7

> . . . Within sixty calendar days after a report is submitted or is required to be submitted pursuant to section 1543(a)(1) of this title, whichever is earlier, the President shall terminate any use of United States Armed Forces with respect to which such report was submitted (or required to be submitted), unless the Congress (1) has declared war or has enacted a specific authorization for such use of United States Armed Forces, (2) has extended by law such sixty-day period, or (3) is physically unable to meet as a result of an armed attack upon the United States. Such sixty-day period shall be extended for not more than an additional thirty days if the President determines and certifies to the Congress in writing that unavoidable military necessity respecting the safety of United States Armed Forces requires the continued use of such armed forces in the course of bringing about a prompt removal of such forces. . . .

Source: War Powers Act, 1973

7 Based on this document, state **one** way in which the War Powers Act could limit United States involvement in foreign conflicts. [1]

_____

_____

Score ☐

Document 8

> . . . Fourteen years after the last United States combat units left Vietnam, at least 15 men who were there have made their way into Congress.
>
> **Each Draws His Own Lesson**
>
>   Some are Republicans, like Representative David O'B. Martin of upstate New York; some are Democrats, like Representatives H. Martin Lancaster of North Carolina and John P. Murtha of Pennsylvania; some are conservatives, and some are liberals. Each has drawn his own lesson from having participated in the war, and each applies the experience in his own way to the issues of foreign policy he confronts as a legislator.
>
>   Some support military aid to the Nicaraguan rebels, some oppose it. A few favored sending the Marine contingent to Beirut in 1982, though most say they had grave reservations. Some see the Soviet threat in larger terms than others.
>
>   But the Vietnam experience has given almost all of them a sense of seasoned caution about using American military power without having the broad support of the American people. And this translates into some sober views on the limitations of force, especially in impoverished countries torn by internal strife. . . .

Source: David K. Shipler, "The Vietnam Experience and the Congressman of the 1980's," *New York Times*, May 28, 1987

8 According to this article, how has the experience of many Congressmen who served in Vietnam affected their views on when to use American military force? [1]

_____

_____

Score ☐

Document 9

Comments on United States participation in Operation Desert Storm and Persian Gulf War, 1991

"By God, we've kicked the Vietnam syndrome once and for all!" So said President George Bush in a euphoric [joyful] victory statement at the end of the Gulf War, suggesting the extent to which Vietnam continued to prey on the American psyche more than fifteen years after the fall of Saigon. Indeed the Vietnam War was by far the most convulsive and traumatic of America's three wars in Asia in the 50 years since Pearl Harbor. It set the U.S. economy on a downward spiral. It left America's foreign policy at least temporarily in disarray, discrediting the postwar policy of containment and undermining the consensus that supported it. It divided the American people as no other event since their own Civil War a century earlier. It battered their collective soul.

Such was the lingering impact of the Vietnam War that the Persian Gulf conflict appeared at times as much a struggle with its ghosts as with Saddam Hussein's Iraq. President Bush's eulogy for the Vietnam syndrome may therefore be premature. Success in the Gulf War no doubt raised the nation's confidence in its foreign policy leadership and its military institutions and weakened long-standing inhibitions against intervention abroad. Still it seems doubtful that military victory over a nation with a population less than one-third of Vietnam in a conflict fought under the most favorable circumstances could expunge [erase] deeply encrusted and still painful memories of an earlier and very different kind of war. . . .

Source: George C. Herring, "America and Vietnam: The Unending War," *Foreign Affairs*, Winter 1991/92

9 According to this document, what was **one** impact of the Vietnam War on United States foreign policy? [1]

_____

_____

Score [ ]

Part B
Essay

Directions: Write a well-organized essay that includes an introduction, several paragraphs, and a conclusion. Use evidence from *at least five* documents in the body of the essay. Support your response with relevant facts, examples, and details. Include additional outside information.

Historical Context:

Since World War II, conflicts in Asia have played a major role in the Cold War. One of these conflicts arose in Vietnam. United States involvement in this conflict was sometimes controversial. The decision to send troops to Vietnam had a major impact on American society and on United States foreign policy.

Task: Using information from the documents and your knowledge of United States history, write an essay in which you

- Explain the reasons for United States involvement in Vietnam
- Discuss the impact of the Vietnam War on American society
- Discuss the impact of the Vietnam War on United States foreign policy

Guidelines:

In your essay, be sure to:
- Develop all aspects of the task
- Incorporate information from *at least five* documents
- Incorporate relevant outside information
- Support the theme with relevant facts, examples, and details
- Use a logical and clear plan of organization, including an introduction and conclusion that are beyond a restatement of the theme

UNITED STATES HISTORY AND GOVERNMENT
January 2007

ANSWER SHEET

Student . . . .

Teacher . . . .

School . . . .

Write your answers for Part I on this answer sheet, write your answers to Part III A in the test booklet, and write your answers for Parts II and III B in the separate essay booklet.

FOR TEACHER USE ONLY

Part I Score _____

Part III A Score _____

Total Part I and III A Score

Part II Essay Score _____

Part III B Essay Score _____

Total Essay Score

Final Score
(obtained from conversion chart)

Part I

1.........	26.........
2.........	27.........
3.........	28.........
4.........	29.........
5.........	30.........
6.........	31.........
7.........	32.........
8.........	33.........
9.........	34.........
10.........	35.........
11.........	36.........
12.........	37.........
13.........	38.........
14.........	39.........
15.........	40.........
16.........	41.........
17.........	42.........
18.........	43.........
19.........	44.........
20.........	45.........
21.........	46.........
22.........	47.........
23.........	48.........
24.........	49.........
25.........	50.........

No. Right